ORGAN DONATION AND THE DIVINE LIEN IN TALMUDIC LAW

This book offers a new theory of property and distributive justice derived from Talmudic law, illustrated by a case study involving the sale of organs for transplant. Although organ donation obviously did not exist in late antiquity, this book posits a new way, drawn from the Talmud, to conceive of this modern means of giving to others. Our common understanding of organ transfer (transplant) as either gift or sale is trapped in a dichotomy that is conceptually and philosophically limiting. Drawing on Maussian gift theory, this book suggests a different legal and cultural meaning for this property transfer. It introduces the concept of the "divine lien," representing an obligation to others in need that is built into the very definition of property ownership. Rather than a gift or sale, organ transfer is shown to exemplify an owner's voluntary recognition and fulfillment of this latent property obligation.

Madeline Kochen is a public interest lawyer and former professor at the University of Michigan Law School. She has a B.A. *magna cum laude* in Judaic Studies and a law degree from Yeshiva University, as well as an interdiscliplinary Ph.D. in Religion and Political Philosophy from Harvard University. After a stint at the Legal Aid Society, Kochen worked as an attorney for the New York Civil Liberties Union, where she eventually founded and directed the NYCLU Reproductive Rights Project. In addition to Michigan, Kochen has taught at Harvard and at Stanford Law, where she was an assistant dean. Her fellowships include the Harvard Center for Ethics and the Professions, the Frankel Center for Advanced Judaic Studies, and the Revson Fellowship at Columbia University. Her publications have appeared in *Aramaic in Postbiblical Judaism and Early Christianity*, *The Encyclopedia of the Bible and Its Reception*, the *New York Law Journal*, and the *Jewish Law Association Studies*.

Organ Donation and the Divine Lien in Talmudic Law

MADELINE KOCHEN

CAMBRIDGE
UNIVERSITY PRESS

CAMBRIDGE
UNIVERSITY PRESS

32 Avenue of the Americas, New York, NY 10013-2473, USA

Cambridge University Press is part of the University of Cambridge.

It furthers the University's mission by disseminating knowledge in the pursuit of education, learning, and research at the highest international levels of excellence.

www.cambridge.org
Information on this title: www.cambridge.org/9780521493383

First published 2014

A catalog record for this publication is available from the British Library.

Library of Congress Cataloging in Publication data
Kochen, Madeline, 1957– author
Organ donation and the divine lien in Talmudic law /
Madeline Kochen, J.D., Ph.D.
pages cm
Includes bibliographical references and index.
ISBN 978-0-521-49338-3 (hardback)
1. Donation of organs, tissues, etc. (Jewish law) 2. Human body in rabbinic literature. I. Title.
KBM3116.K63 2013
296.1'88362197954–dc23 2013030424

ISBN 978-0-521-49338-3 Hardback

For my grandfather, Jacob Isaac Kraminer, z"l (1900–1993), who was born in the Ukrainian town of Sokal on the banks of the River Bug, ate only hard-boiled eggs when he traveled, and kvelled over my learning even though I was a girl.

Contents

Preface *page* xi

Acknowledgments xv

Introduction 1

1 **Beyond Gift and Commodity: Rethinking the Compartmentalization Approach to the Problem of Commodification** 20

1.1 The Apparent Problem: Money and Markets 22

1.2 Gift v. Commodity: Bridging the Historical Divide 30

1.3 Gift v. Commodity: Bridging the Rhetorical Divide 36

1.4 Interrogating the Social Meaning of Monetary Exchange 38

2 **Alternate Property Conceptions: The Donor's Lien** 43

3 **"From the Table of the Most High": Divine Ownership and Private Property in Talmudic Law** 60

3.1 Basic Conceptions 62

3.2 Two Overlapping Realms of Ownership 66

3.3 The Realm of Divine Ownership and Exchanges Therewith 71

3.3.1 Direct Gifts to God: Sacrifices and Vows 79

3.3.2 Gifts from God: Priestly Gifts and Workers' Rights 81

3.3.3 Gifts to God, to the Poor 100

3.3.4 Other Transfers Involving the Divine Realm: *Shemitah*, *Yovel*, and *Hefker* 107

3.4 The Distinct Legal Category of "Divine Gifts": Distributive Justice Instantiated in the Definition of Property Ownership 111

4 "And Your Brother Shall Live with You": The Divine Lien and the Obligation to Save Human Life 121

4.1 Votive Institutions: *Neder*, *Hekdesh*, and *Tsedakah* 122
4.1.1 *Tsedakah* and *Neder* 124
4.1.2 *Tsedakah* and *Hekdesh* 129
4.1.3 The Rabbinic Construction of *Tsedakah* as Quasi-*Hekdesh* 131
4.1.4 *Tsedakah* as *Hekdesh* during the Medieval Period 136
4.2 The Sustaining/Saving of Human Life as a Gift to and from God 146
4.2.1 The Obligation to Sustain Human Life 147
4.2.2 *Tsedakah* as a Transfer through the Divine Realm 151
4.2.3 Fulfilling the Obligation to Save Human Life – The Divine as Primary Recipient 159
4.2.3.1 The Dualistic Obligation to Save Human Life 159
4.2.3.2 Rendering Visible the Operation of the Divine Lien 164
4.2.4 Saving Human Life – The Question of Payment 167
4.2.4.1 Who Bears the Costs of the Rescue? 167
4.2.4.2 Other "Costs" to the Rescuer 174

5 Returning a "Lost Body" with One's Own Body: Organ Transplantation as Retrocession and (Re)consecration of the Body 178

5.1 Organ Transfer and the Fulfillment of the Divine Lien 183
5.2 What Is Given Goes (First) to God – The Human Body as *Hekdesh* 190
5.2.1 The Body as an Object of Dedication and Retrocession 190
5.2.2 Tithing the Body: Biblical Antecedents as Conceptual Analogues 192
5.2.3 Limits to Bodily Destruction, Harm, and Sale 193
5.3 The Erroneous Application of the "Pious Fool" Idiom 195

5.4 The Question of Permissible Payment 201
5.4.1 The Prohibition against Getting Paid to do a *Mitzvah* 203
5.4.2 Concerns of Unjust Enrichment 209
5.5 The Free and Obligatory Gift, and the Question of Human Ownership 211

Conclusion and Public Policy Implications 218

Glossary 229
Bibliography 235
General Index 249
Index of Biblical and Talmudic References 255

Preface

A popular (mis)conception regarding the Jewish tradition dating to ancient times assumes that, for the Jew, anything and everything is for sale. Thus, in William Shakespeare's *The Merchant of Venice*, the Jewish character Shylock appears fully prepared to enforce a contract by which he is entitled to obtain a pound of flesh in payment for an outstanding monetary debt. Outside intervention is required in order to avoid this outcome. The Shylock character, a symbol for the venal Jew, exemplifies an invidious stereotype that has persisted for generations.

It is possible to probe this idea on a theoretical level.[1] The moral and legal principles presented within the voluminous Jewish textual tradition provide a basis upon which to assess the contention (or accusation) that, for the Jew, there is nothing wrong with regarding everything as for sale and money as paramount. The legal tradition articulates normative principles that dictate the degree to which people can or cannot consider themselves free to act for purely monetary purposes, as well as ideas concerning property and social relations that delineate the individual's prerogatives and responsibilities with respect to property.

The "pound of flesh" contract at issue in *The Merchant of Venice* (not surprisingly) is not to be found in this rich legal tradition;[2] nevertheless, it is interesting to analyze how a case involving something resembling the sale of a human body part would fare. The contemporary scenario of organ transfer,[3]

1 Of course, how people behave, or have behaved, is a different matter entirely. See, e.g., Derek Penslar, *Shylock's Children: Economics and Jewish Identity in Modern Europe*, Berkeley: University of California Press (2001).

2 But see Shlomo Zevin, "*Mishpat Shylock*" [Hebrew: The Case of Shylock], in *Le'or Hahalacha*, Jerusalem: Beyt Hillel (1946), pp. 311–335, which analyzes precisely this hypothetical question of whether the contract at issue in *The Merchant of Venice* would be enforceable under Jewish law. He decides it would not be, based on the principle that humans do not own their bodies.

3 Rather than the phrase "organ donation," which assumes answers to the very questions explored here, the phrase "organ transfer" will generally be used in this book.

with the possibility of payment of a market price, provides just such a nonhypothetical setting for examining this question under Jewish law.[4] One might be tempted to argue that this is not a fair test, for it hardly seems likely that the well-developed legal/religious system of Jewish law would permit something that is condemned by most people as immoral and is legally banned worldwide. As it turns out, while relatively little has been written on this particular question (which is interesting in and of itself), much of what has been written seems to suggest that there is essentially nothing wrong with the sale of human organs (for purposes of transplantation) according to Jewish law.[5]

Along with this counterintuitive proposition, there is a puzzling empirical fact relating to Jews and organ transfer. If there is any generalization that one can accurately state regarding this tradition, it is that it places paramount importance on the value of human life, so much so that it permits the transgression of all but three prohibitions[6] if necessary to save a human life.[7] One might, therefore, expect a very high rate of organ transfer among Jews; that is what I had assumed when I began working on this topic. As it turns out, quite the opposite is true.

While I was working on this book, my mother died very suddenly of a stroke. She had signed her organ donor card, and I experienced the process of organ transfer firsthand, from the perspective of the donor family. What I found out, to my surprise, was (1) that Jews generally donated fewer organs than any other demographic group in the New York area, (2) that in Israel the rates of donation

4 I do not use the term "Jewish law" in a traditional religious sense (with a presumption of teleological or evolutionary development or causality); nor do I mean to imply the existence of a hypostasized, unitary entity. Rather, I use it in a generic sense to refer to the contents of a body of legal literature that was produced by Jews (often males and rabbis) that spans nearly two thousand years and great geographical distances. These texts embody many variegated approaches. I make no assertions as to how the disparate parts relate to one another. In contrast to "Jewish law," I use the term "Talmudic law" to refer to the legal contents of Talmudic, or "rabbinic," literature attributed to the Tannaim and Amoraim, circa 200–600 C.E.

5 See, e.g., Zalman Nechemiah Goldberg, *Kinyanim Bemechirat Kelayot* [Hebrew: Acquisitions in the Sale of Organs], in *Ateret Shelomo*, Jerusalem: Machon Madaei Technologi Lehalacha (5757/1997), pp. 49–55; Shlomo Goren, "*Mechirat Kelayot Lehashtalah al pi Hahalacha*" [Hebrew: The Sale of Organs for Transplant According to Jewish Law], in *Torat Harefuah: Mechkarim Hilchati'im Benosei Refuah*, Jerusalem: Ha-idra Rabah (5761/2001), pp. 127–148; Israel Meir Lau, "The Sale of Organs for Transplantation," in Daniel B. Sinclair (ed.), *Jewish Law Association Studies*, volume 15, Binghamton: Global Academic Publishing (2005), pp. 285–305 (translated from the Hebrew in *Tehumin* 18 [5758/1998], 125–136.); Yitzchak Zilberstein, "*Mechirat Kalya Lephar'on Chovot*" [Hebrew: Sale of Organs for the Payment of Debts], *Yated Ne'eman, Musaf* (Dec 30, 1994/27 Tevet 5755), p. 7.

6 These three exceptional prohibitions entail (1) idolatry, (2) certain prohibited sexual acts, and (3) murder of another person. See Babylonian Talmud ("B.T.") Sanhedring 74a.

7 The saving of the life of another is the greatest act one can perform; it is described as being tantamount to saving the entire world (B.T. Sanhedrin 37a).

were among the lowest in the world, and (3) that Israel is renowned for its high rate of participation in the worldwide black market in human organs.[8]

One can speculate as to why Jews might not donate in greater numbers. A possible explanation is the common intuition that, given the prohibition against maiming the human body (alive or dead), it might not be permitted under Jewish law. Yet, in view of the tradition's stress on the importance of saving human life, and its structural tendency to generate (a sense of) obligation for others, this hardly seems a likely or sufficient explanation.

Further puzzling is the fact that there is other evidence that suggests that, at least under some circumstances, Jews will donate, even at an unusually high rate. For example, in 2002, a man named Samuel Berger, who was in dire need of a new kidney, advertised in various Jewish newspapers in New York in search of a donor. The enticement to prospective donors was not money, but the opportunity to do the greatest *mitzvah*[9] there is – saving a human life. An astounding number of strangers – twenty-eight in all – responded to his ad and offered to donate their kidneys (*gratis*). This was an overwhelming response rate, which is what made the story newsworthy.[10]

The Berger story does seem to provide a clue – that willingness to donate might have something to do with community building and social bonding. In fact, that incident places in stark relief my final encounter with the way in which organ transfer is institutionalized in contemporary society. My mother did, in fact, donate her liver, to a person who would have died in a few days without it. About a month after the surgery, I called my contact person at the New York Organ Donor Network and made what I thought was a rather simple request – to visit the person (still hospitalized) who had received my mother's liver. The question elicited a lengthy silence on the other end of the line. I was

8 One report of an investigation into the international organ trade noted that "To those who monitor organ trafficking, it was no surprise that Israel should emerge as the focal point of a syndicate. Organ transfer rates in Israel are among the lowest in the developed world, about one-third the rate in Western Europe, in large part because of what Health Ministry officials and doctors describe as a widespread impression that Jewish religious law prohibits transplants as a 'desecration of the body.' In reality, religious law is far more nuanced. But influential Orthodox rabbis have been reluctant to make public statements that would encourage either live donors or the harvesting of organs from the deceased." Larry Rohter, "Tracking the Sale of a Kidney on a Path of Poverty and Hope," *New York Times* (May 23, 2004), pp. A1, A8. See also Dominick, Tao, "Worldwide Market Fuels Illegal Traffic in Organs," *New York Times* (July 29, 2009), p. A26 (Forty-four people arrested in FBI sting includes an Orthodox Jewish business man from Brooklyn, who is accused of trying to sell a human kidney for $160,000.)

9 The word "*mitzvah*" is translated colloquially as a good deed. More accurately, it connotes the fulfillment of a Jewish legal obligation (whether mandatory or voluntary). For more on the definition of the word *mitzvah* see p. 15 n. 44.

10 For a similar, more recent case, see http://m.ynet.co.il/Article.aspx?id=4406117.

finally told, in a tone of amazement, that no one had ever asked that question before. The wasted opportunity for human contact surrounding this event, the very element that might be likely to foster organ transfer, was striking.

So what is the "Jewish" approach to organ transfer,[11] and what, if anything, does it offer that might contribute to contemporary debates and problems surrounding this issue? The relevant legal texts can clarify the answer to this question. It is most interesting to read them against the backdrop of the empirical and anecdotal evidence described above. The apparent lack of a prohibition against organ sales, coupled with the paucity of organ transfers by Jews, could be perceived as an uncomfortable echo of the selfishness and venality represented by Shylock. Yet, there is other evidence that seems to indicate something very different. The Samuel Berger incident hints not only at the underappreciated importance of sociality in this context, but also at the possible effectiveness of a tradition that, at least in theory, aims to cultivate a sense of obligation to sustain the lives and well-being of (some?) others.

That which is suggested by the anecdotal evidence finds resonance in the traditional texts. This book will show that Jewish law can serve as a model for a new approach to addressing the dire need for organs for transplant. It is more complicated (but perhaps more practical and realistic) than the perceived narrow, dichotomous choice: to either rely on "pure" altruistic gift giving or to allow the market to help solve the problem by introducing money as an incentive. For, the question of the permissibility of "organ sales" under Jewish law is not at all straightforward. It calls for an exploration of questions of obligation, reward, incentive, property ownership, and self-ownership, an inquiry that proves illuminating as to the Jewish legal perspective on organ transfer and for the contemporary debate over the "commodification" aspect of this issue. What comes to the fore is the importance, in this realm, of social bonding (the absence of which is one of the very problems resulting from excessive commercialization and commodification) and the idea of tapping into a third possibility: envisioning and encouraging a gift that is both free and obligatory (if not simply obligatory), and the possibility of some form of compensation. This study develops this theory and offers it as a different perspective on the ethical dilemma presented by the shortage of organs for transplant.

[11] The phrasing of this question is somewhat rhetorical. I do not mean to suggest that there is one "Jewish" response to organ transfer (or to anything else), or that it necessarily relates to the narratives recounted here.

Acknowledgments

This book came out of a lifelong love for learning ancient texts. My interest and devotion could not have been piqued and nurtured, however, without the support of many many people from my childhood to now.

First I would like to say thank you to my graduate committee at Harvard: Jay Harris, Moshe Halbertal, Michael Sandel, and Michael Waltzer.

While at Harvard I had the privilege of teaching a faculty Talmud group for four years. This group kept my juices flowing and my ideas coming as we methodically dissected the most difficult parts of the Babylonian Talmud – Chapters 4 and 5 of Tractate Bava Metzia. Wholehearted thanks go to these people, who were my students, my role models, and my inspiration: Alan Dershowitz, Charles Donahue, Catherine Krupnick, Hilary Putnam, Ruth-Anna Putnum, Joseph Singer, Avi Soifer, Martha Minow, Harvey Cox, and the late Steven J. Gould.

Appreciation goes to those at the University of Michigan Law School who were supportive and helpful: Reuven Avi-Yonah, Evan Caminker, Robert Howse, Douglas Laycock, Jessica Litman, the late Brian Simpson, and James Boyd White, as well as Lois Harden, John Lloyd, and Laura Harlow.

Thanks go to the many great scholars from whom I derived inspiration simply by being in their presence at Harvard University, U.C. Berkeley, the Graduate Theological Union, Princeton University, the Shalom Hartman Institute, the Institute for Advanced Study, the University of Michigan, and elsewhere. Special thanks go in particular to Daniel Boyarin, Caroline Walker Bynum, Robert Chazen, Soelve Curdts, Yaacov Elman, Geoff Ely, Isaiah Gafni, the late Clifford Geertz, the late Oleg Grabar, Alyssa Gray, Jennifer Hasty, the late Albert Hirschman, Bernard Jackson, Regina Morantz-Sanchez, Mika Natif, Rachel Neis, the late Charles Nelson, Anita Norich, Naomi Seidman, and Aharon Shemesh.

I would also like to thank the wonderful members of my family, all now deceased, who fostered, in one way or another, my love for studying Jewish texts and my search for justice in the world: my grandfather, Jacob Isaac Kraminer (1900–1993); my cousin Lissie, Elise Deborah Rosen Odenheimer (1958–1995); my father, Dr. Joseph Abraham Kochen (1931–2012); and my mother, Elizabeth Kraminer Kochen, (1931–2000) who helped me survive her own sudden death by donating her liver to save the life of someone who had only a few days to live. Special mention must also be made here of two people who were, effectively, family – the late Jacob Aaron Vogelman (1988–2012) and the late Debbie Friedman (1951–2011). All of these people loved me best and believed in me most. Their love is a continuing source of nourishment.

Thank you to my adoptive family – the people who have made the final publication of this book possible with their love and encouragement – Lynn Saul and everyone at CBS in Tucson, Raquel and Zakai Gibly, David and Mary Vine, Hallie Bongar White, and last, but not least, Yitzhak Zamir.

There are countless others to whom I owe a debt of gratitude for their support, ideas, and encouragement during the course of the intellectual path that led to my writing this book especially Saul Berman, the late Rhonda Copelon, Ruhama Fixler Erenberg, Nancy Garber, Susan Kahn, Judith Levin, Judith Paikin, and Maria Slowiaczek.

I would like to thank the following Fellowship programs, whose support was invaluable to the completion of this project: the Wexner Graduate Fellowship; the Harvard Center for Ethics and the Professions; the Harvard University Graduate Society Fellowship; the Barney and Anne B. Malloy Memorial Fellowship at Harvard University; the Alan M. and Katherine W. Stroock Fellowship at Harvard University, the Frankel Institute for Advanced Judaic Studies, and the N.E.H. Summer Program in "Aramaic in Post-Biblical Judaism and Early Christianity."

Finally, and despite the impropriety of thanking someone for doing a *mitzvah*, I must thank my wife, Annie Ringo Vine, for saving and sustaining my body and my soul for the past four years. Without you, Ringo, this book likely would never have been published.

Introduction

In modern capitalism, all are "brothers" in being equally "others."[1]

Benjamin Nelson, *The Idea of Usury*

"Would it be wrong of me to sell my kidney?" For many people, the answer to this question most certainly would be yes. Practical concerns about the potential for abuse, coercion, and exploitation hardly account for this near-visceral reaction. What seem to fuel this response are deeply rooted attitudes regarding human dignity, the meaning of money, and boundaries between people and property. Even in nonreligious discourse, this reaction is often explained by invoking the idea of "sacredness," referring perhaps to both the special status of the property at issue and the meaning associated with the act of transfer itself.

The nearly universal worldwide ban on the sale of human organs for transplant is a classic example of a moral limit to the market, enacted into law.[2] It illustrates the "compartmentalizing" approach to resolving problems of markets and morals, pursuant to which transactions deemed ill suited to a commercial milieu are relegated to the nonmonetary sphere; in other words, such items are expected to be gifted, or given without remuneration.

The results of the prosaic ban on organ sales illustrate the way in which the compartmentalization approach can be insufficient and even problematic. The immense discrepancy between the number of organs needed to save lives and the number of donated organs available has caused contemporary theorists and policy makers to consider whether some form of payment ought not to be

1 Benjamin Nelson, *The Idea of Usury*, Chicago: University of Chicago Press (1969), p. xxv.

2 It could also be referred to as the "blocked exchange" of a "contested commodity." See, e.g., Michael Walzer, *Spheres of Justice*, New York: Basic Books (1983); Margaret Jane Radin, *Contested Commodities*, Cambridge: Harvard University Press (1996).

permitted. For indeed, notwithstanding the murkiness of the term "sacred" as used in ordinary (nonreligious) parlance, what is clear is that the very "sacredness" of the human being that theoretically renders payment for organs off limits is desecrated by the tens of thousands of deaths each year of those unable to secure organs within a system dependent on altruistic donation.[3]

As is true with many of the issues raised by problems of markets and morals (and by what are often related advances in science and technology), the ethical conundrum of "organ sales" is played out through the complications it presents and the ambiguities it highlights regarding the legal and philosophical meanings and boundaries of the concepts of property, ownership, personhood, and individual autonomy.[4] This theoretical puzzle is not solved but, rather, is further complicated by the prevalent perspective that appears to allow for only two options: a market in human organs or exclusive reliance upon (insufficient) altruistic donations. The impracticality and arguable immorality of the restrictive choice of either commodity or free gift hints at a deeper truth – that many of the ideas articulated in the contemporary debate over commodification are rooted in silent assumptions that surreptitiously overdetermine the very questions that they pretend to answer.

This book takes as its starting point the problem of "commodification," using the hypothetical lens of "selling" body parts for transplant. It is this case that perhaps best represents the rich intellectual complexities of a larger dilemma, providing a locus for the intersection of the most significant theoretical and philosophical issues involved in the problem of commodification. Chapter 1 introduces the way in which questions such as these have caused scholars to interrogate "the market" and to theorize about what limits, if any, ought to be imposed thereon. While the literature is replete with critiques of the theoretical underpinnings and political structures that support the

[3] There are other ways in which the status quo is claimed to be immoral. For example, under the current system, everyone involved in an organ transplant, including the doctor, is paid (or benefits in some substantial way) except the person providing the organ. See Stephen J. Dubner, "Flesh Trade: Why Not Let People Sell Their Organs," *New York Times Magazine* (Jul 9, 2006), pp. 20–21.

[4] The theoretical confusion this problem generates is manifest, for example, in the way arguments from "sacredness" quickly become self-contradictory or even mutually exclusive. On the one hand, a concern for that which is "sacred" (human life? the human body?) is said to demand a ban on organ sales; on the other hand, the imperative to protect "the sanctity of the individual" – the "first principle" of Western society that guarantees near-absolute sovereignty over one's body – would seem to militate in the opposite direction. See e.g. *McFall v. Shimp*, 10 Pa.D. & C.3d 90 (1978) (Intractable moral quandries illustrated in a case where the court refuses to compel someone, who had previously consented, to submit to a bone marrow transplant necessary to save the life of a relative).

market,[5] it is clear upon closer examination that those arguing on both sides of this question, anti-commodifiers as well as those who are pro-market, are caught up in a certain way of thinking about these issues. Entrenched in a particular discourse (organs are either gifted altruistically or sold), even those scholars (particularly anti-commodifiers) who recognize the impoverished nature of traditional conceptions underlying markets (such as social-contract theory) have offered few if any theoretical alternatives.

This quandary, and the paucity of practical and theoretical options, invites consideration of other analytical constructs. One way of getting out of this discursive and theoretical bind is to tap into the "potentially subversive possibilities" of anthropology.[6] Comparative analyses invoking the perspectives of other traditions represent an ideal way to try to address category-challenging moral dilemmas such as "organ sales." Applying a comparative approach to analyze novel scenarios can help elucidate foundational ideas in our tradition that are not readily visible. Marilyn Strathern's observation, that models from other cultures can turn out to be "more appropriate to the post-industrial Western world than outdated models of private ownership and possession,"[7] might be particularly true in this context.

With this in mind, this book explores certain legal aspects of exchange, payment, and property relations in Jewish law, particularly in the realm of the sacred. The theories and ideas elucidated by this case study provide a different conceptual framework for analyzing modern-day problems associated with commodification, such as those related to organ transfer and possible payment for organs. Through a proposed alternative approach illustrated by the model of Jewish law, this book exposes, challenges, and rethinks some of the assumptions associated with our market-based society. While articulating a new theory of the economy of the sacred in Jewish law, it supplies the theoretical grounding for a different perspective on contemporary questions of markets and morals.[8]

5 Critiqued constructs include social-contract theory, a specific theory of the person, theories of distributive justice, and (limited) notions of obligation.

6 Alexandra Ouroussoff, "Illusions of Rationality: False Premises of the Liberal Tradition," *Man* 28/2 (Jun 1993), pp. 281–298 at 282.

7 Chris M. Hann, "Introduction: The Embeddedness of Property," in Chris M. Hann (ed.), *Property Relations: Renewing the Anthropological Tradition*, Cambridge: Cambridge University Press (1998) at 44.

8 Anthropological literature is replete with comparative projects that come to be relevant to our own cultural predicaments. The work of Marcel Mauss, in his essay entitled *The Gift: The Form and Reason for Exchange in Archaic Societies* (New York: W. W. Norton and Co. [1990]), is an example of such an enterprise. Like this book, it is based, in method and in substance, on literary texts and ancient practices. This examination of property and obligation in Jewish law builds upon some of the themes and concepts at work in *The Gift*.

While one might expect there to be more inhibitions on the use of money in the realm of the sacred within the religious Jewish legal system, there actually appear to be far fewer. In fact, among the underexamined questions that are brought to light by the contemporary problem of organ sales is the role and meaning of money in Jewish law. This phenomenon highlights a ubiquitous yet rarely noticed aspect of Jewish law: that in most contexts, the transfer of money has little legal effect; neither will it render permissible that which is prohibited, nor is it likely to render prohibited something otherwise permitted. Indeed, the payment of money often does not even register on the legal radar screen as a juridically significant event.[9]

This might explain why, while there is a considerable amount written about organ transfer and Jewish law (considering relevant prohibitions, such as the prohibition against mutilating the human body), there is relatively little mention in the literature of the impact the introduction of money has on the legality of the transaction.[10] In one of the few statements by a contemporary Jewish legal decisor, Rabbi Israel Meir Lau, wrote, during his tenure as Ashkenazi Chief Rabbi of Israel (1993–2003), that in any situation where organ transfer is otherwise permissible (e.g., to save a life), there is no impediment under Jewish law to the "sale" of human organs for transplant.[11] Noting the potentially troublesome consequences of this finding, Rabbi Lau conceded that Jewish law would abide the development of a market in human organs.

This only confirms what might seem instinctive to some, that Jewish law might be an inappropriate candidate for this comparative project regarding the sale of organs for translplant, given Judaism's popular association with private property and the market.[12] However, to so understand the Jewish tradition and its historical

[9] Of course, one reason for the relative lack of concern regarding many of the problems that fall under the rubric of invidious commodification is the fact that the rabbinic tradition predates capitalism. As the material in Chapter 1 makes clear, however, this fact in no way delegitimates a comparative examination of Jewish laws on the question of money and exchange regarding contemporary questions.

[10] This issue has begun to receive slighly more attention in the past few years.

[11] Lau, Israel Meir, "The Sale of Organs for Transplantation" (Hebrew), *Tehumin* 18 (1998), pp. 125–136.

[12] See, e.g., Werner Sombart, *The Jews and Modern Capitalism*, New York: Collier Books (1951); Wolf Heydebrand (ed.), *Sociological Writings of Max Weber*, New York: Continuum (1984). Even Jonathan Parry assumes that Jewish law epitomizes an association with money when he remarks somewhat critically, "[i]t is not I think coincidental that the ideology of the 'pure gift' is accorded such prominence among groups – such as the Jews and the Jains – which have a particularly close historical association with market trade, for the two spheres ('pure gift' and sale) define each other"; Jonathan Parry, "The Gift, the Indian Gift and the 'Indian Gift'," *Man* 21/3 (Sep 1986), pp. 453–473 at 469. Parry's remark can be viewed as one instance within a tradition of scholarship concerning the relationship between Jews and money, some of which includes invidious stereotyping. Some of the books that deal critically with this tradition include Hillel Levine, *Economic Origins of Antisemitism*, New Haven: Yale University Press

association with money matters is to mistake accident for cause. While it is true that many Jews in medieval Europe were involved in trade and business, this was not a product of the Jewish tradition but, rather, was related to severe externally imposed restrictions on the kinds of economic activities in which they, as legal aliens, could engage.[13] Thus, while engaging in economic activity that results in the accumulation of capital is certainly within the bounds of Jewish law,[14] the historical impression ought not to be confused with the larger conceptual framework envisioned or imagined by this legal system. Moreover, looking in isolation at the situation during a few medieval centuries in Eastern Europe, which represent but a fraction of Jewish history, both historically and geographically, is to present a skewed image of the Jewish tradition. It is also to insufficiently attend to the canonical legal texts upon which Jewish law is founded. The canon produced in late antiquity – that is, Mishnaic and Talmudic literature (upon which ensuing Jewish legal decisions rest) – will be studied here to uncover the basic conceptions upon which later developments are based.

Rather than pointing to its supposed proto-capitalist character, it is more likely that the reason Jewish law has not been the source for this type of project on commodification is due to the nature of Jewish Studies scholarship, much of which tends to focus almost exclusively on critical-historical questions, literary and philosophical matters,[15] and internal legal analysis. To the extent that there is literature that draws on ancient Jewish texts to address contemporary problems, it primarily takes the form of religious legal Responsa (*she'elot* and *teshuvot*) and internal religious discourse. As illustrated in the context of organ sales, present-day traditional scholarship can also fail to sufficiently ground itself in the conceptual matrix of the ancient texts; ironically, contemporary religious decisors can be unreflectively influenced by their modern liberal cultural environments. At the same time, there is also a well-trodden conventional approach to choosing and analyzing those precedents deemed relevant that can lock the decisor into what is often a very narrow, and ultimately peripheral or tangential, way of dealing with some of the deeper issues at stake.

This study of Jewish law explicitly attempts to avoid these pitfalls. In so doing, it suggests a different approach in Jewish law, one that can also help extend the debate over commodification beyond the deep discursive and theoretical

(1991); Derek J. Penslar, *Shylock's Children: Economics and Jewish Identity in Modern Europe*, Berkeley: University of California Press (2001); James Shapiro, *Shakespeare and the Jews*, New York: Columbia University Press (1996).

[13] See, e.g., Jacob Katz, *Tradition and Crisis*, Syracuse: Syracuse University Press (2000), chapters 6 and 7.

[14] Although, as the noted historian Jacob Katz points out, this was by no means the only way in which Jews made a living during the medieval period. *Id.*

[15] Jewish Studies is a relatively young field and is still heavily influenced by the founders of the *Wissenschaft des Judentums* tradition, a nineteenth-century historical method.

constraints described earlier. Conceptions borrowed from law (e.g., the notion of the "lien") and anthropology (e.g., neo-Maussian ideas of gift exchange) are invoked to help analyze Talmudic texts and to aid in the elucidation of a new theory of the Jewish sacred economy, a theory that, in fact, suggests a way to reconceptualize the so-called donation versus sale of organs for transplant. By highlighting the embeddedness of exchange practices in the obligatory framework of law, and in building on the idea of obligatory gifts as an integral form of social relations, this book provides a different perspective on this question. As a more general matter, Jewish law is offered as a model that enables us to move beyond the sharp divide between gift and commodity, and some of the constraints implicitly imposed by that dichotomy.

Some of the background principles used in this analysis of Jewish law, traceable primarily to the work of Marcel Mauss, are developed in Chapter 2, "Alternative Property Conceptions: The Donor's Lien." Renowned as "the inventor of the gift in anthropology,"[16] Mauss conceives of a gift as something other than the voluntary, free gift of contemporary Western usage. According to Mauss, a gift is an obligatory act; the practice of gift giving is characterized by a set of interlocking obligations: the obligation to give, the obligation to receive, and, most important for present purposes, the obligation to reciprocate, or to make a "return gift." Through his study of "ancient societies," he established that gifts are part of a web of interconnected obligations, and, as such, they play a critical role in social bonding.

Critical about Mauss's approach, for purposes of this book, is his claim that the character of most exchanges is neither purely altruistic nor purely self-interested.[17] He highlighted the interrelational focus of exchange, whereby the interests of both parties to a transaction are always and at once taken into account. This perspective reflects a kind of hybrid morality that is characterized by the fact that both "generosity and self-interest that are linked in giving."[18] This hybrid morality, where the "life of the monk, and the life of a Shylock are both equally to be shunned,"[19] is at the heart of the Jewish legal approach to organ transfer and sales that is outlined in this book.

[16] Marilyn Strathern, "Divisions of Interest and the Languages of Ownership," in C. M. Hann (ed.), *Property Relations*, Cambridge: Cambridge University Press (1998, pp. 214–232) at 220.

[17] This insight is key to Mauss's purpose in reviewing the archaic institution of gift exchange, which was neither to aspire to an earlier evolutionary stage of (pure) gift giving (in contrast to self-interested commodity exchange) nor to show that all exchanges, including those taking the form of gifts, are always about individual (economic) self-interest. His aim was to turn (in part) to ancient society and reveal subtle complexities about gift exchange that continue to be true today.

[18] Mauss (1990) at 68.

[19] *Id.* at 69. Mauss aspires to a society in which people "give, freely and obligatorily." *Id.* at 71.

A second and related theme that underlies this hybrid morality is the paradoxical notion of "freedom and … obligation inherent in the gift."[20] Distinct from but linked to the idea of the combination of interest and disinterest (here meaning lack of self-interest), the paradoxical notion of freedom and obligation being combined in the gift appears with nearly every mention thereof, throughout Mauss's essay. And yet, it is the interest/disinterest idea that is the focus of most discussion of Mauss's work, particularly in the context of the debate over commodification (where the issue involves the character of gift giving as an alternative to sales as altruistic – or not). This is, for example, the critical feature that Jacques Derrida focuses on in his critique of Mauss's exposition on the gift.[21] Even Mauss pays more attention to this facet of his theory in his essay and in his discussion of its possible policy implications.

Indeed, the fact that these two themes (interest/disinterest and freedom/obligation) are separate and distinct in Mauss' essay often goes unnoticed. Yet, for purposes of analysis, the question of (the degree of) altruism – which is the usual focus of attention in matters relating to gifts – and the question of (the degree of) voluntariness point in two different (albeit, at times, overlapping) directions. Although the first theme, of the inextricable mixture of self-interest and generosity, underlies my critique, in Chapter 1, of using the idea of a pure gift as a response to the problem of commodification, it is Mauss's second observation, of the paradoxical mixture of the free and the obligatory that is mixed in giving, that propels and supports my new approach to these questions, as illustrated here by Jewish law.

Marcel Mauss's insights on gift exchange form part of the theoretical framework for this analysis of the sale of organs for transplant under Jewish law, and for the larger theory of property to which it gives rise. His notion of the obligatory "return gift" is particularly helpful in understanding the Talmudic materials. Mauss's work is credited with recognizing the dimension of obligation that inheres in many forms of gift exchange. His analysis does more, however, than simply articulate the prosaic sense of responsibility to reciprocate that one feels, for example, when one is invited to someone's house for dinner. Indeed, the word "obligation," by itself, fails to capture the various facets of what Mauss was describing, which is a duty with the following set of attributes:

(1) it resides in particular property ("*in rem*") – thus, I make reference to this neo-Maussian obligation as a "lien" (on property) or as an "embodied obligation";

[20] *Id.*

[21] See Jacques Derrida, *Given Time*, volume 1: *Counterfeit Money*, translated by Peggy Kamuf, Chicago: University of Chicago Press (1991); see also Jacques Derrida, *The Gift of Death*, translated by David Wills, Chicago: University of Chicago Press (1992).

(2) it is not directly enforceable at law (and, thus, might perhaps better be termed an indefinite obligation or an obligation without a right, in Hohfeldian terms);[22]
(3) it presumes that both the impetus for its fulfillment and the terms thereof (how much, when, whether, to whom, etc.) are dependant upon the volition of the gift recipient; and
(4) its fulfillment is motivated by a mixture of concerns for oneself and for the other (interest and disinterest, generosity and self-interest, are combined).

It is the latter three features of this embodied, indefinite duty (2)–(4) that explain why the act of fulfillment might be described, paradoxically, as both "free and obligatory."

This complex concept, of an act that is both free and obligatory, and interested as well as disinterested, that emerges from Mauss's ethnographic and historical analysis is not readily apparent or recognizable in contemporary society. One can glean, from his essay, an explanation for why, today, it is difficult to perceive or comprehend this phenomenon. He provides a portrayal of so-called primitive societies in order to tell a particular story whereby, in early gift exchange, entities that are, today, presumed to comprise or reflect binary constructs, such as interest and disinterest, or persons and things, were actually fused. Later, these theoretical pairs were split, resulting in the perceived opposition between interest and generosity, sale and pure gift, or people and things. Today, this related set of distinctions as distinctions, between interest and disinterest, freedom and constraint, people and things, are presumed to underlie our conceptions of property and market exchange. It is this set of distinctions that presupposes the problematic twin ideologies of the pure gift and of the purely interested individual pursuit of utility. Tracing the theoretical heritage of these ideas reveals the problem with anti-commodifiers' embrace of the pure gift approach to the notion of organ sales. Endorsing the theory of pure gift reinforces its supposed theoretical counterpart, interested monetary exchange. The alternative response suggested here is to focus on bonding-enhancing exchanges, ones that entail the combinations of interest and disinterest, obligation as well as freedom, and in which the divide between persons and things (as well as between persons and persons) may be understood to be more porous.

The blurring of the lines between people and things, and the mixture of freedom and obligation, is particularly reflected in a key element of Mauss's theory known as "the spirit of the gift." According to this concept emanating from Mauss's empirical findings, it is imagined that when something is gifted, part of the donor – or the "spirit" of the donor – continues to "reside in" the item and yearns to return

[22] See Wesley Newcomb Hohfeld, "Some Fundamental Legal Conceptions as Applied in Judicial Reasoning," *Yale Law Review* 23 (1913), pp. 16ff.

to the donor. This is one way to think about the need for a "return gift" (an obligation that is left to the discretion of the gift recipient to fulfill) that is presumed to accompany every gift. Thus understood, it is possible to see how gift exchange establishes a web of interlocking obligations that create social solidarity.[23]

The notion of the "spirit of the gift" might be conceived of as a sort of nascent lien or claim residing in particular property that creates a bond between persons in its representation of their indebtedness to each other. Defined as a "claim or charge on property for payment of some debt, obligation or duty,"[24] a lien (or, perhaps in this case, something more akin to an equitable lien) communicates the essential element of an obligation to another that resides within particular property, such that the property is implicated by another.

The terms "lien" or "donor's lien" will be used in this book to communicate this concept; it is, of course, not meant to imply the existence of an actual debt enforceable at law by a particular individual – to the contrary, in this context it refers to a duty (or compulsion to give) that is defined precisely, in part, by its indefiniteness, by the openness of some or all of its terms. The property holder is often left to decide whether, when, what, and to whom something ought to be given as a "return." Yet, despite its somewhat open-ended and volitional nature, it is, nevertheless, an *in rem* obligation that is built into the property.[25] Thus, while being in one significant sense an obligation, the return gift is still a gift.[26] This is precisely the explanation for the phenomenon whereby "obligation and liberty intermingle."[27]

[23] Mauss's theory has been seen as providing an alternative to the originary myth of social contract, with the institution of gift exchange seen to arise from human beings' early realization of their reciprocal dependence. As Marshall Sahlins put it, one can see the gift operating as "the primitive way of achieving the peace that in civil society is secured by the State." Marshall Sahlins, *Stone Age Economics*, Chicago: Aldine Publishing Company (1972) at 169. The reason the gift "succeeds in suppressing the Warre of all against all [is] because it creates spiritual bonds between persons by means of things which embody persons." *Id.*

[24] Henry Campbell Black, *Black's Law Dictionary*, 5th ed., St Paul: West Publishing Co. (1979), p. 832. The anthropologist Jonathan Parry mentions the word "lien" in describing this notion of "the spirit of the gift," although he does not develop the legal concept and its relevance to the Maussian gift. In his words, the gift is understood to "contain some part of the spiritual essence of the donor, and this constrains the recipient to make a return." Parry, (1986) at 456. In other words, "because the thing contains" its original owner, "the donor retains a lien on what he has given away ..., and it is because of the participation of the [donor] in the object that the gift creates an enduring bond between persons." *Id.* at 457.

[25] What is meant here is a legal obligation that does not carry with it a corresponding (directly enforceable) legal right. While "a lien is, in essence, an *in rem* obligation," in the sense that it is built into the property itself, not every *in rem* obligation represents a lien enforceable at law by an identifiable party. Jeffrey K. Robison, "Note: The Debtor's Right to Restrict Lienholder Recovery to the Value of the Encumbered Property under Section 506 of the Bankruptcy Code," *Journal of Corporations Law* 11 (spring 1986), pp. 433–455.

[26] As will be demonstrated, while this donor's lien might be more loosely understood as a moral or social obligation, it is nevertheless also possible to conceive of it as legal.

[27] Mauss (1990) at 65.

The legal and anthropological conceptions described above are outlined in the first two chapters of the book. Against the backdrop of these ideas, the latter three chapters undertake an in-depth study of Talmudic sources, focusing primarily on the Talmudic legal institution of divine ownership. In so doing, this book sets forth a novel understanding of the ideas of ownership, people and property in Jewish law. When the idea that God is the original owner and donor of all things is taken seriously as a legal concept, human ownership, even of oneself, is shown in the Talmudic framework to be neither total nor absolute. As subjugated within the "divinely" mandated Jewish legal system, the person is shown to be caught up in a web of responsibilities and obligations that relate directly to limitations on ownership and self-ownership. These limitations inhere in a legal notion of divine ownership, an overarching property conception that can elide people and things as originally owned by God.[28] Chapter 3 elucidates this principle of divine ownership and the connection thereto of myriad legal obligations, thus laying the foundation for a theory of the divine donor's lien as embedded in the Jewish conception of property. As will be seen, in Chapter 4, certain transfers that occur under this rubric of limited ownership can be seen to illustrate complex exchanges that parallel and, in important ways, go beyond those contemplated by the Maussian theory. In Chapter 5, human organ transfer and transplantation are seen to exemplify this type of free and obligatory "exchange."

This book analyzes the Jewish law of the classical rabbinic texts from late antiquity. These texts form a touchstone, or even a foundation, for the Jewish legal tradition that follows. In juxtaposing the ancient, living Jewish legal tradition with the very contemporary problem of payment for organs, this book focuses attention on some of the conceptual foundations of Jewish law that have heretofore been largely unexamined, undeveloped, or unappreciated both in the academic field of Jewish Studies and in the *halakhic* (internal Jewish legal) literature.

[28] Limitations on the Jewish notion of self-ownership are evinced both in the way the person is always imagined as a relational social unit, and also, more concretely, in restrictions and prescriptions relating to the body and its use, including the prohibition against *chavalah* (self-mutilation) and suicide, laws of *peyot* (shaving one's beard), burial, redemption of the firstborn son, circumcision, and the obligation of *pikuach nefesh*. (See e.g. *hatra'ah*, (the rabbinic law that prohibits imposition of the death penalty unless the person is warned, beforehand, that he is about to commit a crime that could result in the death penalty) and, conversely, the rule prohibiting the acceptance of money to save/redeem the life of a convicted murderer.)

The novel and useful perspective that is drawn out of the Jewish legal texts is one that brings to light what is really at stake in the context of organ transfer and payment. Rather than disdain for the payment of money and the desirability of an altruistic gift in lieu of a sale, what is at the heart of the moral dilemma presented by the shortage of organs for transplant are deeper and more disturbing questions of obligation and entitlement. These problems are embedded in the very concept of contingent human property ownership under Jewish law.

In its earliest conception, Jewish law contemplates divine "ownership" in its most literal legal sense. On the one hand, all that is worldly – people and things – are seen as grants from the divine. Furthermore, classic rabbinic literature sets forth a system of property law that is essentially two tiered;[29] in addition to mundane (human-owned) property law, there is a separate body of law related to property owned by God (retained or received through the ancient Temple).[30] With the legal institution of *hekdesh* – sanctified property – there exists a category of property that is seen to be legally owned by God and from which no human is permitted to benefit.

Property transactions between people and God are ubiquitous in rabbinic literature.[31] Talmudic law provides explicit legal mechanisms by which a person is able to "give" objects, animals, money, and possibly persons into God's

[29] There are also some types of property, or some property at different stages of transition between the two categories of *hekdesh* (sacred) and *chullin* or *hedyot* (secular), that either possess intermediary levels of sanctity and/or represent hybrids containing aspects of both or shared (human/divine) ownership.

[30] The rabbis of the Talmud frequently learned from the body of "divine" property law to other areas of law, often by analogy or by distinction. Even though they may not actually have had Temple-like *hekdesh*, this category functions for them as a real legal counterpoint to secular property. And indeed, specific aspects of "divine" property law are rooted in the rabbi's conception that it is God who legally is thought to be the owner. For instance, whereas a transfer of (secular) property between people is not considered irrevocable until the merchandise is actually moved, property can be transferred to God through the use of words alone. (Mishnah Kiddushin 1:6: "An uttered dedication to the Temple is tantamount to an act of delivery to an ordinary person.") This is explained elsewhere by the fact that, since all property is already in God's domain (inasmuch as God owns the entire world), there is no need to actually move the property to signify its shift from one domain to the other. See p. 73, *infra*.

[31] This idea is found elsewhere, as well. For example, the Italian scholar, rabbi and poet Leon (Judah Aryeh) de Modena (1571–1648) referenced this idea in the epitaph (which he penned) that appears on his gravestone. Using the language of a legal document, the epitaph avers that the four cubits of land in which de Modena was buried had been acquired (הקנו) by him from God (ממעל) forever. (Thank you to Naomi Seidman for pointing out this reference). The epitaph states in full:

קרקע בחצר זה אגב קנין סודר מימות עולם הקנו ממעל ליהודה אריה ממודינה בזה נסתר ונעלם ארבע אמות

"Four cubits of ground in this [grave]yard, by means of acquisition by kerchief (*kinyan sudar*), were permanently acquired by Judah Aryeh of Modena from God (lit. from above). In these [four cubits] he hid himself and disappeared." Isidore Singer (ed.), "Tombstones", *The Jewish Encyclopedia*, New York: Funk and Wagnalls Co. (1916), p. 192.

ownership in a fully legal, this-worldly sense. Conversely, there are mechanisms by which sacred property (or people, e.g. the firstborn male) can be transferred or redeemed (i.e., removed from divine ownership), often through the use of money. These rules are not merely semantic curiosities, but represent a body of law that serves to make apparent deep philosophical (and theological) concepts of obligation in property in Jewish law. Furthermore, these concepts (or their influence) are shown to be reflected in the development of various relevant legal institutions after the Temple was destroyed.[32]

In the Jewish legal imagination, there is a conceptual strain in the legal texts that echoes the Maori notion "spirit of the gift," whereby all things and people are understood to have originated as gifts from God, and thus to contain what I call a "divine lien,"[33] which creates a bond between the donor (God) and the recipient. The original institutional focus of divine ownership (as a concrete legal matter) was the ancient Temple in Jerusalem, where the quintessential obligatory gift was made to God in the form of a sacrifice. This book shows that the original bond between the donor and recipient at times gets reinscribed as a bond between persons, as various provisions or institutions of Jewish law systematically deflect obligatory gifts to God (his expected "return") by transposing them, in whole or in part, onto certain human beings.

Chapter 3 sets forth legal texts that bear out this idea that God, as original "donor," has a lien on everything. This, in turn, gives rise to obligations that are written into the very notions of property (ownership) under Jewish law, obligations to share or to give (either to God or, devolving from the debt to God, to other people) as preconditions to taking ownership, as well as obligations to share or to give that run conterminously with, and thus inherently limit, ownership. Three such categories of obligations are built into the notion

[32] In Temple times, the institution of *hekdesh* implied giving directly to God via the Temple, for example, through dedicating and offering an animal for sacrifice, or making a donation for Temple upkeep. Yet, long after the destruction of the Temple in 70 C.E., the rabbis of the Mishnah, the Talmud, and beyond continued to imagine, discuss, and develop this legal institution of divine property, even though there was no longer a Temple to stand in for, or to provide a portal for a direct transfer to, the sacred realm of divine ownership. There is reason to believe that the theoretical underpinnings of subsequent developments in other legal institutions, many involving exchange, can be traced, in whole or in part, to conceptions of divine ownership (lien) and gifts to God, which perpetuate the imagined possibility of legally "giving" things (or people?) to God by providing a mechanism by which people might continue to be able to do so, even if possibly only metaphorically.

[33] Everything also has the potential to be returned to God and to become sacred property. As described above, the term "lien" is used here somewhat metaphorically for the conceptual contribution it makes, to communicate the location of a debt within property. Other elements of a standard lien, such as the existence of a formal, legally enforceable debt and the right of a particular person to enforce that debt, are not meant to be implied to be present in this context.

of property under Jewish law: (1) property obligations toward God, as original owner of everything and continuing lien holder;[34] (2) obligations toward certain sectors of society (such as priests);[35] and (3) obligations toward the needy,[36] the latter two categories of people constituting God's representatives or third-party beneficiaries. These obligations written into selves and into property have a social bonding function, as well as a redistributive function with respect to the community at large.

Chapters 3 and 4 explore the way in which certain legal developments and institutions were animated by the concept of God's lien, or by the idea of literally "giving" things to God, so as to inform or help effectuate their particular usually *tsedek*- or justice-related purposes. Mauss himself hinted obliquely at this theory in Jewish law. In *The Gift*, he made mention of the rabbinic notion of *tsedakah* (commonly (mis)understood today to mean "charity" or *caritas*), noting that it harks back to its (biblical) root meaning of *tsedek* – justice.[37] Mauss mentions *tsedakah* in the context of his explanation as to how "a theory of alms can develop."[38] According to Mauss,

> [a]lms are the fruits of a moral notion of the gift and of fortune on the one hand, and a notion of sacrifice on the other. ... This is the ancient morality of the gift, which has become a principle of justice. The gods and the spirits accept that the share of wealth and happiness that has been offered to them and had been hitherto destroyed in useless sacrifices should serve the poor and children (emphasis added).[39]

A roughly similar theory of alms, which traces certain entitlements of the poor (and others) to God's demand for sacrifices, can be borne out in Jewish law. For example, in a postclassical rabbinic development, *tsedakah* began to

[34] E.g., laws of *shevi'it* (*shemitah*) and the Jubilee year, *orlah* (laws governing the first fruits of trees that must be followed before enjoying the fruit is permitted), *bechorot*, certain sacrifices, the benediction required before eating (in which God's creation of the world and its fruits are acknowledged) lest one be guilty of theft from God, redemption of the first-born son, and possibly even *brit milah*. See Jon D. Levenson, *Death and Resurrection of the Beloved Son*, New Haven: Yale University Press (1993).

[35] E.g., tithes and portions of sacrificial offerings given to the priests. This might also include *ma'aser sheni*, which must be consumed by the owners in the city of Jerusalem.

[36] E.g., *peah* ("rights" of the poor to freely take from the corners of the field), *ma'aser ani* (tithes for the poor) and certain labor laws.

[37] Mauss (1990) at 18. This linguistic derivation of *tsedakah* suggests that the debt to the poor is akin to some sort of property right. The significance of the (justice-related) meaning of *tsedakah*, as opposed to the popular (Christian) understanding of charity (*caritas*) as a purely altruistic gift, will be developed throughout the book. Because of this difference in meaning, whenever the word charity is used in this book to refer to *tsedakah* it will appear in quotation marks.

[38] Mauss (1990) at 18.

[39] *Id.*

be referred to as *hekdesh* – sanctified property (owned by God). Moreover, Chapter 3 demonstrates, by way of illustration, that this theory is played out on a larger scale, possibly accounting for Jewish legal phenomena and institutions in a variety of contexts, relating not just to the poor. Chapter 3 analyzes analyze certain legal rules and institutions that illustrate this development, such as (1) the aforementioned application to *tsedakah* of the legal notion of *hekdesh* (divinely owned property), (2) the institution of vows (*nedarim*) using the concept and language of sacrifice,[40] and (3) the legal institution of *hefker* (ownerless property), whose development was possibly related to both notions of a divine realm of ownership and the idea of sacrifice to God, and which itself formed the basis for judicial power to redistribute property in the interest of justice (*hefker beit din hefker*).[41]

Paralleling Mauss's studies of Melanesian practice, Roman law, and Indo-European law, this exploration of Jewish law illuminates and extends aspects of Mauss's hypothesis in ways that are relevant to contemporary ethical questions. Indeed, it is likely that the appropriateness of Jewish law in this regard is no coincidence. As Mary Douglas points out, the seeds for Mauss's idea for *The Gift* might well lie in his earlier work on animal sacrifice.[42] Just as there is a conceptual evolution evinced in Mauss's work from sacrifice theory to a broader moral theory of gift exchange, so too is there a historical evolution in Jewish law from sacrifice and Temple property to, for example, "charity" and related legal concepts, reflecting a similar conceptual theme involving the interrelationality of property and the bond between people.

After exploring a broader theory of property and obligation as conceived in foundational texts of Jewish law, Chapter 4, "And Your Brother Shall Live

40 Regarding *nedarim* (vows), see, e.g., Moshe Benovitz, *Kol Nidre: Studies in the Development of Rabbinic Votive Institutions*, Atlanta: Scholars Press (1998); Moshe Benovitz, "*Kol Kinuyey Nedarim*" (Hebrew: Substitute Vow Formulae), *Sidra* 12 (1996), pp. 5–25.

41 A possible connection to *hefker beit din hefker* is seen through the use of the language of *cherem*. Regarding *tsedakah* and *hefker*, see, e.g., Ephraim Urbach, "'*Hefker*' – On the Place of *Derelictio* in Historical Reality" [Hebrew], *Shenaton Ha-Mishpat Ha-Ivri* 6–7 (1979–1980), pp. 17–28; Shamma Friedman, "The Scholars' Dictionary of Tannaitic Hebrew, A Critique of the Entry: *Hefqer/Hevqer*" [Hebrew], in *Sidra: A Journal For the Study of Rabbinic Literature*, volume 12, Jerusalem: Daf-Noy Press (1996), p. 113, and Moshe Benovitz (1998). Also relevant are certain legal institutions that (seem to) allow for the commodification or monetary valuation of persons during Temple times such as laws of restitution, redemption (*pidyon*), consecration of a person's worth to the Temple ("*arakhin*"), marriage, and slavery.

42 Douglas said that it is "likely that Mauss [got] the idea of a morally sanctioned gift cycle upholding the social cycle from the Vedic literature that he studied in [his] first major research," his "early book with Henri Hubert (1889) on Sacrifice." Douglas, "Foreword," in Mauss (1990), pp. vii–xviii at ix–x. See Henri Hubert and Marcel Mauss, *Sacrifice: Its Nature and Functions*, Chicago: University of Chicago Press (1964).

With You: The Divine Lien and the Obligation to Save Human Life," focuses on the particular circumstances involved in the context of organ transfer – the imperative to save human life and the special status of health and the human body. Like Chapter 3, this chapter is implicitly framed by the fact that tension points produced by the problem of commodification and taken for granted as problematic under United States law, such as payment for saving a life by supplying an organ, have a very different resonance under Jewish law. While an organ transfer to save a life is both permitted and desirable,[43] payment in this context is not necessarily problematic. Does Jewish law thus allow for the "sale" of human organs? Significanly, what becomes apparent is that this formulation is oversimplified and overdetermined.

Chapters 4 and 5 analyze the appropriate legal characterization and moral understanding of whatever payment might be permitted as compensation (not necessarily purchase money) in a context such as organ transplantation. In the course of this analysis, which draws upon the principle of divine ownership and the related principle of *tsedek* (justice) described in Chapter 3, what is offered is an account of monetary exchange and its desacralizing effect (if any) on good acts (*mitzvot*)[44] and sacred property under Jewish law is offered.[45] To ascertain the role and impact of money in the domains of the sacred, particularly sacred acts, the chapter investigates the meaning and legal treatment of certain payments in the context of a *mitzvah*, such as (1) monetary compensation for the performance of a *mitzvah*; (2) the doctrine of *schar batalah* (whereby a rabbi or other *mitzvah* doer, who is otherwise not allowed to be paid, can be given the money that he theoretically would have made had he spent his time working and earning a salary instead of performing the *mitzvah*); (3) the extent to which

[43] Organ transfer is only permitted under these circumstances. Bodily mutilation is otherwise prohibited under Jewish law.

[44] In fact, the word *mitzvah* (the singular form of *mitzvot*), when used by itself, is frequently understood in Mishnaic Hebrew precisely as giving to *tsedakah*. As a general matter, the meaning of the word *mitzvah* is actually quite complex. It is used in various ways in rabbinic literature (e.g. it can mean commandment or legal or moral obligation). See Arye Edrei, "*Mitzvah al Hayetomim Lifro'a Chov Avihem*" (Hebrew: Orphans' Obligation (*Mitzvah*) to Pay Their Father's Debt), in Arnold Enker and Sinai Deutch (eds.), *Iyyunim Bemishpat Ivri Uvehalachah* (Hebrew: Studies in Hebrew Law and Halacha), Ramat Gan: University of Bar Ilan Press (1998, pp. 19–51). It is used, in this book, to connote a legal obligation, as that phrase is or can be understood in Jewish law.

[45] In this regard, Chapter 4 explores, for example, payment for the duties of those who regularly perform *mitzvot* such as rabbis, doctors, judges, and witnesses. The rabbis formulated a theory that permitted payment of a sort even in what might be seen as the quintessential case in which one ought not be paid for that which comes from God – the situation of passing on to another the Torah that one has learned or acquired, with respect to which the Talmud states (B.T. Bechorot 29a) that since Moses received (or taught) it for free, so should others teach (or be taught) for free. See Section 5.4.1, *infra*.

practical considerations ("if there is no payment, no one will do this *mitzvah* or necessary act") are taken into account, and how this is conceived; (4) payment for the opportunity to do a *mitzvah* (such as participating in ritual services); and (5) circumstances where what appears to be a (prohibited) "payment for a *mitzvah*" is nevertheless permitted in order to satisfy other public-policy concerns, such as avoiding unjust enrichment and incentivizing good acts.

Chapter 5, "Returning a Lost Body with One's Own Body: Organ Transplanation as Retrocession and (Re)consecration of the Body," brings these issues, and the Jewish property theory developed in Chapters 3 and 4, to bear upon the particular issue of the transfer of organs for transplant. Indeed, the resulting hypothesis as to what obligations and prohibitions are implicated in this context under Jewish law carries the argument in the previous chapters full circle.

What is demonstrated is that, in analyzing organ transfer under Jewish law, contemporary religious decisors turn to a sixteenth-century Responsum by the Radbaz (Rabbi David ben Zimra, 1479–1573) involving a hypothetical scenario that (for our purposes) is far less productive, analytically, than its Shakespearean contemporary.[46] The heavy focus on this Responsum obfuscates the significant insight that an analysis of organ transfer and sale can shed on rabbinic conceptions of obligation and ownership.

As might be expected, there are few direct legal precedents for organ transfer and "sale" in the ancient Jewish legal system. The much-cited Responsum of the Radbaz results in an implicit downplaying of any legal or moral obligation a Jew might have to give his or her bodily material to save or improve the life of another.[47] The scenario offered by the Radbaz is of a cruel ruler threatening to kill one person if another does not agree to have a limb cut off. The Radbaz rules that one is not obligated to forfeit one's body part in this case.

The Radbaz is generally taken to be perhaps the only direct Jewish legal precedent for the contemporary scenario of organ transfer. This is despite the fact that this scenario can hardly be seen as comparable. Regarding the question of obligation, the case of a tyrant threatening, on a whim, to kill someone unless another agrees to have a limb chopped off – a situation akin to paying ransom to a kidnapper or turning someone over to a terrorist – is hardly analogous to the situation in which a life-threatening illness can be cured thanks to someone's relatively safe donation of an organ or bodily material.

46 *The Merchant of Venice* was written in 1596.

47 See Rabbi David ben Zimra, (1479–1573), *Radbaz, Responsa III* #627 (re: sacrificing organs) and II #1052 (re: endangering oneself to save another). For example, in a decision that might be misguided, Rabbi Joel Roth of the Jewish Theological Seminary cites the decision of the Radbaz as precedent for a principle of self-ownership or bodily autonomy that dictates that a person is not even under an obligation to donate blood to save the life of a person standing before him who needs the blood to survive.

The popular perspective among contemporary academics and rabbinic decisors that accompanies the virtually wholehearted adoption of the approach of the Radbaz might be attributable, in part, to the influence of liberal conceptions of personhood and property. For it reflects a focus on individual self-preservation, or in contemporary terms, on individual self-ownership and bodily integrity, which fails to give sufficient weight to relevant concepts that are shown here to be at the core of the Jewish legal tradition: limits to self-ownership resulting from divine ownership of the human body and human life, and the obligations to others that flow therefrom.[48] It regards the act of donating as, at best, a (mere) act of piety, or charity (as popularly construed; *caritas*), as opposed to an obligatory act of giving. This mistake in assessing the meaning of organ transfer becomes apparent when the question of organ sales is posed; absent a direct basis for prohibition, one is relegated to opining that the decision to sell one's organs, like the decision to donate, is entirely up to the autonomous individual, an outcome that is perceived as troubling by many.

An alternative approach to the novel phenomenon of organ transfer is suggested by the legal analysis applied by the twentieth-century scholar Rabbi Shlomo Zevin to another literary precedent, the so-called pound-of-flesh contract in Shakespeare's *The Merchant of Venice*.[49] In contrast to the case described by the Radbaz, which contemplates circumstances of torture and extortion and militates against requiring one to give up one's limb (or life?) to save the life of another, this contract represents an arrangement that is (at least initially) mutually agreed upon by both parties and thus might to some extent provide a more apt analogy to today's consensual organ transfers. Nevertheless, Zevin declares that Shylock's contract (which does not entail saving a life) would be unenforceable under Jewish law due to the divine ownership of the human body, which renders human beings juridically incapable of "selling" their body parts.[50]

48 Chapter 3 demonstrates that divine ownership is a legal principle that implicitly limits the Jewish legal understanding of private property, building obligations (both legal and moral) to others into the very notion of property ownership. Inasmuch as the notion of the divine lien has particular applicability to protecting and sustaining human life and the human body (see Chapter 4), it would have a similar obligation-generating effect here in limitations on self-ownership.

49 See Zevin (1946).

50 By invoking Zevin's analysis of the Shylock case, I do not mean to endorse his legal analysis. Indeed, as should be clear from Chapters 3 and 4, I would argue that the questions of self-ownership and limits thereto are much more complicated than suggested by Zevin. Nor do I mean to imply that Zevin's hypothesis is undisputed in the literature. See, e.g., Shaul Yisraeli, "*Tikrit Kivyeh L'or Ha-halacha*," *Ha-Torah ve-ha-Medina* 5 (1953–1954), pp. 71–113, who disagrees with Zevin's argument.

The notion of a divine lien, which has largely been overlooked in the Jewish legal literature, implies that more of an emphasis ought to be placed on the obligation to donate for necessary transplants. Echoing Zevin's approach, this book suggests that the element of divine ownership challenges the unreflective use by contemporary rabbinic decisors of the term "sale" to describe a transaction involving human organs that includes some sort of payment. Indeed, this phenomenon of failing to precisely typologize what concededly might be a permissible payment by simply calling it a "sale" might again reflect the influence on contemporary rabbinic decisors of contemporary liberal ideas and assumptions regarding property and markets.

Although the legal concept of divine ownership is invoked by contemporary religious decisors in the context of organ transfer to explain the limitation on the degree of self-endangerment to which one might be permitted or forced to expose oneself,[51] the more productive or affirmative implications of this obscure legal concept have not been explored.[52] In any event, it drives home the necessity of stressing the importance of organ transfer within the Jewish community, and its meaning as perhaps the quintessential return gift to God.

This examination of ancient Jewish law provides a conceptual vehicle for expanding the narrow confines that characterize much contemporary discussion concerning markets and morals. It provides a specific and concrete illustration of how ideas gleaned from the comparative study of premarket or nonmarket systems can be used to better understand and to reform the contemporary market system.[53] The question of commodification of human organs, analyzed in the context of Jewish legal institutions, raises issues of deep philosophical importance that are not otherwise readily recognizable.

[51] See, e.g., Elliott N. Dorff, "Jewish Law and Lore: The Case of Organ Transplantation," *The Jewish Law Annual* 12 (1997), pp. 65–114 at 82–86.

[52] Chapter 3 grounds the concept of divine ownership more broadly in the larger Jewish legal infrastructure and elucidates the obligation-generating aspects of the notion of divine property (a notion that has particular but not exclusive applicability to human life and the human body). Ancient legal institutions, such as *hekdesh*, priestly dues, and sabbatical-year produce, make plain the existence of the category of divinely owned property, the breadth of the concept's applicability, and the property-related obligations – to God and to other human beings – that flow therefrom. These ancient institutions themselves and their potential theoretical relevance to contemporary legal and ethical questions (despite their possible technical legal inapplicability at this point in history) have not received much, if any, attention in the contemporary literature.

[53] As Evans-Pritchard said in his introduction to *The Gift* with respect to ancient economies, there is value in asking "not only how we can understand these archaic institutions but also how an understanding of them helps us to better understand our own, and perhaps to improve them." E. E. Evans-Pritchard, "Introduction," in Marcel Mauss, *The Gift: Forms and Functions of Exchange in Archaic Societies*, London: Routledge (1974), pp v-x.

This book demonstrates an approach to the problem of commodification that sees beyond the fact of the (possible) involvement of money in a transaction. As an approach that is geared to a concern for greater social interrelationality, it calls for the conceptualization of more porous notions of property and of the self – of property as more inclusive, and of a self not as an atomized individual but as a self always already implicated by the other.

The ethical or philosophical anxiety provoked by the problem of commodification is largely perceived or described as the fear of treating persons or other "sacred" entities as objects (something whose value is set in "mere" pecuniary terms). In fact, that which is referred to as the problem of commodification is a symptom of this deeper problem, a symptom that ought not to be confused with the underlying pathology. Indeed, the problem can be exacerbated by responses that attempt to repress the symptom (by simply blocking certain exchanges), as opposed to those designed to attend to the pathology itself. What underlies the problem of commodification is the lack of social relationality that is, in part, engendered by the market system, its philosophical underpinnings, and the illusions it perpetuates.

Inasmuch as the fear of commodification is related to the slippage of the person or things held sacred into mere objects, the seemingly counterintuitive approach of seeing personhood implicated in objects turns the problem on its head by actually finding a solution in the apparent problem, suggesting, ironically, that blurring the boundaries between person and person, and between thing and person, is (under the right conceptual circumstances) not necessarily bad. Recognition and development of the phenomenon of embodied obligation reveal the way in which people relate to one another through seeing selves as or in property. The theory of property that has begun to be developed in this book contributes to the debate about the questions of commodification and organ transfer and has broader implications for matters of distributive justice.

1

Beyond Gift and Commodity: Rethinking the Compartmentalization Approach to the Problem of Commodification

In what is undoubtedly one of the saddest of modern phenomena, in the United States more than 119,000 people are waiting for someone to die so that they might have a better life or a better chance to live.[1] As candidates for organ transplant whose lives are in jeopardy, they live day to day hoping and praying that an organ will become available. Medical science has miraculously made it possible to help people who, a few decades ago, would have had no hope of survival. In yet another example of society being unable to keep up with technology, the promise offered by modern medicine is, at this point in time, entirely dependant on the willingness of other people – often strangers – to help others. How many viable organs are buried each day? What can and should be done in the face of this calamitous situation? In the absence of a better solution, some have suggested that people ought to be paid for their organs – that a market in human organs, something that is currently prohibited around the world, ought to be permitted. Meanwhile, like it or not, a black market in organs flourishes as poor people supply the organs necessary for those who can afford to pay.

The ethical quandaries posed by the shortage of organs for transplant in general, and by the payment for organs in particular, do not lend themselves to easy solution. Much has been written in the debate over these issues; this book does not survey the literature nor does it thoroughly examine the myriad arguments that have been made on the subject. It contributes to the debate by offering a perspective rooted in Talmudic law, a perspective that could offer a new way to think about this problem.

The old way of thinking about the problem is relatively straightforward. People are dying while waiting for organs; the urgency of the need is beyond

[1] This is the number according to the United States Department of Health and Human Services in August 2013. See http://optn.transplant.hrsa.gov.

dispute. The logical suggestion of providing some form of remuneration, as an incentive for organ transfer, presents itself as one (if not the) obvious solution. This idea, however, triggers a larger concern that is itself the subject of debate – that of commodification, a problem that is at its most blatant in the context of a market in human organs. The visceral negative reaction to selling organs gives rise automatically to the moral expectation, mirrored in law, that organs will be donated or gifted altruistically. The status quo, in which nearly 120,000 people are in dire need, is the result of a simple calculation: the unreflective conceptual move directly from (invidious) "sale" to (altruistic) gift. It is this simple, dichotomous calculation that this book means to disrupt.

The critique to this approach to organ sales proceeds at two levels. First, attention is focused on the step that is taken almost unconsciously – the reflective move from sale to gift. Whence does this move come? Is it necessary? Is it legitimate? Focusing on this almost instinctive equation (if sale is bad, what is called for is gift) forces one to take into account the ramifications of the exclusive turn to gift and to question the basic assumption that monetary payment will taint the transaction. More importantly, by upsetting that move from the abhorrence of sale to the locking in of altruistic gift as the only option, one opens the door to the possibility of approaching the problem of the shortage of organs from perspectives other than those rooted in the contrast between charity and commerce. This leads to the second level of critique, which posits that the problem is not one of process (should there or should there not be an element of reciprocity or *quid pro quo* with the organ transfer), but of substance. This is not a problem of (rules of) exchange but of property and obligation. Rather than taking for granted the correctness of the perspective of private property presupposed by the sale versus gift approach to this question, this book suggests an entirely different perspective, one that asks how people do and ought to feel about their bodies, given that they have the chance to use them to save a human life. This larger question, of the meaning of property and of one's sense of self and obligation to others, is susceptible to guidance by policy choices, such as those mentioned in the Conclusion, that could be enacted into law.

The concrete vehicle for this new perspective on organ sales is offered in the form of an analysis of Talmudic law. It differs in form, content, and approach from contemporary legal and ethical Jewish writings, offering something genuinely new and yet old to this ongoing debate. This Talmudic analysis fits squarely with the two-part critique described above. First, there is no anti-commodification principle in Talmudic law. While there are particular rules concerning the use of money, ranging from prohibitions on bribery or profiting (e.g., from an interest-bearing loan) to the introduction of money in the realm of the sacred (e.g., allowing "sacred" property to be "redeemed" with money), there is no general sense in which money is perceived to have an inherently tainting effect. In the absence of specific prohibitions, acts are not deemed illegal or unethical simply because money has changed hands. Given this background feature of Talmudic law, not only is the exchange of money removed as the salient, if not definitive, focus of analysis when the question of organ sales is presented, but in the context of the real focus of analysis – ought one give of oneself to save the life of another – the possible propriety of some form of monetary compensation in the interest of fairness and justice becomes a topic that needs to be explored.

As a prelude to the eventual examination of this book's approach to this question, this chapter investigates the prevalent contemporary approach that demands that organs be given, altruistically.

1.1 THE APPARENT PROBLEM: MONEY AND MARKETS

Along with the ever-increasing trend toward commercialization, monetization, and commodification, there is an ever-burgeoning literature in the fields of law, political science, anthropology, and sociology regarding the meaning of money in our society, and debating what limitations, if any, should be placed on the market. Some of the most poignant areas of debate entail the sale of humans in some form – for example, surrogate motherhood, and the sale of organs, blood, sperm, eggs, and even babies.[2] In the opinion of many prominent economists, there is essentially nothing wrong with permitting the individual to decide whether to enter into transactions such as these; indeed, many argue that this is precisely what liberal guarantees of individual freedom and autonomy are all about.[3]

By contrast, theorists who might be called "anti-commodifiers" find many of these monetary exchanges troubling. They point to these issues as evidence that there are, or ought to be, moral and legal limits to the market. Illustrative of this view is Michael Walzer, who proffers the notion of "blocked exchanges" – specifying those goods that ought to be distributed by criteria other than money.[4] In a similar vein, Margaret Jane Radin argues that property that is deeply connected with an individual's "personhood" ought not be commodified; she proposes a ban on the sale of such property, which she claims should be valued for its own sake, as its value cannot be measured by

[2] Richard Posner has supported the suggestion for a market in human babies. Richard A. Posner and William A. Landes, "The Economics of the Baby Shortage," *Journal of Legal Studies* 7 (1978), pp. 323–348.

[3] See, e.g., Richard A. Posner, "The Regulation of the Market in Adoptions," *Boston University Law Review* 67 (1987), pp. 59ff; Gary Becker, *The Economic Approach to Human Behavior*, Chicago: University of Chicago Press (1976).

[4] Walzer (1983).

money.[5] Elizabeth Anderson puts forth a theory of "value pluralism," pursuant to which certain goods that ought not be subjected to or governed by market norms should be excluded from market relations.[6]

This book calls into question the use of the compartmentalization approach[7] (taken as a whole) as a response to the problem referred to as "commodification." This approach is shown to bolster the rigid bifurcation of gift and commodity (and related binaries) and, therefore, runs the risk of being deeply counterproductive, in the long run, from the perspective of the anti-commodifiers. This critique is supported by the work of certain exchange theorists, including Marcel Mauss, whose theories and findings challenge the assumptions and strategy underlying the impulse to block certain exchanges. Taking its strength, in part, from similar comparative analyses of exchange and property relations in different cultures, this critique complicates and problematizes the category-based approach to anti-commodification and suggests an alternative approach that entails a focus on obligation rather than polarization and compartmentalization.

The various approaches proffered by anti-commodifiers share the suggestion of blocking certain monetary exchanges, in an effort to shield from the market certain goods or services that they contend should not be exposed or subjected to market norms. These excluded goods tend to be identified based on their inherent meaning, on their relation to the individual, or on a theory regarding the just distribution of resources.

Laws banning the sale of human bodily material provide the classic example of a blocked exchange. Foreshadowing the dispute over human organ sales, in 1971 Richard Titmuss wrote, in his famous study contrasting blood collection systems in the United States and England, that money ought not to be exchanged for human blood.[8] In addition to arguing that a system of unremunerated blood donation is more efficient, Titmuss suggested that the medical need for human blood provides the perfect opportunity for the performance of acts of altruism (defined as the giving of a pure gift) and, for this reason, ought to be legally preserved as such. He asserted that individual freedom is augmented by institutional support for what he calls "fellowship

[5] Margaret Jane Radin, *Contested Commodities*, Cambridge: Harvard University Press (1996). Radin's discussion of "incomplete commodification," does, in some respects, eschew the all-or-nothing nature of the compartmentalization approach.

[6] Elizabeth Anderson, *Value in Ethics and Economics*, Cambridge: Harvard University Press (1993).

[7] This is Radin's term.

[8] Richard M. Titmuss, *The Gift Relationship: From Human Blood to Social Policy*, New York: New Press (1997).

arrangements."[9] His suggestion – that the government should mandate that blood be given as a gift, not sold for money as a commodity – might be seen as the quintessential "blocked exchange."

Certain practical and theoretical limitations to the blocked-exchange approach are evident in Titmuss's own proposition. He suggested, in essence, that blood "donation" be shifted from the category of (quasi-) commodity to the category of pure gift. One might query the long-term efficacy of attempting, by fiat, to shift socially desirable (if not necessary) transactions into the "gift" column by simply blocking the transfer of money. For as it turns out, precluding the transfer of money does not, by itself, seem to induce altruistic behavior, or encourage the type of fellowship relationships across the board as Titmuss might have envisioned (at least in the context of our market economy). Unfortunate evidence for this is provided by the immense shortage of human organs needed for transplant, a shortage that continues to grow in the context of a near-universal worldwide ban on the payment for organs, leaving policy makers struggling to come up with a solution.[10]

Beyond immediate practical questions,[11] there are theoretical ones as well. Those attempting to block exchanges operate (either implicitly or explicitly) squarely within the rubric of the classic binary of gift versus commodity, an oppositional construct that is the subject of a great deal of debate among contemporary anthropologists and sociologists.[12] There is sound basis upon which

[9] Titmuss argued that even though institutional supports for fellowship relationships, like bans on compensation for blood, appear to restrict individual autonomy by limiting freedom of contract, they can actually advance individual liberty and find support in the ideology of individual rights. He asserted that "[i]n the interests of the freedom of all men they should not ... be free to sell their blood ..." *Id.* at 310.

[10] See, e.g., Kenneth J. Arrow, "Gifts and Exchanges," *Philosophy and Public Affairs*, 1/4 (summer 1972), pp. 343–362; Richard A. Epstein, "Organ Transplants: Is Relying on Altruism Costing Lives?" *The American Enterprise* 4 (Nov/Dec 1993), pp. 51–57. See also Richard A. Epstein, "Are Values Incommensurable, or Is Utility the Ruler of the World," *Utah Law Review* 3 (1995), pp. 683–715.

[11] The limits of the compartmentalization approach also become apparent when one steps outside the realm of those goods that, unlike body parts and derivatives, might not readily be classified as "sacred." See, e.g., Ted C. Fishman, "A Simple Glass of Water," *New York Times* (Aug 23, 2001), p. A21.

[12] Arjun Appadurai has described the gift/commodity binary as comprising the following set of assumptions: "[g]ifts, and the spirit of reciprocity, sociability and spontaneity in which they are typically exchanged, usually are starkly opposed to the profit-oriented, self-centered, and calculated spirit that fires the circulation of commodities. Further, where gifts link things to persons and embed the flow of things in the flow of social relationships, commodities are held to represent the drive – largely free of moral or cultural constraints – of goods for one another, a drive mediated by money and not by sociality." Arjun Appadurai, "Introduction: Commodities and the Politics of Value," in Arjun Appadurai (ed.), *The Social Life of Things: Commodities in Cultural Perspective*, Cambridge: Cambridge University Press (1986) at 11–12.

to question the extent to which this paradigmatic construct, a theoretical fiction emanating from Western discourse and ostensibly reflecting the cultural reality of Western liberal democracy,[13] is a useful tool.

What partly underlies the gift-versus-commodity binary is a largely unexamined assumption as to the meaning and power of money, something embedded invisibly in contemporary debates about the legal and moral limits to markets. Money is presumed to be so meaningful, to carry such weight, that its mere presence in a transaction is almost always taken to signify commodification and the governance of market norms. This idea is reflected in the usual framing of the inquiry regarding the problem of commodification: how ought we (morally if not legally) limit (the reach of) the market? The question itself evokes the type of spatial imagery vividly conjured up by the suggestion of Michael Walzer and others that there is or ought to be a separate "sphere" of money and commodities. It implies that the presence of money defines the nature of an exchange and, moreover, that it is possible to cordon off the realm of money such that, when properly defined and circumscribed, it will pose no threat to other spheres of human interaction.

In 1913, the sociologist Charles Cooley observed, "it is impossible to mark off sharply the pecuniary sphere from that of other kinds of value. It is always possible that the highest as well as the lowest things may be brought within its scope."[14] Nearly a century later, with the expansion of market capitalism, perhaps it is worthwhile to take Cooley's suggestion to heart and to reconsider whether we ought to be approaching the question of limits to markets by attempting to draw a circle around the realm within which money plays a proper role and within which goods can be treated as "mere commodities." Is it really possible to formulate a clear list of exchanges for money that ought to be "blocked," in such a way as to enable the construction of parallel realms of justice that can exist and flourish side by side? Is the only option to compartmentalize – to attempt to cut out exceptional cases in which the supposed amorality of monetary exchange, which otherwise has free reign, should not be the governing force? Given the nature of market society, is it reasonable to rely on a theory that assumes that, once contained, money and its supposedly nasty effects can be neutralized?

Appadurai notes that "many of the essays in [his edited] volume ... are designed to show that this is a simplified and overdrawn series of contrasts."

[13] See Marilyn Strathern, *The Gender of the Gift: Problems with Women and Problems with Society in Melanesia*, Berkeley: University of California Press (1988).

[14] Charles H. Cooley, "The Sphere of Pecuniary Valuation," *American Journal of Sociology* 19/2 (Sep 1913), pp. 188–203 at 192.

Like assumptions regarding the meaning and power of money, the gift-versus-commodity binary itself – whereby gifts and commodities are thought to be polar opposites – is also commonly taken for granted. Indeed, it is a theoretical construct that gains strength from, and serves to reinforce, the powerful meaning associated with money. As such, it is an intellectual fiction that seems to become more entrenched the more monetized and commercialized society becomes. Ironically, as concerns about commodification increase, suggested responses that bolster the perceived opposition between gift and commodity could intensify the invidious meaning-power of money itself.

Walzer invokes the gift-versus-commodity binary as part of the "blocked exchanges" approach set forth in *Spheres of Justice*. He proposes that it is possible to "properly mark[ ] off"[15] the world of monetary and commodity exchange, a sphere characterized by bargaining and self-interest, while opposing it to gift exchange, a realm marked by altruism.[16] Indeed, Walzer approvingly cites Titmuss's suggestion that blood ought to be donated as an unremunerated gift to illustrate his approach of blocking certain exchanges.

Walzer alludes to the problem inherent in straightforwardly applying the compartmentalization approach to the use of money when he admits that money is something that uniquely cuts across all spheres.[17] Yet, without resolving this basic complication, he nevertheless maintains that it is necessary, and therefore presumably possible, to "fix its boundaries."[18] Perhaps this is one reason it is hard to be satisfied with the notion of "blocking exchanges" – the idea that by delineating those things that ought not to be alienable for money, one can successfully relegate money to its appropriate sphere. One need only peruse Walzer's list of "blocked exchanges"[19] to get the sense that it is not necessarily so simple.[20] Seemingly imponderable questions of definition and

15 Walzer (1983) at 283.

16 Walzer endorses the distinction between two such realms, making reference to Branislaw Malinowski. See, e.g., Walzer (1983) at 123–128. It is suggested later in this chapter that, although it is common to read Mauss as agreeing with Malinowski in setting up this contrast, in fact, Mauss challenges this presumed binary and would suggest that it is dangerous, even as a rhetorical device. It is interesting to speculate what Walzer might have said differently in his chapter on money and commodities had he considered this alternative, non-Malinowskian understanding of Mauss.

17 "The list [of blocked exchanges] repeats or anticipates other chapters, for it is a feature of the sphere of money that it abuts every other sphere; that's why it is so important to fix its boundaries." *Id.* at 100.

18 *Id.*

19 Walzer (1983) at 100–114.

20 See, e.g., Judith Andre, "Blocked Exchanges: A Taxonomy," *Ethics* 103/1 (Oct 1992), pp. 29–47.

boundary drawing nearly jump off the page, concerning both the content of the different categories and the relations among them. For instance, the first category of a blocked exchange – "buying and selling human beings" – raises the question: why *do* we prohibit slavery but permit payment for labor? How does this "blocked category" help us analyze new arrangements, such as surrogate motherhood, the sale of bodily fluids, or the ancient profession of wet nursing?[21] How do we know when payment connotes the invidious "sale of a person" as opposed to just and proper compensation? And is it really true, as Walzer maintains, that religion and money do not mix?

The sheer difficulty of compiling a coherent list of those things that simply should not be "for sale" hints at a deeper problem, one inherent in the very attempt to cordon off "money and commodities" as a self-contained "sphere of justice." For it is an approach that silently condones and strengthens the unexamined tendency to take the social meaning and function of money at face value, as something *sui generis*.[22] Upon closer examination, there is reason to fear that this approach might undercut the concerns and ultimate goals of the anti-commodifiers.

Titmuss might also have been hinting at these deeper aspects of the problem of "commodification" when (unlike many contemporary anti-commodifiers) he described the dilemma regarding blood sales not in terms of abstract concerns about human "personhood" or the "sacredness" of blood *per se*, but rather in terms of the question of the type of *relationships* that society ought to be fostering. This socio-relational concern does not take a prominent role in the contemporary debate over limits to markets. Much of the analysis put forth by both sides in the debate over commodification starts with and goes no further than the atomistic perspective of the individual who seeks to alienate his property or spend his money. Of primary (if not exclusive) concern are questions of freedom and autonomy, rights to property ownership, freedom of contract, matters of personhood, and fairness of (centralized) distribution.

As opposed to Titmuss's reliance upon altruistic gift giving, his purposeful focus on the relational aspects of social exchange is a major insight that ought to be developed in the contemporary debates about limits to markets.[23]

21 See Valerie Fildes, *Wet Nursing: A History From Antiquity to the Present*, Oxford: Basil Blackwell (1988); George D. Sussman, *Selling Mother's Milk: The Wet-Nursing Business in France 1715–1914*, Urbana: University of Illinois Press (1982).

22 See Bernard Barber, "Absolutization of the Market: Some Notes on How We Got from There to Here," in Gerald Dworkin, Gordon Bermant, and Peter Brown (eds.), *Markets and Morals*, Washington, D.C.: Hemisphere Publishing Corp. (1977), pp. 15–31.

23 Indeed, it could be argued that Titmuss accurately learned from Marcel Mauss that what matters is the issue of relationality and social bonding, but that he erred in reading Mauss as supporting a proposal involving pure gifts. For, as will be shown, it is possible that Mauss's

Although his specific policy recommendation relies upon, and arguably reinforces, the contested and problematic dichotomy of (pure) gift versus commodity, the thrust of Titmuss's project points in a different direction, inviting consideration of the body of literature whose subject is the study of the phenomenon of exchange across time and across cultures.

Walzer's more general theoretical insights point in a similar direction. He premises his theory of complex equality on the express requirement of respect for the full range of social goods and social meanings. One might, perhaps, proceed from where Walzer leaves off[24] in his chapter on the sphere of money and commodities by investigating an approach that seeks to temper, if not regulate, monetary exchange while taking Walzer's initial premise very seriously. A different approach to conceiving of "limits" to markets, one explicitly designed to uncover and account for the varied social meanings of exchange, might call for a reexamination of some of the assumptions that underlie many of the approaches suggested heretofore, such as the following:

- the assumption that whenever money is involved in a transaction, it necessarily bears the invidious characteristics commonly associated with market exchange;[25]
- the tendency (bolstered by the above assumption) to assume that a corrective policy can focus on the money alone – and that (other) problematic aspects of transactions or relationships can be ignored (or even shielded from examination) when no money is involved;
- the concomitant assumption that, by regulating (usually banning) money in certain realms all problems will have been solved – that the theoretical perspective of concern about markets does not force consideration of the negative practical consequences that might result therefrom (e.g., shortage of human organs available for transplant);
- the assumption that cherished values cannot survive monetary exchange, not even in the face of compelling problems of human welfare;
- the assumption that the "market economy" operates autonomously and brings in its tow an amorality in the realm of exchanges involving money that can go unquestioned; and finally,
- the idea that the problem of commodification can be addressed without questioning basic assumptions regarding the meaning of "ownership" and "property."

theory would suggest the opposite: that pure gifts do little to increase social bonding, and that something else is needed, a "gift" that is recognized as free and obligatory.

24 Walzer's aim, to consider all social meanings, is advanced by the application of the non-Malinowskian rereading of Mauss that will be suggested *infra*.

25 See Anderson (1993).

This critique of the current state of thinking regarding limits to markets echoes Viviana Zelizer's succinct observation that "the power of the market has been overestimated – we need further research on its limits."[26] In other words, a response to the perceived dangers inherent in certain kinds of exchange that resorts exclusively to the cordoning off of money runs the risk of "leav[ing] the cultural independence and power of money unquestioned,"[27] and of giving money too much power, which is precisely what critics of what Zelizer terms "monetary imperialism," like Walzer, fear.

The suggestion made here, of an alternative framework for the debate over commodification, draws upon a reading of Marcel Mauss's essay *The Gift: The Form and Reason for Exchange in Archaic Societies* that differs from that of Titmuss, Walzer, and others. This approach places the spotlight on the relational aspects of exchange behavior and invites a broader, less atomistic view of the web of human exchanges in society. It suggests a nuanced response to problems of "commodification," problems for which the presence of money is, arguably, no more than a red flag. Before exploring this approach, it is useful to briefly introduce some of the basic theories of exchange, along with relevant empirical findings regarding money and markets that themselves help to undercut the premises of a binary approach to the problem of commodification.

Anthropologists "[u]nderstand … exchange [to be] much more than a subfield of economic activity. It is a pervasive principle of social life that underpins all human relationships."[28] The writings of Bernard Barber, Jonathan Parry, Maurice Bloch, Mary Douglas, Viviana Zelizer, and other anthropologists, sociologists, economic historians, and political theorists provide insights regarding the phenomenon of exchange that support a serious critique of the compartmentalization approach. As an effort to constrain some of the invidious effects of the market, it fails to adequately account for the varied social meanings of money and exchange. Literature on exchange can fill this lacuna and, in so doing, help inform the contemporary political debate over how

[26] Viviana A. Zelizer, *Markets and Morals: The Development of Life Insurance in the United States*, New Brunswick: Transaction Books (1983) at x.

[27] Viviana A. Zelizer, *The Social Meaning of Money*, Princeton: Princeton University Press (1997) at 5.

[28] Chris Hann, *Social Anthropology*, London: Hodder and Stoughton Ltd. (2000) at 76. Exchange theory is the main topic that has occupied economic anthropologists until relatively recently. Chris M. Hann, "Introduction: The Embeddedness of Property," in C. M. Hann (ed.), *Property Relations: Renewing the Anthropological Tradition*, Cambridge: Cambridge University Press (1998) at 34. "Exchange" refers to the flow of goods and services as well as intangible transfers. Hann (2000), *ibid.* Economic anthropology, which itself is a subfield of social and cultural anthropology, identifies four "economic subfields" – work, exchange, property, and consumption. *Id.* at 62.

society ought to respond to the problem of the pervasiveness of the market and to the concomitant invidious commodification of many of the things that society considers sacred.

1.2 GIFT v. COMMODITY: BRIDGING THE HISTORICAL DIVIDE

Underlying the contemporary debates about the moral and legal limits to markets are certain fundamental concepts, oppositions, and factual assumptions about markets and their role in society. For example, a staple of the Western philosophical tradition has been the notion that money has "the *intrinsic* power to revolutionize society and culture" – in the view of some, primarily for evil (e.g., Aristotle, Aquinas, Marx) or, in the view of others, for good (Adam Smith) or a mixture of both good and evil (Georg Simmel).[29] Related to these assumptions regarding the power of money is the idea that gift exchange and commodity or market exchange are in fundamental opposition to each other. The commodity is often defined by its contrast with its supposed counterpart: the gift. The flip side of the coin, so to speak, of a commodity is thought to be a transfer that is ostensibly unremunerated, one that is done for purely altruistic reasons.[30]

Until relatively recently, the above assumptions have been largely taken for granted. Neither the market itself (as an idea and as a social institution) nor its fundamental assumptions have been the subject of much scrutiny by economists.[31] Noting that "[t]he history of economic thought shows a surprisingly small amount of attention given to the idea of the market,"[32] the sociologist Bernard Barber points out, moreover, that "the concept of the market has all the tendency to absolutization, to reification, to the fallacy of misplaced concreteness that established paradigms ... always have ...."[33] Indeed, he cites Titmuss as an example of the fact that a focus on altruism, in the context of polarizing debates about the market, can be just as narrowly absolutist.[34]

29 Jonathan Parry and Maurice Bloch, "Introduction: Money and the Morality of Exchange," in Jonathan Parry and Maurice Bloch (eds.), *Money and the Morality of Exchange*, Cambridge: Cambridge University Press (1989) at 2–4 (emphasis added). See, e.g., Aristotle, *The Politics*, Harmondsworth: Penguin Books (1962); Georg Simmel, *The Philosophy of Money*, London: Routledge and Keegan (1978); Richard H. Tawney, *Religion and the Rise of Capitalism*, Harmondsworth: Penguin Books (1972).

30 See, e.g., Titmuss (1997).

31 See Barber (1977).

32 *Id.* at 18.

33 *Id.* at 16.

34 He states that, in Titmuss's *The Gift Relationship*, "one can see the author reacting strongly against the market as ideology ... with the burden of the market as ideology weighing heavily upon him, he must proclaim an ideology of altruistic exchange, which has some of the same

Social scientists have studied the market, as a social institution that provides a system of one form of social exchange among others, only to a limited extent. The initial "Formalist" paradigm, used by anthropologists in the early twentieth century to study exchange, essentially took market assumptions for granted. It was premised on the universalist assumptions of neoclassical economics that all people behave "rationally" by making choices that are designed to maximize utility. More broadly, the Formalist approach posited that the general conceptions in the modern economists' tool kit[35] are universalizable and can legitimately be applied to the entire range of human societies, at all times and in all places.

A new "Substantivist" paradigm developed as a direct challenge to the Formalist model, originating in the work of economic historian Karl Polanyi (1886–1964).[36] In his famous work, *The Great Transformation*, Polanyi used concepts such as "economy" or "economic" in a substantivist, empirical sense, not in a formalist sense. Polanyi took as his starting point the distinction, first posited by Aristotle and later picked up by Marx, between householding and moneymaking. He asserted that the word "economic" had two different meanings. Its Formalist meaning was that put forth by the neoclassical economists – the maximization of utilitarian conditions of scarcity. In its Substantivist sense, it meant simply the study of how people interact with their environment to satisfy their needs and wants, that is, those activities that relate to the "material provisioning of a society."

Polanyi established a triadic typology of transactions or structures of exchange that, he claimed, exist alone or in combination in all societies: reciprocal, redistributive, market exchange. According to Polanyi, pre-industrial societies were primarily characterized by reciprocity (epitomized by gift exchange) and redistribution (by a central authority). Significantly, Polanyi described these "premodern" economies, in which market exchange did not predominate, as "embedded" in the rest of society, that is, regulated by society's basic moral structure, by larger social, moral, and political constraints. Because precapitalist (so-called moral) economies were embedded in their own social and political contexts, according to Polanyi they needed to be

tendencies to absolutization as the ideology it is combating." *Id.* at 17. See also Bernard Barber, "Function, Variability, and Change in Ideological Systems," in Bernard Barber and Alex Inkeles (eds.), *Stability and Social Change*, Boston: Little, Brown (1971), pp. 244–262 at 247.

35 E.g., economic actors as individuals who maximize their return in terms of exercising choice, marginal theory of utility, returns, utility costs, factors of production, etc.

36 See contributions by Karl Polanyi to Karl Polanyi, Conrad M. Arensberg, and Harry W. Pearson (eds.), *Trade and Market in the Early Empires: Economics in History and Theory*, Glencoe: Free Press (1957).

analyzed on their own (substantive) terms by means of their own distinct sets of tools; one could not simply apply the tools of the modern economist.

Polanyi hypothesized that a "great transformation" was brought about when the industrial revolution of the late eighteenth century produced "market economies" – economies that, for the first time in history, were characterized not by three different types or spheres of exchange[37] but by only one – the market form of exchange. This factor signified, for Polanyi, a significant difference between modern and premodern economies in terms of their "embeddedness" and accounted for what Polanyi termed the "great divide" between modern and traditional economies. He claimed that "prior to capitalism, commodity exchange was subordinated to the principles of reciprocity and redistribution; in other words, ... [commodity exchange] was socially embedded and hence regulated rather than self-regulating."[38] With the onset of industrialization, economies were released from the social and political constraints in which they had previously been "embedded." Thus, whereas "traditional" societies, with their mixture of various forms of exchange, were "embedded," the "modern" market economy is "disembedded," cut loose from the "moral" regulation of society.

Polanyi's notion of the "disembedded" market economy is of "an economic system controlled, regulated, and directed by markets alone; order in the production and distribution of goods is entrusted to this self-regulating mechanism."[39] He contended that in a "modern" economy monetary exchange represents a separate domain, one not subject to society's moral laws. Polanyi thus created the image of the market economy as autonomous, impersonal, and self-regulating, and of a market society in which other institutions and

37 "Spheres of exchange" are "culturally defined categories of things readily exchangeable for other things in the same categories, but not exchangeable, without moral opprobrium, for things in other categories." Thomas Barfield (ed.), *The Dictionary of Anthropology*, Oxford, Blackwell Publishers Ltd. (1977) at 329. See, e.g., Richard Firth, *Primitive Polynesian Economy*, Hamden: Routledge and Kegan Paul, Ltd. (1965), pp. 343–344. There are distinct (often ranked) spheres of exchange in most, if not all, societies. Parry and Bloch, (1989) at 12. Another Substantivist theorist, Paul Bohannan, wrote about the "spheres of exchange" that exist in different societies (e.g., different spheres are represented by marriage, luxury goods, and other goods), and the relationship among these different spheres. See Paul Bohannan, "Some Principles of Exchange and Investment Among the Tiv," *American Anthropologist* 57/1 (1955), pp. 60–70. See also Mary Douglas and Baron Isherwood, *The World of Goods: Towards an Anthropology of Consumption*, New York: Basic Books (1979), regarding hierarchically ranked spheres of exchange in modern market society.

38 Chris A. Gregory, "Exchange and Reciprocity," in Tim Ingold (ed.), *Companion Encyclopedia of Anthropology*, Oxford: Routledge (2000), pp. 911–939 at 920.

39 Karl Polanyi, *The Great Transformation*, Beacon: Boston (1957) at 68.

values are wholly dependant upon, or themselves embedded in, the market economy.

The "great divide" said by Polanyi to exist between "traditional" and "market economies" had certain practical and methodological ramifications. It implied that each of these two different entities must be studied on its own terms. Whereas traditional, embedded economies must be examined on the basis of their own substantive content (hence Substantivism), when it came to the study of economic life in modern industrial societies, Polanyi conceded that the scientific tool kit of the economist (put forward by Formalists for use in analyzing all cultures) is appropriate. Moreover, the wall erected by the "great divide" also implied that it is not legitimate to learn from premarket to market economies. Finally, the set of assumptions and distinctions composing Polanyi's "great divide" also serve to undergird the popular "model used to compare the West with exotic societies ... [perpetuating a] great divide between modern and savage."[40]

One of the key features of Polanyi's theory was its evolutionary aspect. While Polanyi was influenced by Marx, this aspect of Polanyi's theory can also be traced to anthropologists such as Mauss[41] and Malinowski,[42] who had studied "gift economies," which were claimed to be the apparent precursors to "market economies." Traditional anthropology follows the ideas of scholars like Polanyi and Malinowski in seeing "'pure gifts' as being antecedent to market exchange,"[43] and in seeing a sharp break between precapitalist and capitalist societies.[44] There are those who (as I will argue later, mistakenly) interpret

[40] Alexandra Ouroussoff, "Illusions of Rationality: False Premises of the Liberal Tradition," *Man* n.s. 28/2 (Jun 1993), pp. 281–298 at 295n2. This supposed cultural "divide between modern and savage" will be discussed and critiqued *infra*.

[41] As will be discussed *infra*, in the common reception of his essay, *The Gift: The Form and Reason for Exchange in Archaic Societies*, Mauss's ideas were merged with above-described theories expressed by Polanyi, Malinowski, and others. For Mauss also talked about societies in which gift exchange predominates as distinct from those dominated by market exchange. I offer a different reading of Mauss in Chapter 3.

[42] Branislaw Malinowski, *Argonauts of the Western Pacific*, London: Routledge and Kegan Paul (1922).

[43] Maurice Bloch, "The Symbolism of Money in Imerina," in Parry and Bloch (1989), pp. 165–190 at 169.

[44] The neo-Marxist approach in economic anthropology, which utilizes a political economy paradigm, entails a similar theory of historical transformation. Like Polanyi, Marx also saw a historical shift in the economic structure of society whereby capitalism destroyed embedded social forms. Neo-Marxist anthropologists criticized both the Formalists and the Substantivists for focusing exclusively on exchange, and for failing to grasp the deeper issues regarding production. For an interesting comparison of Mauss and Marx on the symbolism of money, see Bloch (1989) at 168–174.

Mauss to be making the same point. Noted theorists such as Paul Bohannan, George Dalton,[45] and Marshall Sahlins utilize Polanyi's typology and reiterate that there was a historical transformation from societies that included all three types of exchange (but where market exchange was peripheral), to one characterized almost exclusively by market exchange – that societies moved from "gift economies" with multiple spheres of exchange to "market economies" with one sphere of exchange, "even though pure gifts are seen as surviving in an attenuated form in market society."[46]

Nevertheless, today, most historians[47] and anthropologists[48] reject Polanyi's contention that there is a "great divide" between pre- and postindustrial economies. While acknowledging that change has taken place over time, they reject the rigid bifurcation[49] that implies (1) that it is appropriate to analyze the modern economy using the economist's tool kit, and (2) that it is inappropriate

[45] See, e.g., George Dalton, "Theoretical Issues in Economic Anthropology," *Current Anthropology* 10/1 (Feb 1969), pp. 63–102; Harumi Befu, "Social Exchange," *Annual Review of Anthropology* 6 (1977), pp. 255–281.

[46] Bloch (1989) at 169. The supposed historical evolution from gift economies to market economies is part of what lies at the foundation of the rhetorical opposition between gift and commodity, which itself is contested. One contemporary defender of the gift-versus-commodity binary who relies on Marcel Mauss in this regard is C. A. Gregory. See C. A. Gregory, *Gifts and Commodities*, London: Academic Press (1982). Tracing some of the themes highlighted by Mauss, Gregory depicts a sharp divide between market society and gift societies in which gift exchange predominates. He notes that, unlike our culture in which a person has alienable rights over everything she owns and there is a significant differentiation between people and property, people in gift-exchange cultures have no alienable rights over things. As a result, objects are never completely separated from the people who exchange them, resulting in the formation of a strong bond between people through gift exchange. By contrast, commodity exchange creates a bond between things, not between people. In a notion related to that set forth by Polanyi, Gregory – citing Bohannan (1955) – asserts, "a gift economy has multiple spheres of exchange while a commodity economy has only one sphere." Gregory (1982) at 23.

[47] Hann (1998) at 10.

[48] Hann (1998) at 32–33.

[49] Studies demonstrate "continuities between what now appear to have been increasingly complex subtleties of exchange in the past." *Id.* Even many of those who generally accept the opposition between gift exchange and commodity exchange critique the assumption "that commodity-based economies displace gift economies, or that the two economies may be regarded as successive phases within an evolutionary scheme." Pnina Werbner, "Economic Rationality and Hierarchical Gift Economies: Value and Ranking Among British Pakistanis," *Man* n.s. 25/2 (Jun 1990), pp. 266–285 at 268, citing Gregory (1982); N. Long, "Commoditization: Thesis and Antithesis," in N. Long et al. (eds.), *The Commoditization Debate: Labour Process, Strategy and Social Network*, Pub. Dept. Sociol. 17, Wageningen: Agricultural University (1986), pp. 8–23. Gift-exchange systems have been shown to flourish alongside capitalist, commodity-based economies. *Id.* For example, Werbner focuses on "the systematics of gift economies and the way such economies come to be embedded both in capitalist, market economies and in plural societies." *Id.* at 267.

to apply concepts, categories, or ideas from traditional so-called moral economies to so-called market economies.

Not only do theorists reject Polanyi's hypothesis of a "great divide," but many also use an aspect of his theory precisely to subvert any supposed "divide" between traditional and market economies; they embrace his notion of "embeddedness" and extend it to the present-day market economy.[50] It is useful precisely in debunking the myth of the "disembedded" market economy.

There is a good deal of ethnographic and sociological evidence documenting the "embeddedness" of the contemporary market economy. [51] This embeddedness can be traced (normatively and descriptively), at the very least, to the fact that it operates within the framework of legal institutions of property, contract, and so on. Some of the social-scientific evidence, as well as the significance of germane legal theories, will be explored below. In line with this perspective of embeddedness, research demonstrating that money is not universally powerful, and documenting the more complex and ambiguous social meaning of money and of monetary exchange, lays the groundwork for a less absolutized and polarized assessment of the various institutions of social exchange that exist in contemporary society.[52]

Scholarship on monetary exchange calls into question the presumed transformative power of money, upon which the theory of "the great divide" as well as the perceived opposition between gift and commodity are based. Before examining this material, it is useful to consider a contemporary critique of the stereotypical divide between gift and commodity and all that this presumed opposition presupposes. This analysis illuminates the danger inherent in utilizing such intellectual constructs to analyze or categorize societies, such as

50 For instance, Chris Hann notes that Polanyi's "conception of industrial economies as 'disembedded' was exaggerated and perhaps largely illusory. Many historians no longer accept his view, yet his "notion of 'embeddedness' may still prove fruitful." Hann (1998) at 10.

51 See, e.g., William James Booth, "On the Idea of the Moral Economy," *American Political Science Review* 88 3 (Sep 1994), pp. 653–667 at 661. Barber points out "the basic sociological fact that all types of exchange institutions are interdependent with their environing value patterns and other institutional systems," and "[c]alling market exchange *disembedded* leads attention away from analyzing just how it is interdependent with other parts of its societal system; it gives a false kind of analytical, as well as concrete independence." Barber (1977) at 27.

52 As anthropologists Maurice Bloch and Jonathan Parry observed in their introduction to their edited volume, *Money and the Morality of Exchange*, "[g]iven that money is held to have [a] profound impact on society and culture ... it is hardly surprising that there is a tendency to postulate a fundamental division between non-monetary and monetary economies (or even *societies*) ... [or that] this opposition gets elided with a series of other dichotomies – 'traditional' and 'modern,' pre-capitalist and capitalist, gift economies and commodity economies ... with money acting as a major catalyst of the 'great transformation' between them," Parry and Bloch (1989) at 7.

the detrimental effect such fictions can have on our ability to understand and learn from other cultures, by exposing the tendency of fictional constructs such as the gift/commodity binary to reify, mystify, and conceal.

1.3 GIFT v. COMMODITY: BRIDGING THE RHETORICAL DIVIDE

As noted above, contemporary social theorists dispute the accuracy or usefulness of the basic rhetorical opposition between gift and commodity – a binary that has been used not only to mark temporal transitions but also to distinguish between modes of exchange and between types of economies and societies.

There is a significant view that argues that there has been an "exaggeration and reification of the contrast between gift and commodity in anthropological writing."[53] Arjun Appadurai, a proponent of this view, admits that "the tendency to see these two modalities of exchange as fundamentally opposed remains a marked feature of anthropological discourse." Yet, in what has been described as "perhaps one of the most influential volumes in recent years,"[54] Appadurai has collected a series of essays that challenge "the view that the spirit of the gift and that of commodity are deeply opposed ... [and that] gift exchange and commodity exchange are fundamentally contrastive and mutually exclusive."[55] A good deal of literature subsequent to Appadurai has followed his critique of the gift/commodity dichotomy.[56]

Like the rejection of the "great divide" (a move that opens the door to learning from so-called moral or premarket economies to market economies), a critique of the presumptions concerning the opposition between (pure) gift and commodity and the power and meaning of money has certain methodological implications. One element of methodological significance becomes clear when these studies are read against the backdrop of the contemporary culturalist approach in anthropology. This approach stresses the need to avoid the ethnocentrism that is necessarily entailed in applying models developed in Western society to other cultures. Recognizing that theorists cannot completely avoid the use of concepts, language, and ideas developed in the West to analyze other societies, this approach stresses that Western social scientists and theorists should, at the very least, make sure they are cognizant of

53 Appadurai (1986) at 11.

54 Hann (1998) at 31. See Arjun Appadurai (ed.), *The Social Life of Things: Commodities in Cultural Perspective*, Cambridge: Cambridge University Press (1986).

55 Appadurai (1986) at 11.

56 D. Miller, "Consumption and Commodities," *The Annual Review of Anthropology* 24 (1995), pp. 141–161 at 147.

and explicit about the fact that their analytical constructs are artifacts originating in Western culture and consciousness. This perspective suggests that in the debate over the rigid divide between gift and commodity, as with other presumed binaries, what is important is not to decide who is "right," but to expose those things that the binary operates to mystify or conceal – in this case, the fact that money can have various social meanings and that both gift exchanges and commodity exchanges can entail mutual obligation and social bonding.

In her book *The Gender of the Gift*, Marilyn Strathern stresses the importance of this critical perspective while examining a variety of analytical constructs, including the opposition between gift and commodity, that are used by Western social scientists to describe other cultures.[57] She applies this approach to the supposed opposition between gift and commodity.[58] Pointing out that this binary is a heuristic fiction "rooted in Western metaphysics,"[59] she insists that her goal is to expose the "contextualized nature" of analytical constructs such as these,[60] and to make visible the way they work as self-referencing and self-validating strategies that, in turn, serve to expose Western assumptions, purposes, and interests.[61]

There is a significant limitation in the comparative account of another culture that relies on the gift/commodity opposition. It can distort one's vision

57 Strathern does not refrain from using the analytical constructs of contemporary anthropology, so long as "there is nothing surrogate or covert about the antinomies [she] use[s]," and she is explicit about and conscious of the fact that "they [are] deliberate artifice." Strathern (1998) at 220. According to Strathern, it is necessary to ask "what [a particular] analysis makes meaningful … [W]hatever uses [a particular] distinction might have for organizing social analysis, there were bound to be some things it left unexplained. The question becomes how to construct an analytical vocabulary that would make evident those elements previous analyses have hidden. Any choice would entail its own concealments in turn." *Id.*

58 Strathern's "own interest has been in [the] distinction between individual and society that has driven much anthropological enquiry." *Id.* She suggests that Westerners ought to stop thinking about all cultures as based on that antinomy.

59 Strathern (1988) at 7.

60 *Id.* at 8

61 The perceived dichotomy of gift and commodity arises directly from Western discourse. As described by Strathern, this "pair of terms provides an axis for considering a range of contrasts between [other societies] and the societies of the Western world from which the analytical constructs of social science in the first place derive." Strathern (1988) at 143. As analytical constructs, gift and commodity are deliberate fictions; they represent categories of analysis used to elucidate various social systems and to posit a "fictional division" of societies. *Id.* The contrast supplies "terms for a single cultural pair within Western political-economic discourse." *Id.* at 18. As Strathern notes, the concept of the gift is a "fiction to be deployed in its relational definition vis-à-vis its counterpart, the commodity." *Id.* at 134. It is in this regard and for this reason that "[t]he metaphor of the 'gift' … holds a particular place within Western formulations." *Id.* at 19.

of other cultures while concomitantly reinforcing certain assumptions about Western culture. Thus, the so-called gift economy (such as that claimed to exist in Melanesia) is "an inverse construction … [that] derive[s] from the symbolic practice of a commodity economy … What is hidden are techniques of reification, conventionalized assumptions which have consequences for the conduct of people's lives."[62] Knowledge produced about other cultures using this opposition "is not commensurate with the form that knowledge takes there."[63] From the perspective of other cultures, "what is missing is real time."[64]

One might also ask to what extent is "real time" also "missing" in studies of Western society by the presumptive opposition between gift and commodity. What aspects of Western society are hidden and reinforced by this theoretical construct? More specifically, how knowledge is produced about Western society is undermined or disrupted by the bundle of fictions that make up or underlie that binary (such as the distinctions between people and things and between interest and disinterest, and the meaning of ownership and private property). As it turns out, money and markets are themselves fictions that conceal meanings that can be illuminated through empirical examination.[65]

1.4 INTERROGATING THE SOCIAL MEANING OF MONETARY EXCHANGE

In contemporary society, where the purview of the "market" is seemingly all encompassing, there is a tendency to regard any exchange that entails the transfer of money as a "sale" or "purchase." To the extent that some thing (a good or a service) can be seen as moving from one person to another alongside or in conjunction with the passage of money – the universal medium of exchange – notions of sale, contract, and commodification immediately come into play. The item or act for which the money is paid is seen to be commodified, implicating market norms, with all of the accompanying invidious connotations of commodification, including degradation, objectification, and depersonalization.[66] It is a presumption that, in most contexts, arises *sua sponte* and requires rebutting in order to avoid triggering the array of value-laden assumptions that accompany the notion of "sale."

It is true that the presence of money can be an accurate indicator that a certain set of values and assumptions is at play in a transaction. Yet, it is worth

62 *Id.* at 175.
63 *Id.* at 344.
64 *Id.*
65 This is also true of the institution of gifts, whose social and philosophical meaning will be explored in the next chapter.
66 See, e.g., Anderson (1993).

examining whether assigning meaning to the presence of money in so sweeping a fashion is accurate, and whether it advances the project of preserving the values threatened by commodification. Seeing money not as just a possible indicator of invidious commodification but also as a necessary signifier of it could obfuscate what is really taking place in a particular transaction. The consequence could be not only to reinforce the very perceptions that are seen to be invidious, but also to render off limits various resources and approaches that could otherwise be marshaled in the drive to contain the troublesome aspects of the market.

Some theorists suggest that this tendency to see all transactions involving money as "commodifying" gives too much power to "money" as a social good and misreads a great deal of what goes on in Western culture. If that is true, this all-or-nothing approach might impede an accurate assessment of the problematic reaches of the market, making it difficult to ascertain where and how it ought to be limited and, at times, leading to unintended consequences of injustice (e.g., by denying someone just compensation, or by exacerbating life-threatening shortages through the barring of monetary incentives).

In fact, the meaning of money is culturally determined. Money does not necessarily possess the intrinsic meaning and power that Western theorists have traditionally ascribed to it – neither across all cultures,[67] nor across all realms within our own culture.[68] Social scientists have begun to map the social meanings of money and of various types of exchange in different societies (both ancient and modern). A good deal of the findings, concepts, debates, and perspectival shifts that have emerged from this field of study can be very useful to political and moral philosophers seeking to trace and delimit the role money plays in contemporary society. A thicker account of the social characteristics of money, and of the goods or services for which money can be seen to be transferred in any particular setting, could serve as the basis for a different kind of approach to "limiting" the reach of the market.

Money "is often credited with an *intrinsic* power to revolutionize society and culture"; and, yet, studies such as those contained in the volume edited by Jonathan Parry and Maurice Bloch, *Money and the Morality of Exchange*, cast doubt on the common assumption that money acts "as an incredibly powerful agent of profound social and cultural transformations."[69] Noting how infrequently the assumption regarding the power of money is questioned or examined, Parry and Bloch state, "[m]oney, we believe, is in nearly as much

67 See, e.g., Parry and Bloch (1989).

68 See, e.g., Viviana A. Zelizer, *The Social Meaning of Money*, Princeton: Princeton University Press (1997).

69 Parry and Bloch (1989) at 3.

danger of being fetishised by scholars as by stockbrokers."[70] Their collection of cross-cultural studies forcefully demonstrates that money does not play as powerful a role in all societies as is commonly believed.

This compilation of ethnographies demonstrates that money has no immutable, intrinsic meaning or power; that the meaning ascribed to money depends upon the cultural matrix in which it is incorporated, and that, in different cultures, money can often operate in different spheres of exchange – for example, even in the realm of the sacred.[71] Money is not universally seen, and need not operate, as inherently dangerous or powerful. For example, the volume includes a study of a culture in which gifts are seen as poisonous and commercial profits are morally neutral.[72]

Studies regarding the role and meaning of money and market transactions in other cultures have clear ramifications for Western society.[73] Findings similar to those yielded by cross-cultural anthropological studies are also being reached by sociologists analyzing the state of affairs in the United States. For example, Viviana Zelizer's work highlights the tendency of most people in our society, including academics, to attribute too much power to money; she challenges the view that regards money as something that carries its own meaning, a meaning that floods any situation it encounters and one that is necessarily invidious.

In her book *The Social Meaning of Money*, Zelizer explores the social characteristics of money based on its use in the United States between 1870 and 1930. Her study casts doubt on assumptions regarding the cultural independence and power of money. Challenging the traditional utilitarian view of money, she "proposes an alternate, differentiated model of money as shaped and reshaped by particular networks of social relations and varying systems of meanings."[74] By tracing the various ways in which money was earmarked – that is, ways in which "values and social relations reciprocally transmute[d] money by investing it with meaning and social

[70] *Id.*

[71] See e.g., David Lan, "Resistance to the Present by the Past: Mediums and Money in Zimbabwe," in Parry and Bloch (1989), pp. 191–208.

[72] See Parry (1989).

[73] Alexandra Ouroussoff notes that, despite their effort to undermine rigid assumptions regarding the meaning of money (and to reject Polanyi's idea of a "great divide"), Parry and Bloch are among those who "unwittingly perpetuate" the related idea of the "great divide between modern and savage" by failing to include Western ethnographies in the model used to compare the West with exotic societies. As she points out, like "virtually all major volumes of comparative anthropology," their work lacks any study that tests the validity of assumptions regarding the meaning and power of money in contemporary Western society. *Id.*

[74] Zelizer (1997) at 18.

patterns"[75] – she proves that the classic economic approach of "focusing exclusively on money as a market phenomenon ... fails to capture the very complex range of characteristics of money as a social medium."[76] Among other things, Zelizer shows that money is able to enter numerous nonmarket realms (such as personal relations) without having the feared commodifying effect that is generally expected. In fact, she demonstrates that money can take on even sacred meanings.[77]

Followed to their logical conclusion, studies such as these explicitly challenge the usefulness of the analytical constructs of "the market" and "market exchange." The growing body of literature challenging the notion of the "disembedded market economy" and the gift-versus-commodity binary indicates a deepening anthropological critique of some of the most basic assumptions made by economists.[78] What is presented is "growing empirical support for the idea that the pure market relations presupposed as foundational to modern

[75] *Id.*

[76] *Id.* at 19.

[77] Zelizer explores the intersection of monetary interests and noneconomic (even "sacred") concerns in two other works, *Markets and Morals: The Development of Life Insurance in the United States*, New Brunswick: Transaction Books (1983) (studying the history of life insurance in the United States), and *Pricing the Priceless Child*, Princeton: Princeton University Press (1994) (in which she examines the changing valuation of the child). In *Markets and Morals*, she traces the gradual acceptance of life insurance in the United States in the late nineteenth and early twentieth centuries. Zelizer reveals that, in an interesting parallel to present-day discussions of issues such as the sale of human organs for transplant, initially "putting death on the market [through life insurance] offended a system of values that upheld the sanctity of human life and its incommensurability." Zelizer (1983) at 43. Life insurance was seen as "sacrilegious because its ultimate function was to compensate the loss [of a human life] with a check." *Id.* at 45. In a transformation that Zelizer shows is attributable in part to independent noneconomic factors, life insurance became an accepted institution by the early twentieth century – an institution built on a "continuing tension between [the] contradictory demands and expectations" of the "simultaneous goals" of altruism and commercialism. *Id.* at 153 (crediting Robert K. Merton). At the early stages of its development, life insurance thus went from being stigmatized for its desacralization of the value of human life to a morally acceptable (if not laudable) mechanism that enables people to prepare themselves and their family for dealing with death. In fact, "money became sacralized by its association with" life and death. *Id.* Whereas life insurance went from being seen as the sacrilegious commodification of human life to a respectable social and economic institution, the "value" of the child underwent a transformation in the opposite direction at the turn of the century. In *Pricing the Priceless Child*, Zelizer traces the "cultural process of 'sacralization' of children's lives.... While in the nineteenth century, the market value of children was culturally acceptable, later the new normative ideal of the child as an exclusively emotional and affective asset precluded instrumental fiscal considerations." Zelizer (1994) at 11.

[78] As the sociologist Jon Lie notes, "the problem with neoclassical economics is that the gulf between the concept [of the market] and the social reality is often bridged by fiat." John Lie, "The Concept of the Mode of Exchange," *American Sociological Review* 57/4 (Aug 1992), pp. 508–523 at 509.

consumption may simply not exist, even within highly developed consumer markets."[79]

In casting doubt on the presumed intrinsic transformative power of money, these studies also implicitly cast doubt on the related assumptions regarding the radical difference between market and nonmarket economies.[80] In sharp contrast to the economic paradigm depicted, for example, in the work of Gary Becker,[81] this body of work documents what Zelizer describes as "the *interrelation* between economic and noneconomic factors, specifically between the market ... and personal or moral values."[82]

Interestingly, this perspective echoes Polanyi's idea of "embeddedness," a conception that can actually be very useful for analyzing exchange as a social institution in all societies.[83]

In sum, the insights of sociologists and anthropologists studying exchange suggest an analysis that does not rely on the rough and obfuscatory constructs of money, "market," and the distinction between gift and commodity but, rather, one that instead highlights the interactive, social meaning of different types of exchanges. An approach that focuses on the relational (bonding) aspects of exchange necessitates the exploration and evaluation of the deeper structural and normative framework governing property relations within which the market economy is embedded.

79 Miller (1995) at 151 (citations omitted). Miller goes on to note that, "previously, anthropologists tended to accept the concept of the market as a model of metropolitan societies.... In the future, there probably will be increasing emphasis on this critique of basic terms such as the market and even capitalism." *Id.*

80 See Parry and Bloch (1989); Bloch (1989) at 167.

81 See, e.g., Becker (1976).

82 Zelizer (1994) at 18.

83 As noted above, many of the theorists who reject the "exaggerated and reified" opposition between gift and commodity, and Polanyi's related theory of the "great divide," explicitly retain and build upon this notion of embeddedness, in part to refute Polanyi's claim that the market economy is disembedded. See, e.g., Hann; Booth (1994); John Davis, *Exchange*, Buckingham: Open University Press (1992). Foreshadowing the insights of contemporary scholars, Charles Cooley wrote in 1913 that "[p]ecuniary values are members of the same general system as the moral and aesthetic values, and it is part of their function to put the latter upon the market. To separate them is to cripple both, and to cripple life itself by cutting off the healthy interchange among its members. Our line of progress lies, in part at least, not in over commercialism but through it; the dollar is to be reformed rather than suppressed ... Our next task seems to be to ... enlarge and humanize the system by bringing it under the guidance of a comprehensive social and ethical policy." Charles H. Cooley, "The Sphere of Pecuniary Valuation," *American Journal of Sociology* 19/2 (Sep 1913), pp. 188–203 at 203. Also anticipating and refuting Polanyi's assertion that the market is autonomous, Cooley wrote that "the sphere of pecuniary valuation" is "an institution, like another, having important functions, but requiring, like all institutions, to be brought under rational control by the aid of a comprehensive sociology, ethics, and politics. It has no charter of autonomy, no right to exemption from social control." *Id.* at 197.

2

Alternate Property Conceptions: The Donor's Lien

It might be suggested that the contrast between gift and commodity, and its importance, have been overstated thus far. After all, many who employ it are aware that it does not describe all transactions and exchanges. What it represents, however, is something many consider troubling: the notion (of relatively recent vintage[1]) that transactions geared toward individual self-interest make up the engine that drives and guides the proper functioning of society. This blanket presumption of self-interest and its deleterious effects are what prompt the anti-commodifiers to turn to a conception of disinterested, altruistic exchange. The critique offered here asserts that such a move serves only to bolster the victory and acceptance of self-interest as the default mode of social exchange.

Comparative exposition demonstrates that these limited choices – self-interested market exchange or disinterested gift exchange – are not, and need not be, the only modes or institutions of exchange. Implicated in the problem at the heart of contemporary debates over markets and morals are deep philosophical assumptions intrinsically linked with the notion of exclusive private property. These assumptions, such as the related and sometimes mutually exclusive ideas of the autonomous individual, persons as distinct from things, freedom versus constraint, and liberty (and rights) versus obligations, extend well beyond the meaning of money and market exchange.[2] These

1 See Albert Hirschman, *The Passions and the Interests*, Princeton: Princeton University Press (1977).

2 Strathern notes the way in which the "Western paradigm of property ownership ... is so very much bound up with a special view of the person." Marilyn Strathern, "Subject or Object? Women and the Circulation of Valuables in Highlands New Guinea," in Renee Hirshchon (ed.), *Women and Property – Women as Property*, New York: St. Martin's Press (1984), pp. 158–175 at 158. Elsewhere she also observes that how we define and understand people, property, and ownership is not merely an academic issue. She predicts that "[t]he way in which people organize their relations to one another as a matter of control not just over

fundamental conceptions and oppositions, which go largely unquestioned, silently limit the range of options and hide what is at stake in the debate over commodification.

In contemporary debates over commodification and "limits to markets," questions of whether there are or should be different categories of property vis-à-vis market exchange, the extent to which the notion of obligation (as opposed to rights) should come into play with respect to certain property transactions, and the broader questions of how people relate to property, and to one another through property, are all at issue. All of these questions come under the general rubric of property relations – how they are defined, conceived, and actualized in our society.[3] Indeed, the institution that most directly and concretely embodies the notion of liberty being protected by the fictional gift/commodity binary, and by popular assumptions regarding the market, money, and the autonomous individual, is private property.[4]

Certain basic conceptions regarding the institution of private property are taken for granted in contemporary Western society.[5] In what might best describe the popular conception of property ownership, Felix S. Cohen has

things ('property' in the Supreme Court's sense) but over aspects of life (that define 'people') will loom large in the world agenda over the next decade. We can expect an explosion of concern with ownership." Strathern (1998) at 216.

3 Chris Hann notes that, "[i]n comparison with the attention paid to money and to markets, property has not attracted the attention it deserves from economic anthropologists." Chris M. Hann, "Introduction: The Embeddedness of Property," in Chris M. Hann, (ed.), *Property Relations: Renewing the Anthropological Tradition*, Cambridge: Cambridge University Press (1998) at 34. In the Introduction to his edited volume, Hann argues for a shift in attention to property relations, the area that underlies exchange theory (which has until relatively recently been the main focus of economic anthropologists) *Id.* at 29. There has, in fact, been a reorientation of exchange literature since the 1980s that has brought the topic closer to property. This shift has drawn on Mauss, among others, since "[w]hen he constructed a model of a type of exchange, Mauss also constructed a model of the relationship between people and objects, which is to say a construction of a kind of property." James G. Carrier, "Property and Social Relations in Melanesian Anthropology," in C. M. Hann,(ed.), *Property Relations*, Cambridge: Cambridge University Press (1998), pp. 85–103 at 88.

4 A shift in the focus from exchange theory to the deeper social/political/legal structure entailed in property relations that underpins it will elucidate some of the concepts, ideas, and beliefs that provide the backdrop for the phenomenon of exchange, such as the view of the person (as more or less atomistic) and the possible interrelationality of property. "A concern with property relations requires investigation into the total distribution of rights and entitlements within society, of material things and of knowledge and symbols. It requires examination of practical outcomes as well as ideals and moral discourses." C. M. Hann, "Introduction: The Embeddedness of Property," in C. M. Hann (ed.), *Property Relations: Renewing the Anthropological Tradition* Cambridge: Cambridge University Press (1998) at 34.

5 One alternative to the traditional approach to these issues is illustrated by a response to the question of organ sales found in Jewish law. The study of Jewish texts, in Chapters 3 and 4, will illustrate a distinct notion of property, and of the rights and obligation related thereto.

summarized it as follows: "[T]hat is property to which the following label can be attached: 'To the world: Keep off X unless you have my permission, which I may grant or withhold.'"[6]

The dominant liberal paradigm of property, originating in the seventeenth-century writings of Hobbes and Locke, is often associated with the notion of "possessive individualism."[7] There is a tendency (which might date back even further[8]) when characterizing "the legal concept of property in the definitional sense in the West, ... to agglomerate in a single person ... the exclusive right to possess, privilege to use, and power to convey a thing."[9] This "great bundle of exclusive rights, privileges, and powers"[10] can be described with a parallelism and simplicity reminiscent of Hohfeldian conceptions: "Western law tends to ascribe to the possessor of a thing: the right to possess the thing with a duty in everyone else to stay off, the privilege of using the thing with no right in anyone else to prevent him ..., a power to transfer any and all of his rights, privileges, and powers."[11]

This idea of exclusive and near-absolute ownership of private property is a foundational concept that creates "the well-grounded illusion that the value of symbolic goods is inscribed in the nature of things."[12] Many regard the institution of private property to be almost natural[13] and consider the effect

[6] Felix S. Cohen, "Dialogue on Private Property," *Rutgers Law Review* 9 (1954), pp. 357–387 at 374.

[7] See Crawford Brough Macpherson, *Political Theory of Possessive Individualism*, Oxford: Oxford University Press (1962).

[8] See Charles Donahue, Jr., "The Future of the Concept of Property Predicted from Its Past," in J. Roland Pennock and John W. Chapman (eds.), *Property*, Nomos 22, New York: New York University Press (1980), 28–68 at 34.

[9] *Id.* at 32.

[10] *Id.* at 33.

[11] *Id.* at 32. See Wesley Newcomb Hohfeld, "Some Fundamental Legal Conceptions as Applied in Judicial Reasoning," *Yale Law Review* 23 (1913), pp. 16ff. The classic idea of the right to property has been described, at its core, as the right to exclude. See J. E. Penner, *The Idea of Property in Law*, Oxford: Oxford University Press (2000).

[12] Pierre Bourdieu, *Outline of a Theory of Practice*, Cambridge: Cambridge University Press (1997) at 183. At the same time, some legal scholars are also documenting a "collapse of the idea of property" – Thomas C. Grey, "The Disintegration of Property," in J. Roland Pennock and John W. Chapman (eds.), *Property*, Nomos 22, New York: New York University Press (1980), pp. 69–85 – and are, in fact, predicting "an uncertain future for the Western concept of property." Donahue (1980) at 58. They are also attempting to expose "something important" that is obscured or denied by our "political rhetoric, court opinions and scholarly discourse" – the fact that there is a tension in our property system between liberty and obligation and the fact that "owners have obligations as well as rights." Joseph William Singer, *The Edges of the Field*, Boston: Beacon Press (2000) at 16.

[13] Private property might be described, in Pierre Bourdieu's terms, as *doxa*: a construct that operates to "naturalize" (limit) the "arbitrariness" of the established order in Western liberal society. *Id.* at 164. It operates at a deep level to make "the natural and social world appear[]

this property system has on the economy to be neutral. These two factors are presumably part of what the "divide theorists" and neoclassical economists rely on in deeming the market economy "disembedded" – unbounded by social, political, and moral constraints. Yet, as G. A. Cohen explains, the liberal paradigm entails a "moralized definition" of liberty as lack of constraint,[14] combined with a confusion or conflation of this idea of freedom with that of private property (defined as exclusive rights and virtually no obligations).[15] It is this moralized definition of liberty (practically reified as a particular view of private property) that underlies the dominant discourse concerning money, markets, and exchange in this society. Exploring nonmarket societies can expand our understanding of ones in which the market predominates and can illuminate many commonly held perceptions that reflect the dominance of the exclusive concept of property.[16]

As a general matter, anthropologists have demonstrated that a shift to the broader perspective of property relations brings to light the fact that property is a "political relationship between people," something that is really "a three-way matter: that is, a relationship between people in relation to a thing."[17] Thus, for example, as distinct from "the liberal (neoclassical) paradigm in economics," which "tends to emphasize the 'thingness' of property," anthropology emphasizes "the essentially relational, social character of property ownership."[18] Rather than focusing, in the moralized fashion described by Cohen, "on relationships with *things*," anthropologists emphasize "the social web in which they are held."[19] In contrast to the impression created by rigid categories of ownership and private property established in law and political philosophy,

as self-evident," resulting in what appears to be "a quasi-perfect correspondence between the objective order and the subjective principles of organization." *Id.*

14 G. A. Cohen, "Capitalism, Freedom and the Proletariat," in Alan Ryan (ed.), *The Idea of Freedom*, Oxford: Oxford University Press (1979), pp. 9–25 at 12.

15 *Id.* at 11. Cohen states, "The marriage of liberty and private property requires not only a moralized definition of liberty but also a moral endorsement of private property." *Id.* at 12.

16 Chris Hann, and those who contributed to the volume he edited entitled *Property Relations*, undertake the type of comparative project described above. Rather than focusing on exchange, Hann "approach[es] property as a key category in cross-cultural analysis." Hann (1998) at 9. One of the things he points out is that there is an interesting parallel between perceptions of private property and popular attitudes toward money. *Id.* at 32. "Like property, money is seen in Western thought, both negatively, as 'the root of all evil,' and positively, as the source of autonomy and liberty." *Id.* Hann concurs with the finding of Parry and Bloch that, in fact, "money cannot itself be the cause of radical social changes." *Id.*

17 Alan MacFarlane, "The Mystery of Property: Inheritance and Industrialization in England and Japan," in C. M. Hann (ed.), *Property Relations: Renewing the Anthropological Tradition*, Cambridge: Cambridge University Press (1998) at 113. See 44n.3, *supra*.

18 Hann (1998) at 6.

19 *Id.*

"[a]nthropologists take it for granted that people's attitudes towards objects and the ways in which they are used to create meaning are culturally and historically variable."[20]

Anthropological and sociological research lays the groundwork for a critical discourse regarding property relations, particularly by helping to expose what Pierre Bourdieu might call "the arbitrariness of the taken for granted."[21] Comparative studies have the effect of disrupting the apparent universality and, indeed, the perceived "naturalness" of the classical liberal idea of private property and of ownership (as an element integral to individual freedom).[22] They support explicit rejection of the dominant paradigm whereby "the established cosmological and political order" of absolute and exclusive property ownership "is perceived not as arbitrary, i.e. as one possible order among others, but as a self-evident and natural order which goes without saying and therefore goes unquestioned."[23] By demonstrating the varied possibilities of property conceptions and patterns of relations, comparative projects help to supply at least the "symbolic means of rejecting the definition of the real that is imposed" by a certain moralized definition of liberty and property.[24] Immersion in an alternative system that is not rooted in the categories, binaries, and assumptions that conceptually flood the market economy (e.g., the gift-versus-commodity binary, the intrinsic power of money, the exclusivity of property and the "moralized definition" of liberty) helps to expose what is not readily visible in contemporary market society.[25]

[20] *Id.* at 3. Anthropologists try to avoid "the crude dichotomies of individual or collective systems." MacFarlane (1998) at 201.

[21] Bourdieu (1997) at 169.

[22] As Evans-Pritchard points out in his Introduction to Mauss's essay, "[w]e take our own social conventions for granted and we seldom think how recent many of them are and how ephemeral they will perhaps prove to be. Men at other times had … different ideas, values and customs, from a study of which we may learn much that … may be of value to ourselves." Evans-Pritchard (1974) at ix–x.

[23] *Id.* at 166.

[24] *Id.* In this vein, one might say this book hopes to offer a "critique which brings the undiscussed into discussion, the unformulated into formulation," and makes "the arbitrary principles of the prevailing classifications appear as such." *Id.* at 168, 169.

[25] Thus, for example, one of the insights that emerged from studies examined earlier, such as those of Douglas, Zelizer, and Ouroussoff, was that, whatever liberal philosophy says about the meaning of private property and private ownership, in actuality our society does evidence what are seen to be attributes of the so-called gift economy, including the relationality of property, the role its transfer plays in binding people together and in creating obligations, the (often hierarchical) categorization of property on the basis of values implicated by the property or its transfer, and, finally, a less atomistic, more porous, notion of the individual. These studies highlight different value structures that are present, albeit not readily apparent, in Western culture.

Cross-cultural comparative studies provide alternative models for use in describing and rethinking the larger social, moral, and political frameworks that inform and shape behavior in a market society. Some are particularly apt with respect to the property theory introduced here. For example, an anthropological study by James Carrier provides a useful typology. Looking to the literature on exchange practices in Melanesia in order to understand Melanesian norms of property, [26] he introduces the terms "inclusive" and "exclusive" property. He explains that in Melanesia, "one of the central conceptions of the relationships between people and things … [entails] an *inclusive* notion of property, wherein an object is embedded in and reflects durable relationships between those people implicated in its past."[27] He explains that "[t]his attribute is taken to distinguish Melanesia from the modern West, where property is taken to be *exclusive*, under the sole control of and associated only with the person who happens to own it at the moment."[28]

Transposing this rough categorization onto contemporary society is useful. The powerful notion of exclusive private property, concomitant with the

[26] Carrier, (1998). Carrier explains that "[i]n addressing the way people identify and relate themselves to one another through the giving and taking of things, the literature on exchange necessarily includes some information on [Melanesian] notions of property." Carrier (1998) at 86.

[27] *Id.* Indeed, Carrier explicitly notes that Mauss posits a particular "construction of a kind of property," something that illustrates his category of inclusive property. Carrier points out that Mauss's essay "contains a model of property that stresses its inclusive nature," *Id.* at 90, whereby "[t]hings are not construed solely as neutral, alienable chattels under the control of the person who happens to have them at the moment in the manner of exclusive conceptions of property. Rather, they are '… part of the self …' … the object is construed as bearing and being part of one's relationship with others, in the manner of inclusive conceptions of property. (citations omitted)." *Id.* at 88.

[28] *Id.* Like other theorists who have been discussed in this paper, Carrier asserts that assumptions about "the West" "exist in a dialectical relationship with" assumptions about other societies. *Id.* at 101. This oppositional stance, fueled by "twinned essentialist assumptions," distorts assessments of "the West" and of other cultures. *Id.* He points out that just as there is "voluminous work that indicates that transactions in the West are not so uniform" as is indicated by the essential rendering that reduces Western societies to "impersonal commodity transactions and a wholly exclusive view of property," *id.* at 101–102, the existence of commodity-like exchanges in Melanesian society "gets swamped by the traditional structure of the Maussian society of the gift." *Id.* at 103. Echoing other theorists, Carrier observes, "the basic Melanesian distinction between gift and commodity systems can be seen … as a surrogate for an essentialist simplification of the distinction between the modern West and Melanesia … it distorts the reading of each area." *Id.* at 102. Yet it should be noted that, like Strathern, who articulates a similar anti-essentialist critique of the opposition between gift and commodity, Carrier "is not arguing that the distinction between gifts and commodities should be abandoned, as Arjun Appadurai [1986] suggests. Rather [he thinks] it should be applied with greater sensitivity." *Id.*

myths of the atomized individual and a liberal definition of freedom, underlie the reification and absolutization of the "autonomous" market. This also accounts for the tendency of even the anti-commodifiers to use the individual as the relevant analytical unit in formulating a response to the pervasiveness of the market.[29] Furthermore, the view that regards the market economy as disembedded depends upon the same perceptions regarding money and market exchange that defend, and are integrally related to, the moralized liberal ideals regarding freedom, the autonomous individual, and private property.[30]

James Woodburn supplies another useful alternative model of property relations.[31] Woodburn depicts a hunter-gatherer society (the Hadza of Tanzania) whose dominant form of property relations is "sharing." When a hunter kills a large animal, a portion of it belongs to God, and the rest is considered "people's meat," neither category belonging initially to the hunter. What is significant is that the obligation that the property be shared is *in* the property itself – it does not arise as an obligation of exchange.

Woodburn explains that "sharing" is not merely a form of exchange. It is not, for instance, an example of "generalized reciprocity" described by Marshall Sahlins whereby one gives in order to one day receive a return. Nor is sharing a matter of generosity. Recipients are simply entitled to their share, with no obligation to reciprocate. Sharing is a political ideology that stresses the entitlement of all group members. It is an ethos that informs the way people relate to one another through property.[32]

Another anthropologist whose theory suggests the possibility of a new way to think about property is Marcel Mauss. Mauss's contribution to property theory can be gleaned from his writing on gifts.[33] A brief foray into these ideas will yield insights that will prove critical to the upcoming analysis of Jewish law. Indeed, the ideas offered in his essay, *The Gift: The Form and*

[29] One of the things called into question by studies such as those done by Zelizer and Ouroussoff is the traditional liberal view that society is made up of rational, utility-maximizing individuals acting in their own self-interest. See Zelizer (1994), Introduction.

[30] As Hann notes, "[t]he liberal paradigm is predicated on a separation of political, economic and legal spheres ... [T]his separation is fictitious ... [It is] a myth ... At the end of the day, ... judicial concepts are necessarily bound up with questions of embedded culture and political economies." Hann (1998) at 45–46.

[31] Woodburn, "Sharing Is Not a Form of Exchange: An Analysis of Property-Sharing in Immediate-Return Hunter-Gatherer Societies," in C. M. Hann (ed.), *Property Relations*, Cambridge: Cambridge University Press (1998), pp. 48–63.

[32] See Hann (1998) at 34.

[33] In his fascinating book, *Toward an Anthropological Theory of Value*, David Graeber laments the fact that "almost no one nowadays seems aware of Mauss' importance as a political [thinker]." David Graeber, *Toward an Anthropological Theory of Value: The False Coin of Our Dreams*, New York: Palgrave (2001) at 152.

Reason for Exchange in Archaic Societies,[34] will provide the backdrop for the analysis, which will be undertaken in Chapters 3–5, of the particular notions of property at play in the Talmudic materials, notions that, themselves, offer a different type of solution to the dilemma of the sale of human organs for transplant.

As noted above, Polanyi and his followers claimed support for their theory from Mauss's essay. Titmuss, as well as Walzer, also claimed to be building on Mauss. All of these approaches conjure up the perceived sharp contrast between the ideology of the market and the ideology of altruistic exchange. There is, indeed, a tendency to associate Mauss with this opposition. This reading fails, however, to appreciate the thrust and broader implications of Mauss's theory regarding the gift.[35] Mauss does describe an evolutionary transition from "gift economies" to modern market economies;[36] and yet, in so doing, he does not reinforce the above contrast. To the contrary, as I read him, Mauss explicitly problematizes much of what is implied or entailed in the gift-versus-commodity distinction.[37]

Gift exchanges described by Mauss do not entail unilateral acts of altruism; rather, they are part of a web of interconnected obligations. As such, they play a key role in cementing community. The critical combination of self-interest and generosity emblematic of gift exchange is shown by Mauss to form the basis of many transactions and institutions in the societies he studied. His thesis is that, throughout much of human history, the predominant transfer of property has taken place via such systems of gift exchange.[38]

Salient for purposes of this book is Mauss's focus on the transfers as something that, as he puts it, are both free and obligatory. With respect to certain transfers, despite being called "gifts," there is a sense in which they are not voluntary. Nor are they strictly obligatory – hence the denomination "gifts." The mixture of the free and the obligatory is a notion that is intriguing and

[34] Marcel Mauss, *The Gift: The Form and Reason for Exchange in Archaic Societies*, New York: W. W. Norton and Co. (1990).

[35] Mauss's groundbreaking essay has been described as "perhaps one of the most fundamental yet most misunderstood texts in anthropology." Parry and Bloch (1989) at 168.

[36] Some align this transition with other dichotomies or dualities in social theory, such as Tonnie's transition from *Gemeinschaft* to *Gesellschaft*, and Henry Maine's description, in *Ancient Law*, of the transition from "status" (in early societies, in which law of persons and things tended to be conflated) and "contract" (modern societies characterized by the institution of contract and informed by individual rights, the idea of ownership, etc.).

[37] Mauss (1990) at 68. Cf. Mary Douglas, "Foreword," in Marcel Mauss, *The Gift: The Form and Reason for Exchange in Archaic Societies*, New York: W. W. Norton and Co. (1990), pp. vii–xviii; Parry and Bloch (1989); Parry (1986); Bloch (1989); Appadurai (1986).

[38] My use of Mauss is conceptual, not historical or empirical.

paradoxical.[39] This seeming incongruity is partly why Jacques Derrida declares the gift an impossibility as a philosophical matter.

Mauss demonstrates that, in the ancient societies he studied, while the form might be of a gift generously offered, the accompanying behavior shows that exchange is based on obligation. Thus, while gift giving might appear voluntary, disinterested, and spontaneous, it is, in fact, also both an obligatory and an interested act. Specifically, the gift is characterized by a set of interlocking obligations: (1) the obligation to give, (2) the obligation to receive, and (3) the obligation to reciprocate. Mauss describes an ethic of generous gift exchange, under which lies a logic of self-interested gift giving combined with the notion that it is necessary to return what has been given.

What renders this transfer a "gift" is definitely not the purity of an altruistic motive; that is precisely what is imagined in the "pure gift" but lacking in the Maussian gift. Rather, it is its nature as a voluntary (albeit, paradoxically, obligatory) transfer. Focusing entirely on the issue of motive (interest v. disinterest), as occurs in the turn toward gift giving as a response to the problem of commodification, while critical for thinkers like Titmus, is misleading. The presumed sharp divide between interest and disinterest, or self-interest and selflessness, as Mauss helps demonstrate, is a false dichotomy. What is important to highlight is the related but conceptually different characteristic of the gift – its voluntariness, while exposing the fact that it is also obligatory – hence, significantly, its nature as a "free and obligatory" act.

Mauss himself at times elides what are really two separate characteristics possibly attributable to gifts – voluntariness and altruistic intent. This, in turn, leaves Mauss open to the critique of Jacques Derrida. Derrida also meshes the two separate facets of the gift: motive (self-interested or disinterested – or both) and voluntariness (free or obligatory – or both). It is worth reviewing Derrida's assessment of the Maussian idea of the gift while keeping in mind the need to separate the element of altruism (not a necessary factor in the gift) and its (peculiar obligatory) voluntariness.[40] With respect to this latter quality, which, as distinct from altruism, will be significant to the Jewish theory of property to be discussed, Derrida's insights are helpful.

39 I use the term "Maussian gift" as a shorthand term to refer to the paradoxical free and obligatory property transfer described by Mauss. Its essence lies in its locus of entanglement in a set of interlocking obligations. By contrast, I use the phrases "pure gift" or "free gift" to describe an altruistic gift. It is the notion of pure gift that is intended when reference is made to the classic opposition between gift and commodity.

40 Derrida's critique, with which I do not agree to the extent that it purports to undermine altogether the notion of the obligatory (or "Maussian") gift, is useful for exploring the thrust of the theoretical insight Mauss makes on the basis of empirical ethnographic and literary

Derrida points to its apparently contradictory nature to proclaim the gift impossible – indeed, "[n]ot [only] impossible, but *the* impossible."[41] He operates with an ironclad conception of the pure gift: a transfer is not a gift unless it is given and received without any thought of reciprocation.[42] Further, the gift must occur spontaneously, as a surprise. It cannot be planned; nor can it be given out of a sense of generosity. Yet, Derrida explains (in reliance, in part, on Mauss's work) that such an "event" is impossible. Thus, the gift is something that can only be imagined – it cannot really exist.

Derrida concedes that, despite its character as "another name of the impossible ... we still think [the gift], we name it, we desire it ... [w]e intend it"; he observes that "the gift itself will never be confused with the presence of its phenomenon."[43] It can be "imagined" as something that is given (with no desire for a return, etc.) but then immediately forgotten by all parties. For (as Mauss demonstrated) the very recognition of the gift gives rise to a debt or contemplation of a return; therefore, if one recognizes something as a gift, "this simple recognition suffices to annul the gift. ... The simple identification of the gift seems to destroy it."[44] The gift "not only must not be repaid but must not be kept in memory, retained as symbol of a sacrifice, as symbolic in general. For the symbol immediately engages one in restitution."[45]

With his thesis of impossibility, Derrida takes very seriously the paradoxical notion of the free and obligatory gift described by Mauss. He notes that "we require simultaneously of the gift that it appear and that it not appear in its

historical evidence. See Jacques Derrida, *Given Time*, volume 1: *Counterfeit Money*, translated by Peggy Kamuf, Chicago: University of Chicago Press (1991); see also Jacques Derrida, *The Gift of Death*, translated by David Wills, Chicago: The University of Chicago Press (1992). Derrida's analysis of Mauss is but one piece of the complex interdisciplinary discussion of gifts that has been inspired by Mauss's essay. See, e.g., Robyn Horner, *Rethinking God as Gift: Marion, Derrida, and the Limits of Phenomenology*, New York: Fordham University Press (2001); Alan D. Schrift (ed.), *The Logic of the Gift: Toward an Ethic of Generosity*, New York: Routledge (1997); John D. Caputo and Michael J. Scanlon (eds.), *God, the Gift, and Postmodernism*, Bloomington: Indiana University Press (1999).

41 Derrida, *Counterfeit Money* at 7.

42 In Derrida's words, "for there to be a gift, it is necessary that the donee not give back, amortize, reimburse, acquit himself, enter into a contract, and that he never have contracted a debt." *Id.* at 13. (Interestingly, this description comes close to what is expected in the Jewish legal prohibition against usury; apart from the return of the borrowed money or item itself, no benefit on behalf of the giver/lender is to be generated whatsoever.)

43 *Id.* at 29.

44 *Id.* at 7, 14. Or, as he states in *The Gift of Death* (p. 29), "a gift that could be recognized as such in the light of day, a gift destined for recognition, would immediately annul itself."

45 *Id.* at 23.

essence … *that it obligate and that it not obligate*" (emphasis added).[46] At the same time, he works with a surprisingly essentialist idea of the gift as something that is absolutely pure, a notion implicitly rejected by Mauss. Derrida's criticism of Mauss is that he fails, ultimately, to speak of (what Derrida conceives as) the gift. With this argument, Derrida seems to reject or dismiss Mauss's deeper theoretical project (discussed below) of the disruption of the conceptual building blocks of contemporary discourse regarding exchange.

In a sense, Derrida's vivid articulation of the impossibility of the pure (altruistic) gift supports or helps explain Mauss's rejection thereof. What Derrida does not accept or acknowledge is Mauss's effort to move beyond this (impossible) conception of the (pure) gift to something that is altogether different. Perhaps, as Derrida points out and as Mauss concedes, the word "gift" is inapposite in this context. Semantics aside, what Mauss seeks to describe is clear: it is an exchange that is different from a pure gift, but that is also neither a contract nor a sale.

The Gift recounts a particular story whereby, in ancient "economic and legal systems,"[47] transactions involving goods (and people) primarily took place in the form of gifts – transfers that were voluntary in theory but that were "in reality … given and reciprocated obligatorily."[48] Mauss explores this interesting phenomenon from both relevant perspectives of freedom (or voluntariness) and obligation. On the one hand, he examines the "so to speak voluntary character" of exchanges that were "apparently free and disinterested but [were] nevertheless constrained and self-interested."[49] At the same time, he explores what it is that "compels the gift … to be obligatorily reciprocated" or, more specifically, "what power resides in the object that causes its recipient to pay it back."[50]

Pursuant to the system of gift exchange typified by the Maori, something Mauss calls "total services," everything "is there for passing on, and for balancing accounts."[51] Technically, this is presented as an archaic form of contract that is characterized by three interlocking obligations: an obligation to give,

46 *Id.* at 27.

47 Mauss (1990) at 5. The earlier societies he describes preceded modern forms of sale and contract, as well as the use of money, although these cultures were not altogether lacking in economic markets. *Id.* Following his description of the Maori, Mauss traces a similar system of gift exchange among the Melanesians, where "the notion of money emerges much more clearly." *Id.* at 20.

48 *Id.* at 3.

49 *Id.*

50 *Id.* In the course of this two-pronged inquiry, Mauss succeeds in exposing the contingent nature of the relatively recent array of assumptions that underlie current ideas of contract and exchange.

51 *Id.* at 14.

an obligation to receive, and an obligation to reciprocate (as discussed above). Despite, or alongside, these obligatory elements, there is a voluntariness to these exchanges that imparts significant meaning. This aspect is expressed, for example, in a description, quoted by Mauss, of a similar institution among the Andaman Islanders: "these presents do not serve the same purpose as commerce and exchange in more developed societies. The goal is above all a moral one, the object being to foster friendly feelings between the two person in question, and if the exercise failed to do so, everything had failed."[52]

Mauss's essay begins with a discussion of what he calls "Maori law and religion."[53] A key idea entails the *hau*, or the "spirit" that is contained in every object (*taonga*). Once an object (*taonga*) is given to another, its *hau* – a force related to the giver – continues to reside in the object and to impel a return of some sort to the giver.[54]

The deep significance of this set of conceptions is summarized by Mauss as follows:

> in Maori law, the legal tie, a tie occurring through things, is one between souls, because the thing itself possesses a soul ... to make a gift of something to someone is to make a present of some part of oneself ... to accept something from somebody is to accept some part of his spiritual essence.[55]

[52] *Id.* at 19, quoting Brown, *Andaman Islanders* (1922) at 83.

[53] Without defining them, Mauss freely makes use of terms such as "law," "religion," "morality," and "economy." There is no room, here, to examine the presumptions underlying these categories, particularly as they are used across cultures and historical epochs. On its face, Mauss's apparently uncritical utilization of these terms can be seen as problematic. While insufficiently examined by Mauss, his terminology bolsters the sense he creates, of a blurring of boundaries that are taken for granted in contemporary thought. The comingling of conceptions of law, religion, morality, etc. in Mauss's essay can and should be unraveled, although there is no room here to do so. Nevertheless, this seemingly paradoxical or at least counterintuitive blending of concepts illuminates, and is illuminated by, the theory of the voluntary/obligatory gift developed in Chapters 3–5, taking it beyond Mauss's conception and in a way that responds to Derrida's critique of Mauss. Mauss's use of imprecise contemporary theoretical categories, uses that seem somewhat out of place, is evidenced, for example, in his frequent mention of "principles of law and economics" governing the ancient system of gift exchange (see, e.g., p. 21); in his description of the link between persons and things as entailing a form of "contractual morality" (p. 4); and in his mention of Maori "law," "magic," and "religion" (pp. 10 and 12) or the "mythical jurisprudence" of the Maori (p. 26), and the "religious nature of the things exchanged" by the Buin and Banaro tribes, "particularly that of money" (p. 31).

[54] As described by Mauss, "[w]hat imposes obligation in the present received and exchanged, is the fact that the thing received is not inactive. ... it still possesses something of [the giver]. Through it the giver has a hold over the beneficiary just as, being its owner, through it *he has a hold over the thief.* This is because the *taonga* is animated by the *hau* ... the *hau* follows after anyone possessing the thing. ... the *hau* wishes to return to its birthplace" (emphasis added). *Id.* at 11–12.

[55] *Id.* at 12.

Following his examination of the Polynesians and Melanesians, Mauss examines another system of gift exchange, the *potlatch*, practiced by Native Americans in the American northwest.[56] Here again, Mauss highlights the key element – the implicit obligation to make a return gift. He states that "[t]he obligation to reciprocate constitutes the essence of the potlatch."[57] More specifically, Mauss explains that "in the things exchanged during the potlatch, a power is present that forces gifts to be passed around, to be given, and returned."[58] Echoing his description of Maori law, he describes the drive to make a return gift in the *potlatch* as follows: "by giving one is giving *oneself*, and if one gives *oneself*, it is because one 'owes' *oneself* – one's person and one's goods – to others."[59]

Mauss's premise is that persons do not stand wholly in opposition to the things exchanged.[60] To the contrary, for Mauss the "spirit of the gift" suggests that every gift contains an element of the donor, something that inherently gives rise to the obligation to make a return gift. Mauss describes the lack of clear separation between the person and the item exchanged as "an indissoluble bond of a thing with its original owner." Indeed, he partially attributes the obligations that flow from the giving of a gift to the idea that, in giving a particular object, the person is giving a piece of him/herself – hence the obligation to reciprocate.[61]

[56] Mauss describes the *potlatch* as a system of gifts exchanged that differs only slightly, and in certain ways, from that of the Melanesians. Interestingly, one such difference resides, according to Mauss, in a "lack of juridical concepts … the juridical and economic concepts possess less clarity and less conscious precision," although, in practice, "the principles are positive and sufficiently clear-cut." *Id.* at 35.

[57] *Id.* at 41.

[58] *Id.* at 43.

[59] *Id.* at 46.

[60] One of the critical elements of this ancient system of exchange that emerges from this description is the mitigation of an opposition between persons and things; indeed, there is a lack of rigid boundaries, thus permitting (or nurturing) the relation of people to things and, through things, to one another. This comes across very early in Mauss's essay, where he traces the basis for obligation to reciprocate.

[61] Mauss sees value in facilitating the ability of people living today to recognize the bond between a thing and its owner, creator or donor, and thus between people through things. (This also entails a more porous notion of the self, another important aspect of Mauss' political philosophy.) The inseparability of persons and things is elemental to Mauss' exposition of traditional society; their eventual (theoretical) separation is a key to which Mauss points explicitly to account for the transition to modern concepts of property and exchange. The dismantling of the presumed separation between people and things, something portrayed as natural in contemporary law, might be difficult to conceive today. Nevertheless, it is one among an array of contrasts, binaries, and dichotomies that Mauss aspires to break down in order to (if nothing else) make it easier to learn from the ancient morality of gift exchange.

Mauss demonstrates that, in the ancient societies he studied, there is a deep sense in which people relate to one another through property. Ideas such as the "spirit" of the gift, or the notion that some part of the donor continues to reside in the object given, eloquently portray a perspective that, unlike our own, did not presume a rigid divide between people and things. There was as sense of porosity of the self and inclusivity of property.[62] This system of exchange (in contrast to "the mere exchange of useful goods") was a significant site of social bonding in the ancient cultures he studied.

Mauss's analysis, in some ways, parallels the property models described by Carrier and Woodburn earlier in this chapter. His study of ancient societies renders complex our simple conceptions related to property and ownership, recognizing that they can include, or even be defined by essential elements of obligations and entitlements inhering in non-"owners."[63] He did not coin terms like "inclusive property" or "sharing," but Mauss identified an obligation or compulsion to give back that is inherent in gifted property. Tracing it, metaphorically, to the essence of the donor that remains in the gift and yearns to return, he articulated a kind of latent property claim belonging to someone

62 The philosophical notion of person and self, which undergirds the autonomous individual, is of a discrete, bordered and closed unit, albeit one which interacts variously with other such units or "closed subjectivities." This notion of autonomous selfhood is in fact the overwhelming bequest of the modern Western philosophical and political traditions, although it has been questioned, if not undermined by various twentieth century thinkers (such as Levinas, Merleau-Ponty, Lacan, Foucault, and arguably Mauss). The basic concept of the self, person, or individual, although taken for granted in our society, has a meaning that is culturally variable. See Appadurai (1986) at 12 n.3; Ouroussoff (1993).

63 This comes across clearly, for example, in his discussion of the Trobriand Islanders' well-developed and "noble" system of gift exchange, known as the *kula*. Mauss describes the *kula* as an institution that provides for the continuous circulation of property that entails a particular idea of ownership. Mauss makes clear the different conceptual framework that governs this system of exchange: "it is indeed ownership that obtains with the gift that one receives. But *it is ownership of a certain kind*. One could say that *it partakes of all kinds of legal principles that we, more modern, have carefully isolated from one another.* It is ownership and possession, a pledge and something hired out, a thing sold and bought, and at the same time deposited, mandated and bequeathed in order to be passed on to another. For it is only given to you on condition that you make use of it for another or pass it on to a third person … Such is the nature of this economic, legal, and moral entity." *Id.* at 23–24 (emphasis added). Elsewhere Mauss states that the Melanesians did not "isolate and divide up their economic and juridical concepts" the way we do; they "have no conception of either selling or borrowing, but nevertheless carry out juridical and economic operations that fulfill the same function. … [they] exchange things of great value, under different forms and for different reasons from those with which we are familiar." *Id.* at 32–33. The full text of the earlier part of this quote is likely meant to be ironic. Mauss states, "The stumbling block that these laws and, as we shall also see, Germanic law, came up against, was their inability to isolate and divide up their economic and juridical concepts. But they had no need to do so."

other than the nominal "owner" of property. This concept of the obligatory return gift (underlying the basic notion of the "free and obligatory" transfer) will be very important as we turn to the Talmudic analysis in Chapter 3. With the help of that textual analysis, this phenomenon will be further conceptualized and labeled. I will refer to it as a "donor's lien" that is built into all gifted property.

Concededly, there is a risk of confusion in the use of the term "lien," or even in the term "obligation," in reference to the impetus to which Mauss refers, to make a return gift. There is no obvious debt (lien) or obligation in the technical legal sense; there exists no corresponding, directly enforceable right in another person to demand or receive something in return. Nor is any definite or direct reciprocity or mutuality anticipated or relied upon with the act of giving. Indeed, its uncharacteristic indefiniteness is a salient feature of this obligation.

Despite the fact that no legal debt technically exists, the term "donor's lien" (as a charge or encumbrance on property accruing to the benefit of the donor) has intuitive metaphorical appeal. In a sense, it communicates the aspect of the "spirit of the gift" that, in its literal recitation, borders on a type of anthropomorphization of property, positing that something of the donor resides in the gifted property and yearns to return. This aspect of the duty to give, its presumptive and implicit presence within the (gifted) property, suggests another term – it can also be described and referred to as an "embodied obligation."

The peculiarity of this duty (which explains why the labels "lien" and "obligation" might, at first blush, seem inapposite) inheres in its open-endedness. As noted, this is not a directly enforceable "return" obligation, and there is technically no "right" in another person corresponding to this duty. To the extent that the duty will be fulfilled, it will be because the actor has chosen voluntarily to do so, using whatever property the actor chooses to give in return. As understood in the Maussian framework, this indefiniteness should in no way render the obligation nugatory. To the contrary, this degree of voluntariness or open-endedness is its distinguishing feature, one that is intimately connected to the spatial factor that regards this (sense of) duty as arising from within the property (or within its recipient). Open are the questions of when, what, how much, to whom, and, indeed, whether the duty will be fulfilled. In this sense, it is not really obligatory at all – and yet, in the sense described by Mauss, it is. This explains its paradoxical essence as something that is both free and obligatory. Being volitional but driven by a sense of duty, it is, as Mauss puts it, "where obligation and liberty intermingle."[64]

[64] Mauss (1990) at 65.

What is this phenomenon that Mauss traces – something that is not a legal obligation but that nevertheless exists as more than an idea, something whose existence and role in society can be tracked empirically? It can be conceived as a sociological observation made by Mauss in the intellectual tradition of his uncle, Emile Durkheim, who regarded his charge as that of uncovering the forces or compulsions that precede and undergird social life. The notion of an implicit obligation "within" gifted property (or its holder) is a type of compulsion to reciprocate, found (as Mauss demonstrates) across cultures and across time, that is not determined by – and, indeed, prefigures, the categories and binaries that are taken for granted and that filter the way social ordering is understood. Much like the intuitive sense that one must repay a dinner invitation with a return invitation, the gift recipient described by Mauss senses a responsibility – one that is not legally enforceable – to give something back. It is this force, this presocial compulsion referred to as the "spirit of the gift," that upsets the popular conception of a gift as "free" and supplies the obligatory component in the institution of gift exchange.

The obligatory element of gift exchange is what accounts for the gift's interrelational aspect and the active role it plays in social bonding. Unlike pure gifts, understood as completely disinterested acts of altruism that spring entirely from a sense of freedom and absolute dominion over property, these acts are prompted by a sense of duty or responsibility, as well as some self-interest. It is a response to some intuitive recognition that the other is implicated in the property. And unlike contracts, where a well-defined and externally imposed obligation can prompt discrete and unreflective action, the indefiniteness of the embodied gift obligation conduces to ongoing relationships via cycles of giving and the freewheeling exercise of judgment and concern for others. Rather than vitiating the beneficial social effects of gifts, the self-interested, indefinite, and unenforceability elements that characterize this peculiar notion of obligation – the paradoxical "free and obligatory" duty – make up the engine that drives the institution of gift exchange as a healthy and potentially productive aspect of social life.

Using his language, Mauss's normative argument can be summarized as follows. The morality of gift exchange is characterized by the dual themes of "the freedom and the obligation inherent in the gift, of generosity and self-interest that are linked in giving."[65] Aspiring to a society in which people "give, freely and obligatorily,"[66] Mauss envisions a "hybrid" morality, where the "life of the monk, and the life of a Shylock are both equally to be shunned."[67]

65 Mauss (1990) at 68.

66 *Id.* at 71.

67 *Id.* at 69.

The analysis of Jewish law in Chapters 3–5 draws upon many of Mauss's insights, takes his aspirations seriously, and develops the policy implications of his theory and suggestions further than he did at the conclusion to his essay. Positing, as a theoretical matter, that God (or nature, etc.) is the original "donor" of all things, the Jewish legal theory of property set forth below posits a preexisting and continuous obligation to reciprocate (to God and/or to other persons) that is resident in all property; it is an obligation that, in turn, corresponds to and instantiates a larger theory of justice. Jewish law thus provides an example "of, precisely, [this] 'hybrid,' which defies the oppositions permitting one to construct concepts."[68]

Incorporating some of the counterintuitive Maussian ideas described in this chapter, the theory of the divine donor's lien described in Chapters 3–4 establishes a real basis for obligation in the realm of the voluntary, an obligation that is grounded in, and itself grounds, principles of justice. The final chapter will return to the question of organ transfer, where these ideas will become manifest in a concrete contemporary context. According to the law in the United States, one's body is regarded as perhaps the exemplary private property, over which the individual has the utmost control and total ownership rights, indeed as the seat of his/her autonomy. As a result, organ transfer is almost intuitively understood as either a volitional act of beneficence (gift) or as a part of a contractual exchange (commodity). By contrast, under Jewish law there are clear limits to the understanding of ownership and self-ownership, which, in turn, give rise to certain obligations and entitlements that lead to a very different understanding of what it means to give an organ, and what it means to receive compensation. The ancient texts suggest that, stemming from the idea of divine ownership (and a resulting "donor's lien"), there is a sense in which human ownership is seen to be internally limited by obligations to give to others, obligations that actually inhere *in* the property, and even *in* the person (as subject or object). It is to the study of these texts that we now turn.

[68] *Id.* at 55.

3

"From the Table of the Most High": Divine Ownership and Private Property in Talmudic Law

The vexed question of Jews and money is one that has haunted the West for nigh two thousand years. From the New Testament to Shakespeare, from Sombart and Weber to the modern Kibbutz movement, the relationship between Judaism and the twin cornerstones of capitalism – money and private property – has long been the subject of stereotype and debate, both within and without the Jewish community. The Jewish tradition has variously been condemned as a recipe for venality, heralded as a blueprint for free enterprise, and cited as a basis for socialist ideology.

In fact, the problem of characterizing the role of money and private property in the Jewish tradition is quite complicated. The overall picture that emerges from the Jewish sources does not lend itself to easy categorization, certainly not along the lines of condemnation or approbation. Private ownership of property appears to be a basic tenet of Jewish law, and there is not much to suggest that money is seen as something invidious – in fact, it plays a key role in certain sacred transactions, even taking on the status of consecrated property. Yet, foundational legal institutions – ones that provide substantive definition to deep structural conceptions – lend strong support to an argument that suggests that the notion of "ownership," in the conventional sense of near-absolute individual sovereignty over property, does not really exist.

These apparently contradictory indicators help explain why diametrically opposed views ranging from Socialism to neoliberal capitalism claim to (and, indeed, do) find support in the same literature. These very conceptual tensions provide the key to understanding the peculiar paradigm of property relations envisioned by the rabbis of late antiquity, whose writings form the intellectual basis for present-day traditional forms of Judaism. For it becomes clear, upon closer examination, that the contrasting (if not contradictory) impulses regarding the question of ownership that emerge from early rabbinic literature signify an array of approaches embodying neither private nor communal ownership, but something more nuanced and, in certain ways, quite different.

The Bible sets forth a complicated framework surrounding the individual's initial and continuing entitlement to enjoy of the fruits of the earth. A full accounting of the complicated rabbinic understanding of property ownership and the broader implications thereof are beyond the scope of this book. This analysis of the biblical scheme (or, rather, the form it takes in the rabbis' interpretation and elucidation thereof) aims to explain at least two of its most puzzling elements: (1) the meaning and character of human ownership, given the totalizing concept of divine ownership of everything worldly, and (2) the strange mix of the free and the obligatory that characterizes a significant element in the realm of property relations within the Jewish legal tradition.

The contemporary problem of whether one can charge money for an organ needed for transplant provides a basis for teasing out the coterie of legal conceptions that, when juxtaposed, depict a rather complex rabbinic understanding of the meaning, limits, and responsibility of human dominion over property and over persons, including selves. These larger questions will be explored against the theoretical backdrop of the problem of organ sales, which, itself, will await specific examination until the end of the book.

Before continuing, what follows is a brief introduction to late antique rabbinic literature, which will be the subject of analysis in the remainder of the book.

The *Mishnah* is the first major written compilation of the "oral Torah," which supplements the "written Torah" (the Bible). It records the views of the *Tannaim*, who were Palestinian rabbinic sages who date from approximately 10-220 CE. Written mainly in Mishnaic Hebrew, with some Aramaic, the Mishnah was redacted circa 220 CE by Rabbi Yehudah ha-Nasi. It contains 64 tractates, which are grouped under six "orders" (*sedarim*). The orders and their subjects are: *zeraim* (seeds), dealing with prayer and blessings, tithes and agricultural laws (11 tractates); *moed* (festival), dealing with the laws of the Sabbath and the Festivals (12 tractates); *nashim* (women), concerning marriage and divorce, some forms of oaths and the laws of the Nazirite (7 tractates); *nezikin* (damages), dealing with civil and criminal law, the operation of the courts and oaths (10 tractates); *kodashim* (holy things), dealing with sacrificial rites, the Temple, and the dietary laws (11 tractates); and *tehorot* (purities), dealing with the laws of purity and impurity, including the impurity of the dead, the laws of food purity and bodily purity (12 tractates).

The *Tosefta* is a supplement to the Mishnah. It parallels the Mishnah in its language and structure and contains tannaitic material that does not appear in the Mishnah (hence its title Tosefta, which means "supplement" or "addition"). Its dating is a matter of dispute but it is thought to have been redacted concurrently with, or shortly after, the Mishnah.

The *Talmud* is a combination of (1) the Mishnah and (2) the *Gemara*. The Gemara follows the structure of the Mishnah, and records the teachings of the *Amoraim* (Palestinian and Babylonian rabbinic sages from approximately 200–500 CE), who elucidate the Mishnah and other tannaitic material. The Jerusalem Talmud ("J.T.", also known as the Palestinian Talmud or the *Talmud Yerushalmi*), written mainly in Jewish Palestinian Aramaic, was compiled in the fourth-fifth centuries in Palestine; the Babylonian Talmud ("B.T.", also known as the *Talmud Bavli*), written mainly in Jewish Babylonian Aramaic, was redacted in the sixth century in Babylonia.

3.1 BASIC CONCEPTIONS

As in many societies, the simple notion that "what is mine is mine and what is yours is yours" is the postulate thought to underpin common, interhuman property relations under Jewish law.[1] The institution of private property at its most basic has been described as deriving from common sense, as it is thought to be self-evidently necessary to the preservation of the social order. As in many legal systems, a standard web of rules regulating people's interactions in the realms of sale and exchange, theft and trespass take this basic proposition for granted.

Such appears to be the case under normal circumstances with respect to ordinary property owned by human beings. All in all, the usual characteristics of property ownership are part of a larger body of Jewish civil (and, to some extent, criminal) law that, notwithstanding certain doctrinal differences, does not look all that different from its counterparts in many, if not most, other legal systems. In biblical and rabbinic law, people can own property, property can have monetary value, and property can properly be bought, sold, bartered, or given away. The institution of property ownership is presumed in the biblical prohibition against theft and in the obligation to return lost property. The

1 Mishnah Avot 5:13 ארבע מדות באדם האומר שלי שלי ושלך שלך זו מדה בינונית ויש אומרים זו מדת סדום שלי שלך ושלך שלי עם הארץ שלי שלך ושלך שלך חסיד שלי שלי ושלך שלי רשע
There are four character types among people: [1] the one who says "what's mine is mine and what's yours is yours." This is an average character, and there are those who say this is the character of Sodom. [2] "What's mine is yours and what's yours is mine." [This is an] *am ha'aretz* (uneducated person) [3]. "What's mine is yours and what's yours is yours." [This is a] *chasid* (pious person). [4] "What's mine is mine and what's yours is mine." [This is a] *rasha* (evil person)." (Note that translations from Hebrew or Aramaic to English throughout the book are mine.)

ability to hold and to transfer ownership implicitly underlies the range of civil and criminal laws establishing legal and ethical parameters within this realm of social relations.

And yet, under the rabbinic scheme, notions of property ownership and expectations regarding exchange are different from those assumed by present-day institutions of "private" or even "communal" property. Moreover, the Jewish legal system, as conceived by the rabbis, is not about social order alone. An overriding vision of the divine, reflecting a particular normative framework, was thought to inform the way social/property relations ought to be conceived and managed. Seen in this light, there are ways in which property ownership can turn out to have great significance. For example, under certain circumstances – as in the famous Talmudic story of two men in a desert with only one jug of water[2] – property ownership can dictate who shall live and who shall die. Yet in general, the significance, within the ancient Jewish texts, of general assignations of "ownership"[3] (apart from the original allocation of property among the twelve tribes of Israel) emerges not as an explicit ideological stance or normative prescription, but rather as a presumed axiom of social relations.[4] The definitional core of Talmudic conceptions of ownership and property, and of the rights and obligations related thereto, lies in the underlying premise that God is the original (and, in some sense, the continuing) "owner" of everything.

The breadth of what the concept of divine ownership is understood to encompass has its origin in the Bible. By way of a wide array of legal institutions, the biblical scheme portrays an ideal understanding of human property ownership and distribution that originates in, and regularly returns to, ultimate ownership by the divine. A snapshot of this picture is provided, for example, at the end of the book of Leviticus.

[2] B.T. Bava Metzia 62a:
שנים שהיו מהלכין בדרך וביד אחד מהן קיתון של מים אם שותים שניהם מתים ואם שותה אחד מהן מגיע לישוב.
דרש בן פטורה מוטב שישתו שניהם וימותו ואל יראה אחד מהם במיתתו של חבירו עד שבא רבי עקיבא ולימד
וחי אחיך עמך חייך קודמים לחיי חבריך
Two [people] were walking on the road [far from civilization], and [only] one of them possessed a pitcher of water. If they both drank [from it] they would both die, but if one of them drank [from it] he would reach civilization. Ben Patura explained: it is better that they both should drink [from the pitcher] so that one [person] will not witness the death of his companion. [This was the rule] until Rabbi Akiva came and taught, "your brother shall live with you." [This verse, Lev. 25:36 dictates that] your life takes precedence over your companion's life.

[3] That is, excluding designations of property such as those dedicated to priests or the poor. See *infra*.

[4] See, e.g., the area of inheritance law, where the rabbis created legal vehicles (effectively, a will) that allow a property owner to subvert the planned pattern of inheritance outlined in the bible.

Chapter 25 sets forth certain boundaries of human ownership that are tied, explicitly, to the all-encompassing idea of divine ownership. These limits are made manifest in concrete obligations and limitations that operate as regular reminders of that idea. In a key biblical articulation of the general claim of divine ownership, in verse 23 God makes a simple and clear declaration: "And the land shall not be sold in perpetuity, for the land is Mine; for you are strangers and settlers with Me."[5] Permanent ownership of the land is, accordingly, precluded by the *yovel*, the Jubilee (fiftieth) year, when all slaves are freed, all debts forgiven and all land is returned to its original owners (Lev 25:8–13). Similarly, the laws of *shemitah* – according to which, during every seventh year, the land must lie fallow, and produce is deemed ownerless and free to anyone – is yet another reminder of the continuing hold of divine ownership as a fundamental constraint on the institution of human property ownership (Lev 25:1–7). Ensuing passages, such as those calling explicitly for the prevention of poverty (e.g., demanding lending without interest), and providing rules as to the treatment of those enslaved from impoverishment ("For they are My servants" [not the servants of servants[6]]; Lev 25:42), by their juxtaposition with the earlier statements regarding real property, can be understood to describe additional limitations on human sovereignty that stem from divine sovereignty.[7]

Chapter 27 of Leviticus deals specifically with the general rules of giving property to (or back to) the (legal) realm of the divine.[8] Persons (i.e., their worth), animals, and real property can be pledged to God by means of a vow. These are the items, given to the Temple, that the rabbis call *hekdesh* (sacred property), donated for purposes of either animal sacrifice or to support Temple maintenance; upon their consecration they are considered to belong to God (via the Temple), having been transferred from the human to the divine realm of ownership. Chapter 27 also discusses the possibility (or lack thereof) of redeeming items (including persons) from God's ownership.

[5] In the original Hebrew, Lev 25:23 provides:

והארץ לא תמכור לצמתת כי לי הארץ כי גרים ותושבים אתם עמדי

[6] Lev 25:42, 55, provides:

כי עבדי הם אשר הוצאתי אתם מארץ מצרים לא ימכרו ממכרת עבד . . . כי לי בני ישראל עבדים

"For they are My [God's] servants, whom I brought forth out of the land of Egypt. They shall not be sold as slaves .... For the children of Israel are My servants." And see B.T. Kiddushin 22b, quoting and interpreting Lev 25:55:

כי לי בני ישראל עבדים ולא עבדים לעבדים

"'for the children of Israel are My servants' and not servants to servants."

[7] While there is no room to explore it here, there are (sometimes obvious) relationships between this book's theory of divine ownership and all of the rules outlined in Lev 25 and 27. (The theoretical relationship is obvious, for example, with respect to the requirements to lend without interest and to charge a "just price".)

[8] See, e.g., Lev 27: 14, 16.

Further, in addition to items that people own and choose to donate to the Temple, Lev 27:26 describes something that belongs to God from birth – firstlings of animals (*bechorot*). Finally, the series of mandatory tithing obligations, all of which entail the giving of property to human beings, are also explicitly described as belonging to God: "And all of the tithes of the land, from the seed of the land [and] from the fruits of the trees, belong to God; they are sacred [belonging] to God .... And all of the tithes of the herd or the flock, all who pass under the rod, the tenth will be sacred [belonging] to God."[9]

Beyond the specific property rules described above is a deeply rooted assumption that is ubiquitous in Jewish literature and at the theoretical core of the institution of property law within the Jewish tradition, positing that God is, in some sense, the owner of everything. The notion is referenced repeatedly in rabbinic texts with more than just homiletic or theological effect. In many contexts it is understood precisely as a declaration of the status of property as being within the divine legal realm. While it is couched as a legal expression and is often used literally (or as a legal fiction) in that sense, the proposition of divine ownership (particularly of an all-encompassing sort) is not well developed as a legal principle in Talmudic literature (or in contemporary scholarship). Moreover, while the notion that God is the "owner" of everything is a motif often mentioned in Jewish legal and homiletic literature, and one that can be "substantiated by *halakhic* [Jewish legal] norms,"[10] there has been no systemic scholarly work delving into its parameters, ramifications, and legal/philosophical significance.[11]

It is possible to track the complicated legal interplay between the seemingly all-encompassing institution of divine ownership and the institution of human property ownership, with which it somehow overlaps and, indeed, often runs in parallel. Beyond the categories of property (such as *hekdesh* – property owned by the Temple) that are recognized as being "*shel gavohah*" (of the Most

[9] Lev 27:30, 32.

[10] Isador Twersky, *Studies in Jewish Law and Philosophy*, New York: Ktav Publishing House (1982), p. 126n16. As Twersky explained, "[w]e are accustomed, on the basis of *halakhic* [Jewish legal] terminology and conceptualization, to thinking of God as the ultimate 'recipient' or 'beneficiary' of all things 'consecrated' for the Temple or other religious causes, all priestly gifts (tithe, heave-offering, etc ...) God (usually designated as *gavohah*) is the juridical personality that is the 'owner,' agent, or trustee and all legal procedures are based on this fact." *Id.* at 112.

[11] One variation of this idea is the rare discussion of when or whether property, such as *hekdesh*, is considered to have a legal personality (*ishiyut mishpati*) of its own. See, e.g., Asher Gulak, *Yesodei Hamishpat Ha'ivri* [Hebrew: Foundations of Hebrew Law], Berlin: Devir (1922); Shwartz, *supra*; David Fink, "The Corporate Status of *Hekdesh* in Early Sephardic Responsa," in *Jewish Law Association Studies*, volume 1, ed. B. S. Jackson, Atlanta: Scholars Press (1985) pp. 17–24. To the extent that this question is tied to the larger question of ownership by the divine as a real legal phenomenon, the analysis usually fails to go beyond very technical legal questions.

High), completely or predominantly owned by the divine, there is a range of items that are legally implicated in the realm of divine ownership although not considered to be fully owned by God. Far more common in Mishnaic and Talmudic literature (particularly in Tractates Zeraim and Kodashim) are hybrid categories of property, owned partially by God and partially by human beings (with greater and lesser degrees of "*kedushah*" – holiness or divine ownership). There are also categories of property recognized as coming from (or returning to) the original realm of divine ownership (during which time they are specifically not within the domain of any particular person) that are not owned by God *per se* and thus do not have *kedushah* in the technical sense.

3.2 TWO OVERLAPPING REALMS OF OWNERSHIP

As mentioned above, there is something of a doctrinal paradox presented by the contemporaneous existence of the possibility of human ownership and the idea that God owns everything. A section (known as a pericope or "*sugyah*") of Talmudic discussion at the beginning of the sixth chapter of Tractate Berakhot (B.T. Berakhot 35a–b) confronts this problem head on and, in solving it, reveals the way in which divine ownership can be seen to ripple throughout all human property ownership.[12] The paradox or apparent contradiction is embodied in the alignment of two separate verses from Psalms:

> Rabbi Levi contrasted [two texts:] It is written, "*The earth and all that is in it belongs to God*" [Psa 24:1], and it is also written, "The heavens are the heavens of the Lord, but *He has given the earth to the children of men*" [Psa 115:16]. (emphasis added)
>
> רבי לוי רמי כתיב לה' הארץ ומלואה וכתיב[תהלים קט"ו] השמים שמים לה' והארץ נתן לבני אדם

[12] B.T. Berakhot 35a-b:
אמר רב יהודה אמר שמואל כל הנהנה מן העולם הזה בלא ברכה כאילו נהנה מקדשי שמים וכתיב [תהילים כ"ד] לה' הארץ ומלואה. . . .אמר רבי חנינא בר פפא : כל הנהנה מן העולם הזה בלא ברכה כאילו גוזל להקדוש ברוך הוא וכנסת ישראל. . . .תנו רבנן אסור לו לאדם שיהנה מן העולם הזה בלא ברכה וכל הנהנה מן העולם הזה בלא ברכה מעל
"Rav Yehudah said in the name of Samuel, anyone who benefits from [something in] this world without [first reciting] a blessing is tantamount to one who benefits from sacred property belonging to heaven, as it is written [Psa 24] 'The earth and all that is in it belongs to God'.... Rabbi Hanina ben Papa said, anyone who benefits from [something in] this world without [first reciting] a blessing is tantamount one who steals from God and the congregation of Israel .... Our Rabbis taught: one is prohibited from benefitting from [something in] this world without [first reciting] a blessing and anyone who benefits from [something in] this world without [first reciting] a blessing has committed [the illegal act of] *me'ilah*." The beginning of this *sugyah* is analyzed here; the continuation of this *sugyah* deals with pertinent matters relating to balancing of basic principles and concerns within this overall plan for the just satisfaction of human need and the regulation of greed, and forms part of the same literary unit analyzed in this section. This latter part of the text will be analyzed in Chapter 5.

What prompted this question was Rav Yehudah's reliance (earlier in the *sugyah*) on the former verse as the source for Samuel's uncontested Tannaitic proposition that "benefitting from anything of this world without a [first reciting a] blessing is tantamount to benefitting from sacred property belonging to heaven."

אמר רב יהודה אמר שמואל כל הנהנה מן העולם הזה בלא ברכה
כאילו נהנה מקדשי שמים וכתיב [תהלים כ"ד] לה' הארץ ומלואה

Elsewhere in the *sugyah*, the prohibited act of tasting anything before reciting a blessing is likened to "robbing the Holy One, blessed be He," and is characterized as an act of *me'ilah* (the technical name of the crime of benefitting from divinely owned property (*hekdesh*).

תנו רבנן אסור לו לאדם שיהנה מן העולם הזה בלא ברכה
וכל הנהנה מן העולם הזה בלא ברכה מעל

The Talmud, at B.T. Berakhot 35a–b, offers a simple solution to Rabbi Levi's apparent textual conflict:

> There is no contradiction: the first [verse, "the earth and all that is in it belongs to God" describes the situation] before a benediction [has been recited, whereas] here [the verse "He has given the earth to the children of men" applies] after [a benediction has been recited].

לא קשיא כאן קודם ברכה כאן לאחר ברכה

Simply stated, the explanation of how to reconcile both verses (1) one connoting divine ownership, and (2) the other describing human ownership of things in this world) turns on the phenomenon of the benediction ("*bircat nehenin*," benediction of pleasure) that the rabbis require to be made before one may obtain certain enjoyment from things (e.g. before eating). Thus, verse (1) refers to the legal state of affairs before an individual has made the benediction, and (2) explains the situation after the benediction has been recited. It is as if ownership of the item shifts from God to the person once the benediction has been recited. Why should that be the case?

The generic benediction to which the text refers is a statement expressing the fact that God is the creator and original owner of the item. For example, the benediction that must be recited before eating an apple is "You are blessed, God King of the Universe, the creator of the fruit on the tree." The benediction is not an expression of gratitude. It is a simple assertion of the fact that God created, and thus owns, the apple.

This simple reconciliation of the two verses communicates a profound rabbinic realization, one that, notably, was arrived at, according to the Talmudic text, through "*sevarah*" (human reason) alone. This philosophical/ theological insight echoes concepts discussed in Chapter 2: notwithstanding contingent human rules governing property ownership, individuals do not fully acquire anything gifted by God (which is everything) unless and until all requisite "returns" (in the Maussian sense) have been given to the original donor. The benediction operates like a tithe or Maussian "return" in a similarly ironic and almost paradoxical way. One acquires ownership by verbally professing God's ownership (i.e. by professing one's lack of ownership). In the case of tithes and other "returns," ownership takes place when one acknowledges one's lack of ownership by retroceding (giving back to its true or original owner) all or part of the property.

The Mishnah upon which this Talmudic text is commenting explains the different benedictions appropriate to different categories of food (e.g., depending on whether it grows on trees or in the ground). The Mishnah (Berakhot 6:1) does not explicitly express the underlying obligation to make such a benediction; its existence is implicitly taken for granted.[13] As is common in the Talmudic *sugyah*, the text is first arranged in order to inquire as to the source of the obligation itself. The *sugyah* reviews a series of items that are thought to contain potential support for this general obligation. All involve a specific requirement of "returns" to (or on behalf of, as will be seen later) God as (pre) conditions to taking ownership, such as the redeeming of fourth-year grapes (*kerem revai*), which are considered sacred; leaving certain grapes in the vineyard for the poor (*olelot*) (which are not sacred); and giving a portion to the priests from standing grain. While all of these gifts to God and to other persons fit within the general scheme of mandatory giving, as pre-conditions of acquisition or ongoing periodic conditions of continuing ownership, none is found by the rabbis to provide a specific source for the broad rule that a final, additional "return" to God in the form of a benediction is required before one may legally own and ingest any type of food. However, the fact that these examples are looked to for the possible derivation communicates a categorical commonality between these items of "return" and the benediction.[14]

[13] Tosafot (a medieval commentary on the Talmud) sees this precondition to taking ownership as a rabbinic rather than a biblical requirement because of a conflict elsewhere in the text. Tosafot to B.T.Berakhot 35a, *d"h lefanav lo kol sheken*.

[14] There is more than symbolic significance to the fact that this confrontation, in Tractate Berakhot, between the divine and human realms of ownership occurs in the context of eating. For one clear pattern that emerges in the attempt to track the boundaries and transactions between these two domains is that the most basic transactional moment is the moment of ingestion. In cases ranging from sacrifice to labor laws and to vows, the moment of eating (or the theoretical moment of eating) is the point at which a status change in the nature of the property occurs.

The prohibition against eating without first reciting a benediction makes the point in the extreme, vividly demonstrating the operation of this principle of "returns" by tracing it to its logical conclusion: no matter how legitimate and secure one's legal claim to ownership (both in terms of mundane property requirements and even in terms of the array of deity-related "returns" – such as mandatory tithes – that can be understood as legal preconditions to acquiring rights of ownership vis-à-vis God), a final act of "return" (even if only verbal) is necessary before one may legally take complete ownership by means of consumption; thus, no matter how strong one's claim to ownership of the apple, the act of eating will be considered tantamount to theft (from God) until the appropriate benediction, as a final ritual of return has been made.

The idea of acquiring ownership from God is not at all clear-cut. In rough correspondence with the continuing donor's lien in the neo-Maussian paradigm Talmudic law, in general, includes overlapping levels of ownership by God (reflected to some extent in differing levels of sanctity of property) that never cease to exist. In some sense, God continues to own everything, which in this context means that, notwithstanding the strength or legitimacy of a person's legitimate claim on property, in the final instance it is the case that to enjoy anything in this world without making a benediction is like stealing from God. This is a vivid rendition of the paradox of property relations at the heart of the neo-Maussian scheme of exchange. Part of the original donor remains, somehow, within the donated item. This, in turn, gives rise to the obligation of the recipient to make a return. Apart from the fact that this seems to lead inevitably to an endless cycle of giving, the initial gift leaves all human parties, at all times, less than absolute owners.

Thus, in the final analysis, the rabbis in Talmud Berakhot conclude that no textual source for the obligation of a final benediction is necessary. The rabbis confidently conclude that, given the encompassing nature of the principle of divine ownership, it is a matter of logic or reason (*sevarah*) that it is forbidden for a man to enjoy anything of this world without saying a blessing. The *sevarah* that resolves the apparent contradiction between contemporaneous divine and human ownership anticipates the neo-Maussian theory of exchange. The rabbis thus understood that, in some sense, a divine claim or lien continues to exist in all property. The requirement to make a benediction before eating even food that one "owns," lest one be considered a thief of God's property, relates to something that will be seen later involving the institution of *hekdesh*, that is the idea that everything continues (even after the giving of all requisite tithes, etc., and/or legal purchase from another), to some extent, to belong to God.

As a general matter, the notion of divine ownership appears in Talmudic law in many contexts as a relatively straightforward concept, one that confers a status on property that is significant and legally meaningful. While scholars, both academic and religious, have acknowledged the existence of the legal principle of divine ownership,[15] there has not been much attention paid to its significance in terms of evolving legal principles, categories, and theories set forth by the rabbis of the Talmud (and thereafter).

Before delving into the largely unexamined concept of property owned by the divine in Talmudic law, it is useful to make note of two significant legal categories of property that are ideationally related to the category of divinely owned property, but are not coextensive therewith: property that is called *kadosh* or *hekdesh* (sacred) and property denoted as *issurei hana'ah* (property from which humans are denied the right to benefit).

As will be shown, the category of items that come from, return to, or pass through the divine realm of ownership is not coextensive with the category of goods that are technically considered *kadosh* (sacred). Similarly, the category of *issurei hana'ah* contains a subcategory of goods that are clearly linked to the category of divinely owned property;[16] at the same time, items can have an *issur hana'ah* (a prohibition against human benefit) without being *kadosh* (indeed, some seem to be the opposite of property that is *kadosh*[17]). Furthermore, although things that are *kadosh* carry with them an *issur hana'ah*, there are items that one receives from God, that can even have some sacred status, but that are considered the property of the recipient, with no *issur hana'ah* (e.g., *terumah* in the hands of a priest).

All of this is simply to demonstrate that there are a number of legal categories regarding the status of property[18] that are not coterminous but overlap and intersect in interesting ways. While it is beyond the scope of this book, it would be would be interesting to try to make sense of these different ideas

[15] See, e.g., Twersky (1982); Elliott Dorff, "Jewish Law and Lore: The Case of Organ Transplantation," *The Jewish Law Annual* 12 (1997), pp. 65–114.

[16] A very basic iteration of the interconnection of these concepts is in Mishnah Nedarim 4:3: "[The Sages] said to him, what is the difference between an [animal that is] impure (*temeah*) [and one that is] pure (*tehorah*)? He replied to them, the life of a pure [animal] belongs to heaven [God], but the body is his own; but an impure [animal] belongs, body and life to heaven [God]. They said to him, the life of an impure [animal] also belongs to heaven [God] and the body is his. For if he wishes, he can sell it to a non-Jew or feed it to dogs."

אמרו לו מה בין טמאה לטהורה אמר להן שהטהורה נפשה לשמים וגופה שלו וטמאה נפשה
וגופה לשמים אמר לו אף הטמאה נפשה לשמים וגופה שלו שאם ירצה הרי הוא מוכרה לעכו"ם
או מאכילה לכלבים

Attribution of ownership of the body of the animal, as between a human being and God (heaven – *shamayim*), turns on whether the human is able to get any benefit from the animal. (Note also the presumption that the animal's life, in any event, belongs to God, and the assumption that, in some cases, the body of the animal itself could also belong to God.)

[17] Certain prohibited property, such as things used for idol worship, represent one category of items that carry a probation against benefit.

[18] Categories such as *kadosh*, *mamon gavohah*, or *shel shamayim* and *issurei hana'ah*.

by, for example, outlining the taxonomy of property according to degrees of holiness, or (levels of) human and divine ownership, and of tracking the prohibitions against benefit, to see the way all these concepts relate to one another. But it is important, for our purposes, to keep in mind that (a) the realm of divine ownership and the category of property that is technically considered sacred (*kadosh*) are not coextensive, and (b) while also not reflecting coterminous categories, there is a complicated relationship, both legally and philosophically, between those items from which a person or people can not benefit and the realm of divine ownership.

In any event, what is immediately relevant is that the notion of divine ownership, originating in legal institutions that are integrally related to categorical limits to human ownership such as *shemitah* and *yovel*, can be seen to implicitly underlie broad areas of rabbinic law that have to do with the initial acquisition of as well as continuing obligations related to property ownership. Many of these obligations of or limits to ownership operate through the mechanism of (mandatory as well as voluntary) transfers of property, both to and from God.

3.3 THE REALM OF DIVINE OWNERSHIP AND EXCHANGES THEREWITH

The existence of the legal category of property that is (literally or by means of a legal fiction) owned by the divine is taken for granted throughout the corpus of rabbinic literature. It is labeled by terms such as *hekdesh* (sacred) or *shel gavohah* (of the Most High) and is set off from property that is *shel hedyot* (of the ordinary), which is within the human realm of ownership.

Whether regarded as a legal fiction or as a matter of ontological fact, the idea of divine ownership is a conception that, even more than the usual connotation of "ownership domain," is purely legal, without necessarily having a physical dimension.[19] For example, the essential element defining an act of theft from God (*me'ilah*) is not physical removal of an object but rather the (unauthorized) obtaining of human benefit, however slight, from property owned by God (*hekdesh* – sacred property). And, as will be shown, to

19 Some have ascribed this lack of physical dimensionality with respect to divine ownership to the desire to avoid any hint of anthropomorphism. However, many Talmudic conceptions do imply a kind of active, physical role on God's part, such as *mitah beyedei shamayim* (death at the hands of heaven). Issues of anthropomorphism aside, it would be interesting, from the perspective of jurisprudence, to attempt to discover the extent to which the rabbis of late antiquity took legal conceptions involving God's active (physical?) participation in the world literally. What is clear is that the notion of a particular realm of divine ownership that property can move into and out of was taken very seriously, at least as a legal fiction if not as something imagined to be more concrete.

accommodate the absence of the Temple – the imagined portal through which material objects could actually pass into God's realm – the rabbis also developed vehicles for giving things to the divine realm in a somewhat different sense, such as self-imposed obligations that are taken on (as substitute sacrifices to God[20]) by a similar process of oral declaration.[21]

This mix of the physical and legal in the realm of transactions with God is quite nuanced. For example, the statement that everything "belongs" to God can itself be understood, in part, as an expression of the idea that there is no physical domain that is not within God's domain. As Bernard Jackson has pointed out, unlike Greek, Roman, and Hellenistic Law,

> [biblical and Jewish Law] did not restrict the offence of sacrilege to theft from a sacred site...The reason why the Jewish conception of sacrilege was wider than that which prevailed in the Hellenistic-Roman world derives from the very wide Jewish concept of what constituted holy property. Such property was often possessed by a private citizen. *Indeed,a man could make his property holy merely be declaring it to be dedicated.* (empahsis added)[22]

The fact that an item could be moved from one legal realm of ownership to another by the simple means of an oral declaration is significant for another reason. For within the Jewish legal tradition there is a basic requirement (with some exceptions[23]) that property be *physically moved* (even if only slightly, to symbolically signify transfer between property domains) in order to perform an effective act of acquisition (*kinyan*). In the face of this general rule, the Mishnah in Kiddushin makes the clear statement,[24] אמירתו לגבוה כמסירתו להדיוט, "One's oral statement to

[20] See Moshe Benovitz, *Kol Nidre: Studies in the Development of Rabbinic Votive Institutions*, Atlanta: Scholars Press (1998).

[21] E.g., *neder, cherem* and possibly *hefker*. Interestingly, the contemporary case of organ transfer might, in some sense, be considered the first approximation of the gifting (physically) of holy property since the time of the Temple (see Chapter 5).

[22] Bernard Jackson, *Theft in Early Jewish Law*, London: Oxford University Press (1972), pp. 77, 79.

[23] See, e.g., Ranon Katzoff, "Oral Establishment of Dowry in Jewish and Roman Law: *D'varim Haniknim Ba'amira* and *Dotis Dictio*," in *Critical Studies in Ancient Law, Comparative and Legal History*, ed. John Cairns and Olivia Robinson, Oxford: Hart Publishing (2001), pp. 157–171. Interestingly, Katzoff does not mention this principle of *amirah legavohah kemesirah lehedyot* (an oral statement [giving property] to God is the functional equivalent of a [physical act of] transfer to a human being), despite the fact that the main point of his article is to stress the "exceptional, but not unique" category of *devarim haniknim be'amirah* (items acquired with an oral statement [alone]). This might reflect an across-the-board reluctance, if not failure, in the academic study of Jewish law to pay attention to perfectly legitimate legal concepts that differ when dealing with God's property. In fact, one possibility that Katzoff fails to raise is that the reason the case of dowry seems to be "exceptional" in permitting an oral self-imposed obligation might have something to do with the fact that the institution of marriage (*kiddushin*) is implicitly tied, somehow, to the divine realm of *kedushah*. This is another topic warranting further study.

[24] Mishnah Kiddushin 1:6.

God (lit: *gavohah*, the Most High) is equivalent to one's act of delivery to an ordinary person (*hedyot*)." Or as explained more fully in Tosefta Kiddushin 1:9,

> One's word of mouth to the Most High is equivalent to one's act of delivery to an ordinary person. How so? [If one states,] "this ox is sanctified" [or] "this house is sanctified" – *even if it is [located somewhere] between here and the end of the world, hekdesh* [the property domain of God and the Temple] *has made acquisition wherever it is located.* But [when property is being tranferred to] an ordinary person, he makes acquisition only when he has physically taken possession. (emphasis added)
>
> אמירתו לגבוה כמסירתו להדיוט כיצד שור זה הקדש ובית זה הקדש אפי' מיכן ועד סוף העולם קנה הקדש בכל מקום שהוא אבל בהדיוט לא קנה [עד] שיחזיק

Thus, an oral declaration – technically known as a vow, or "*neder*" – is the means by which one donates one's property to the Temple. By verbally[25] designating an item as dedicated to God (for sacrifice or Temple upkeep), the owner transfers the item from the ontological realm of human ownership to that of divine ownership, changing its character from ordinary (*chullin*) to sacred (*hekdesh*) property. The Gemara ascribes this significant difference in the legal procedure of property transfer to the fact that, since the world and all that is in it belongs to God, there is no need to *physically move* the item as if to enact a shift from one domain to another. (Jerusalem Talmud ["J.T."] Kiddushin 1:6). The domain of divine ownership is a legal, not a circumscribed physical, one (albeit perceived as having full and distinct ontological significance).

The conception, and worldwide parameters, of a divine property realm are explored in B.T. Chullin 139a. The relevant *sugyah* involves the following question: what happens if a bird is sanctified (given to the Temple) and then flies away? Does it continue to have sacred status or not?[26] Samuel's position is, "wherever [the bird] happens to be it is in the divine property realm (lit.

[25] Oral designation accomplishing status change is emblematic of shifts of property from the human to the divine realm and the self-imposition of an obligation on an individual that can be seen to be attached to some item (in contradistinction to an oath (*shevuah*), which is understood to be a personally binding promise to God). This practice of transferring an item to God by means of a speech act that constitutes a vow (*neder*) is how property (or oneself, e.g., as a *nazir*; see Chapter 4, *infra*) was sanctified (made *hekdesh*) at the time of the Temple. As will be discussed, it was imagined that, even after the Temple was destroyed, the institution of vows enabled a continuation (at least symbolically) of the practice of "transferring property" as gifts to God. See Benovitz (1988). Similarly, the separating of tithes that, as will be shown, also constitutes an act of giving to God is accomplished by means of an oral declaration (*koreh shem*).

[26] Samuel and Rav disagree regarding the status of a bird sanctified only for its value (for Temple maintenance), but they agree that a bird sanctified for the altar is sacred wherever it may happen to be. In support of his position (that any bird sanctified, for whatever purpose,

God's treasury), for it is written (Psalms 24:1): 'The earth and all that is in it belongs to God'" בבי גזא דרחמנא איתיא דכתיב לה' הארץ ומלואה. This text goes beyond the passage in Tosefta Kiddushin in that it makes explicit mention of the domain of divine ownership, which is referred to here as "God's treasury" (*bei gaza de'rakhmanah*).

This same term for and conception of the divine property domain, as "divine treasury" or "storehouse" (*bei gaza de rakhmanah*, i.e., the place to which an object is automatically transferred once it has been sanctified or given to God and the Temple), is also mentioned explicitly by Pseudo-Jonathan's Targum, or Aramaic translation to Deut 23:22. This verse, establishes a timing (a "do not delay") requirement with respect to the fulfillment of vows.[27] In his targumic "translation" of the verse into Aramaic, Pseudo-Jonathan adds the following words of explication to the biblical text: "In the offering there shall not be guilt or deficiency *for it is considered as already in the treasury (hiptik) of the Master of the Universe*" (emphasis added);[28] בקורבנא לא יהי חוב ופסולא דבהפתיק מרי עלמה קאי. In other words, immediately upon orally pledging a particular animal to God and the Temple for sacrifice (and prior to

remains sanctified after flying off), Samuel reasons: "*Wherever it happens to be it is in God's treasury, for it is written*: 'The earth and all that is in it belongs to God' [Psalms 24:1]. And so, too, did Rabbi Yohanan say: It is like the case where a man consecrated his hen to the Temple treasury, and afterwards it broke loose. Thereupon Rabbi ben Lakish said to him: Surely as soon as it breaks loose its sanctity has gone! – He replied: '*Wherever it happens to be it is in the God's treasury, for it is written: 'The earth and all that is in it belongs to God'* [Psalms 24:1]." (emphasis added).

27 Deut. 23:25 "When you make a vow (*neder*) to the Lord your God, do not delay in fulfilling it because the Lord your God will require it of you, and [if you have not fulfilled it on time] you will have incurred guilt." כי תדר נדר לה' אלקיך לא תאחר לשלמו כי דרש ידרשנו ה' אלקיך מעמך והיה בך חטא

28 Translation of Pseudo-Jonathan is from Ernest G. Clarke, *Targum Pseudo-Jonathan: Deuteronomy* (The Aramaic Bible, Volume 5b), Collegeville, MN: The Liturgical Press (1998), p. 65. B.T. Chullin and Pseudo-Jonathan are clearly working with the same conception, although they use different language. Pseudo-Jonathan uses the word הפתיק (*hiptik*), which comes from the word אפותיקא (*apotika*), where the Babylonian Talmud spoke of the בי גזא דרחמנא (*bei gaza de'rakhmanah*) – these are different (Aramaic) terms for the same concept. Note that, as a general matter, the relationship between Targum Pseudo-Jonathan and rabbinic literature is not clear. See, e.g., Joseph M. Baumgarten, "Qumran and the Halakha in the Aramaic Targumim," in *Proceedings of the Ninth World Congress of Jewish Studies: Panel Sessions, Bible Studies and Ancient Near East*, Jerusalem: Magnes Press (1985), pp. 45–60; Joseph M. Baumgarten, "The Laws of Orlah and First Fruits in the Light of Jubilees, the Qumran Writings and Targum Pseudo Jonathan," *Journal of Jewish Studies* 38/2 (1987), pp. 195–202; Moshe J. Bernstein, "The Aramaic Targumim: The Many Faces of the Jewish Biblical Experience," in *Jewish Ways of Reading the Bible*, Oxford: Oxford University Press (1994), pp. 133–165; Moshe Bernstein, "The Halakhah in the Marginalia of Targum Neofiti," in *Proceedings of the Eleventh World Congress of Jewish Studies (Jerusalem, June 22–29, 1993): Division A: The Bible and Its World*, Jerusalem: World Union of Jewish Studies (1994), pp. 223–230; Jose Faur, "The Targumim and Halakha," *Jewish Quarterly Review* 66 (1975–1976),

actually bringing the animal to the Temple) it is considered to have been automatically transferred (by words alone) to the divine property domain – to "God's treasury".

The notion that property can be moved easily (orally) into the divine realm because it is *already* in the divine realm is one of the surface paradoxes that renders the division between divine and human property ownership somewhat fuzzy. The lack of clarity is compounded by the fact that different combinations or hybrids of property ownership (divine and human) are possible. Nevertheless, there are places in Talmudic law where the outlines and mechanics of the spectrum of ownership possibilities (including outright divine ownership) become visible. In undertaking the technical task of determining classifications of ownership, the rabbis at times reveal and attempt to make sense of the complexities posed by the idea of divine ownership for the Jewish (human) property system. This often occurs when the need for more precise classification of property is occasioned or necessitated by a separate legal question, of which the issue of ownership is determinative.

pp. 19–25; Steven Fraade, "Rabbinic Views on the Practice of the Targum, and Multiligualism in the Jewish Galilee of the Third–Sixth Centuries," in *The Galilee in Late Antiquity*, ed. Lee Levine, Cambridge: Harvard University Press (1992), pp. 253–286; A. Geiger, *Ha'Mikra V'Targumav* [Hebrew: The Text and Translations of the Bible], Jerusalem: Mossad Bialik (1950); Bernard Grossfeld, "Targum Onqelos, Halakha and the Halakhic Midrashim," in *The Aramaic Bible: Targums and Their Historical Context*, ed. Beattie and McNamara, Journal for the Study of the Old Testament supplement series 16, Sheffield: Sheffield Academic Press (1994), pp. 228–246; Joseph Heineman, "Early Halakhah in the Palestinian Targumim," *Journal of Jewish Studies* 25/1 (1974), pp. 114–122; David Henschke, "*L'tiv Zikato shel HaTargum HaMeyukhas L'Yonatan Lemidrashe Ha-halakha: L'parshayot Ama Ivriyah*" [Hebrew], *Tarbiz* 68 (1998–1999), pp. 187–210; Yishayahu Maori, "*Al Yachaso Shel Targum HaTorah HaMeyukhas L'Yonatan ben Uziel L'mekorot HaHalakhah*" [Hebrew: The Relationship of Targum Pseudo-Jonathan to Halakhic Sources], *Te'uda*, volume 3: *Studies in Talmudic Literature in Post-biblical Hebrew and in Biblical Exegisis*, ed. M. Friedman, A. Tal, and G. Brin, Tel Aviv: Tel Aviv University (1983), pp. 235–250; Yishayahu Maori, "*HaTargumim Ha-Arami'im LeTorah U'midrash Hazal*" [Hebrew: The Aramaic Targum and Rabbinic Exegesis], in *Proceedings of the Ninth World Congress of Jewish Studies: Panel Sessions, Bible Studies and Ancient Near East*, Jerusalem: Magnes Press, (1985), pp. 1–12; Yishayahu Maori, *The Peshitta Version of the Pentateuch and Early Jewish Exegesis* [Hebrew], Jerusalem: Magnes Press (1995); Avigdor Shinan, *Targum V'aggadah Bo: Ha'agadah B'targum HaTorah Ha'arami Ha-Meyukhas L'yonatan ben Uziel* [Hebrew: The Embroidered Targum: The Aggadah in Targum Pseudo-Jonathan of the Pentateuch], Jerusalem: Hebrew University (1992); Willem F. Smelik, "The Rabbinic Reception of Early Bible Translations as Holy Writings and Oral Torah," *Journal for the Aramaic Bible* 1 (1999), pp. 249–272. For a more in-depth analysis of these tests, and of the question of what light these texts might shed on the question of divine ownership (at least with respect to Pseudo-Jonathan), see Madeline Kochen, "Property and Its Limits: Jesus, the Pharisees, the Rabbis and the Targumists," in Eric Meyers and Paul Flescher, eds., *Aramaic Studies in Judaism and Early Christianity*, Winona Lake, Indiana: Eisenbrauns (2010).

Areas in which the decision as to whether a person can or does own a particular item is pursued as matter of course are those in which the question of ownership will determine whether a status change of biblical significance has occurred. For example, the decision of whether a valid marriage has taken place is a question with serious legal ramifications.[29] One of the prerequisites for marriage to take place is that the groom give the woman something *that he owns* (and that has more than *de minimus* value). The question of whether something can be used to accomplish *kiddushin* (marriage) is thus often a touchstone for determining whether a person can or does own a particular item. For this reason, the parameters of property ownership are of serious concern in the area of marriage. It is critical for these purposes, as a categorical matter, to ascertain exactly what types of property can or cannot be "owned" by a human being (as opposed to being owned by God). Thus, for example, a series of Mishnayot in Tractate Kiddushin (Marriage) evaluate different types of property possibly owned by God to determine whether they can be used to accomplish *kiddushin*.[30]

Similarly, the biblical law, as interpreted by the rabbis, dictates that one has the power to consecrate (to give to God and the Temple) only that which one owns. As in the case of marriage, serious biblical questions hinge on whether property is considered sacred (*kadosh*) or ordinary (*chullin*) (e.g., whether its improper use constitutes *me'ilah*, a serious act of desecration that is regarded as an act of theft from God). This is another context in which determining ownership is a decision that implicates the question of biblical ownership at the most fundamental level.

There are also concrete situations in which a biblical prohibition applies only to that which one owns, thus requiring a determination of ownership for very practical purposes. For example, serious prohibitions regarding leavened bread on Passover are understood by the rabbis to turn on the question of ownership. As the trigger for a lengthy analysis of the means for determining ownership (vis-à-vis God) in the second chapter of Tractate Pesachim,[31] the rabbis interpret the biblical proscription,

[29] Marital status will determine, for example, whether adultery (which carries the death penalty) has taken place, or whether a person born of a sexual liaison is a *mamzer* (which also carries serious penalties).

[30] See, e.g., Mishnah Kiddushin 2:8, "If a man betrothed a woman with his portion of either the Most Holy Things (*kodshei kodoshim*) or the Lesser Holy Things (*kodshim kalim*), her betrothal is not valid." המקדש בחלקו בין קדשי קדשים בין קדשים קלים אינה מקודשת

[31] The extensive inquiry undertaken in the second chapter of B.T. Pesachim primarily involves the category of "*issurei hana'ah*" (property from which humans are not permitted to benefit), a category that was also significant in the section in Tractate Kiddushin regarding property that can be used for marriage. While the analysis in Pesachim suggests something of an

"and leaven shall not be seen *to you (lecha)*" (ולא יראה לך שאר) (Exod 13:7),

to mean:

> "[On Passover] you may not see [*leavan*] *that is yours*, but you may see [*leaven*] *of others* and *of the Most High*." (emphasis added)[32]
>
> שלך אי אתה רואה, אבל אתה רואה של אחרים ושל גבוה.

The category of property owned by the divine (*shel gavohah*) appears regularly in connection with matters of property and exchange, in realms ranging from the most holy to the most mundane. It is taken for granted as a distinct legal category, one that has special ontological significance. This difference is reflected in certain distinct rules and procedures that apply exclusively to property in this category. For example, numerous requirements or prohibitions that are described in a biblical text as being applicable to interactions between an individual and his or her "fellow" (human being), such as the ban against charging interest on a loan (*ribit*) and the requirement of charging a "just price" (*ona'ah*), are deemed, by the rabbis, to be inapplicable to property transactions with the divine. The obligation of "just price" (*ona'ah*) and the prohibition against charging interest (*ribit*) are found to not apply to property owned by God.

The rules regarding *hekdesh* amount, in essence, to a body of property law that is distinct from, yet parallel to, the institution of property in the human, *hedyot* realm.[33] As the above-described examples illustrate, there are items on both ends of the spectrum – ones that are owned by God (and cannot be owned or used by a human being), and ones that can easily be owned by a person. The former category is epitomized by sacrifices such as *kodshei kodashim* (Most Holy Things). While donating any item to the Temple renders it *shel gavohah* (belonging to God), animal sacrifices, particularly those

equivalence between ownership and the right to benefit, it is clear from elsewhere, including the Mishnayot in Kiddushin, that the categories of *issurei hana'ah* and property that is not owned by a human being are not coextensive. There is a complicated relationship, both legally and philosophically, between the rule against benefiting from certain things and the category of items which are not owned by a human being.

32 B.T. Pesachim 23a.

33 As such, they contain many procedural rules that differ from those applicable in mundane (human) property law. E.g., a general rule of property law requires that, for a transfer of property to be effective, the recipient must perform an act of *kinyan* (acquisition), such as a lifting up or pulling the property that is changing hands. By contrast, according to the Mishnah in Kiddushin 1:6, a physical act is not necessary in order to successfully transfer property into the domain of the divine: "Dedication to Most High [Temple] by word of mouth is equal to the act of delivery to a common person." Indeed, an individual's power to assume an obligation to God, or to transfer property to God, by means of a simple verbal vow or pledge is a procedure that, for the most part, is peculiar to commitments to the ontological realm of the divine.

that are intended entirely for God (and are not shared by a priest or the animal's owner), are essentially understood to be "fed" to the divine.[34]

The text in B.T. Pesachim, among others, makes plain the separate legal existence of the realms of divinely owned and human-owned property. Even more illuminating are texts that track the passage of a transferred item between property domains (between persons and God or between persons and persons). When read together, these cases from different legal contexts offer insight into the way the property claims and transactions involving the divine realm impact on human property ownership.

The exchanges that are most illuminating in this regard are sites where there is an explicit characterization, or attempt to characterize, the nature of the property claim of the person involved in an exchange with the divine. Differences in the mechanics of the transactions also imply different property implications of transactions across these categories. When analyzed side by side, the myriad instances of property transactions with God examined below paint a surprisingly clear picture of what turn out to be very complicated (but in some ways quite simple) property relationships. This picture, comprised of a complicated set of property relationships, reveals the general rubric within which human property rights are conferred and limited by the parameters of ownership by the divine.

The complicated scheme of property transactions involving the divine realm is evidenced by seven paradigmatic cases, which will be analyzed below:[35]

1. Cases in which property owned fully (to the extent possible) by a human being is gifted to God. The transfer of ownership is accomplished simply by the owner's oral declaration. (Case: Consecration of animal for sacrifice)
2. Property that has been directly transferred to God's domain and, from that "location," goes to a particular human being who has a property entitlement thereto, who simply takes his due by eating it; there is no other human designation of the property, nor does the recipient receive other property or rights of ownership beyond what he ingests. (Case: priest eating from God's table [Table of the Most High])
3. Grants of property that appear to come from the realm of human ownership (i.e., from property that has not previously been *explicitly*

[34] While the animal is transferred to divine ownership and converted to *hekdesh* when it is pledged, one might say that, at least metaphorically, it becomes God's property in the fullest sense when it is sacrificed and burnt on the altar. There is a dispute about whether there is a difference between the act of giving to God by deeming the item *hekdesh* and the act of "feeding" God through the slaughter and burning of the animal on the altar.

[35] This list of cases does not cover the full array of possible legal permutations suggested in the rabbinic texts.

transferred to the divine realm) but (according to some) that are deemed to come from God's property. (Case: laborer eating from the fruit he is picking)

4. Grants of property conferred upon certain persons by operation of law (with no eating involved), where the property is considered to be a grant from the divine realm rather than an entitlement arising from the dictates of (human) property or contract law. (Case: priest's entitlement to the robbed property of a convert)
5. Pursuant to requirements related to the legitimate taking and maintaining of ownership, property is set aside by the (initial) owner on behalf of the poor. While it might appear as a gift of property from the owner, it is not; the owner does not own property acquired by the poor, nor does he have the right to select the identities of the recipients (*tovat hana'ah*). The owner separates from his property the portion available to the poor, but the produce is taken by anyone who qualifies as poor, who then receives the full right of ownership. (Cases: *leket*, *shikhechah*, *peah*, and [perhaps some] *ma'aser ani* [poor tithe], etc.)
6. Transactions as described in (4), except that (a) the property is to be made available only to priests, and (b) it is, to a limited extent, considered something of a gift from the initial owner, who does not own the property but who has the right to decide who shall receive this property (*tovat hana'ah*). (Cases: *terumah* [priestly tithe], and [perhaps some] *ma'aser ani* [poor tithe])
7. Property as described in (4), except that the property is available (on the same terms) to everyone, not just to the poor (e.g. *hefker* [ownerless property]). (Case: *shemitah* [Sabbatical year produce])

3.3.1 *Direct Gifts to God: Sacrifices and Vows*

The body of law related to the Temple in Jerusalem (destroyed 70 C.E.) is central to a proper understanding of the conception or legal fiction of divine ownership. For it was property donated to the Temple (for purposes of either (1) sacrifice or (2) *bedek habayit*, Temple maintenance) that was considered, literally, to have been "given" to the divine, transferred from the ontological category of property in the realm of human ownership (*hedyot*) to the ontological category of property belonging to God (property known as *hekdesh*)[36]

[36] The rabbinic scheme entails a kind of hierarchy of *kedushah* (sanctity), with different levels (or completeness of) direct ownership by God. Temple-related property that is, in a sense, most directly owned by or "given to" God are sacrifices that are entirely burnt up and "fed" to God (known as *kodshei kodoshim*, "most holy things"). Nevertheless, once something is donated to

and to other categories of lesser sacredness and hybrid ownership. These gifts, (or, in a neo-Maussian sense, "returns") to God (and to others) were at the theoretical center of pre- and early rabbinic Judaism. A full appreciation of the realm of divine property claims thus requires an understanding of the role played by the Temple in Jerusalem and of the rabbis' perception of its meaning and significance; such an understanding is also necessary in order to be able to identify rabbinic efforts to understand and preserve aspects of what was thought to have been lost with its destruction.

The corpus of Tannaitic and Amoraic literature, which has come to represent the foundational legal texts of traditional Judaism, is a rich artifact of rabbinic culture that captures a significant transitional period in Jewish history from the perspective of the rabbis. Following generations of residence in Palestine, with a greater or lesser degree of autonomy, in a land considered their own, the rabbinic sages in the early centuries of the common era found themselves living (both inside and, later, outside Palestine) in an "exile" that began with and was essentially characterized by the destruction of the Temple in Jerusalem in the year 70 C.E. Beyond the geographic, social, and emotional upheaval wrought by this event, it caused a significant rupture in the intellectual continuity of the tradition of Second Temple Judaism. Many of the tradition's primary (religious and) legal underpinnings[37] were radically unhinged by the physical loss of the Temple and by the accompanying exile. For before its destruction, the Temple (and related institutions) functioned as the practical, metaphysical, and philosophical cornerstone of the power structures, social relations, and spiritual meaning in the Jewish community. Serving as more than a "religious" locus of sacrifice and prayer, it represented what might be characterized colloquially as the seat of government, as it was thought to house the ultimate power (political and otherwise) – the divine sovereign.[38]

It is difficult to know exactly how the Temple functioned. Certainly it seems, from varying accounts,[39] that, as in any contemporaneous Near Eastern temple, the offering of sacrifices stood at the center of its ritual.[40] What is clear from

the Temple, whether for sacrifice purposes or for Temple upkeep (*bedek ha'bayit*), it is considered *hekdesh*, owned by God (and the Temple).

37 Or presumably at least those of certain "sects" or religious group(s).

38 This characterization is obviously not historical fact but is the rabbis' construction and account of their origins and authority.

39 Philo, Josephus, Tacitus, Strabo, etc.

40 The Temple in Jerusalem was supposed to be the only place sacrifices were offered during the late Second Temple period. In contemporary times it is hard to comprehend the meaningfulness of the practice of animal sacrifice. This is not a modern problem. Questioning and even criticism of this ritual began with the prophets of the First Temple period. See, e.g., Amos 5:21–27; Hos 6:6; Mic 6:6–8; Isa 1:11–17; Jer 6:20; 7:21–22; cf. Psa 40:7–8; 50:8–15. Arguably, what was condemned in the prophetic and wisdom literature was not the ritual of sacrifice itself, but

an analysis of rabbinic texts is that the Temple was understood by the rabbis (as it might well have been at the time of the Second Temple, particularly after its enlargement by Herod at the turn of the millennium, and the veritable tourist industry that developed as a consequence) to represent a literal gateway to God's domain, a portal that enabled the giving of gifts directly to God.

The rabbinic construction of the Temple's significance cannot be overemphasized. It served as the focal point for a complex system of social and property relations sketched out in the Bible (with the Bible functioning in a way that might be described, anachronistically, as that of a constitution). For the Temple was perceived by the rabbis as the central locus of implementation, by way of tithes, donations, and sacrifices, of a critical part of the biblical plan for property relations set forth in the Bible. The rabbis developed an intricate legal and theoretical infrastructure, which served to house and to explicate the array of biblically based mandatory and voluntary gift givings to God and, by necessity and implication, related aspects of human ownership and exchange.

In the rabbinic imagination, the divinely dictated Temple-based system of interdomain (human to divine or divine to human) exchange, via sacrifice and the related system of tithes, played an extremely important role in the social order and, more broadly, in the very running of the world. Apart from supporting the class of priests who acted as "representatives of God," the thrust of this system of giving entailed direct gifts to God and gifts deflected from God to the poor and needy. This system of giving was the practical embodiment of vision of distributive justice as mapped out in the Bible.

3.3.2 *Gifts from God: Priestly Gifts and Workers' Rights*

Corresponding to the category of gifts *to* God is the category of gifts from God. This category has an identifiable meaning, beyond the general statement that everything belongs to God and comes to humans as a gift. The gifts from God under discussion here are understood to come directly from the realm of divine ownership; many of them also entail chronologically or legally prior gifts given *to* God from another person.[41] While gifted property

its practice without the proper intent, attitude, and "knowledge of God" (Hos 6:6). This view is certainly borne out in rabbinic literature, where the focus on the requirement of proper intent became critical to the practice itself (see, e.g., Lev 7:18, *piggul*) and reached its apex with Maimonides, who characterized it (in *Moreh Nevuchim* [Hebrew: Guide for the Perplexed], 3:32) as a temporary concession, on God's part, to a people who could not reasonably have been expected to simply abandon, abruptly, a practice that had, at the time of Moses, been a universal custom of worship.

[41] Parts of animal sacrifice eaten by priests illustrate this phenomenon. Thus, while it might appear as if the person donating the animal for sacrifice is feeding the priest, on this view the

in this category need not always be considered "sacred" or *kadosh*, it is always understood that the recipient receives property (and the entitlement thereto) from God's domain (rather than from the human property domain, according to its internal set of principles).

The items in the category of gifts from God vary in terms of degree of ownership and by whom. The numerous possible combinations of property grants result partly from the fact that the range of possibilities is multi-dimensional. It is beyond the scope of this book to do a systematic analysis of all properties and gifts in which God has a part in the property or in the transfer. For immediate purposes I will bring examples to demonstrate general categories or rules. Before embarking on an analysis of these examples, it is useful to separate out the various legal vectors at play in all of these transactions:

1. *Who is the true donor of the gift (who owns the property at the moment it is given), God or a human being?*
2. *If the gift is from God, what is the status of the donated goods in their original state?*

This issue relates to questions such as whether the gift is received from God (or his "table") directly or indirectly (as a "gift" from a human donor), how holy the property is and how restricted is its use. In answer to this question,

(a) some things are deemed to belong to God from the beginning. Exemplifying this category is the firstborn animal, which is considered to be sacred, belonging to God (for the priest) from within the womb.[42]

(b) In another category are goods that are owned (to the extent that full human ownership is possible) by an individual human being who then transfers them to the domain of divine ownership (e.g., animals donated to the Temple for sacrifice).

(c) Finally, there is a category, perhaps in between, of goods that are owned by the human being in a limited sense (e.g., *tevel*, untithed produce), from which a portion of that property must be designated as gifts or donations (e.g., by separating tithes), an act that, in turn, changes the ownership status of the remaining goods by rendering them fully owned by the human being.

animal is giving the entire animal to God and it is from God (or his property domain) that the priest receives the meat to eat. The same two-step transfer of property (from the human donor to God and from God to another human recipient) will be shown to also occur in the context of gifts to the poor.

42 See Lev 27:29; B.T. Arakhin 29a.

3. *What, if any, property rights are conveyed? In other words, how does the property come to the human recipient: does it become his (private) property or does the property that the recipient receives (or is permitted to eat) continue to belong to God?*

While reference is often made to a dichotomy between property owned by God (*shel gavohah*) and property that is owned by humans (*shel hedyot*) (even if regulated or restricted), that binary is not straightforward. For there are various possibilities as to how the recipient might receive the property gifted and what the "ownership" status of the property is. The description of the recipient receiving the gift as "private property" (to use the phrase loosely) might not always mean the same thing. There might be restrictions attached such as to whom it may be sold to or how it may be used. Conversely, while property that continues to belong to God is not the property of the recipient, there are cases in which the recipient is understood to have rights that might, at first blush, seem to suggest private property (e.g., the laborer can take money instead of food from the field). There are also items that seem to be hybrid property with some kind of joint ownership. But there are cases in which the Talmudic text itself describes these two ends of the spectrum – items that remain God's property even as the recipient receives the gift, and items that pass from the divine realm to the recipient in such a way that it becomes "his property" (e.g., it is alienable). These poles of the spectrum of ownership are very helpful in analyzing different kinds of transfers.

4. *What property rights, if any, does the human donor have in the item "gifted"?*

Once the gift has been designated or separated by the human donor, the property does not belong to him; however, there are differences among various types of "gifts" as to whether (or the extent to which) the human donor has some right (monetary or nonmonetary) in the property that is being turned over to another on behalf of God (e.g., whether the human donor has the right to choose the recipient, known as "*tovat hana'ah*").[43]

Despite these variables and the many possibilities they engender, what comes across from the Talmudic texts is a uniform category of gifts that come from, or pass through, the realm of divine ownership on their way to a human recipient.

[43] Another variation on this question is illustrated by a dispute in B.T. Bava Kamma 12b as to whether certain "minor" sacrifices, such as peace offerings, whose flesh is consumed by the original owners, is their private property or whether they are invited guests eating from the divine table. There, Rabbi Jose the Galilean asserts that minor sacrifices are the private property of the human donor, even after the animal has been consecrated. See B.T. Kiddushin 52b. See also B.T. Bava Kamma 109, regarding the status of animals that were donated to the Temple for sacrifice but have not yet been put to death.

Before exploring the relevant texts, it is useful to spell out precisely how such a transfer takes place, using the portions of sacrifices eaten by the priests as an example.

There are many different kinds of animal sacrifices. *Kodshei kodoshim* or most holy things, are animal sacrifices that are entirely burnt (for God) on the altar. By contrast, *kodshim kalim* or lesser holy things or "minor" sacrifices, are not to be burnt and consumed entirely; part of the animal is to be eaten by humans, such as the priest on duty in the Temple or the person who gave the animal for sacrifice. In the latter case the "human donor"[44] of the animal is not considered to be feeding, or giving his property directly to the priests or others who will eat from the sacrifice.[45] In the eyes of the rabbis, two steps are involved. In the first step, (1) with the initial vow of sanctification and animal sacrifice,[46] as described earlier, the animal is understood to move directly from the human donor's ownership to the domain of divine ownership. Then (2), as a second, legally separate transaction, the portions of the animal that are eaten by the priest (and possibly that portion eaten by the initial donor[47]) are seen as having been conveyed directly from God to the priests. Thus, following the human donor's direct gift to God, the portion eaten by the priest represents a gift from the realm of divine ownership, not from the person who originally owned the animal.

The nature of sacrificial portions as gifts from God is readily apparent, as they come from property that has just been given to God by the human donor, bringing the ritual of animal sacrifice (and the gift cycle) full circle. As noted above, while some sacrifices are intended to be ultimately consumed entirely by God (*kodshei kodashim*) by being burnt entirely on the altar, some sacrifices are meant to be eaten (also) by human beings – by priests and/or by the initial donor of the animal, and possibly his guests.[48] The idea of a "gift

[44] For the sake of convenience, I use the term "human donor" when referring to a human being supplying property to God that will, in turn, result in a gift from God to another human being. This is to avoid confusion with the concept of the divine as original and continuing owner of everything, and to be able to speak of this group without worrying (when it is not necessary) about differences in specific property rights as among the human donor, God, and the (human) recipient. Thus, in the case of sacrifices, I call the one who donates the animal for sacrifice the human donor but I do not intend to imply any other connotations of the word "donor".

[45] As noted, some things, such as firstborn animals, start out belonging to God.

[46] The question of the difference between pledging an animal to the Temple and sacrificing the animal, in terms of its *kedushah*, level of divine ownership, etc., is contested. It is not necessary to deal with this question for the purposes of this analysis.

[47] The text in B.T. Bava Kamma 12b implies that this is so, but this question, of whether the portion of the sacrifice eaten by the human donor is to be classified in the same way as the portion eaten by the priest, becomes a matter of dispute. See Tosafot *ad loc.*

[48] For example, the tithing of one's newborn cattle, sheep, and goats, commanded in Lev 27:32–33, results in a sacrifice at the Temple in Jerusalem, with the meat being eaten by the initial owner and his guests.

from God," intended here to describe the second step in the two-step process described above, is made vividly clear by the terminology used repeatedly to describe the transaction. Thus, B.T. Kiddushin 52b states:

> When [the priests] acquire (*ka zakhu*)[49] [their portion], it is from the table of the Most High that they acquire [it] (*ka zakhu*).[50]
>
> כי קא זכו משלחן גבוה קא זכו

According to the plain meaning of this statement, the property transferred to the priest does not belong to or come from the human donor but (directly) from God. This case involves an animal that once belonged to the human donor. He gives it to God, who, in turn, gifts portions from "his table" to the priests.[51] One might also say that in cases in which the priest eats of the sacrifice, the human donor, in giving an animal as a gift to God, is also making a gift of divine property to another human being on behalf of God.

Divine
↗ ↘
Israelite ←··· ···→ Priest

The statement that the priest acquires "from the table of the Most High," used in the context of the priests' share of an animal sacrifice, can be understood to convey, almost literally, the idea that the priest is eating as a guest invited to dine at God's table,[52] that he does not "acquire" unless and until he ingests it. The priest eats from property that actually belongs neither to the human donor nor the human recipient (in this case the priest), but to God. As will be shown,

[49] The word *zokhe* is used consistently to describe the entitlement or the right a person has to property that's been gifted to them in this way. Among the various translations of this word (e.g., obtain, become entitled, acquire), I use the word "acquire," (the word that is usually used to translate the word *koneh*) in order to capture its use here, as a term of art, connoting the complete transfer of property from one to the other. As a gift flowing to the priest directly from God, it is perhaps the strongest type of property entitlement one might have, akin to what some might call a "natural right."

[50] B.T. Kiddushin 52b. See also B.T. Chullin 12a, B.T. Bava Kamma 13a, B.T. Bezah 21a, B.T. Menachot 6a. (Aside from one other appearance regarding priestly gifts, these are the only places this phrase appears in rabbinic literature.) This is one of the more explicit descriptions of the process that, as I will show, takes place for an entire series of gifts, property transfers, and property relinquishments done for the benefit of other human beings that are required as part of the most basic definition of what it means – in terms of rights, responsibilities, and entitlements – for a human being to own property.

[51] Note that this is unlike the case of property that is considered to have *always* belonged to God and must be returned to or redeemed from the divine. See Lev 27:26: "A firstling of animals, which as a firstling belongs to the Lord, cannot be consecrated by anyone; whether ox or sheep it is the Lord's," which is reflected in rabbinic literature at B.T. Arakhin 29a.

[52] This idea even entered the lexicon of later commentators. See, e.g., the commentary of the Ralbag (Levi ben Gershon, 1288–1344) on 1 Sam 2:12, which explains that the reasons the sons

this is how the Tanna Rabbi Meir regards another mandatory gift – the second tithe (*ma'aser sheni*) in B.T. Bava Metzia 90a. We turn, now, to that case.

The biblical scheme requires that a series of tithes must be separated every year (except the *shemitah* – the 7th or Sabbatical – year) as a prerequisite to ownership, so that the remaining produce will be considered, legally, one's own. In addition to the tithes destined for the priests (such as *terumah* and *terumat ma'aser*), there are two other tithes that are given to non-priests, in alternating years of the seven-year cycle. In years one, two, four, and five, the additional tithe is called the "second tithe" (*ma'aser sheni*); in years three and six, in lieu of the second tithe, a "tithe for the poor" (*ma'aser ani*) is separated in addition to the priestly tithes. The rule regarding the second tithe states that, once separated by the owner, the food is considered holy and must be taken to Jerusalem and eaten there. The biblical provision also permits one to exchange one's second tithe produce for money, an act of redemption ("*pidyon*") that transfers the status of holiness from the produce to the money. The (sacred) second tithe money must then be brought to Jerusalem, where it will be used to purchase food (which then acquires the status of holiness, freeing up the money as ordinary property) that must be eaten by the owner in Jerusalem.

Ma'aser sheni (for which *ma'aser ani* is the substitute in some years) has the status of sacred "*kadosh*" property. Like *hekdesh*, it is considered to belong to God. However, whereas the priest's portion (as described above) is understood to be eaten from the table of the Most High, the ownership status of the second tithe that is eaten in Jerusalem is a matter of dispute among the rabbis. After quoting two beraita's (tannaitic texts) that appear to contradict each other in this regard, the Amoraim attribute them to rabbis with different views:

> This [first beraita] represents [the view of] Rabbi Meir, who says that *ma'aser* [*sheni*] is the property of the Most High (*mamon gavohah*). This [second tannaitic text] represents [the view of] Rabbi Yehudah, who says that *ma'aser sheni* is the property of an ordinary person [i.e. the one who separates and eats it] (*mamon hedyot*).[53]
>
> הא והא במעשר שני, ולא קשיא הא רבי מאיר, הא רבי יהודה

of Eli are declared *resha'im* (evil ones) is because of the way they abused their position as priests by eating sacrificial meat improperly, simply to satisfy their own desire for food. They ignored the fact that God's gifts to the priests were designed to enable the priests to be engaged in God's Torah, rather than having to work. According to the Ralbag, by doing so they improperly put "their table" before "the table of the Most High."

53 B.T. Bava Metzia 90a. The law seems to follow Rabbi Meir. But see B.T. Sanhedrin 112b, which states that Rabbi Meir deems *ma'aser sheni* exempt from the obligation of *challah* (to separate a portion of dough for the priests), which only applies to "your dough" (Num 15:20),

הא רבי מאיר דאמר מעשר ממון גבוה הוא הא רבי יהודה דאמר מעשר שני ממון הדיוט הוא

While no mention is made of the table of the Most High, the idea is the same. This, too, is familiar terminology often used to connote the dichotomy between *mamon gavohah*, or property in the divine realm (*reshut gavohah*), and *mamon hedyot*, or property that is within the ordinary, human property realm (*reshut hedyot*). Thus, Rabbi Meir is of the view that, like the priest eating from his sacrificial portion, one eating *ma'aser sheni* is eating property that is sacred, property that belongs God, not to himself.[54] Thus, for instance, he cannot use *ma'aser sheni* in order to betroth a woman, which can only be accomplished with an item that he owns.[55]

By contrast, Rabbi Yehudah is of the opinion that, although *ma'aser sheni* is restricted in that it is not allowed to be eaten outside Jerusalem,[56] it does belong to the possessor and thus could be used by him for betrothal.

We will return to a different scenario, concerning the laborer working in the field, where there is another explicit debate as to whether particular property that one is biblically entitled to eat belongs to God (*shel shamayim*, "of heaven") or to the person doing the eating (*shelo*, "his"). First, however, it is important to pursue the evolution of the concept captured by the phrase "he acquires from the table of the Most High" as it moves along vector number 3 – what, if any, property rights are conveyed when one is "*zokhe*" (when one acquires) from God.

For this inquiry we return to the category of priestly gifts. The priestly portion of sacrifices is just one among many mandated gifts to the priest, not all of which involve eating. Are these other gifts also "acquired from the

because it belongs to God (*mamon gavohah*), whereas the majority of the rabbis consider it ordinary property (*mamon hedyot*) and, therefore, obligated in tithes. It is said that this dispute applies only to the status of *ma'aser sheni* that is in Jerusalem, but that all agree that *ma'aser sheni* that is outside Jerusalem (but in Israel/Palestine) is sacred and thus exempt from the obligation of *challah*.

54 Rabbi Meir also expresses this opinion in Mishnah Kiddushin 2:8. This is a complicated Mishnah that illustrates how difficult it is to classify things within certain categories for various purposes. An analysis of the set of Mishnayot at the end of the second chapter of Kiddushin (particularly when read in conjunction with the second chapter of Pesachim, which also deals with the category of *issurei hana'ah*) is beyond the scope of this book.

55 See B.T. Kiddushin 52a and B.T. Bava Kamma, the inquiry concerning the actual owner of *ma'aser sheni* is triggered by a question concerning the prohibition against muzzling one's cow while it is working in the field. It is determined that the prohibition only applies when the produce being threshed belongs to the person, but does not apply to property (such as that belonging to God) that does not. See B.T. Meilah 13a, where this finding is made on the basis of the biblical verse that establishes the muzzling prohibition, which states, "Do not muzzle an ox in his threshing" (Deut 25:4), with the focus on the word read as "his" threshing (*bedisho*).

56 See Deut 12:17, "You may not eat within your gates [i.e., outside Jerusalem] the *ma'aser* [*sheni*] of your grain."

table of the Most High?" If so, what does that mean (outside the context of eating)?

The one occurrence of the phrase, of "acquiring from the table of the Most High," that appears in connection with a priestly gift other than sacrifice is at the beginning of the seventh chapter of Tractate Arakhin in connection with the priests' entitlement to certain ancestral fields when the Jubilee year arrives.[57] As provided in Lev 27:16, 20-21,

> (16) And if a person consecrates to the Lord (*yakdish*) any ancestral field ... [the property may be redeemed by the person until the year of the Jubilee].... (20) but if he does not redeem the field, or if it has been sold to someone else, it shall no longer be redeemable [by the one who consecrated it]. (21) And when [that] field is released in the Jubilee [year], it shall be holy to the Lord (*kadosh*); like a devoted field (*cherem*). To the priest it shall become his holding (*lakohen tehiye achuzato*). (numbers added).
>
> ואם משדה אחזתו יקדיש איש לה' והיה ערכך ....ואם לא יגאל את השדה ואם מכר את... השדה לאיש אחר לא יגאל עוד והיה השדה בצאתו ביבל קדש 'לה כשדה החרם לכהן תהיה אחזתו

This rule is codified in Mishnah Arakhin 7:3 as follows:

> If a man consecrated [his field] and then [he or his son] redeemed it, it does not go out of his possession in the Jubilee...[otherwise] it goes to the priests...
>
> הקדישה וגאלה אינה יוצאה מידו ביובל; גאלה בנו יוצאה לאביו ביובל; גאלה אחר או אחד מהקרובים וגאלה מידו יוצאה לכהנים ביובל

Elsewhere, in the context of a Talmudic discussion at B.T. Arakhin 24b a question regarding the mechanics of transferring such property to the priest (specifically, whether the priest simply receives the field or must pay to redeem it), Rava asserts,

> at any rate, does it eventually return to the owners? It is to the priests that it goes, and the priests acquire it (*ka zakhu*) *from the table of the Most High*. (emphasis added).
>
> סוף סוף לבעלים מי קהדרא? לכהנים הוא דנפקא, וכהנים משולחן גבוה קא זכו

This case seems to be a (theoretically if not chronologically) later use of this phrase *shulchan gavohah*; the terminology "acquiring from the table of the Most High" used here has taken on (if it did not already have it) the function of a term of art referring to a gift (or at least a property entitlement) received directly from the legal property domain of the Divine.[58] With this discussion of the ancestral

57 Lev 25:13–16 provides that land can only be sold until the the fiftieth, Jubilee year, and that in that year all land reverts to ancestral ownership.

58 The biblical language itself seems to communicate the idea that the ancestral field reverts to God's ownership and, from there, is granted to the priests. Lev 27:21 states, "when the field is

field, especially when read with the parallel case concerning robbed property of a convert (to be discussed below), the legal concept of acquiring property from God is seen to be broader. It describes more than a priestly gift that entails a (limited) right to eat (and nothing more) from property that is sacred and that it stays in God's domain; it also describes something that looks more like a normal grant of title, involving property that is not inherently sacred but that emerges, as a gift, from the realm of divine ownership.

The precise legal elements that constitute a priestly gift from God are more visible in another case from Tractate Arakhin, that involving the "robbed property of a convert." Interestingly, this case is used explicitly in Tractate Bava Kamma (109b) to further illuminate the transaction involving the ancestral field.[59] One thing (among others) that these two cases have in common is that they entail what might be described as residual property entitlements, where the appropriate human recipient is absent; the property thus reverts to divine ownership and, from there, devolves to the priests.

The case (of "the robbed property of a convert") in Arakhin relates to the general rule that one who swears falsely in denial of a monetary obligation, and then confesses and wishes to repent, is required (1) to repay the principle, (2) plus an added surcharge of a fifth of its value, and (3) must bring an *asham* (guilt) offering.[60] Mishnah 9:5 in Tractate Bava Kamma stresses how important it is that the repentant robber actually make the required compensatory payment. It states,

> One who robs his fellow in the value of [even] a [mere] *perutah* and swears [falsely] to him [and then repents] must *pursue* him to return [what he owes] even to [the faraway location of] Media … If [the victim] dies, [the robber] must return [the stolen property] to his heirs …
>
> הגוזל את חבירו שוה פרוטה ונשבע לו יוליכנו אחריו אפילו למדי. . . .
> ואם מת יחזיר ליורשיו . . .

According to Num 5:8, if the victim to whom repayment is due dies without heirs (which, could include any family members, even of distant relation),

released in the Jubilee, it shall be holy to the Lord as a devoted field; to the priest it shall become his holding. (והיה השדה בצאתו ביבל קדש לה' כשדה החרם לכהן תהיה אחזתו)" In this case, either the consecrated field was already in the possession of the Temple (unredeemed), or it was reclaimed by God from the interim owner in the Jubilee year, when all property was supposed to be reclaimed by God from those in possession and returned to the original "ancestral" owners.

59 To use a familiar Talmudic expression applicable here, one might say that the case from Arakhin comes, in Bava Kamma, to teach, and it, itself, is illuminated thereby.

60 See Lev 5:21–26; Num 5:6–8.

and there is no one "to whom restitution can be made, the amount repaid *shall go to the Lord, to the priest.*" (emphasis added).

ואם אין לאיש גאל להשיב האשם אליו האשם המושב ילה לכהן

This verse is understood by the rabbis to dictate that when there are no heirs, the property that was to be returned to the victim or his heirs is to be given to the priests serving in the Temple during the week the robber confesses. The rabbis also read the scenario of a victim without heirs as referring a case where the victim is a convert. Because of the laws regarding conversion, which nullify all previous familial relationships of the convert (who is only likely to have heirs if he has children), the convert is much more likely to die without legal heirs than is a Jew (who, even if childless, is likely to have some family, however distant).

Like Leviticus 27:21 concerning the ancestral field (which states "it shall be holy to the Lord as a devoted field; to the priest it shall become his holding"),[61] this passage also seems to describe the property as moving, literally (in a legal sense), to God, for the priest. In this case, the Talmud does not talk of the priest acquiring from the table of the Most High. However, it invokes the same legal concept with an even more vivid description of the nature of such a transaction.

Initially the Talmud makes clear the nature of this priestly entitlement as one directed by God. Relying on Numbers 5:8 (directing the property be given "to God, to the priest" (לה' לכהן) the texts states: "[concerning] the robbed property of a convert, God [lit. the Merciful One] stated that it is given to the priests"[62] (גזל הגר דקאמר רחמנא נתינה לכהנים). Later, a beraita describes precisely the legal process by which the priest is given this property:

God acquired it and he gave it to the priests of that watch (*mishmar*).[63]

קנאו השם ונתנו לכהנים שבאותו משמר.

This statement reveals the two-step process involved in acquiring from the table of the Most High. First, God "acquires" (*koneh*) the property (in this case, from the robber). Once the property has moved from the robber's property domain to that of the divine, God gives it to the appropriate priests. Later

[61] See 89n58, *supra*.

[62] B.T. Bava Kamma 109b. Numbers 5:8 is cited for this proposition. That verse provides: "If the man has no redeemer [relative] to whom restitution can be made, the amount repaid shall go to God for the priest…" (emphasis added)

ואם אין לאיש גאל להשיב האשם אליו האשם המושב לה' לכהן.

[63] *Id.* In the Temple, the priests were organized into labor divisions called *mishmarot* or "watches". In this manner the priests were on a scheduled rotation in performing the services in the Temple. The watches served for a week at a time and changed on the Sabbath.

in the text, the Talmud uses a different formulation to describe the same transaction (with a truncated description of the multiple steps that are involved):

> God has told [the robber] to give this gift to [the priest].[64]
>
> דההיא מתנה אמר רחמנא דניתיב להו

The payment from the robber to the priest goes through God. In paying the priest, the robber is considered to have given a gift[65] of God's property on God's behalf.

Parallels between the cases of the ancestral field and the robbed property of the convert continue to emerge as the rabbis, in Tractates Arakhin and Bava Kamma, respectively, continue to probe the nature of these priestly entitlements, using similar language, similar reasoning, and even a certain incorporation by reference. Given the linguistic and structural similarities and proof texts, it is clear that these *sugyah*'s are literary parallels likely arising from some common source or tradition. These analyses, to be discussed below, confirm the status of these priestly entitlements as gifts coming directly from God.

In one parallel move, a similar question is posed in both the case of the ancestral field and that of the robbed property of a convert: what happens if a particular priest is in possession of these properties (it is *tachat yado*, literally, "under his hand") when the time comes to give the property to the priests – can that priest keep the property as his (*yehei shelo*), or must he (give it up and then) acquire a portion of it (*zokhe*)[66] along with the other priests? In the case of the ancestral field, the problem is posed in Mishnah Arakhin 7:3 as follows:

> If [before the Jubilee] one of the priests redeemed it [from the Temple treasurer], and it was still in his possession (*tachat yado*) [at the commencement of the year of the Jubilee] then he cannot say: "since it will go to the priests in the Jubilee and it is [already] now in my possession (*tachat yadi*), therefore it

64 *Id.* at 110b. Shortly thereafter the text repeats this idea in the name of Rav Zeira, who states concerning the robbed property of a convert, "this is the gift that God told [the robber] to give [the priests]."

65 A question is raised later as to whether the payment constitutes a gift or an inheritance payment. That will be discussed below.

66 As will be seen, a continuing linguistic pattern is evidenced in these cases whereby the word *zokhe* is consistently used to describe this type of acquisition that is, as if, "from the table of the Most High." This concept is contrasted with the idea of having property in one's possession – *tachat yado* – whether legally or illegally. Later, the notion of *reshut* (domain) will be seen to be used to describe the legal property domain from which the property derives (e.g., the divine domain or the property domain of a particular individual). I have not fully examined the usage of these three legal terms outside this particular context, so I cannot say that the meanings evidenced here are always consistent with their use elsewhere in rabbinic literature.

belongs to me;" rather, it goes out of his possession to be distributed among all his brethren the priests.

גאלה אחד מן הכהנים והרי היא תחת ידו לא יאמר: הואיל והיא יוצאה לכהנים ביובל והרי היא תחת ידי הרי היא שלי אלא יוצאה מתחת ידו ומתחלקת לכל אחיו הכהנים

This situation is elaborated in the ensuing Talmudic text (B.T. Arakhin 34a) as follows:

Our Rabbis taught: [Lev 27:21 states,] "like a devoted field; to the priest (*lakohen*) it shall become his holding." What does this teach? With respect to a field that would go to the priests in the Jubilee year [but] was redeemed [prior to the Jubilee] by one of the priests, from where [is the rule derived] that [this priest] cannot say: Since it goes to the priests [in the Jubilee anyway,] and now is in my possession, let it be mine (*harei he takhat yadi yehei sheli*). And it is logical. If I acquire (*zokhe*) what belongs to others [i.e. unredeemed fields], how much more [am I entitled (*zokhe*) to] what belongs to me?

תנו רבנן: (ויקרא כ"ז כא) שדה החרם לכהן תהיה אחוזתו מה תלמוד לומר? מנין לשדה שיוצא לכהנים ביובל וגאלה אחד מן הכהנים, מנין שלא יאמר: הואיל ויוצאה לכהן הרי תחת ידי ותהא שלי ודין הוא בשל אחרים אני זוכה בשל עצמי לא כל שכן

The same question is presented at B.T. Bava Kamma 109b, using the same legal terminology, concerning the robbed field of a convert as follows:

Our Rabbis taught: consider [the case where] the robber [of the convert who died] was a priest [and he came to the Temple and confessed during the week in which his own *mishmar* (watch) was serving]. From where [is it derived] that he should not say "since [the robbed property of the convert] goes to the priests [in my *mishmar*], and [that which I robbed and must give them] is already in my possession let it be mine (*harei hu tachat yadi yehei sheli*)." And it is logical: If I acquire (*zokhe*) what belongs to others, how much more [am I entitled (*zokhe*) to] what belongs to me?

תנו רבנן הרי שהיה גוזל כהן מנין שלא יאמר הואיל ויוצא לכהנים והרי הוא תחת ידי יהא שלי? ודין הוא: אי בשל אחרים הוא זוכה בשל עצמו לא כל שכן

In both cases (B.T. Bava Kamma 109b and B.T. Arakhin 34a), the conclusion reached is that the priest in question does not acquire (*zokhe*) what he has; rather, the property "leaves his possession (*tachat yado*) and is divided (among all his brethren[67]) the priests."

In both cases, the text distinguishes between property that is (either legally or illegally) in one's possession (*tachat yado*) and property to which one is

67 This part of the statement appears only in connection with the robbed property of a convert. Perhaps this is because he (the robber) does not share in that which is divided among the priests, but the possessor of the field does.

entitled or that acquires (is *zokhe* or, even more explicitly in the case or the ancestral field, is "*zokhe be'alma*"), in this context, from the divine domain. In neither case is the priest in possession deemed to acquire the property; in both cases it is divided among the priests; they are *zokhe* these priestly gifts.

These cases are explicitly linked in B.T. Bava Kamma 109b, as they each implement biblical directives that dictate that the property goes *to* the priest – "*lakohen*." When the case of the robbed convert is learned from the case of the ancestral field on this basis in what might be described as a *gezerah shavah*, it further demonstrates that, procedurally and substantively, these priestly entitlements get transferred to "*lakohen*." The entitlement (*zekhiyah*) of these priestly gifts has nothing to do with the question of who is (legally or illegally) in possession of the property. Rather, it is a *zekhiyah* (or *zekhiyah be'alma*) that is derived from the divine domain.

This last point, as to the derivation of the property entitlement, is supported by more than the fact that, in both cases, the transfer is described similarly as a gift to the priest from the table of the Most High, or as property that God has acquired and given to the priest. For the internal arguments within the cases also make clear that these entitlements are coming from the divine domain. In both contexts,[68] the question is raised as to whether the requirement of Num 5:10, "a man's holies (*kodoshav*, holy sacrifices) shall be his own" (ואיש את קדשיו לו יהיו), does not create an entitlement on the part of the priest in possession of the property at issue. While giving rise to responses that are in some sense opposites, the parallel attempts to apply this biblical mandate create a firm link (here, by contrast) with the basic notion that the priest's sacrifices are *not* his personal property, but are eaten from (and belong, until eaten,[69] to) the table of the Most High.

In B.T. Bava Kamma 109b, Num 5:10 is interpreted as permitting a priest to bring his own sacrifice at any time,[70] and as saying that when he does so, the meat and the skin belong to him (he need not share it with other priests). In another beraita on 109b, the verse dictating that, in the case of a thief who confesses, the "guilt payment is for God, for the priest" is interpreted to require that both the compensatory payment and the *asham* offering are to be given

[68] Numbers 5:10 provides, "and each man's *kodoshav* (holy sacrifices) shall be his; each priest shall keep what is given to him."

ואיש את קדשיו לו יהיה איש אשר יתן לכהן לו יהיה

[69] There is a disagreement as to the point at which the priest actually acquires that which he receives from the table of the Most High; the rabbis do not all agree that it is at the point when he eats the food.

[70] A beraita brought on B.T. Bava Kamma 109b states that, on the basis of Deut 18:6–7, a priest is entitled to bring his own sacrifice at any time, even when his *mishmar* (watch) is not serving in the Temple.

to the priests who are in the *mishmar* (watch) that is on duty during the week the thieving priest confesses.[71] The question is asked, therefore, whether Num 5:10 (which permits the confessing priest to bring his own *asham* sacrifice, and to keep the meat and skin) does not also give the confessing priest the right to the compensatory payment itself, since they are both meant to be given to the same priest(s).

In substance, the Talmud cannot refute the textual argument that, by implication and on the basis of Num 5:10, the confessing priest should have a right to the compensatory payment just as he is permitted to eat the meat from the *asham* sacrifice (when he himself brings it). The explanation as to why the priest has no such entitlement is by learning from the case of the ancestral field, which also states that the property at issue goes to the priest ("*lakohen*") and which is also interpreted to preclude the priest himself from keeping the property in his possession.

The aforementioned decision regarding the ancestral field is made after refuting possible inferences from a number of verses that might have been read to grant the priest in possession the right to keep it even after the Jubilee. In that case, the Talmud successfully refutes any deduction from Num 5:10 that the priest has such a right.

In B.T. Arakhin 34a, Rami bar Chama suggests that Num 5:10 might lead one to think that the priest who redeemed the ancestral field acquires it (is *zokhe*), just as it is stated, with regard to sacrifices that he brings, "a man's holy sacrifices shall be his own." He is promptly rebuffed by the strong statement that these two items, *kodoshav* (sacrifices) and the ancestral field redeemed by the priest, are different regarding precisely the matter that is determinative here:

> How can you compare these? His holy sacrifices are not in his doman/legal possession (*reshuto*), whereas this [redeemed ancestral field] is in his domain/legal possession (*reshuto*).
>
> מי דמי? קדשיו לאו ברשותו, הכא ברשותו

While the priest's sacrificial portions are not in his legal possession (*reshut*) since, as we have seen, they come from and belong to God (the table of the Most High), the ancestral field is in his legal possession – he did not acquire it in the limited way he acquires the sacrificial portion as a gift from God; rather, "here he takes it himself" (הכא קא שקיל ליה *hakha ha shakeil lei*), having legally purchased (redeemed) it, making it his property.

[71] Exceptions are made later in the Gemara, when the confessing priest does not bring the *asham* sacrifice and the compensatory payment during the same week.

The mandate of Num 5:10 reflects the priest's acquisition (*zekhiyah*) of "holy sacrifices" in the form of a right to eat from God's table; the priest does not "own" these "holies," as they continue to belong to God. That mandate is avoided, in the case of the ancestral field, precisely by distinguishing the priest's right to the sacrificial portion (*zekhiyah*), property that ultimately remains in God's domain (*reshut*), from the ancestral field that was redeemed and is owned by the priest (in his *reshut* and *tachat yado*). It is the priests among whom the ancestral field will be divided who are *zokhe* the field as a gift from God. By contrast, in the case of the robbed property of a convert, were it not for the analogy to the case of the ancestral field, one would find a right on the part of the thieving priest to keep the stolen property along with his right to (a *zekhiyah* conferred directly by the table of the Most High) the *asham* sacrifice that it accompanies, for it would then be exactly the type of ownership of a "holy" thing contemplated by Num 5:10.

Nor is there anything unique about the robbed property of a convert (and the ancestral field and sacrifices) and the way the priest comes by them as gifts received from God. The Talmud proceeds to bring all priestly gifts under this rubric at B.T. Bava Kamma 110b. Rava asks whether the priests receive the robbed property of a convert in the capacity of substituted heirs of the convert or as "the recipients of gifts" (*mekabelei matanot*) from God. After some discussion, the *sugyah* resolves this inquiry by quoting a beraita describing *all* of the items granted to the priests as gifts from God. The beraita states that

> [t]wenty-four priestly gifts were given to Aaron and his sons...and these are them: ten of them [are granted] in the Temple and four in [the city of] Jerusalem and ten [anywhere] in the provinces. The ten in the Temple are (1) the animal *chatat* offering and (2) the bird *chatat* offering and (3) the definite *asham* offering and (4) the questionable *asham* offering and (5) the communal *shelamim* offering and (6) the log of oil in *Metsora* and (7) the remainder of the *omer* offering and (8) the two loaves offering and (9) the *panim* bread and (10) the remainder of *minchah* offerings. The four gifts granted in Jerusalem are (1) the firstborn [animal] and (2) the *bikurim* and (3) the [portions] separated from the *todah* offering and [from] the *nazir*'s ram and (4) the hides of the *kodashim*. The ten [gifts granted] in the provinces are (1) *terumah* and (2) *terumat ma'aser* and (3) *challah* and (4) the first of the shearings and (5) the gift portions [of slaughtered animals] and (6) the redemption of the [firstborn] son and (7) the redemption of the firstborn donkey and (8) the [consecrated] ancestral field and (9) the *cherem* [devoted] field and (10) the robbed property of a convert. (numbers added)

עשרים וארבע מתנות כהונה ניתנו לאהרן ולבנו...ואלו הן: עשר במקדש, וד' בירושלים, ועשר בגבולים; עשר במקדש: חטאת בהמה, וחטאת העוף, ואשם ודאי, ואשם תלוי, וזבחי שלמי צבור, ולוג שמן של מצורע, ומותר העומר, ושתי הלחם, ולחם הפנים, ושירי מנחות; וארבע בירושלים: הבכורה, והביכורים, והמורם מן התודה ואיל נזיר, ועורות קדשים; ועשרה בגבולין: תרומה, ותרומת מעשר, וחלה, וראשית הגז, והמתנות, ופדיון הבן, ופדיון פטר חמור, ושדה אחוזה, ושדה חרמים, וגזל הגר

By implication, all twenty-four "priestly gifts" (some of which come from God directly, e.g., sacrifices, and some of which come from the hands of a human donor to whom the property does not belong, e.g., *terumah*) represent acquisitions that come (theoretically) from God to the priests.[72]

Thus, while the priestly gifts are, on one level, interhuman transactions, it is also true that: (1) what is given is understood to come from God's domain and as being given on God's behalf, and, (2) some of the time, the act also entails (or is preceded by) the (sometimes simultaneous) giving of a gift by the human donor to God. Twenty-four gifts from God are understood to be transferred to the priest in like manner as the robbed property of the convert, where God "acquires" (*kena'o* קנאו) the item[73] and where, with the human donor making the transfer at God's direction, God gives the gift to the recipient who is *zokhe*. Items ranging from food and money to real property devolve to the priests, in varying states of ownership, from full-fledged private property to property that is only "acquired," if at all, once it is eaten from God's table.

It is worth examining one more text that makes very clear the fact that among the group of things that people receive as direct gifts from God, some things received as such remain God's property (like sacrificial portions, which are eaten at the table of the Most High), while others become the property of the recipient, with rights of alienability and so on. Mishnah 2:1 in Tractate Bikurim states specifically that two kinds of priestly gifts, the tithe (*terumah*) and first-fruits (*bikurim*), "are the property of the priest (*nikhsei kohen*) ..." Mishnah 3:12 proceeds to list things that the recipient priest can do with this property (such as purchasing real estate). Mishnah 2:1 specifies, however, that this status of (at least quasi-) private property, does not describe the second tithe: "[t]hese rules apply to *terumah* and *bikurim*, but not to [the Second] tithe."

הרי אלו בתרומה ובכורים מה שאין כן במעשר

[72] Some of them, such as *terumah* (tithes), are explicitly said to belong to (i.e., to come from) God. See, e.g., Lev 23:30, 32, regarding *terumah* ("Any tithe of the land, of the seed of the land, of the fruit of the tree, belongs to God; it is holy to God.... Any tithe of cattle or of the flock... the tenth one shall be holy to God").

[73] Unless the items, like firstborn animals, never left the divine realm in the first place.

The Mishnah states that, whereas *terumah* and *bikurim* are conferred upon the priests as their own property (*nikhsei kohen*), Israelites are entitled (*zokhe*) to eat *ma'aser sheni* "from the table of the Most High" and, as such, it remains God's property (*shel gavohah*).[74]

Another biblical entitlement to eat gives rise to a lengthy dispute in the Talmud as to whether that which is eaten belongs to God or whether it is property that belongs to (becomes the property of) the recipient. Sacrificial portions and second tithes are not the only items that are considered to be eaten directly from God's property. A Mishnah in Bava Metzia is interpreted, in the Talmud, to make the same finding regarding a worker's biblical right to eat from the produce with which he works. The Amoraic debate over this proposition, particularly when read in light of the Talmudic discussion concerning priestly gifts described above, provides insight into what the category of gifts from God represents jurisprudentially, in contradistinction to other property entitlements.

A good deal of the seventh chapter of Tractate Bava Metzia is concerned with the parameters of the right of a hired worker to eat (while working) from the produce with which he is working.[75] During this discussion it is taken for granted that, like the priestly portion of a sacrifice or, as will be shown, the forgotten sheaves that are taken by the poor, the fruit eaten by the worker does not belong to the employer (the field or vineyard owner). So to whom does the fruit belong? This becomes the subject of lengthy debate in the Talmud, at B.T. Bava Metzia 92a as the question is asked,

> does a worker eat of his own [property] (*mishelo*) or does he eat of Heaven's (*mishel shamayim*)?
>
> פועל, משלו הוא אוכל או משל שמים הוא אוכל?

The latter alternative echoes the description of the priest eating from the table of the Most High; in fact, it represents roughly the same conception.[76]

[74] See the commentary of Nahmanides (Rabbi Moses be Nahman of Girondi, also known as "Ramban", 1194–1270) to B.T. Yevamot 73a, where he makes precisely this point ("And *nikhsei kohen*". We do not learn [about them] from [second] tithe, because [*nikhsei kohen*] are priestly gifts, whereas [the second tithe, *ma'aser sheni*] the Israelites acquire [*zokhin*] from the table of the Most High.)
(ונכסי כהן. לא גמרינן ממעשר, דהני מתנות כהונה, והאי ישראל זוכין בו משולחן גבוה). See also, e.g., B.T. Sanhedrin 112a (*terumah* in the hands of the priest is his property).

[75] This property entitlement is said to derive from Deut 23:25–26. Something that will be discussed later is the fact that the plain meaning of these verses does not correspond to this particular right.

[76] In order to avoid confusion, it is useful to keep in mind a difference in the contexts that gives rise to these separate but parallel debates about the nature of a possible gift from God. Regarding priestly gifts, the implications of this classification are raised while testing the

Because the characterization of the priest's sacrificial portion went unquestioned, those particular texts did not elaborate on this idea. However, the cases of the ancestral field and the robbed property of the convert did give rise to probative questions that can be aligned with the even lengthier discussion that ensues from the debate concerning the status of the worker's produce.

After much discussion, the Amoraic rabbis conclude that this question as to the nature of the worker's right to eat is a matter of (an earlier) Tannaitic dispute. It is determined that the Mishnah in B.T. Bava Metzia Chapter 7 regards the worker to be eating of God's food, while a separate beraita (also tannaitic) reflects the alternate position, that the food the worker eats is his own.[77] The Mishnah's view provides another clear example of a direct gift from God.

The produce on the employer's property that is eaten by the worker is not seen as coming directly from the employer. To the extent that the field owner, prior to the laborer's choosing to eat, had owned the produce, there is a step (in the nature of a legal fiction) that takes place when the worker puts the apple in his mouth. Between passing from the employer's ownership domain to that of the worker (like the robbed property of a convert), it is acquired by God such that it is from God's realm of ownership that it is given to the laborer. In this sense, the employer may be described as having been directed to gift the produce to the laborer.

The level or degree or nature of property rights conferred by God upon the recipient has no bearing upon the nature of the transaction itself.[78] The question of the worker's food is raised in the context of a query as to whether the worker can assign his "portion" to his wife.[79] Not much else is spoken of when discussing the ramifications, for the laborer, of ascertaining the proper classification of the property entitlement. In this context, alienability of the produce

rights (or lack thereof) of the human being initially in possession (e.g., the robbing priest and the priest who had redeemed the ancestral field). As has been noted, in the context of the laborer, there is no suggestion that the produce eaten by him belongs to the field owner (the "human donor"). What is at issue is the nature and extent of the rights of the recipient – the worker. Despite this difference, both situations involve property that may or may not be direct property transfers from God, in the sense that the property received by the recipient is acquired from God, after having first been acquired by God from the original human donor (such as the donor of the sacrificial animal or the owner of the field).

77 The Gemara appears to follow the usual procedure of regarding the Mishnaic view as more authoritative and, hence, of concluding that the produce eaten by the worker belongs to God.

78 While the dichotomy between eating God's property and eating one's own property is important, it is also worth noting the unimportance (to the theory of divine gifts) of the precise nature of the property rights of the recipient. The degree (or amount) which the worker is free to eat is discussed, for example, in Mishnah Bava Metzia 7:4 and 7:5.

79 B.T. Bava Metzia 92a. "What difference does it make? If he says, 'give it to my wife and my son.'"

למאי נפקא מינה דאמר תנו לאשתי ובני

happens to be the marker for ownership by the laborer (as opposed to by God).[80]

As evidenced by the large category of (24) priestly gifts listed in the *sugyah* in Bava Kamma, all of which have different rules regarding the prerogatives given to the recipient, there exists a range of different types of property entitlements representing divine gifts – from the holiest sacrificial portions (which only priests can eat and which they are entitled only to eat), to gifts that result in what amounts, essentially, to an outright grant of private property (with full alienability, carrying no sacredness), to a variety of categories in between (such as the produce eaten by the laborer, which can be taken by the laborer in the form of money rather than produce, but which cannot itself be alienated). In fact, one opinion mentioned prominently in the Talmud in Pesachim regards certain consecrated sacrificial animals (possibly only those of a certain kind and under certain circumstances) to be the private property of the human donor.[81]

The salient legal feature that is common to all of these cases is that the items pass through the divine realm on their way from human donor (whether of animal sacrifice or of produce before it is tithed or eaten by a laborer) to human recipient. The basic implications of that juridical event are as follow:

1. The property ceases to be (if it was) owned by the human donor, as it is (re)claimed by the divine lien.
2. The human donor's primary obligation is to God, and secondarily, by operation of transference, to the human recipient.
3. The ceding of ownership on the part of the human donor, like the bringing of a sacrifice, is tantamount to giving to God.
4. The recipient has an absolute entitlement to the divine gift;[82] it is not a right derived from ordinary rules regulating property but is part of the definition of the institution of human property ownership.

[80] As will be seen, different prerogatives are associated with the notion of ownership in different contexts. For example, although the produce is attributed to God's domain (up to the moment of ingestion), thus precluding the laborer from being able to transfer whatever rights he might have in the produce to his wife, he *is* entitled to take money from the field owner in lieu of produce, something that would, in other contexts, seem to indicate that the produce is his property, or at least represents some kind of a property interest.

[81] It is suggested that this opinion is intended to cover those animals that, if lost or destroyed after consecration, must be replaced by the human donor. See B.T. Bava Kamma 12b and B.T. Sanhedrin 112b. Of course, declaring an animal to be someone's property because they have a responsibility to replace it when lost or destroyed might not entail the same understanding of ownership at play elsewhere.

[82] Of course, there are different procedures for determining which individual person (which priest, which poor person) has this entitlement. Until that procedure has been carried out, once the property has been "given to God" (another procedure that varies), the property is

5. What the recipient receives can be characterized as a gift from God, and as a gift given by someone else to God that has been redirected to the recipient.

All of this is true without regard to the level of holiness, or degree of restrictedness, ascribed to the property either before or after it passes through the divine property domain (although this is a factor that can be relevant).

3.3.3 *Gifts to God, to the Poor*

Most of the mandated gifts to priests are aimed at supporting priests on a regular basis, chiefly (but not only) by providing them with food. There is a dual purpose underlying this scheme. On one hand, it is clear from the biblical texts that it is intended to establish a needed source of support for those – deemed "holy" representatives of God – who occupy themselves with Temple (public) service (and are thus unable to earn a living). There is a second reason for the priestly entitlements: because the priestly tribe was not granted land along with the rest of the tribes, they are presumptively needy.[83]

Along with gifts for the priests (and for God), provision for the poor and the needy (in a variety of forms) is another significant category of explicit obligations attendant to taking ownership and delimiting property rights in general. One of the regularly scheduled tithes is that designated for the poor, *ma'aser ani*. Along with the numerous priestly gifts, regular requirements of setting aside a variety of properties for the poor[84] – from a portion of the produce of one's land to tithes and other items for the poor – form part of the theoretical basis on which the institution(s) of (divine ownership and) human ownership of property is based.

The poor tithe, *ma'aser ani*, is given in years three and six in the regular seven-year cycle, in place of *ma'aser sheni*, which is given to God in years one, two, four and five. While *ma'aser ani* is a sacred tithe that, as we have seen, might actually "belong" to God, it is not considered "*kadosh*" like *ma'aser sheni*. Nevertheless, like the priestly gifts (which do not all possess the same

essentially held in trust by God on behalf of (the member[s] of) the group entitled to receive it. See, e.g., as stated in Mishnah Shekalim 2:5, "the excess of [property set aside] for poor people must be for poor people – מותר עניים לעניים".

83 See e.g. Deut 14:27 to be discussed below.

84 Such as *leket* (gleanings), *shikhechah* (forgotten sheaves), *peah* (corner of the field), and *olelot* (incompletely formed grape clusters). Also relevant is the regular tithe for the poor, which is not simply set aside but is actually required to be distributed to the poor (although there is a dispute in the Talmud as to whether the homeowner has *tovat hana'ah* (the right to choose the recipient) with respect to *ma'aser ani*; see B.T. Nedarim 84b).

sacred status but are all in the nature of gifts to/from God), the various tithes (*ma'aser rishon*, *ma'aser sheni*, *ma'aser ani*, *terumah*) might have different levels of sacredness but they all pass through the divine domain. That is made plain in Lev 23:30 and 32, which provides that "Any tithe of the land, of the seed of the land, of the fruit of the tree, belongs to God; it is holy to God.... Any tithe of cattle or of the flock... the tenth one shall be holy to God."

From their place within the broader rabbinic structure of mandatory gifts as conditions to initial or continuing ownership, other portions owed to the poor (*leket* - gleanings, *peah* - corner of the field, etc.) also share something in common with portions due to the priests.[85] They are linked to the same divine lien, which under like circumstances operates in like manner – requiring the human donor to forfeit property in favor of another person as a condition of ownership. It is for this reason that gifts to the poor, like other gifts described above, are exempt from tithes – they come as direct gifts from God. This is stated explicitly in a beraita at B.T. Bava Metzia 89b that deals with the laborer's produce:

> Come and hear: Workers who are picking figs, dates, grapes or olives may eat and are exempt [from tithing what they eat], because the Torah entitled them (*zikhtah lahem* – from the word *zokhe*) to the produce.
>
> תא שמע: פועלין שהיו עודרים בתאנים, וגודרים בתמרים, ובוצרים בענבים, ומוסקין בזיתים
> הרי אלו אוכלים ופטורים, שהתורה זיכתה להם

As the medieval biblical and Talmudic commentator Rashi notes, the exemption (from tithing) for the laborer is deduced from a similar exemption for a related category of gifts for the poor: gleanings (*leket*), forgotten sheaves (*shikhechah*) and corners of the field (*peah*).[86] Gifts to the poor, like the laborer's produce and priestly gifts, are conferred upon the recipients through the same legal mechanism of *zekhiyah* (entitlement); as invocations of the divine lien, they are exempt from the obligation of tithes, which represent obligations to make a (divine) gift on behalf of God.

In some contexts, the categories of gifts to the poor and gifts to priests are seen to be effectively interchangeable. For example, in the following texts, gifts destined for the poor may be given to the priests, and property that one might expect would be given to the priests is to be given to the poor. The

[85] While historians and biblical scholars might differentiate between the tithes that were for sacral purposes (Temple upkeep, sacrifices, priestly gifts) and those in the category of philanthropic gifts for the poor, in this sense, the rabbis did not.

[86] See Mishnah Terumot 1:5 ("Tithes are not taken from *leket* or from *shikhechah* or from *peah* or from *hefker*", אין תורמין מן הלקט ומן השכחה ומן הפאה ומן ההפקר) (Note the inclusion of *hefker* in this exemption; the relationship between *hefker* and divine gifts will be discussed *infra*).

former idea is not so surprising for, as noted above, the purpose of priestly gifts is, in part, to provide sustenance to a group of people that received no inheritance. Thus, Deut 14:27 states, "And the Levite that is in your gates, do not neglect him, for he has no portion or inheritance with you."

והלוי אשר בשעריך לא תעזבנו כי אין לו חלק ונחלה עמך

The Tannaitic gloss on this verse that appears in Sifre on Deuteronomy Piska 108 is noteworthy:

> "And the Levite that is in your gates" – wherever you find mention of the Levite, the intent is to instruct you to give him his portion; if he has no portion [due to him], give him poor tithe (*ma'aser ani*); if he has no poor tithe, give him peace offerings (*shelamim*); if he has no peace offerings, sustain him out of (*tsedakah*).
>
> והלוי אשר בשעריך, כל מקום אתה מוצא לוי הזה לומר תן לו מחלקו אין לו חלקו תן לו מעשר עני אין לו מעשר עני תן לו שלמים אין לו שלמים פרנסהו מן הצדקה.

This text assigns *tsedakah* ("charity") funds to support the priest. The next suggests that funds that are normally destined for the priests (robbed property – in this case a son stealing from his father – that cannot be returned to the heirs because there are none) are directed to *tsedakah*:

> Rav Yosef said: [the thief can] even [give payment to] to the coffer of the *tsedakah* fund. Rav Papa said [when giving the money to *tsedakah*] he must say, "this is the robbed property of my father."[87]
>
> אמר רב יוסף: אפילו לארנקי של צדקה. אמר רב פפא: וצריך שיאמר זה גזל אבי.

Priestly gifts and gifts for the poor show a common meaning. Being intended to support people in need, both are written into the very definition of property ownership. Both imply a limit to the property claim of the human donor and an effective claim on the part of the poor. Like priestly gifts, transactions with *tsedakah* pass through the domain of divine ownership. *Tsedakah* is not simply a gift from one person to the other; nor is the worker's food simply an added part of his wages. Both the worker's claim and the entitlements of the poor stem from a divine claim to property in the nature of a demand for return gifts

87 B.T. Bava Kamma 109a. Of course, the thieving son cannot keep the property as his father's heir. While this case is, legally, different in certain respects from the case of the robbed property of the convert, the recognition of the *tsedakah* fund as an entity that is functionally equivalent to the priest's right to that property (like the ancestral field) is unmistakable. In cases such as these, gifts for the poor and for the priests both represent domains that (perhaps like *hefker*; see *infra*) allow for the *de facto* return of property to (a displaced version of) the property's original domain of divine ownership. (I am reading the word *tsedakah* as the functional equivalent of all gifts to the poor. This move will be explained in Chapter 4.)

to God (demanded here in the form of property for the poor). The claims of the priests and the poor are based on (and represent) a continuing lien on property, a divine lien that inures to the benefit of the poor and the needy.

The idea that *ma'aser ani* and other mandatory gifts to the poor are, in this sense, just like *terumah* or *ma'aser rishon*[88] – is reflected, for example, in Mishnah Nedarim 11:3, which provides the following:

> [If one's wife vowed (*konam*) to derive no benefit from human beings (*beriyot*) ... she is allowed to benefit from gleanings (*leket*), the forgotten sheaf (*shikhechah*) and the corner [of the field] (*peah*).
>
> קונם שאיני נהנה לבריות . . . ויכולה היא להנות בלקט ובשכחה ובפיאה

Using the language "*konam alay*," the woman here, by way of a kind of sacrifice,[89] makes benefiting from humanity (*beriyot*) off limits to her like *hekdesh*. What the Mishnah makes clear is that, were she to benefit from these gifts for the poor, she would not, as a matter of law, be violating her vow and benefiting from *beriyot*. While these items might look like they are coming (as gifts) from persons (e.g. the field owner) they are not. Like tithes, *ma'aser sheni*, and priestly gifts, these gifts to the poor come from the domain of divine property ownership. Thus, when the woman benefits from them she benefits from property belonging not to any human being but to God.

That this is the logical implication from the Mishnah is implied by the language itself. The realm from which the wife may not benefit is that of "*beriyot*," which technically means (God's) creations and is almost always used to refer to humanity. In most of the cases in which the word *beriyot* is used in the Mishnah and Tosefta, it is coupled or contrasted with the word *hamakom*, or God. For example, an explicit, dualistic contrasts between *makom* (divine) and *beriyot* (humans) are made in a number of Mishnayot: Shekalim 3:2, Sanhedrin 4:5, Berakhot 3:3, and Avot 3:10 and 6:1. In Tosefta Bava Kamma 7:1, and in the fifth chapter of Tosefta Bava Batra, the terms are not contrasted – they are brought together as a pair. The idea of God as the second part of a dyad is, in fact, implicitly implicated in the word *beriyot* itself. The literal meaning of the *beriyah* emphasizes creation by God; the word *beriyah* (creation) inherently implies the *boreh* (creator).

88 Except as to questions such as whether the human donor has *tovat hana'ah*. See below.

89 The votive phrase "*konam alay*" comes from the words *korban alay*. With this vow or *neder*, whatever is promised by the individual becomes subject to the prohibition *bal yichal* (discussed in Chapter 4) and, in a way that is analogous to a sacrifice or *korban*, is a way of giving something to God. In this case, the vow means that any benefit she would receive from humanity would be like benefiting from *hekdesh*, God's property, and hence is prohibited. It is a backhanded way for making the vowed goods (here, benefit to her from humanity) into that which is sacrificed for God. Vows (*nedarim*) will be discussed more fully in Chapter 4.

By distinguishing that from which the woman *is* permitted to benefit (*leket*, *shikhechah*, and *peah*) and that which is off limits to her (anything that belongs to humans), the Mishnah corroborates the fact that, like the priestly tithes, the gifts to the poor are also gifts to God that are redirected to other people.

After discussing the cases of *leket* and so on, Mishnah Nedarim 11:3 continues as follows:

> [If one's wife] vowed (*konam*) prohibiting priests (Kohanim and Leviyim) from deriving any benefit from her, [priests] may [nevertheless] take [their tithe portions from her] against her will. [However, if she had] vowed (*konam*) prohibiting these [particular] Kohanim and these [particular] Leviyim from deriving any benefit from her, [those priests cannot take their portions but] other [priests] shall take [their tithe portions from her].
>
> קונם כהנים ולוים נהנים לי יטלו על כרחו כהנים אלו ולוים אלו נהנים לי יטלו אחרים

These cases, concerning priestly gifts, speak to the same question from the opposite perspective. Here the woman vows that the priests are not permitted to benefit from her. As in the first part of the Mishnah, the latter section delineates what goods are off-limits to whom, depending on the wording of the vow. Understanding this part of the Mishnah requires a short explanation of the concept of *tovat hana'ah* (literally, benefit of gratitude), which is the right to choose the recipient of a mandatory gift (such as which priest, which poor person, etc.).

It has already been established that priestly gifts (when separated and given over) are not the property of the human donor (they might, depending on the gift, be the property of God or of the priest). There is, however, one (non-property, albeit possibly monetary) right that the human donor does have in the priestly tithe: that is, the right to choose the particular priestly recipient. "*Tovat hana'ah*"[90] is the one, limited "right" that the human donor has with respect to property going to the priests as tithes.[91] This right of choice explains the different outcomes in two cases or two vows described in the latter part of the Mishnah.

While the rule regarding *leket*, *shikhechah*, and *peah* is uncontested in the Mishnah, other rabbinic texts debate the question of whether *ma'aser ani* (the poor tithe) should be one of the items, along with *leket*, *shikhechah*, and *peah*, from which the vowing woman may benefit. That debate turns precisely on

[90] There is also a debate as to whether this right to choose the recipient, *tovat hana'ah*, constitutes a monetary right (for which one might accept remuneration) or merely the pleasure of being able to choose the recipient, which is also a "benefit" to others that the vow taker is not permitted to confer. See B. T. Nedarim 85a.

[91] See B.T. Nedarim 84b–85a.

an analogy with the priestly tithe, to wit: the question of whether the human donor of *ma'aser ani* has *tovat hana'ah* (the right to choose recipients) as he does in the case of *terumah*. (There is, again, no suggestion that the goods being given to the poor belong to the human donor.)

The parallel Tosefta in Nedarim 7:4 is identical to the language of the Mishnah, except that it adds *ma'aser ani* to the list of gifts to the poor from which the woman who has forsworn benefit from humans may benefit:

> [If one's wife] vowed (*konam*) to derive no benefit from human beings (*beriyot*)... she can derive benefit from gleanings (*leket*), the forgotten sheaf (*shikhechah*) and the corner of the field (*peah*), *and from the poor tithe* (*ma'aser ani*). (emphasis added)
>
> קונם שאיני נהנה לבריות . . . יכולה להנות בלקט בשכחה ובפיאה ובמעשר עני

The Jerusalem Talmud (Nedarim 11:3; 42c) examines the two possibilities presented by the Mishnah – whether or not to include *ma'aser ani* among the items from which the woman is permitted to benefit. Without much fuss, the Jerusalem Talmud concludes that *ma'aser ani* should not be listed with the other gifts to the poor, because unlike *leket* and so on, which are simply left in the field for any poor person to come and take (hence denying the human donor any right of *tovat hana'ah*), *ma'aser ani* is given directly by the human donor to the poor person of her choice. "The poor tithe is given by a [conferred] entitlement (*zekhiyah*) and the others [*leket*, etc.] are given by being left [for whomever takes them]."[92]

> מעשר עני ניתן בזכייה ואילו בעזיבה

The woman benefits from the donor's exercise of his right to choose which poor person will receive the *ma'aser ani*.

The Babylonian Talmud explicitly discusses the matter in terms of the question of *tovat hana'ah*. It concludes that some *ma'aser ani* (presumably the type of *maser ani* to which the Tosefta is referring) is merely left for the poor in the field, whereas another type of the *ma'aser ani* is distributed by the human donor to whomever he or she chooses. The latter category would, of course, benefit the human donor (in the form of *tovat hana'ah*) if it was taken by the woman; this could explain why *ma'aser ani* was not mentioned in the Mishnah.

[92] Contrasted with the word *azivah* (left) in one sense, the word *zechiyah* in another sense means the same type of property right for the recipient although the method of transfer from the human donor is different. The category of property left (*azivah*) for the poor is another type of gift from God that, incidentally, is reminiscent of Beit Shammai's view of what the category of *hefker* ought to entail (see *infra*).

From the perspective of the human donor, tithes and gifts for the poor are like priestly gifts in the sense that except for the possible right to choose the recipient (*tovat hana'ah*)[93] (which, if applicable at all, only applies to *ma'aser ani*), the human donor has no ownership rights in the property that is given. Like the property given to the priest, the property given to the poor is given as an obligation to give property to God, who "acquires" it on their behalf and gives it to the poor. At the moment the recipient takes it, he is taking property belonging to God, not to the human donor.

Nor do gifts to the poor differ from priestly gifts because of their (relative) lack of sanctity. Indeed, while some priestly gifts entail property that is sacred (even coming from the table of the Most High and at times continuing to belong to God until eaten), other priestly gifts are not sacred (or are less sacred) by comparison. Gifts to the poor resemble this latter category of priestly gifts that, though not considered "sacred" in the same way as sacrificial portions, are understood to have been given to the recipient (as their property) after having passed through God's domain. These gifts also represent a limit to the ownership of the human donor, and an actual property right in the poor (with the divine domain holding title – albeit without conferring what one usually thinks of as sacred status on the item, in the interim).

The notion that gifts to the poor are, legally, in the nature of priestly gifts and other items that are explicitly classified as gifts from God comes across during the Talmudic debate concerning the property status of the produce eaten by the laborer while working. After the Mishnah declares that the worker's right to eat is from the Torah,[94] the Gemara (B.T. Bava Metzia 87b) proceeds to search for its source. For on the face of it, the verses that are ultimately relied upon do not describe a prerogative that is limited to hired workers.[95] The rabbis cite as the source text Deut 23:25–26, which states:

> When you come into the vineyard of your fellow, then you may eat grapes as is your desire, to your satiety, but you may not put into your vessel. When you come into the standing grain of your fellow, you may pluck ears with your hand, but you may not lift a sickle against the standing grain of your fellow.
>
> כי תבא בכרם רעך ואכלת ענבים כנפשך שבעך ואל כליך לא תתן
> כי תבא בקמת רעך וקטפת מלילת בידך וחרמש לא תניף על קמת רעך

Initially, the Gemara attempts to derive the (more limited) laborer's right to eat from each of the specific cases (vineyard and standing grain) mentioned in

93 This might be a monetary right but is not a property right. Thus, for example, if a priest takes it, he does not have to return it.

94 B.T. Bava Metzia 87a.

95 The fact that the rabbis do not follow the plain meaning of the text, but restrict this right to the laborer, will be discussed below.

the two verses. Both of these attempts are rejected for the same reason: both a vineyard and standing grain are already subject to restrictions that are in the nature of the laborer's right to eat, that is, gifts (of God's property) to another, as part of the network of return gift obligations that are required as (pre)conditions to being able to own or use property. Ownership of the vineyard is constrained by "*olelot*," an obligation to leave certain (incompletely formed) grape clusters for the poor.[96] Ownership of standing grain is constrained by the requirement of *challah*, a portion that must be given to the priest from every dough.[97] Since an obligation that is in the nature of a divine lien already attaches to both the vineyard and standing grain, the right of the laborer to eat from this produce (which, like *olelot* and *challah*, is also in the nature of a gift to and from God) makes perfect sense. But these two categories (the vineyard and standing grain) provide no basis to extend the right of the laborer to eat other produce that is not already specifically subjected to this type of constraint on ownership.[98]

Like *leket*, *shikhechah*, and *peah*, *olelot* is one among a group of gifts that must, as part of the larger network of "return" gifts triggered upon taking ownership, be given to or left for the poor on a regular basis. Just as *olelot* (as indicated for example by the above-described *sugyah*) are seen to be in the same category of gifts from God as priestly gifts and food eaten by the laborer – produce that belongs to heaven (*mishel shamayim*) – in this respect the category of mandatory gifts to the poor is shown here, by implication, to be of the same juridical nature.

3.3.4 *Other Transfers Involving the Divine Realm:* Shemitah, Yovel, *and* Hefker

Gifts to the poor are not the only ostensibly non-"sacred" gifts that pass through the divine realm.[99] There is a category of transfers that can be shown clearly to represent the exercise of the divine lien, despite making property available to an even wider group of ordinary people, and that is: land freed up by the laws of *shemitah* and *yovel*. These regularly occurring curtailments

96 See Lev 19:10.

97 See Num 15:20.

98 It is interesting that, while the text is concerned about finding a way to explain the extension from the vineyard and standing grain to all other produce, it does not seem as concerned with explaining the move from "any person," as implied in the biblical text, to the more limited category of the laborer.

99 They are non-"sacred" in the sense that they are available to a wide swath of people and thus, in the colloquial sense of the term "sacred," they might be seen as less so than priestly gifts (including those that become the priests' personal property).

of owners' property rights might not seem as "sacred" (in the popular sense of separate) as gifts for the priests or even for the poor, given that anyone (even a rich person) is permitted to take from any one's land and produce during *shemitah* and *yovel*. Nevertheless, these institutions (together) represent the most powerful and obvious legal and theoretical expression of the underlying claims of divine ownership and concomitant limitations on human property ownership.

Every seventh (*shemitah*) and, even more extensively, every fiftieth (Jubilee, *yovel*) year the contingency (and fallacy) of across-the-board human ownership is laid bare, as a vast array of what would otherwise be considered property rights are effectively rendered null and void. Involving everything from the ownership of land[100] and produce to entitlement to debt recovery and even propriety over one's slaves, what occurs in the Jubilee – the periodic suspension of entitlements that represent the very underpinnings of the institution of private property – provides a clear statement that God, the original donor, retains a claim and regularly repossesses property. The combination of the broad sweep of divestments that occur during *shemitah* and *yovel*,[101] as well as the mandated returns to God that are transferred to specific people (e.g., priests and the poor), portray unequivocally the significant incursions of the divine lien on the very notion of (human) property ownership.

The institution of *hefker*, or ownerless property, is relevant here. Its two salient features are that (1) a property owner has the legal capacity to render property *hefker* (ownerless) by oral declaration alone (despite the fact, as noted earlier, that property will not normally transfer out of one's ownership domain without an act of *kinyan*, and (2) *hefker* is free; the first person to possess it becomes the owner. Paralleling the reversion of land to God (and thus, possibly, to all people), declaring property *hefker* – like orally dedicating property, taking a vow, or designating a portion of one's goods

[100] Rather than becoming *hefker* like the produce, land goes back to its original owners, which is in and of itself a strong statement as to the limitations on human beings' ability to decide who may actually own land. As noted above, some ancestral fields also revert to God and, from there, to the priests.

[101] While the goods freed up during *shemitah* and *yovel* might not be considered by some to be as "sacred" as gifts that, for example, may only be eaten by priests (or the poor), these more targeted divestments are part of what is contemplated, or at least known to be taken care of, during *shemitah* and *yovel*. For there are, of course, no mandatory tithes for the priests or the poor during those years. Indeed, unlike other years, during *shemitah* the priests (as well as the poor) have just as great entitlement to (*hefker*) property as everyone else and thus have no basis for any special claim.

as tithes – is another way for an individual to change the status of property by reverting it to its original realm of divine ownership. It is true that, on one level, property deemed *hefker* is not technically rendered "sacred" thereby; indeed, it is made available to *all* people. Yet, this is also the case with land that is retroceded to God during *shemitah* and *yovel*, which represents perhaps the quintessential transferring of property to the original domain of divine ownership. While this particular notion of giving items back to God is not like giving God a sacrifice (which carries with it a special sanctity that is inviolable), the practice of giving property back to God by giving it to other people, such as to priests, the poor, or anyone encountering Sabbatical or *hefker* property, presumes a broader (non-Temple centered) conception of what it means for property to pass through or be returned to the divine realm, accommodating levels of sacredness that differ across categories (from types of sacrifices – *kodshim kalim* or *kodshei kodoshim* – to portions eaten by different people to gifts to the priests and gifts to the poor).

There is evidence to support the idea that the legal institution of *hefker* arose as a late (Second Temple or post–Second Temple) development providing another means (along with vow or *neder*) by which one could, by mere oral declaration, give things back to God. Indeed, this *hefker* declaration, resulting in a status change of the property, might be explicitly traceable to the idea of making return gifts to God by *neder*. Shamma Friedman has demonstrated that the word *hefker* derives from the Accadian root meaning retrocession, or "to restore property (to its rightful claimant)" or "to be recovered by the original owner."[102] Along the same lines, E. E. Urbach has suggested that the legal institution of *hefker* developed relatively late as a response to the great need that was created when the "door" permitting the (physical) giving of gifts to God was shut with the destruction of the Temple.[103]

The legal domain of property that is *hefker*, owned by no human being, is, perhaps, precisely what one might imagine as the original (divine) realm from which all gifts from God – all property – came. Nor does the availability of *hefker* to all people suggest a lack of divine direction in terms of its allocation.

[102] Shamma Yehuda Friedman, "*Ha-Milon Ha-Mechkari L'lashon Ha'Ivrit Shel Hatanaaim: Erech Hevker/Hefker; Bikoret* [Hebrew: "The Scholars' Dictionary of Tannaitic Hebrew: A Critique of the Entry: *Hefqer/Hevker*"], *Sidra: A Journal for the Study of Rabbinic Literature* 12 (1996), p. 113.

[103] See Ephraim E. Urbach, "'*Hefker*' – On the Place of *Derelictio* in Historical Reality" [Hebrew], *Shenaton Ha-Mishpat Ha-Ivri* 6–7 (1979–1980), pp. 17–28. (Also appearing in Ephraim E. Urbach, *Me'Olamam Shel Chachamim* [Hebrew: The World of the Sages: Collected Studies]), Jerusalem: Magnes Press [1988], pp. 257–268).

To the contrary, the fact that upon reversion to God it becomes equally available to all people says something about the divine plan regarding property entitlements. Indeed, there was a very early debate between Beit Hillel and Beit Shammai regarding the meaning of *hefker* that supports the idea that *hefker* is explicitly in the category of return gifts to God that take the form of the relinquishment of property to a large group of people.

The question of what, precisely, is the statement made by the possibility of returning property to its original (divine) domain by declaring it *hefker* is exactly what Beit Hillel and Beit Shammai disagreed about in Mishnah Peah 6:1:

> The House of Shammai says, "[property proclaimed to be] ownerless (*hefker*) for the benefit of the poor is deemed ownerless (*hefker*)," and the House of Hillel says, "it can only be deemed ownerless (*hefker*) if it is proclaimed ownerless (*hefker*) [also] for the benefit of the rich, as is the case with Sabbatical year [produce]...
>
> בית שמאי אומרים הבקר לעניים הבקר ובית הלל אומרים אינו הבקר עד שיבקר אף לעשירים כשמטה

The Gemara explains that this debate is a disagreement as to whether property rendered *hefker* is like *shemitah* (available to all, rich and poor alike[104]) or like *peah* (property that is earmarked for the poor). Both institutions (*shemitah* and *peah*) make normative statements about property entitlements regarding property that has been returned to their original state: *shemitah* suggests that property should be equally available to all, and *peah* suggests that it must be made available only for the poor. The confusion regarding the institution of *hefker* seems quite plausible; as yet another way (like *shemitah*) of relinquishing property to its original, divine realm, *hefker* could (as it does) have followed the example of *shemitah*; on the other hand, given the strong (divine) impulse for making property transfers to God into gifts for the poor, it also seems appropriate to go with the Beit Shammai's definition. Their version of how *hefker* should be understood would satisfy the clear agenda in the divine property plan (that will be developed more fully below), that uses the mechanism of return gifts or reversionary interests in the divine to advance an underlying plan of distributive justice that calls for aiding the poor and the needy.

104 The question of how the institutions of *hefker* and *shemitah* fit into the broader theory of divine gifts and the theory of distributive justice that calls for gifts to the poor is more complicated than appears here. See, e.g., Exod 23:11 – "but in the seventh year you shall let it rest and lie fallow, *so that the poor of your people may eat*" (emphasis added) והשביעת תשמטנה ונטשתה ואכלו אביני עמך:

3.4 THE DISTINCT LEGAL CATEGORY OF "DIVINE GIFTS": DISTRIBUTIVE JUSTICE INSTANTIATED IN THE DEFINITION OF PROPERTY OWNERSHIP

Two different types of property claims are suggested by Rava in B.T. Bava Kamma 110 when he inquires as to the legal capacity in which the priests acquire the robbed property of a convert. Are the priests to be considered as (stand-in) heirs of the convert, or are they to be considered gift recipients (*mekabelei matanot*)? This contrast, drawn by Rava, highlights the distinct jurisprudential status of an entitlement conceived as a gift from God.[105]

A categorical contrast similar to that between the erstwhile heir and the gift recipient underlies the debate about the laborer's right to eat; indeed, this is precisely the axis upon which the Talmudic argument over ownership of the produce eaten by the laborer turns.

The possibility that the food eaten by the worker is "his" (as opposed to God's, from whose domain it comes as a gift to the worker) is understood, in a straightforward way, to mean that it is something *earned* by the worker, as a part of his wage; it represents a property obligation flowing directly between the employer and the worker, emerging naturally from their relationship and in accordance with the usual principles of just deserts that lace the institutions of contract and property law.[106] Hence the first assumption made by the text, that if the produce was "his" (part of his salary), its value must implicitly bear a reasonable relationship to the work performed.[107] Along these lines, the text implies elsewhere that if the property was "his," rather than God's, the worker would be considered tantamount to a purchaser (having "purchased" the produce with his labor) as opposed to a gift recipient.

[105] The two separate juridical elements entailed in the transfer of priestly gifts from the donor to God (in cases in which the property initially belongs to the donor) and subsequently from God to the priests are described most openly in connection with one particular priestly gift seen earlier, that is: the robbed property of a convert who died without heirs. The concrete description results partly from a hermeneutic clue (Num 5:8 states that "the returned guilt payment is *for the Lord*, for the priest ..."), (emphasis added), but it is clearly seen as paradigmatic of the 24 priestly gifts listed in the ensuing beraita.

[106] The question of who owns the produce that the worker eats does, by implication, speak to the question of the nature of the field owner's obligation as well. If the produce belonged to the laborer, there is no reason to assume that the payment was anything other than a payment of the employer's property to the laborer.

[107] B.T. Bava Metzia 92a. The Gemara does go on to assert that, even if the property is a gift from God, one would assume, on the basis of principles of fairness, that God would not gift an amount that is greatly disproportionate to the service provided by the laborer. Concerns about fairness and unjust enrichment are, however, categorically different. The text reflects an implicit expectation, emerging from the very notion of a salary, that the property received by the worker bears some relation to the amount of work performed.

The juridical conception of a "gift" transfer (as opposed to payment earned by a worker or owed to a deserving heir) is of an entitlement that would not otherwise flow from the general rules regarding employment relations (or devolution of property). That which the laborer eats (or the priest receives) is his because it is a divine grant or gift of property. As is true with respect to the priestly portion of a sacrifice, only that which is eaten by the laborer belongs to him; there exists no prior or residual property right for the laborer to transfer to another.[108]

Moreover, the required payment does not reflect the regulation of property belonging to the employer.[109] Rather, the employer's property rights are automatically curtailed the moment the worker takes a bite of the apple. For at that moment, a divine lien on the field owner's property kicks in, and ownership of the produce returns to God, from whom it is received by the laborer.

The notion that the priest might receive the robbed property of a convert because he stands in the shoes of the absent heirs (while different in terms of form and other legal implications) parallels that of the laborer eating his own produce in the field. In each case, the property is understood as an entitlement that devolves to the recipient by the usual operation of property or contract law (once the produce is characterized as salary or, in the other case, when the priest is deemed an heir). In the end it is decided that the ordinary rules of human property law do not dictate the outcomes in these cases. Instead, God is understood, after having "(re)acquired" the property, to have directed the robber or field owner to make a property transfer to the priest or laborer and granted it to the priest.

The debates in these cases make obvious the fact that the priestly gifts (and other analogous entitlements) come from a separate legal realm. A clear contrast is drawn between juridical entitlements that derive from the principles governing the ordinary legal institutions that regulate human property ownership, on the one hand, and a direct acquisition/gift from God on the other. It

[108] I use various terms throughout this chapter to refer to gifts that somehow pass through the divine realm of ownership. I loosely use the term "divine gifts" for all transfers in that category. I speak of gifts to God and of gifts from God, either of which can represent an independent and unilateral transfer directly to or from God. However, I also use these terms to describe what is, in essence, a gift to and from God, that is, a transaction in which property passes from human donor to human recipient in two steps, with God, acquiring and gifting the property, imagined as a third player in between them.

[109] Of course, the very existence of the question as to who owns the produce eaten by the worker does, by implication, speak to the field owner's interest therein and the nature of his obligation. If the produce were deemed to belong to the laborer, there would be no reason to assume that the payment was anything other than a payment of the employer's property to the employer; the realm of divine ownership would not be implicated.

is in contrast to the normal (interhuman) property claims that the nature of the claim resulting from a divine gift is to be understood.

Another way to understand the priestly gift or the laborer's right to eat in the field is to see it as a boundary or limit to someone else's property right, as the human donor, in each case, cedes (or, more properly, retrocedes) ownership (back) to God. As opposed, for example, to an earned salary,[110] a gift from God is a property entitlement that supersedes (and precedes) the normal stream of interhuman property relations. Hooking into the divine lien (and what might be understood as the human donor's obligation to make a return, as described by Mauss), these property transfers do not come about as a result of the usual operation of law. They are understood as entitlements that derive from some separate calculation, on the part of the divine, as to who is entitled to what – a particular, substantive vision of distributive justice (*tsedek*).

In the rabbinic imagination, what undergirds the institution of private property is a set of property claims that can be traced to a direct allocation by God. Whatever might be thought to have guided the divine decision regarding initial distributions of property to the tribes, the principles at work with respect to redistribution are very clear: (1) in the Jubilee year, the land is reclaimed by the divine and returned to its original grantees, and (2) in a variety of contexts, property goes (from God) to those in need, such as to priests and to the poor.

Like the return of land to the original owners, the latter type of gifts, or grants of property from God, imposes a categorical (in this case, substantive rather than formal) qualification on the ordinary commercial workings of society (not mere regulations thereof). While gifts to the priests, sacrifices, and other mandatory tithes (such as *ma'aser sheni*) were thought to perform a utilitarian function in sustaining the Temple infrastructure in Jerusalem, the category of gifts to the poor – also a foundational component of the divinely mandated scheme of property and obligations – was based on or defined by particular principles of justice.[111] This *sui generis* legal category, operating on an internally consistent theory of justice, erected a framework within which (even a market) society could operate (more) fairly.

110 The implicit question this matter raises concerning payment of a salary to a rabbi and others who devote their time to doing work that is a *mitzvah* was the subject of intense debate among medieval scholars such as Maimonides and Nachmanides. This will be discussed in Chapter 4.

111 While I describe this category as operating on a substantive view of justice (as is clear from the internal rules governing these grants), this does not preclude a view that would see a utilitarian purpose underlying the mandate to keep people alive.

The initiative of demanding interhuman gifts (tied to or anchored in divine grants of property) to meet a particular view of distributive justice was expressly included as part of the initial distribution of land to the tribes. According to Num 35:1–2, God did not grant a portion of property to the Levites, but did direct that care be taken of them:

> And the Lord spoke to Moshe … saying, *Command the children of Israel, that they shall give to the Levites of the inheritance of their (own) possession* (*minachalat achuzatam*) cities to dwell in; and *you shall give also to the Levites* an open space for the cities around them (emphasis added).[112]
>
> וידבר ה' אל משה . . . לאמר צו את בני ישראל ונתנו ללוים מנחלת אחזתם ערים לשבת ומגרש לערים סביבתיהם תתנו ללוים

As has been noted, that which must be given to the Levites is premised on a claim tied to their relative lack of possession.[113] Wealth disparity, and the mandate to ensure that all have sufficient resources with which to live, was the explanation for the many categories of mandatory gifts to the poor and to the priests. Such property entitlements, whether mandatory or voluntary, established the principle of distributive justice as a significant theoretical qualifier to basic legal institutions that are, for the most part, otherwise class blind.

Whereas the usual rules of the justice system explicitly dictate that one must not favor the poor,[114] there is an altogether different conception of justice in the foundational understanding of property rights (reflected explicitly in the institutions tied to divine gift giving) according to which recognition of wealth disparity is critical. Moreover, it is relevant not only in determining entitlements, but also in determining obligation. For example, the mandate contained in Num 35:8, that the Israelites "give" land to the Levites, includes the following directive:

> And [you shall do as follows in assigning] towns from the holdings of the Israelites [and giving them to the Levites]: *from those that have many you shall give many; and from those that have few you shall give few.* Every one shall give of his towns to the Levites in proportion to the share he recieves. (emphasis added)
>
> והערים אשר תתנו מאחזת בני ישראל מאת הרב תרבו ומאת המעט תמעיטו איש כפי נחלתו אשר ינחלו יתן מעריו ללוים

112 See also Lev 7:35; Num 18:8–29.

113 See Deut 14:27, discussed above: והלוי אשר בשעריך לא תעזבנו כי אין לו חלק ונחלה עמך

114 See, e.g., Lev 19:15 ("You shall not render an unjust judgment; *you shall not be partial to the poor* or defer to the great: with justice you shall judge your neighbor") (emphasis added). לא תעשו עול במשפט לא תשא פני דל ולא תהדר פני גדול בצדק תשפט עמיתך

This same progressive principle of distribution is at play in the implementation of mandatory tithes (given on a percentage basis), gifts to the poor, and, later, *tsedakah*.[115]

Rabbinic texts suggest that the rabbis appreciated the logistical difficulties in integrating the particular view of justice (*tsedek*) reflected in gifts to/from God as a juridical and philosophical concern within (or despite) the institution of private property. In constructing some of the limits on private property imposed by divine ownership discussed earlier, the rabbis were cognizant of the fact that those limits needed to be balanced against countervailing emphases inherent in the institution of private property.[116] This can be seen clearly, for example, in the Mechilta's comment on Exodus 23:11 (the verse directing that in the seventh year "you shall let [the land] rest and you shall abandon it,"[117]), which states as follows:

> [one might say:] and why did the Torah say this? Was it not so that the poor people may eat [the food that grows in the field]? If so, I will just gather in the fruit and distribute it among the poor! [For this reason the Bible] states, "but in the seventh [year] you shall let [the land] rest *and abandon it*," thereby telling us that, to the contrary. He should even make breaches [in the fences of his field to let the poor come onto the land freely]. The sages however,

[115] *Tsedakah* is not discussed in the Bible; it is developed as a legal institution by the late antique rabbis. Interestingly, this progressive approach is in sharp contrast to the annual mandatory payment of half a shekel that went not to the support of other human beings but to Temple maintenance. With respect to this obligation, the Bible states, "Everyone...from the age of twenty years up shall give the Lord's offering [of a half-shekel]; the rich shall not pay more and the poor shall not pay less than half a shekel when giving the Lord's offering" (Exod 30:14–15).

[116] *Prozbul* can be explained this way, as opposed to how it is interpreted by some as evidence of the importance placed by the rabbis on private property and free economic relations. But to the contrary, *Prozbul* is an example of the rabbis navigating the delicate balance between private property and the realm of divine, distributive justice that dictated that all loans be forgiven. They did so in favor of the concerns for distributive justice, by making it possible, as a practical matter, for the poor to receive loans. In fact, they did so utilizing the power they claimed as implementers and protectors of this divine dictate of distributive justice, and it is for this reason that their enactment did not constitute uprooting the Torah (*akirah*). This is an example of an extension of the theory of divine grants of property in the name of distributive justice, which underlies much of what the court does by means of the private-property-undermining principle of *hefker beit din hefker* (property declared ownerless by the court is ownerless).

[117] Exodus 23:11 provides, "but in the seventh [year] you shall let [the land] rest and abandon it. And the poor of your nation shall eat of it, and what they leave let the animals of the field [eat]. You shall do the same with your vineyards and your olive groves."
והשביעת תשמטנה ונטשתה ואכלו אביני עמך ויתרם תאכל חית השדה כן תעשה לכרמך לזיתך
As noted, the dictate to abandon it was translated, in rabbinic literature, in to a directive that the land be deemed *hefker*.

allowed him to keep it fenced in for the sake of *tikun olam* [keeping social order, lit.] repairing the world. (emphasis added).

והשביעית תשמטנה ונטשתה מפני מה אמרה תורה לא שיאכלו אותה עניים הרי אני מכניסה ומחלקה לעניים תלמוד לומר והשביעית תשמטנה ונטשתה מגיד שפורץ בה פרצות אלא שגדרו חכמים מפני תקון העולם.[118]

This text reflects the tension between the vast relinquishment (and undermining) of private property contemplated by the institution of *shemitah*, and the regular institution of private property. The maintenance of fences (perhaps the quintessential rhetorical image of the institution of private property) during the sabbatical year is permitted as a necessary gesture toward the stability and social order that respect for people's property rights provides during the entire seven-year cycle. The concern that this sensibility will be lost during the sabbatical year is what explains the possible permissibility of fences during the seventh year.[119] Just as symbolically important is the statement that during the *shemitah* year, with the Mechilta's interpretation, the Bible expects the landowner to actually make breaches in the fences to enable anyone to enter what would otherwise be considered his land.

There is another example, among the institutions discussed in this chapter, of the rabbis' sensitivity to the fact that, with these institutions, they are rendering a delicate balance between what can amount to two conflicting ideologies – strict rules of private property rights and a theory of distributive justice that allows for the transfer (or confiscation) of property from the wealthy (or everyone) on behalf of the poor (or everyone). As noted above, the laborer's right to eat from the produce with which he is working is said to derive from verses in Deuteronomy (23:25–26) – verses that, according to their plain meaning, seem to dictate something quite different:

When you come into the vineyard of your fellow, then you may eat grapes as is your desire, to your satiety, but you may not put into your vessel. When you come into the standing grain of your fellow, you may pluck ears with your hand, but you may not lift a sickle against the standing grain of your fellow.

כי תבא בכרם רעך ואכלת ענבים כנפשך שבעך ואל כליך לא תתן
כי תבא בקמת רעך וקטפת מלילת בידך וחרמש לא תניף על קמת רעך

[118] Mechilta d'Rabbi Yishmael Mishpatim, Masechta Dekaspa, Mishpatim Parsha 20.

[119] There is a debate over whether those eating produce during *shemitah* from the field of another must do so with the landowner's acknowledgment or consent (*betovah*). See Mishnah Eduyot 5:1; Mishnah Sheviit 4:2. This question also seems to reflect a concern about ensuring that practices during the sabbatical year do not lead to a complete lack of respect for private property rights (a kind of lawlessness) during the six other years.

With the qualifying caveats that one may not put grapes into one's vessel or lift a sickle against standing grain, these verses, on their face, would appear to bring about precisely the sort of social disruption that was of concern to the rabbis in the above-quoted Mechilta. A right of anyone to enter and eat from anyone's field or vineyard at any time would effectively eradicate fences and seriously undermine the institution of private property.[120] Where one might think to interpret these verses from Deuteronomy literally (as in Luke 6:1, Mark 2:23 and Mathew 12:1), the rabbis limited the right to the hired worker, thereby constructing a rule that seems designed to reconcile the twin demands of what they perceived as the divine design, limiting individual property rights to ensure that people are fed, while at the same time preserving the larger schemata of private property (except during the sabbatical year). In fact, the view that would read the verses from Deuteronomy literally, and the countervailing expression of concern for what that would mean for a stable social order that is capable of maintaining humanity, is expressed by Rav in the following text at B.T. Bava Metzia 92a:

> Rav said: I found a hidden scroll in the house of Rabbi Chiya, and in it was written [the following]: [the Tanna] Issi ben Yehudah says: [In the verse Deut 23:25] "when you come into the vineyard of your fellow [then you may eat grapes as is your desire …]," the text is speaking of any person [being allowed to come and eat, not just the laborer]. And Rav remarked: *Issi has not left life for any creature.* (emphasis added)
>
> אמר רב: מצאתי מגילת סתרים בי רבי חייא, וכתוב בה: איסי בן יהודה אומר
> כי תבא בכרם רעך בביאת כל אדם הכתוב מדבר. ואמר רב: לא שבק איסי חיי לכל בריה.

While the institution of private property is accomodated, apparantly for pragmatic, utilitarian reasons, it has an over-arching ideological and practical limit. That limit is embodied in the form of the continuing divine lien, and it operates via the kind of divine property claims discussed in this chapter. The divine lien, the original donor's lien, injects a powerful dimension of distributive justice into the very heart of that institution. Divine property claims and gifts not only operate as regular reminders that one should not feel that one is an absolute owner of one's property. They also build into the very notion of property ownership a theory of justice that is explicitly concerned with wealth disparity.

In the biblical text, two types of property grants are explicitly conferred by God with respect to the land of Israel – (1) direct distributions of inherited

[120] *Hefker beit din hefker* poses a similar theoretical undermining of the institution of private property. Although there is no room to expand upon it here, this legal mechanism is also deeply connected to the divine directive of distributive justice.

portions among the tribes (and ensuring their continued holding thereof with the institution of the *yovel*), and (2) a requirement that those with an inheritance give property to the landless Levites. These can be seen as models for the two different types of property-limiting obligations that have been discussed in this chapter. The first type is self-executing; it takes effect automatically. Thus, like the grants of property to the tribes, (1) the automatic ownerlessness of property in the sabbatical year, (2) the priest's right to the unredeemed ancestral field, (3) the priest's right to the firstborn animal, and, perhaps, (4) the priest's right to eat the sacrificial portions all represent property rights coming directly from (the table of) God, as part of this legal system's definition of first order property ownership.

The second type does not come directly from God, as it were. It entails a request (or demand) by God that those with property transfer some of it to those without, or with less. Like the directive that the Levites be given cities by those who have an inheritance, gifts for the priests and the poor (and the priest's entitlement to the robbed property of a convert) come from a human donor (to God and then as a gift to the recipient) at the request of God.

This second prong of what might, overall, be labelled "divine property law" is not limited to mandatory directives to transfer property. It describes a singular category of transfers, both obligatory and voluntary. The "divine lien" and the underlying concern of wealth disparity render certain transactions – even if performed voluntarily – as necessarily gifts from God. When gifted by the human donor, certain property, or property given under certain circumstances, is automatically taken up by the property claim of the divine on its way to the human recipient. The human donor gives a divine gift on God's behalf.

At the time the rabbinic texts were written, the Temple had been long gone. The rabbis saw gifts to the priests[121] and to the poor to also entail gifts to (and from) God. They saw, in these gifts to other persons, a means for the post-Temple continuation of this function of sacrifices – of retrocessions of property, of return gifts to God. The property transfers examined in this chapter parallel the function of the ritual of sacrifice, which operates as a type of *matir* – something that must take place before humans are allowed to eat from the sacrificial meat. Just as the sacrifice cannot be eaten before the animal

[121] In the context of discussing the equivalence (perhaps symbolic) of the actual bringing of a sacrifice and the priests eating their portions, after the destruction of the Temple, the rabbis note that, postdestruction, the priests had more property rights in their gifts than they had before. This helps to demonstrate that differences in the nature of the property rights received by the recipient of a divine gift (e.g., whether technically considered sacred or not) has no bearing on the way in which these gifts function in a way that is similar to sacrifice.

is given to God (by slaughtering, sprinkling the blood, etc.), so, too, is one mostly prohibited from eating produce until the tithes are separated.[122]

The mandatory gifts to (or to and from) God that are required as a condition or precondition to ownership operate legally, like the sacrificial ritual and tithes, as a *matir*, granting (relatively) definitive title to, or rendering permissible, property that one does not, in some sense, fully own. Whether mandatory or voluntary, these gifts pass through the divine realm.

The priestly gifts are, indeed, repeatedly linked to Temple offerings. For example, the sacrificial service in the Temple, which included a process of salting, was referred to, in Lev 2:13, as the performance of a "salt covenant" with God.[123] Similarly, in the final verse in the biblical passage that lists the twenty-four priestly gifts (Num 18:8–19), God said to Aaron, "I have given [them] to you and your sons and daughters with you as an internal portion; it is an eternal salt covenant before God." On that basis, the beraita in B.T. Bava Kamma 110b listing the priestly gifts says,

> Come and hear: Twenty four priestly gifts were given … in a salt covenant (*brit melach*). One who upholds [these gift mandates] is [considered] as though he has upheld … a salt covenant; one who transgresses them is [considered] as though he has transgressed a salt covenant.
>
> ת"ש: עשרים וארבע מתנות כהונה ניתנו לאהרן ולבניו וכולן ניתנו . . . בברית מלח כל המקיימן כאילו מקיים . . . ברית מלח כל העובר עליהם כאילו עובר על . . . ברית מלח

The giving and receipt of priestly gifts – including the act of the priest eating the *terumah* (even in the absence of the Temple, which was destroyed in 70 C.E.) – is tantamount to performing sacrifices in the Temple.[124] This is made explicit in the passage from the Sifre (Piska 116) to Num 18:7, which states,

> "I will give you the [Temple] service of the priesthood as a gift". Eating the *kodshim* (holy things) in the provinces is equivalent to [performing] the service in the Temple. Just as with the service in the Temple one sanctifies his

[122] Before the separation of tithes, the produce is known as *tevel*; eating *tevel* is considered a very serious transgression (although there are a few exceptions, such as the laborer's right to eat in the field and the permissibility of munching in the field *akhilat ara'i*).

[123] Lev 2:13 states, "You shall salt all of your meal offerings with salt; you may not discontinue the salt of your God's covenant from your meal offering; on your every offering shall you offer (*takriv*) salt."

וכל קרבן מנחתך במלח תמלח ולא תשבית מלח ברית אלהיך מעל מנחתך על כל קרבנך תקריב מלח

[124] Indeed, this text points out that the gift to God does not inhere only in the act of donation made by the human donor; the priest performing the sacrifice is giving a gift (on behalf of the human donor) when he performs the service (eating from God's table).

hands and [only] afterwards performs his service, so too the eating of *kodshim* in the provinces requires the sanctification of his hands [see Mishnah Hagigah 2:5] and [only] afterwards may he eat. Once Rabbi Tarfon was delayed from coming to the [rabbinic] academy. Rabban Gamiliel said to him, "what was your reason for delaying?" He said to him, "I was performing a [Temple] service." [Rabban Gamiliel replied,] "your words make no sense! Is there any service now[adays, since the Temple has been destroyed]?" He said to him, "God said, 'I will give you the [Temple] service of the priesthood as a gift'." Eating the *kodshim* in the provinces is equivalent to [performing] the service in the Temple. Rabi [also] said eating the *kodshim* in the provinces is equivalent to [performing] the service in the Temple.

עבודת מתנה אתן את כהונתכם לעשות אכילת קדשים בגבולים כעבודת מקדש במקדש מה עבודת מקדש במקדש מקדש ידיו ואחר כך עובד אף אכילת קדשים בגבולים מקדש ידיו ואחר כך אוכל. וכבר נשתהא ר׳ טרפון מלבא לבית המדרש אמר לו רבן גמליאל מה ראית להשתהות אמר לו שהייתי עובד אמר לו הלא כל דבריך תימה וכי יש עבודה עכשיו אמר לו הרי הוא אומר עבודת מתנה אתן את כהונתכם לעשות אכילת קדשים בגבולים כעבודת מקדש במקדש. ר׳ אומר לעשות אכילת קדשים בגבולים כעבודת מקדש במקדש

The rabbis set in motion a system that preserved the phenomenon entailed in sacrifice with more than just priestly gifts. With the practice of vows in general, and the giving of *tsedakah* in particular, the idea of sacrifice/gifts to God was thought to continue well beyond the destruction of the Temple. And it continued in both of the forms described above: (1) obligatory gifts and (2) voluntary gifts that hook into the divine lien. The conceptual backdrop of gifts to the poor as gifts to (and from) God continues, as does the specific mandate underlying the worker's right to eat and gifts to the poor in general – the obligation to keep people alive. This idea is on display, in B.T. Bava Metzia 88b, when the rabbis explain (somewhat comically) that there is a difference between the laborer's right to eat on the job and the prohibition against muzzling one's cow while it is threshing (two biblical directives that seem, conceptually, identical). They note that the former rule is undergirded by the biblical obligation to keep other humans alive. There is no such obligation with respect to animals because, afterall, "the verse [Lev 25:35] states: 'And your brother shall live with you', your brother, but not an ox."

אמר קרא (ויקרא כה:לה) וחי אחיך עמך אחיך ולא שור

The next two chapters will continue to examine the nature of divine gifts, with a specific focus on (1) situations involving the saving of human life, and (2) situations in which what might be gifted is part of the human body. Informed by the general theory set forth in this chapter, this more directed study will reveal what is really at stake in the context of organ transfer.

4

"And Your Brother Shall Live with You": The Divine Lien and the Obligation to Save Human Life

In the previous chapter, I began to describe the subtle but significant way in which the obligation of gifting property to God laces the matrix of relationships between people and property, and people and one another. A preexisting obligation to "give" to the needy (as part of or as a substitute for one's obligation to give to God) inheres in all property. Accordingly, this sort of "giving," which plugs into the divine lien, represents an act of returning to others that to which they are entitled.

In this chapter, I trace certain implications of this theory as a prelude to analyzing the act of organ transfer and the parameters and meaning of permissible payment in Chapter 5. The theory already interweaves gifts to God and to others, gifts from God, and property entitlements. What makes this task complicated and interesting is that, by means of the phenomenon of organ transplantation, factors that are otherwise separate are, or appear to be, elided: the giver and that which is given, that which is jeopardized or maimed and that which is saved, and the rights and the obligations of self-ownership. Moreover, the site of this elision is the human body, something whose status (as property?), character (as sacred), and ownership (by God or man) is itself not self-evident.

An analysis that yields a thick description of the act of organ transfer will help clarify these and other questions. In implicating the life and body of two persons simultaneously, organ transfer, by definition,[1] spotlights the inextricable link between body and life, and between bodies and lives (of different people).

[1] For reasons that will become clear, removing an organ from a live human being is only legitimate in a situation in which a human life is at stake.

In this chapter, we demonstrate the rabbis' conceptualization of *tsedakah*, in general, and acts of *pikuach nefesh*[2] (saving a life) in particular, to be in the category of interhuman gifts "to and from God" that implicate the divine lien, as described in the previous chapter. In the next, we pursue the implications of this theory to analyze organ transfer, including its possible status as obligatory (and under what circumstances), as well as the question of whether and/or what kind of remuneration might be permissible.

4.1 VOTIVE INSTITUTIONS: *NEDER, HEKDESH,* AND *TSEDAKAH*

What lies at the heart of the institution of *nedarim* (vows) is the divine lien, which animates the property transfers discussed in the previous chapter. It represents the theoretical calculation that, because God owns everything, a dedicatory gift (to God or to certain persons) entails giving back to God that which is already his. Not coincidentally, this theme comes across quite clearly with respect to donations to the Temple and, later, donations to the synagogue.

It is recounted in Chronicles, for example, that when King David was donating funds for the construction of the Temple (the worldly portal for the actual "giving of gifts" directly to God) he asks rhetorically,

> Who am I, and who are my people, that we should be able to make this type of freewill offering? *For all things come from you, and from your own hand have we given to you*.... Oh Lord our God, all this abundance that we have provided for building you a house for your holy name *comes from your hand and all belongs to you*. (emphasis added).[3]
>
> וכי מי אני ומי עמי כי נעצר כח להתנדב כזאת כי ממך הכל ומידך נתנו לך...
> ה׳ אלקינו כל ההמון הזה אשר הכינונו לבנות לך בית לשם קדשך מידך היא הוא ולך הכל

Historian Tessa Rajak provides evidence that such was also the conception of the donations that were made to the late antique Sardis Synagogue.[4] Mid twentieth-century excavations (1958–1975) revealed inscriptions concerning more than thirty donors to the synagogue.[5] These texts reflected the idea of donation as giving back to God what is his. Rajak reads this formula, of giving what are termed "gifts of God" being returned to him, as "an acknowledgement of God as the source of all wealth." Moreover, she finds this practice to be not what one would otherwise expect, since the average Greek donor in

2 For the sake of convenience, I use the phrase "*pikuach nefesh*" to connote the obligation or *mitzvah* of saving a human life. This phrase was not generally used in Talmudic literature, but began to be used by later rabbinic decisors.

3 1 Chron 29:14, 16.

4 Tessa Rajak, "The Gifts of God at Sardis," in Martin Goodman (ed.), *Jews in a Graeco-Roman World*, Oxford: Clarendon Press (1998), pp. 229ff.

5 The Sardis Synogogue might date to as early as the second century, with inscriptions ascribed to the third or fourth centuries.

any city in the Roman Empire expressed great pride in making a donation, thinking that they deserved to be thanked. Rajak thus concludes that, "[i]t can only be a wholly deliberate departure when the Jews declare that it is God who should be thanked." This is reminiscent of Josephus's description, in *Against Apion* 1.167, of an oath that is to be found nowhere except among Judeans alone …."[6] He notes that the oath is called *korban*, and that it "translate[s] from the Hebrew's language [as] 'gifts for God.'"

For the rabbis, every vow is (or is tantamount to) giving a sacrifice or gift to God's domain. This particular operation of a vow – changing the nature of particular property – is precisely what defines the *neder*, and as what distinguishes it from another binding verbal declaration: the oath, *shevuah*.[7] As explained by Saul Lieberman,

> [t]he differences between [the *neder* (vow) and *shevuah* (oath)] … are essentially theoretical. An oath … is a personal obligation to do or not to do something (I swear I shall do something, shall abstain from something), whereas a vow makes an item forbidden to the person (this shall be forbidden to me). The vow is a development from the original vow … when the man dedicated an object to God, which he could not consequently enjoy any more.[8]

Whereas an oath is a personal obligation, the vow operates *in rem*, altering the status of property, making it forbidden by rendering it to be (or to be like) *hekdesh*, divinely owned property from which a human being may not benefit. The status-changing capacity of the *neder* is its defining feature. Epitomized by the sanctification and sacrifice of an animal, the *neder* is the means by which a human is considered able (in a literal-legal sense) to gift property to God, to shift something into the ontological property realm of the divine (thereby changing the status of the property).

This is the theoretical import of all vows, including the particular type of *neder* that is the subject of Talmudic Tractate Nedarim – something also known as a "prohibitory vow." This type of vow is effectuated by the use of the word *korban* (or a substitute formula, such as *konam*), among other terms. It employs the language and legal mechanism of dedication to create a

6 John M.G. Barclay, *Flavius Josephus: Translation and Commentary, Vol. 10: Against Apion*, Leiden: Brill (2007), pp. 98–99.

7 See Num 30:3: "If a man takes a vow (*neder*) to God, or swears an oath (*shevuah*) to establish a prohibition upon himself, he shall not desecrate his words and he must do all that he has pledged (lit: all that has come from his mouth.)"
איש כי ידר נדר לה׳ או השבע שבעה לאסר אסר על נפשו לא יחל דברו ככל היצא מפיב יעשה

8 Saul Lieberman, "Oaths and Vows," in *Greek in Jewish Palestine*, New York: Jewish Theological Seminary (1941), pp. 115–143 at 117. Lieberman proceeds to note, "in practice the people seem not to have discriminated between these two terms." However, for legal and philosophical purposes, an understanding of the distinction is critical.

prohibition in the following way: the votary utters a pledge that declares that a particular item (the item[s] for which he intends to create a prohibition) will be a *korban* (i.e., *hekdesh*) when and if he benefits therefrom. What is posited is that the item will becomes *hekdesh* – something from which an individual may not benefit – simultaneously with its being (illegally) enjoyed, hence the resulting prohibition against enjoyment.

The aim of the so-called prohibitory vow is not to transfer the particular item mentioned into God's domain; in fact, the hope is that the person will keep the vow by avoiding its benefit, in which case the transformation of the property will never take place; rather, it is oneself, metaphorically – one's forgone bodily enjoyment of a particular thing – that is intended as the gift to God. For this reason, there have been differing opinions as to whether what Moshe Benovitz calls this type of "paradoxical offering" is to be regarded as an offering at all.[9] And yet, to regard the *neder* as merely something that creates a prohibition, to disregard the *in rem* nature of the way it operates, is to essentially nullify its theoretical differentiation from the prohibition-creating oath. Nor does the fact that the status change of the property occurs ("paradoxically") simultaneously with its enjoyment make it unusual in the pantheon of ways a *neder* is understood to operate.

Among the rabbis there was an early, and a continuing, understanding of this type of *neder* as one that, while prohibitory in intent and effect, was, nevertheless, dedicatory in kind. For example, Tosefta Nedarim records the opinion of Rabbi Meir that one who violates a so-called prohibitory vow is guilty of *me'ilah* (desecration of *hekdesh*), something with which Rabbi Shimon disagrees.[10] The very fact that this question was seriously discussed, debated, and answered in the affirmative by some indicates that there is no reason not to take seriously the plain meaning of the words used in this vow.[11] The use of the dedicatory language is unequivocal, and the use of the dedicatory mechanism is precisely what operates to create a prohibition.

4.1.1 Tsedakah *and* Neder

In rabbinic literature, only two types of dedications could be made directly to the Temple (rendering property *hekdesh*): (1) the donation of an item (e.g.,

9 See Moshe Benovitz, *Kol Nidre: Studies in the Development of Rabbinic Votive Institutions*, Atlanta: Scholars Press (1997).

10 Tosefta Nedarim 2:9.

11 Through close analysis of the votive formulas, Moshe Benovitz has demonstrated that all vows are dedicatory vows, including the ones that are prohibitive in effect – the vow results in a prohibition by declaring that the consecration takes place at the very moment it is violated. Benovitz calls this a paradoxical Temple offering and thinks that the rabbis see it as some kind of metaphor. I disagree, and would argue that they saw it as a real dedicatory *neder* qua *neder*, even if it does not result in *me'ilah* (as we will see, there are *nedarim* involving property transfers to God that do not result in actual *hekdesh* but that trigger the prohibition against *me'ilah*).

animal) to be used for sacrifice, and (2) a contribution of money or property (and persons?[12]) to Temple funds used for its maintenance and upkeep (*bedek ha-bayit*). However, the mechanism of dedication, the *neder*, *qua* juridical institution was conceived more broadly, to refer to the entire category of status-changing declarations including those described in the previous chapter.[13] This is made explicit in various rabbinic texts that each offer a precise word-for-word interpretation of Deut 23:22–24, which are the biblical statements setting for the prohibition against "delay" in fulfilling one's vow:

> When you make a vow [*ki tidor neder*] to the Lord your God, *you shall not be late in paying/fulfilling it*, for the Lord your God will demand it from you, and [if you are late] there will be a sin in you. If you refrain from vowing [altogether] there will be no sin in you. You shall observe what emerges from your lips and carry out as you vowed [*nadartah*] a voluntary offering [*nedavah*] to the Lord your God, which you spoke with your mouth. (emphasis added)
>
> כי תדר נדר לה׳ אלקיך לא תאחר לשלמו כי דרש ידרשנו לה׳ אלקיך מעמך והיה בך חטא וכי תחדל לנדר לא יהיה בך חטא מוצא שפתיך תשמר ועשית כאשר נדרת לה׳ אלקיך נדבה אשר דברת בפיך

In addition to what is known as the "do not delay" (*bal te'akher*) prohibition that applies only to vows, a second prohibition (applicable to both vows and oaths[14]) is derived from the phrase in Num 30:3 (quoted above), "do not desecrate [your] words." The plain meaning of this latter prohibition, known as *bal yichal*, (do not desecrate) corresponds precisely to the theoretical significance of the *neder*. Hooking into the binary of the "ordinary" versus the "sacred" (*hekdesh* v. *hedyot*, or in other contexts, *hekdesh* v. *chullin*), the prohibition goes beyond the procedural admonition (that one must fulfill one's pledge in a timely fashion) to the

[12] See Chapter 5, Section 2; see also sources mentioned in Benovitz (1997), p. 9n1.

[13] In its technical meaning, in the context of animal sacrifice, the *neder* is a pledge to give something (a sacrifice, a monetary contribution, etc.) to God, or to the Temple. The verbal act of transferring an item to the divine domain on the spot was called a *nedavah* (a "free-will offering"). However, as explained in the first Mishnah in Tractate Kinim, there is no difference between the two vows except with respect to the question of who is responsible if the pledged item (e.g., a cow) dies or is stolen – the person who made the vow, or the Temple. In discussing bird offerings, Mishnah Kinim 1:1 states, "whether they were vow-offerings [*nedarim*] or free-will offerings [*nedavot*], both must be offered in the manner prescribed for whole offerings [*olot*]. What is a vow offering? When one says 'I pledge (lit: take upon myself, *harey alai*) a whole-offering.' And what is a freewill-offering? When one says, 'this is [hereby deemed] (*harey zeh*) a whole-offering.' What is the difference between vow-offerings and freewill-offerings? Only that with vow-offerings one is responsible for them [and must replace them] if they die or are stolen, but with freewill-offerings one is not answerable if they die or are stolen."
בנדרים ונדבות כולן עולות איזהו נדר האומר הרי עלי עולה ואיזהו נדבה האומר הרי זו עולה מה בין נדרים לנדבות אלא שהנדרים מתו או נגנבו חייבים באחריותם ונדבות מתו או נגנבו אין חייבין באחריותן

[14] There is no room, here, to explore the theoretical implications of the inclusion of oaths in the *bal yichal* ("do not desecrate") prohibition.

heart of what a violation of the *neder* would entail: the rendering of something otherwise, or meant to be, *kadosh* (sacred), into something *chol* (ordinary), a state whose nature is understood precisely in its lack of sacredness.

The phenomenon of a *neder* (vow), which effectively transfers property to (or through) the divine domain, is key to the argument in this book. Hence the question: what counts as a *neder*. The rabbis turn explicitly to the task of coming up with such a list in the context of explicating the "do not delay" prohibition. Appearing, in slightly different versions, in the Sifre to Deuteronomy,[15] the Babylonian Talmud,[16] and the Jerusalem Talmud,[17] the rabbis parse verses 22 and 24 of Deuteronomy chapter 23 to come up with the following list of pledges or "gifts" that are covered by the "do not delay" requirement:

- (voluntary) vow and freewill offerings
- obligatory offerings of valuation (money) and dedication (of property) to the Temple[18]
- obligatory sacrifices to God (such as sin offerings and guilt offerings[19])
- gleanings, forgotten sheaves, and corners of the field
- *tsedakah*[20] ("charity"[21]),

[15] Sifre, Piska'ot 264 and 266.

[16] B.T. Rosh Hashanah 4a–b.

[17] These interpretations appear in full, and in the same sequence, in both the Sifre and in the Babylonian Talmud. In the Jerusalem Talmud (Rosh Hashanah 56a–c), only certain portions of them appear (sometimes separately, in different contexts). A fuller analysis comparing and analyzing the three different appearances of the same interpretive passage, in the Sifre, the Jerusalem Talmud, and in the Babylonian Talmud, although beyond the scope of this book, would be quite interesting. The Jerusalem Talmud sees the following as included in the Deuteronomic verses regarding *neder*: sin offerings, guilt offerings, freewill offerings, and contributions to the Temple for Temple upkeep.

[18] For complicated reasons that, for reasons of space, cannot be explained here, it appears that according to the Sifre (Piska 264), this category also includes some donations (*charamim*) made to the priesthood, not just for Temple maintenance, which is not the case in the Babylonian Talmud (B.T. Rosh Hashanah 5b).

[19] In addition to sin offerings and guilt offerings, the Babylonian Talmud includes in this category burnt offerings and peace offerings.

[20] The most similar, and extensive, rendering of these verses in Deuteronomy is found in the Sifre and in B.T. Rosh Hashanah. In both cases, two verses (verses 22 and 24 in Deut 23) are mined for categories included in this prohibition against delay, and in both cases a number of these categories are repeated (interpreted to appear once in each of the two verses). The most distinct difference between the version of this text found in the Babylonian Talmud and that found in the Sifre (which was presumably the earlier version) is that the Talmud also includes one other category: "*tsedakot*, tithes and firstborn (cattle)." Note that, regardless of this variation, both the Sifre and the Talmud include *tsedakah* at least once in this listing of categories to which the "do not delay" obligation of *neder* applies.

[21] When, for the sake of convenience, I use the word charity to define *tsedakah*, I put it in quotation marks to remind the reader that this term (as commonly understood in line with the Christian notion of *caritas*) is neither an accurate translation of the term (which comes from the word justice), nor an accurate description of the rabbinic understanding or meaning of this legal category of giving.

- tithes, and
- the firstborn animal[22]

In a separate beraita in B.T. Rosh Hashanah 4a–b (one that omits the Sifre's overtly interpretive hermeneutic), this category is set forth very straightforwardly:

> Our Rabbis taught: [With respect to t]hose who are liable for monetary valuations [*damin* and *arakhin*[23]], for *cherem* devoted property for consecrations [*hekdeshot*], for sin offerings, trespass offerings, burnt offerings and peace offerings, *tsedakot* ["charity" contributions], tithes, first born and tithe of cattle, paschal lamb,[24] gleanings, forgotten sheaves and corners of the field – as soon as one year [lit. three festivals] has elapsed [they are considered to have] transgressed the [precept of] "do not delay" [if they have not yet completed their vows].
>
> תנו רבנן: חייבי הדמין והערכין החרמין וההקדשות חטאות ואשמות עולות ושלמים צדקות ומעשרות בכור ומעשר ופסח לקט שכחה ופאה כיון שעברו עליהן שלשה רגלים עובר בבל תאחר

In all versions of the above-described beraitot, the category of *neder* is essentially coterminous with the category of gifts that pass through the divine domain, those constituting what were described above as divine gifts. Each of the items listed – gifts to God, to the Temple, to the priests, and to the poor – is transacted via a "vow to the Lord your God": a legal mechanism by which one changes the status of the property by theoretically shifting it to (or through) the divine realm.[25]

[22] These last two items of tithes and the firstborn (which are listed, as a threesome, along with the second mention of *tsedakot*) appear in the Babylonian Talmud but not in the Sifre.

[23] The procedure for making a monetary donation to the Temple was not a simple promise of cash ("I pledge X amount") Rather, it entailed the pledging of the value of a person ("I pledge the value of John Doe"). This rule is quite interesting from a number of perspectives (such as (1) the role of money in Jewish law – was it considered somehow uncouth to pledge an amount in currency?; and (2) the question of commodification of the body in Jewish law – this is a strange and ambiguous echo to the phenomena of humans as property and human sacrifice.) Also interesting are the technicalities of this procedure. According to the rabbis there are two types of such monetary donations or "valuations" that could be made to the Temple, both using the value of a named person as a measure and each signified by it's own phraseology. (1) *Damim* represents the (more relative?) price the person would fetch in the slave market. (2) *Arakhin* use the (somehow intrinsic?) values set forth in Lev 27:1–8, that are based on the age and gender of the person dedicated.

[24] The Talmud concludes (in the name of Rav Chisda) that the this item was mistakenly included in this list (it was mentioned "for no [legal] purpose"), since the year-long duration allowed before one is considered to have "delayed" fulfilling one's vow does not appear to apply to this sacrifice, which must be given at a particular time – the afternoon of the fourteenth of Nissan. B.T. Rosh Hashanah 5a.

[25] It should be noted that this is not an exhaustive list of all transfers considered to operate that way. There is, for instance, no mention of the obligation to allow the laborer to eat from the produce with which he is working. This omission makes perfect sense; the "do not delay" prohibition is inapplicable here, as it is a transfer of property that, by definition, must happen on the spot (while the laborer is working). Yet, as demonstrated in the previous chapter, similar to

The inclusion of *tsedakah* in the "do not delay" to fulfill your vow category is striking. Unlike all of the other institutions listed (many if not all of which were analyzed in Chapter 2 to conceptualize the category of "return" gifts to God), *tsedakah* is not explicitly mandated in the Bible; in fact, it is not mentioned in the Bible at all. Yet, *tsedakah* is unequivocally included among transfers effectuated by means of a vow. This is significant as it indicates that the pledge to *tsedakah* is the functional equivalent of a pledge to God. *Tsedakah* appears in numerous lists such as the one quoted above: it appears once on the list in the Sifre, and twice on the list in the Babylonian Talmud (and in other beraitot), either on its own or in a group with tithes and the obligation of the firstborn cattle, a version that overtly expresses the rabbinic identification of *tsedakah* with the category of gifts theorized in Chapter 3, earlier.

These texts, along with others, reveal quite explicitly the way the early rabbis constructed and conceptualized the postbiblical institution of *tsedakah*. Interestingly, it is almost as if the rabbis have smuggled *tsedakah* in and "biblicized" it. Of course, it is logical to assume that *tsedakah* would be classified in the same theoretical category as other gifts to the poor (the poor tithe, gleanings, forgotten sheaves, corners of the field, etc.). These passages demonstrate not only that the rabbis did so, but also the plausibility (if not the likelihood) that they did so with an awareness and intention regarding the full theoretical import of this equivalence.

As described in the previous chapter, the very particular meaning of a gift to God is reflected in an apparent incongruity of a gift that is obligatory. It emerges from the paradox of overlapping domains of property ownership (human and divine) and explains the mechanics of transactions between them. Inherent in the very definition of property given by vow is the idea of a gift that, by right, ought to be given. Such is also the understanding of property given by vow to human beings.

According to Franz Rosenthal, this is precisely the philological origin of the word *tsedakah*.[26] He suggests that at some point in the second century B.C.E., and possibly as early as the fifth century, the Aramaic word *sdk*, which meant right-privilege-grant-gift, was combined with the usual Hebrew meaning of *tsedek*, justice. In this original usage connoting "charity", what it meant was "giving a stipulated gift as the appropriate course of action" – precisely the sense intended by the notion of gift as voluntary and obligatory. The rabbis retain this more technical and specific meaning of *tsedakah*.

the priest who, when consuming tithes, eats from "the table of the Most High" (*ochel mishulchan gavohah*), the laborer eats of God's produce (*mishel shamayim hu ochel*).

26 See Franz Rosenthal, "Sedaka, Charity," *Hebrew Union College Annual* 23, part 1 (1950–51), pp. 411–430.

4.1.2 Tsedakah *and* Hekdesh

Tsedakah resembles other (biblically-enumerated) gifts to the poor; like those other gifts, *tsedakah* is a *neder*, a vow, a transfer that (theoretically) entails a (return) gift to God.[27] This point is made overtly in a separate beraita, in Tractate Arakhin, in which the rabbis are explicit in their use of the conception of *neder* as definitional for their conceptualization of *tsedakah*. In B.T. Arakhin 6a, an axiomatic statement is set forth in the name of Rava in the following beraita:

> A *neder* is *tsedakah*, but *hekdesh* is not *tsedakah*.
>
> נדר צדקה ואין הקדש צדקה

If we stop here, prior to the Amoraic unpacking of this cryptic statement, the only way to make it comprehensible is in accordance with the conceptualizations outlined here. Indeed, the statement essentially expresses this theory in the form of an axiom. And, in fact, in the ensuing text, later rabbis discuss the meaning of this statement as follows:

> What does this mean? Neither *neder* nor *hekdesh* is *tsedakah*! Rather, is this not what it means to say, [that] *tsedakah* is included [in the prohibition] "do not delay [to fulfill your *neder*]," but is unlike *hekdesh*, for [*hekdesh*] is forbidden to be used, whereas *tsedakah* is allowed to be used.
>
> מאי קאמר? לא נדר ולא הקדש צדקה! אלא לאו הכי קאמר: צדקה הרי היא בבל תאחר ואינה כהקדש דאילו הקדש אסור לאשתמושי ביה, ואילו צדקה שרי לאשתמושי ביה

On its face, the equation set forth in the beraita (*neder* = *tsedakah*; *hekdesh* ≠ *tsedakah*), thus explicated, sets forth, quite plainly, the way in which the rabbis understood *tsedakah* as a legal institution. Indeed, it expresses a subtle insight into the broader category of "avowed" items, one that embodies an important distinction in the rabbis' general conceptualization of the sacred:[28] there is a categorical difference between the level of sanctity (measured by the degree to which something is off limits to humans, and by whom or how many),

[27] A pledge of *tsedakah* can, perhaps, be understood as a type of "prohibitory vow" in favor of the poor. Other Talmudic texts analogize *tsedakah* and the *neder*. See, e.g., B.T. Nedarim 7a.

[28] On the historical shift of the Amoraim toward the synagogue as sacred territory. See generally, Lee Levine, *The Ancient Synagogue: The First Thousand Years*, New Haven: Yale University Press (1999), and the scholarship cited therein. Incidentally, although there is no room to explore it in this book, there are many ways in which the synagogue-as-sacred, and as a sort of substitute for the sacred locale of the Temple, parallel the postdestruction development of *tsedakah* as the possible theoretical legatee of the institution of sacrifice. Illustrative instances of these parallels include rules regarding the sale of the synagogue building (see B.T. Megilah chapter 4), and the status of donations to the synagogue that, in medieval times, were (in tandem with *tsedakah*) referred to as *hekdesh*.

as to which there is a range, on the one hand, and the question of whether something is in the category of gifts to, or to and from, God, as described in Chapter 2, on the other.

Thus understood, this short beraita represents perhaps the best global statement regarding sacredness that can be made in six words. It communicates that *tsedakah* has the type of sacredness attached to all property given to God (however temporary its presence in the divine domain, as it might just be passing through); yet, at the same time, the range of "separateness" sacredness is most clearly depicted by contrasting the two ends of the spectrum: *hekdesh*, which, once donated, cannot be used by human beings (with the exception of those who eat from the "table of the Most High"), and *tsedakah*, which is available to anyone who is needy and, as will be shown, possibly for certain other uses related to a *mitzvah* or perhaps even for communal purposes.[29]

Interhuman transfers such as tithes and *tsedakah* included in the prohibition against being late to fulfill one's vows (also) represent gifts to God (hence the status change in the vowed property), but in terms of being "off limits" to humans, they do not have the same "sacredness" status of *hekdesh* – sacrifices and funds for Temple maintenance. Whereas the latter point is made regarding *tsedakah* in the beraita equation quoted above, the former point is demonstrated by other passages, to be discussed below, in which the funds held for orphans (a category of funds that most resembles, or are perhaps a subset of *tsedakah*) are called *hekdesh* and treated much like *hekdesh*.

The evolution of the prohibitive vow provides another opportunity to trace the continuity between offerings to God/the Temple and pledges to *tsedakah*. For example, Benovitz points out that "just as actual donations to charity no doubt replaced offerings to the Temple in the popular mind, the prohibitive vow that took the form of a paradoxical[30] Temple offerings was

[29] As to this "separateness" sacredness (which is commonly associated with the very idea or definition of the sacred in the Jewish tradition), there are even levels of sanctity within sacrifices. For example, *kodshei kodashim* are sacrifices meant to go entirely to God from which no human can benefit, whereas *kodashim kalim* are given to God, who, in turn, shares a portion with certain human beings. It is with this sliding-scale conception of separateness sanctity that it is possible to make sense of opinions such as the one mentioned *infra*, that *kodashim kalim* are to be treated as *hedyot* (ordinary property). Indeed, an appreciation of the "relativity" character of sacredness helps explain a good deal in the Tractates of Kodashim and Nezikin. One thing that one might say all sacred items have in common is that they are not free to anyone to use or enjoy. It is in this sense that gifts to the poor – property that is set aside only for the poor or needy – are sacred even according to this "separateness sacredness" scale, pursuant to which they are recognized as less sacred than donations to the sanctuary.

[30] Paradoxical in the sense that the "offering" in a prohibitory vow will not technically take place unless and until the person named violates the prohibition established by the *neder*.

replaced by a prohibitive vow that took the form of a paradoxical donation to charity."[31]

Substantiating this claim is a fascinating passage from Origen, a Church Father writing in the second century, describing how a Jewish friend had explained to him the idea of a prohibitory vow:[32]

> Sometimes, he said, creditors who are faced with stubborn debtors who are able to repay their debts but do not care to so, *dedicate the debt to the poor*, for whom money is donated to the treasury by anyone who wishes to share (*koinonein*, literally: "hold in common") his property with the poor. They would say to their debtors in their own language, "*what you owe me is korban*," *i.e. gift*, "*for I have dedicated it to the poor* out of fear of God." Then the debtor, who now owes his debt not to men but to God and the fear of God, is forced to pay his debt not to the creditor, but to God, to the poor fund, in the name of the creditor. And that which the creditor did to the debtor, sons sometimes did to their parents, saying "the benefit which you would have derived from me, father or mother, you must now receive from the korban, i.e. from the poor fund dedicated to God. The parents, upon hearing that that which was to be given to them is korban, dedicated to God, do not wish to take it from their sons, even if they are in desperate need of food. (emphasis added)[33]

This demonstrates that the prohibitory/dedicatory vow described in Mishnah Nedarim continued to be used, albeit with property donated to *tsedakah*, rather than to the Temple.

Benovitz also brings additional, philological support for the connection between sacrifices and "charity" as gifts to God that are both transferred by means of a *neder* or a vow of consecration. His theory as to the derivation of the term *konam*, the substitute formula for *korban* in what look like prohibitory vows, is that it comes from the Greek word *koinos* (meaning "common" or "shared"), which refers to property donated to "charity".

4.1.3 *The Rabbinic Construction of* Tsedakah *as Quasi*-Hekdesh

Returning to the list of *neder* items, it is useful to examine the larger context of the list in B.T. Rosh Hashanah 4a–b. That, in turn, requires us to take account of how the rabbis were situated, historically, vis-à-vis this list of votive institutions. For while the list posits a group that is logically coherent (if not obvious), it combines legal institutions that date from different historical periods; in fact, it

[31] Benovitz (1997) at 124.

[32] Parenthetically, this passage also sheds light on the prohibitory vow (here called korban) mentioned in Matthew 15:1–9 and Mark 7:1–3.

[33] Benovitz (1997) at 123, quoting Origen.

includes many institutions that were no longer in existence during the rabbinic period. As for the specific institution of *tsedakah* being analyzed here, it is likely that the form it took, and its importance, during the rabbinic period was different from that of the Temple period.[34]

At the time the bulk of rabbinic literature developed, the institution of *tsedakah* was thought of less as an obligation incumbent upon each and every individual and more as a fund collected and managed by the community to help the poor. Given the lack of evidence (with the possible exception of tithes[35]) of the systematic fulfillment of the biblical framework for aiding the needy (e.g. poor tithes, gleanings, corners of the field, etc.) at that time, the *tsedakah* fund likely took on central importance in this area of social management and organization. This supposition is also supported historically by the increasing involvement of the rabbis in the community in the third century C.E.[36]

In B.T. Bava Batra 8–10, questions are raised that revolve around the inherent limits to the community's ability to divert these funds for other purposes – an issue that would not have presented itself with any of the biblically dictated set-asides for the poor (which were handled on an individual, not a communal, basis), nor would they have arisen (at least with a great degree of importance) with respect to the Temple *tsedakah* institutions of *kupah* and *tamchui*, which (at least according to the rabbis' description) were meant to provide for the day-to-day and, at most, week-to-week needs of the poor. Moreover, as will be seen, questions about the use of the funds continued, as *hekdesh* took on even greater importance in Jewish communities during the Medieval period.

The authors, or editors, of classic rabbinic literature lived after the destruction of the Temple; it can, thus, be fairly said that in some sense, through their literature they were "reconstructing" the Temple and its institutions (such as sacrifice). At the same time, both parallel with and derivative of this particular project, they were conceptualizing and developing legal institutions that were ongoing, such as vows, certain aspects of tithes, and *tsedakah*. The beraita at B.T. Rosh Hashanah 4a–b (see p. 126, *supra*) groups historically diverse items in the "do not delay" requirement. As such, it provides an excellent example of a methodological point that is critical to the study of rabbinic literature and legal institutions – that is, to properly grasp their construction

[34] During Temple times, *tsedakah* was comprised of two vehicles: the *kupah* and the *tamchui*. The *kupah* was a communal fund for the poor. Monetary distributions to the poor were made therefrom every Friday. The *tamchui* was a food bank, from which distributions were made to people without food every day. See Mishnah Peah 8:7; B.T. Bava Batra 8b.

[35] See, e.g., Shaye Cohen, "The Place of the Rabbi in Jewish Society of the Second Century," in Lee Levine (ed.), *The Galilee in Late Antiquity*, New York: Jewish Theological Seminary of America (1991), pp. 157–173.

[36] *Id.*

of contemporaneous, developing, and evolving legal institutions (such as *tsedakah*), an appreciation of the rabbis' conceptual, imaginative work related to the Temple is critical; the obverse is also true.

This perspective sheds added light on the meaning and significance of the inclusion of *tsedakah* among the biblically-based votive institutions. In the absence of the Temple, gifts to the poor were essentially all that remained of the broader theoretical framework enabling gifts and offerings to God. Without the system for aiding the needy that was constituted (to the extent that they existed) by poor tithes, gleanings, corners of the field, and so on, the institution of *tsedakah* – as a fund collected and managed by the community – was obviously central to this aspect of social organization.

While the obligation of *tsedakah* remained one that fell on each individual, the communalization of *tsedakah* by the establishment of a central fund, to be collected and distributed by members of the community, resulted in an entity (a pot of *tsedakah* funds) whose legal status had to be constructed or construed. Rabbinic texts concerning the rules of *tsedakah* amount to rabbinic construction and conceptualization of this evolving legal institution. As noted above, the *tsedakah* fund was functionally analogous to the biblically mandated institutions designed to help the poor, which were themselves conceived as deflected gifts to God. Logistically, the *tsedakah* fund bore a greater resemblance to another category of gifts to God – funds in the Temple treasury that were collected for Temple maintenance.

There was a basis for confusion about how to regard the entity of *tsedakah*. Their ultimate purpose was to support the poor, not to render a particular item *hekdesh*. On the other hand, being in the category of *neder*, as described above, the property transfer is hooked into the divine lien. It is in the context of discussion of these basic questions that the axiomatic beraita of B.T. Arakhin 6a appears. What is taken for granted throughout the entire *sugyah* and what is, indeed, confirmed in the beraita that equates *tsedakah* with *neder* is that the status of the property does change automatically, by operation of law, with the utterance of that statement or vow. Given *tsedakah*'s status as vowed property, the idea that there were limits on how the funds could be used before they reached the hands of the poor (i.e. while in that liminal stage, somehow in/passing through the divine domain on the way from human donor to ultimate human recipient) was also taken for granted.

Given the basic propositions set forth in B.T. Rosh Hashanah 4a–b and B.T. Arakhin 6a, which classify *tsedakah* as a *neder* pledge, in the same legal category as mandatory offerings to God and the poor, the next logical questions raised in B.T. Arakhin 6a–b, and even more directly in Bava Batra 8–10, have to do with the technical requirements of collection and distribution and, perhaps more importantly, the implicit limits regarding how these vowed funds can be used (aside from being given directly to the poor). The text in B.T. Rosh Hashanah distinguishes between their usability when they are still in the hands of the votary, as opposed to their status once they have reached the hands of the communal *tsedakah* collector. Specifically, the question was whether, and within what parameters, a community is allowed to decide to divert these funds for other *mitzvah*-related or communal purposes – an issue that would not present itself with the biblically dictated set-asides for the poor (which were handled on an individual, not a communal basis).[37]

The text in B.T. Arakhin 6a–b comes to the following broad conclusions with respect to this question of diversion. It is first established (as seen in the axiomatic beraita from Arakhin quoted above) that unlike *hekdesh*, no blanket prohibition against use applies to *tsedakah* funds (*sharei le'ishtamushei bei*).[38] Thereafter, two distinctions are posited, setting forth the parameters of the answer to the narrower question[39] of whether the funds can be diverted to another use (a question that is the subject of explicit debate in Bava Batra 8–10). First, a clear limit on diversion kicks in when the funds reach the hands of the "charity" collector.[40] It is agreed, as set forth in the following beraita, that

[37] Nor would it likely arise (at least with any great degree of importance) with respect to the Temple *tsedakah* institutions of *kupah* and *tamchui*, which (at least according to the rabbis' description) were meant to provide for the day-to-day and, at most, week-to-week needs of the poor. This same question did come up with respect to items donated to the synagogue. See, e.g., B.T. Rosh Hashanah 6b, concerning one who donates a *menorah* to a synogogue.

[38] The text states, "*tsedakah* is allowed to be used" (שרי לאשתמושי ביה). One other, technical distinction between *hekdesh* and *tsedakah* is also at issue: does the particular language used in the vow make a difference for purposes of the diversion or usability question? This question is resolved as follows: whether phrased as a *neder* ("I pledge that I will donate funds to the poor") or as what, in the context of pledges to the Temple, would be called a *nedavah* ("I hereby designate these funds to the poor"), the new status of the funds is the same. In either case it is the amount, not the particular coins, that is changed or sanctified (shifted theoretically into the divine domain).

[39] It is important to note that *tsedakah* is contrasted with *hekdesh* in the B.T. Arakhin text only insofar as "usability" (*leishtamushei bei*) is concerned. The simple statement here, that *tsedakah* is not *hekdesh*, goes no farther than establishing that the blanket prohibition against benefit (*issur hana'ah*) that applies to *hekdesh* does not apply to *tsedakah*. The other part of that axiom, deeming *tsedakah* something otherwise categorically similar to vowed property (such as *hekdesh* funds), and the question of lesser restrictions on its use – such as whether, when, how, and by whom they can be diverted (*lishnota*) – is yet to be determined. Indeed, the "divertability" question regarding *tsedakah* is answered in much the same way as it is with respect to a particular category of property that is explicitly called *hekdesh*: orphans funds – the "charity" collector can do with the funds only that which will benefit the intended beneficiaries (orphans and the poor, respectively.) (Regarding limits on the use of orphan funds that are, in some ways, analogous to the use of *tsedakah*, see, e.g., B.T. Bava Metzia 70; B.T. Bava Batra 8a.)

[40] Of course, there are other limits that apply to whether, how, and by whom the pledged funds can be used before they reach the hands of the "charity" collector, although they are not quite as stark or categorical.

> [If one says] "this *sela* [coin] is for *tsedakah*," as long as it has not yet come into the hands of the [*tsedakah*] collector, one is permitted to divert it; once it has come into the hands of the collector, one is prohibited from diverting it.[41]
>
> סלע זו לצדקה עד שלא באתה ליד גבאי מותר לשנותה משבאתה ליד גבאי אסור לשנותה

Second, the limit on diversion applicable at this stage is flexible (precisely how flexible is one of the issues discussed in Bava Batra 8–10) so as to permit uses that will benefit the poor.[42] Even a cursory reading of the relevant passages here and in B.T. Bava Batra reveals that the axis around which much of the argumentation revolves is precisely the question discussed here: Given the somewhat murky status of *tsedakah* funds as *hekdesh*-like, and the status of the fund managers as effective stand-ins or place-holders for "the table of the Most High," how are *tsedakah* funds to be conceptualized (1) in terms of their holiness/*kedusha* status (what, if any, limitations are there on their usability), and (2) in terms of their ownership status while they are in the liminal state of belonging neither to the donor nor to any particular poor person.[43]

What little textual evidence that exists for the Gaonic period suggests that, during that time, *tsedakah* continued to be regarded as a *neder*, with the same theoretical significance described above.[44] For example, one Gaonic Responsum (number 2 in *Otzar Hageonim, Nedarim*) states that, when dedicating something to *tsedakah* for the poor, there is no need to state explicitly

41 B.T. Arakhin 6a.

42 The text in B.T. Arakhin 6b questions the conclusion that diversion is impermissible once the funds are in the communal pot: "Is this so? But Rabbi Yannai [a *tsedakah* collector] would borrow [*tsedakah* money] and later repay [it to the fund]! [The explanation is that] Rabbi Yannai is different, for [what he did] was agreeable to the poor, because as long as [Rabbi Yannai] delayed [in repaying the *tsedakah* fund], he could coerce [people to donate more by saying that the tsedakah fund was short on money] and [thereby] bring in [more funds for the poor]." איני? והא רבי ינאי יזיף ופרע. שאני רבי ינאי דניחא להו לעניים דכמה דמשהי מעשי ומייתי להו.

43 There is also no room in this context to explore a much larger issue that is raised by this reading of Bava Batra 8–10, to wit: the implications of *tsedakah* and divine ownership for the developing notions of community power and authority. It would be interesting to explore the links among vowed property (particularly *cherem* property, set aside by the community), the divine domain, its possible link to the realm of *hefker* (abandoned property discussed in the previous chapter), and the great power that the court/community has over private property, namely the principle of *hefker beit din hefker* (that which is declared ownerless by the court is ownerless), a power that the Talmud (B.T. Gittin 36b) derives from Ezra 10:8, where property is threatened to be rendered *cherem* by Ezra. (Another biblical source for this principle, Josh 19:51, is also offered by the rabbis at B.T. Gittin 36b).

44 See generally Shalom Albeck, "*Yesodot Mishtar Ha'kehilot b'Sefarad ad Ha-RaMah* (1180–1244)" [Hebrew], *Zion* 25/2, (1959), pp. 85–121; Moshe Gil, "Introduction," in *Documents of the Jewish Pious Foundations From the Cairo Geniza*, Leiden: Brill (1975), pp. 1– 118.

that the item is dedicated to *hekdesh*; the obligation obtains once one simply states that the item is for the poor:

> One who *consecrates property* ["*demekadesh kodashim*"] to the poor or to the synagogue does not [need to] mention [the word] *hekdesh*, but rather can [simply] say, "this is for the poor" or "for the synagogue"(emphasis added).[45]
>
> מאן דמקדש קדשים לעניים או לבית הכנסת לא יזכיר שום הקדש אלא לימא הרי זו לעניים או לבית הכנסת

Similarly, other Responsa are said to explain that

> *tsedakah* is like *nedarim* and *nedavot*, (therefore, [one who] decides definitively in his heart to give *tsedakah*, even though [the pledge itself] has not left his mouth [he is] obligated.)[46]
>
> צדקה כנדרים ונדבות דמי (הילכך גמר בלבו ליתן צדקה אף על פי שלא הוציא בפיו חייב)

When it came to the early Medieval period, it would seem that that the definition of *tsedakah* as *neder* and, hence, as a kind of *hekdesh*, is the source for the label applied to these funds, which were called *hekdesh*. Indeed, this nominal identification of *tsedakah* and *hekdesh* elicited genuine judicial concern regarding this (possible) conceptual link and its implications, if any, for the legal status of *tsedakah* itself. In fact, the medieval rabbis took seriously, from both a legal and from a philosophical perspective, the classification of *tsedakah* as a form of *hekdesh* to a striking degree. On this basis, there were rabbis who ruled that the serious biblical prohibition against usury did not apply to *tsedakah* funds, just as it did not (in the days of the Temple) apply to divinely owned *hekdesh* funds.[47]

4.1.4 Tsedakah *as* Hekdesh *during the Medieval Period*

There is documentary evidence for the fact that, beginning at least in the early medieval period, roughly the tenth century, "*hekdesh*" (or *kadosh*) was the name used to denote money and property donated[48] to the Jewish community and the synagogue in Egypt, Spain, and elsewhere.[49] The term later came to

45 B. M. Lewin, *Otzar Hageonim* [Hebrew: Thesaurus of the Geonic Responsa and Commentaries Following the Order of the Talmudic Tractates], *Nedarim*, Haifa & Jerusalem: Hebrew University Press (1931) #2.

46 *Id.* at #4.

47 B.T. Bava Metzia 70a.

48 Funds also came from fines and bequests.

49 See generally Mark Cohen, *The Voice of the Poor in the Middle Ages: An Anthology of Documents from the Cairo Geniza*, Princeton: Princeton University Press (2004); Mark Cohen, *Poverty and Charity in the Jewish Community of Medieval Egypt (Jews, Christians, and Muslims from the*

be used to refer to community property in general, or to hospitals for the poor; but between the tenth and the fifteenth centuries, the word *hekdesh* simply meant *tsedakah* or, as it was also called, *hekdesh aniyim* (*hekdesh* of the poor).

In the Medieval institution of *hekdesh*, the actual funds or property set aside for the needs of the poor were generally collected from donations, bequests, and sometimes fines or taxes. Managers appointed by individual donors or by the community variously administered them. The institution of *hekdesh* spread from the Sephardic world throughout Europe, and its meaning evolved. It began to be associated with the place where care for the poor was provided: the shelter, hospice, or hospital for the poor. In the German lands, the earliest use of this meaning of the word *hekdesh* can be traced to 1381. In Spain, it began to be attested in the early fifteenth century. By the seventeenth century, communities all over Central and Eastern Europe had a *hekdesh* for the sick and the poor.[50]

Ancient to the Modern World), Princeton: Princeton University Press (2004); Yehuda Galinsky, "Jewish Charitable Bequests and the Hekdesh Trust in Thirteenth-Century Spain," *Journal of Interdisciplinary History* 35/3 (winter 2004), pp. 423–440; Mark Cohen, "*Halacha U'm'tsiut B'inyaney Tsedakah B'tekufat Hagenizah*" [Hebrew], in *Ha'Islam V'olamot Hashezurim Bo*, Jerusalem: Hebrew University (2001), pp. 315–323; Jonathan Cohen, "Charitable Contributions, Communal Welfare Organizations and Allegiance to the Community According to the Rashba," *Hebrew Union College Annual*, volume 72, Cincinnati: HUC (2000), pp. 85–100; Frank M. Loewenberg, *From Charity to Social Justice*, New Brunswick: Transaction Publishers (2000); Yom Tov Assis, "Welfare and Mutual Aid in the Spanish Jewish Communities," *Moreshet Sepharad* 1 (1991), pp. 318–345; Ephraim E. Urbach, "*Magamot Datiyot V'chevaratiyot B'torat Ha'tsedakah shel Chazal*" [Hebrew: Political and Social Tendencies in Talmudic Concepts of Charity], *Zion* 16 (1950), pp. 18–27 also appearing in Ephraim E. Urbach, *Me'Olamam Shel Chachamim* [Hebrew: The World of the Sages: Collected Studies], Jerusalem: Magnes Press (1988), pp. 97–124; David Fink, "The Corporate Status of *Hekdesh* in Early Sephardic Responsa," in B. S. Jackson (ed.), *Jewish Law Association Studies* volume 1, Atlanta: Scholars Press (1984), pp. 17–24; Yitzchak Baer, *A History of the Jews in Christian Spain*, Philadelphia: Jewish Publication Society of America (1977); Yitzhak F. Baer, "Hayesodot v'Hahitchalot Shel Irgun ha'Kehila haYehudit b'Ymei haBeynaim" (Hebrew: The Foundations and Origins of the Jewish Community in the Middle Ages), Zion 15 (1950), pp. 1–41. Moshe Gil, *Documents of the Jewish Pious Foundations from the Cairo Geniza*, Leiden: Brill (1975); S. D. Goitein, "The Local Jewish Community in the Light of the Cairo Geniza Records," *Journal of Jewish Studies* 12/3–4 (1960), pp. 133–158; S. D. Goitein, "Jewish Community Organization in the Light of the Cairo Geniza Documents" [Hebrew], *Zion* 26/2 (1960), pp. 170–179; Shalom Albeck, "*Yesodot Mishtar Ha'kehilot b'Sefard ad Ha-RaMah* (1180–1244)" [Hebrew], *Zion* 25/2 (1959), pp. 85–121; Jacob R. Marcus, *Communal Sick-Care in the German Ghetto*, Cincinnati: Hebrew Union College Press (1946); Salo Baron, *The Jewish Community*, volume 2, Philadelphia: Jewish Publication Society of America (1941), pp. 266, 329–329; Ephraim Frisch, *An Historical Survey of Jewish Philanthropy*, New York: MacMillan Company (1924).

50 This is a very brief recitation of the history of the legal institution of *hekdesh* during the medieval period. Note that, in this discussion, I do not purport to present a concrete account of the realia of the institution of Medieval *hekdesh*. As was true with my examination of rabbinic literature, my work looks chiefly at the literature of the medieval rabbis and should not be construed as presenting a picture of the life on the ground in medieval Jewish communities. Of course there are historical implications that could be drawn from rabbinic literature, albeit with great methodological

Surprisingly, there is not much secondary literature regarding medieval *hekdesh*. There are two primary sets of sources for studying this phenomenon in the tenth through the fourteenth centuries, and how it was variously conceived. There is a wealth of documents from the Cairo Genizah that provide direct evidence of its use and its institutionalization in Fustat, Egypt, in the ninth through the twelfth centuries.[51] The other literary source regarding *hekdesh* is Responsa, the predominant genre of Jewish legal literature from the medieval period.

A number of contemporary scholars, such as Moshe Gil and Yom Tov Assis, have studied these texts and, in speculating as to the origin of the institution of *hekdesh*, have compared it variously to the Islamic waqf and to the Christian pious foundation, respectively. However, the comparative research does not sufficiently explain the phenomenon of *hekdesh*, particularly in terms of its legal (possibly sacred) status.

The primary sources reveal an ambiguity in the eyes of the rabbis regarding the legal status of these funds.[52] It is clear from the medieval codes and from the way the medieval decisions were couched that these were not like ordinary funds.[53] Questions posed to rabbinic decisors[54] ranged from whether *hekdesh*[55]

caution. See, e.g., Haym Soloveitchik, "Can Halakhic Texts Talk History?" in *AJS Review*, volume 3, Cambridge: Association for Jewish Studies (1977), pp. 153–196. Thus, I do not mean to suggest that we can extrapolate from the medieval rabbinic discourse about *tsedakah* funds that the poor were well cared for; to the contrary. The historian Yom Tov Assis theorizes, for example, that *chevrei kadisha*, private holy societies that began to form in the late thirteenth century, were a response to the *insufficient* care provided the poor by the community, as many communities did not have a *hekdesh* fund. See Assis (1991). In any event, the historical reality is unclear (and there are historians such as Mark Cohen who are working on this in Egypt), but we do know that, despite the institution of *hekdesh*, the poor were not always well taken care of in medieval Jewish communities.

51 See Goitien (1961); Gil (1975).

52 In fact, there was, during the medieval period, and there is today among Jewish Studies scholars, genuine ambiguity regarding the legal status of these Medieval *hekdesh* funds. For example, regarding the question of whether *hekdesh* was considered a legal person, see the difference of opinion between Albeck (1959) and Gil (1975). Although there is no place to explore this here, I disagree with the view articulated by Fink (1984).

53 To some extent (and according to some decisors, such as the Rashba, see *infra*.), the funds belonged to the poor who would eventually benefit therefrom; yet for most decisors and under most circumstances, they were not considered to be owned by them until the poor actually took possession. Yet, despite the fact that there were no claimants for the money – no individual who could step forward and assert "this is mine" – once the money was donated to *hekdesh*, a number of categorical rules kicked in. Real and significant restrictions on the making, retractability, and spending of *tsedakah* funds were presumed to take effect automatically.

54 The early medieval period witnessed a proliferation of questions concerning the precise status of *hekdesh*. Unlike tithes for the priests and gifts for the poor that, in earlier times, tended to pass directly to the human recipient, the funds of the medieval *hekdesh* existed as a separate entity. Legally, they were in a liminal state – frozen in precisely that moment when they belonged neither to the human donor nor to any particular poor person.

55 In some of this discussion of the medieval period, I use the word *hekdesh* to refer to the *tsedakah* fund, as this is what it was called at that time.

funds could be used for a purpose other than helping the poor (and if so, for what) to whether they could be given out as interest-bearing loans in apparent violation of regular usury laws, to what sort of liability was owed by someone who negligently allowed *hekdesh* funds to be stolen, to whether they should be considered a source for tax collection. Many issues like these came down to a relatively simple question: after the money or property was donated, and before it reached the hands of the poor – who was its owner; what was its status?[56] What, if any, ideational significance was there to the fact that this fund was called *hekdesh* – presumably "it was not for nothing that it was called *hekdesh*."[57]

The connection between – if not equation of – medieval *hekdesh* with its earlier namesake (Temple *hekdesh*) is made quite explicit early on, by Rabbi Joseph ibn Migash (1077–1141), also known as the Ri Migash. As an early twelfth-century scholar from Muslim Spain, he was writing at a time when the subject of *hekdesh* does not yet appear very much in the Responsa. In his commentary to the Babylonian Talmud, he asserted that,

> since we no longer have the Temple, in this day and age the unspecified consecration of property (*stam hekdesh*) is for synagogues or for the poor.[58]
>
> כיון שאין לנו עכשיו בית המקדש סתם הקדש בזמן הזה לבתי הכנסיות הוא או לעניים.

[56] At that time there were no developed concepts of trusts or corporate legal entities. In fact, one interesting question worth pursuing concerns the relationship between the early development of the notion of the English trust and the blossoming of the institution of *hekdesh* across the three major religions – the waqf in the case of Islam and the pious foundations in the case of Christianity. What is the relationship, if any, between these somewhat parallel religious institutional developments? Might they share a common origin, perhaps in the earlier (Second Temple and late antique rabbinic) incarnations of *hekdesh*? What are the conceptual connections between "charity" and sacrifice, as described above? The origins of the waqf and the Christian pious foundations are unclear. (For example, an early twentieth-century thesis by C. H. Becker, whereby the waqf was seen to be influenced by the *piae causae* in Byzantine law, was later shown to be unconvincing by C. Cahen. See J. O. Hunwick, "Wakf," in Bearman, Bianquis, Bosworth, van Donzel, and Heinrichs [eds.]), The *Encyclopaedia of Islam*, volume 11, Leiden: Brill (1999), p. 60.) With respect to Christianity, scholars have, for example, speculated that its deep concern for the poor can be traced to that of early Judaism; see, e.g., Peter Brown, *Poverty and Leadership in the Later Roman Empire*, Hanover: University Press of New England (2000). While the subject of charity has been dealt with extensively within the context of Christianity, its study is only beginning to flower with respect to Islam, and it has barely begun in terms of Judaism.

[57] This is a quotation from Ran Responsa #2. This Responsum will be discussed and partially translated, below.

[58] Ri Migash, B.T. Bava Batra 102b. See also Rashba, Responsa V #135; *Sefer ha-Terumot* 46:4; *Bet ha-Behira*, B.T. Avoda Zara 13b. As will be shown, this statement had concrete legal import. Thus, while some considered a statement of dedication to *hekdesh* to still create actual *hekdesh* after the Temple was destroyed, others, such as the Ri Migash, ruled that only if a person were to state specifically that the dedication was for the altar or the Temple funds would the property be deemed actual, sacred *hekdesh*, with all of its attendant prohibitions. See also, Shulchan Arukh Y.D. 248:1 and commentaries thereto.

In other words, as a matter of law according to the Ri Migash, in the absence of specification a dedication to *hekdesh* was *per se* deemed a dedication to *tsedakah*. The Rashbash (Rabbi Solomon ben Simon Duran, c.1400–1467) went even further, stating in Responsa #361 that "even if he said 'this is *hekdesh* to heaven' [we deem that] his intention is for *tsedakah*."

A series of early medieval Sephardic rabbis saw an equivalence between medieval *tsedakah* funds and Temple sacrifices in this (and other) respects. Leading authorities such as the Rif (Rabbi Isaac Alfasi, 1013–1103, of eleventh-century Morocco and then Spain) and Maimonides (the Rambam, Rabbi Moses ben Maimon, 1135–1204, of twelfth-century Spain and mostly Egypt) ruled that the very same votive institution of *nedarim* was involved in both types of gifts and, therefore, that the rules applicable to Temple dedications applied to medieval *hekdesh*,[59] such as the fact that once uttered they take effect immediately and cannot be retracted (as the status of the property is automatically changed thereby).[60] In his Mishneh Torah (Laws of Gifts to the Poor, chapters 8 and 9), Maimonides sums up the precise status of *tsedakah* in a manner that reflects much of the Talmudic material discussed earlier. On the one hand, *tsedakah* is a *neder*; as a result, once pledged, the property has a special character, with attendant restrictions:

> VIII (1)*Tsedakah* is in the category of *nedarim*. Therefore, one who says, "I obligate myself to give a *sela* to *tsedakah*," or "This *sela* [belongs to] *tsedakah*," is obligated to give it to the poor immediately ... (4) Whether one says "This *sela* [belongs to] *tsedakah*," or "I obligate myself to give a *sela* to *tsedakah*" and sets it aside, if he wishes to substitute another [*sela* coin] for it, he may do so. However, once that particular *sela* [coin] has reached the hand of the *tsedakah* collector [substitution is] prohibited.
>
> פרק ח הלכה (א) הצדקה הרי היא בכלל הנדרים לפיכך האומר הרי עלי סלע לצדקה או הרי סלע זו צדקה חייב ליתנה לעניים מיד....(ד) אחד האומר סלע זו צדקה או האומר הרי עלי סלע לצדקה והפרישו, אם רצה לשנותו באחר מותר ואם משהגיע ליד הגבאי אסור

On the other hand, because *tsedakah* is not absolutely sacred in the manner of *hekdesh* funds belonging to the Temple, those managing the funds and the community itself, have some leeway with respect to the management and use of the funds:

> VIII (5) If the poor would benefit by the money remaining in the hands of the [*tsedakah*] collector longer, in that it might cause others to contribute

59 In *Mishneh Torah, Hilchot Matanot Aniyim* [Hebrew: Laws of Gifts to the Poor 8:1], Maimonides writes, "*Tsedakah* is in the category of vows (*nedarim*)."
הצדקה הרי היא בכלל הנדרים

60 See generally Maimonides, *Mishneh Torah, Hilchot Matanot Aniyim* [Hebrew: Laws of Gifts to the Poor], chapter 8. One who says, "I obligate myself to give a *sela* in alms," or "This *sela* is to be for alms," is obligated (see below). See also See Rif, *Sefer ha-Halachot*, B.T. Bava Kamma 36b; Ran, B.T. Nedarim 29b; Radbaz, Responsa I #802; Shulchan Arukh Y.D. 258:13.

> [more], that [*tsedakah*] collector may borrow this money of the poor and repay it [later], because *tsedakah* is not like [Temple-owned] *hekdesh*, from which the derivation of benefit is prohibited....
>
> IX (7) The residents of the town are permitted ... to divert [*tsedakah* funds] to any public purpose they may choose
>
> פרק ח הלכה (ה) היה לעניים הנאה בעיכוב המעות ביד הגבאי כדי לעשות לאחרים ליתן, הרי אותו הגבאי מותר ללוות אותם המעות של עניים ופורע שהצדקה אינה כהקדש שאסור ליהנות בו.... פרק ט הלכה (ז) רשאין בני העיר לעשות קופה תמחוי, ותמחוי קופה, ולשנותן לכל מה שירצו מצרכי צבור

By contrast, the Rashba (Rabbi Shlomo ben Avraham ibn Aderet, 1235–1310, of Barcelona), the primary legal authority of the crown of Aragon in Christian Spain in the latter part of the thirteenth century who wrote a good deal about *hekdesh*, ruled the opposite – that donations to the poor were fundamentally unlike donations to God; therefore, verbal utterance alone was not enough to effectuate the gift.[61] On the other hand, the Rashba found that *hekdesh* funds were the property of the poor people who would eventually receive them and, therefore, for the townspeople to transfer these funds to any other purpose would constitute theft from the poor.[62]

As noted, one very significant dispute that turned on the status of *hekdesh* funds concerned the question of whether the biblical ban against lending money at interest applied to them.[63] In what might seem like a strange rule, according to B.T. Bava Metzia 57b, Temple-owned *hekdesh* was exempt from the otherwise universal prohibition against lending money for interest. No real consensus ever formed on the question of whether this exemption applied to medieval *hekdesh* for the poor. For example, Rabbi Isaac ben Moses of Vienna (1200–1270) ruled that

> the law of [Temple] *hekdesh* applies to *tsedakah* and there is no prohibition against earning interest. Accordingly, when people contribute money and stipulate that the capital is to be preserved but the income distributed to the poor, the law of [Temple] *hekdesh* certainly applies to such capital and it may be lent against fixed interest that is [otherwise] prohibited by biblical law.[64]

Many medieval scholars disagreed with this opinion. Meir of Rothenburg, Germany, a thirteenth-century rabbi (c1215–1293), also known as the Maharam,[65]

61 See, e.g., Cohen, (2000), pp. 85–100, and the Responsa discussed therein.

62 See, e.g., Rashba Responsa #617 5:269 ,תריז. This sounds like a prototrust, hinting again at the possible connection between the development of the legal idea of trust and the idea of a religious or divine lien.

63 This question obviously arose when the fund managers wanted to invest the funds for the benefit of the poor.

64 *Or Zarua*, Hilchot Tsedakah, section 30.

65 The name Maharam stands for Moreinu Harav Rabbi Meir.

ruled against it. In one of his decisions, he bemoaned the fact that "by reason of our sins, the matter [of lending *tsedakah/hekdesh* funds with interest] has spread and become permissible throughout the kingdom."[66] He went on, in great frustration, to note that, given that the practice was so widespread, "the *gaba'im* [fund managers] sin, but not for their own sake, because it is the sin of the whole community; I have not the power to protest, for it is better that it be done by them inadvertently and not intentionally."[67] He did, however, tell future questioners that they should refrain from this practice.

One medieval Responsum explicitly addresses the question of the theoretical (sacredness) status (if any) of *tsedakah/hekdesh* funds. It is written in response to a question addressed to the Ran (Rabbi Nissim ben Reuven of fourteenth-century Christian Spain, 1320–1380),[68] inquiring as to whether the communal *hekdesh* funds for the poor represent a source of funds from which taxes should be drawn (theoretically, on "behalf of" the poor). The lengthy Responsum explores the different rulings on the questions discussed earlier, such as whether the law against usury applies, whether a town can apply them to a different purpose, and so on. It also deals explicitly with the various arguments regarding the analogy to Temple-related *hekdesh* funds.

The analysis in this Responsum is particularly clear, providing a good illustration of the way the medieval rabbis grappled with the categories, rules, and principles regarding *hekdesh, tsedakah,* and gifts to God left to them in the Talmud. The step-by-step analysis provides a clear effort to classify *hekdesh,* by using the various categories of sacred property.[69] What follows is a summary of the findings of the Responsum.

66 Maharam Responsa, ed. Lemberg, number 478.

67 *Id.*

68 This Responsum is cited everywhere as Ran Responsa #2, but the preface to the text says it was written by a *sofer* (copier). I quote from this particular Responsum, which is consistent with other work by the Ran and other medievalists who work on this problem, because its analysis of the issue is very clear and thorough.

69 The relevant portion of Ran Responsa #2 provides: "The law of *hekdesh* funds for the poor is like [the law regarding] funds for orphans, and whenever the property of orphans is like Temple-related *hekdesh,* so too are *hekdesh* funds for the poor like *hekdesh*....[Based on this ruling] there are those who permit *hekdesh* funds for the poor to be loaned out even at fixed interest, for they equate them to pure [Temple-owned] *hekdesh,* however it is certain that neither *hekdesh* for the poor nor the property of orphans are pure [Temple-owned] *hekdesh,* for with regard to those funds one cannot say what is said regarding the priests, that they 'acquire from the table of the Most High,' and it for this reason that what the priests receive is considered to be pure [Temple-owned] *hekdesh,* since the [human] donor gives [the animal] to the Most High, and [priests] acquire from the table of the Most High; however in this case, the donor gives to the [realm of] ordinary property. And there is no difference between [these funds] and ordinary property, for it does not make sense that today's [medieval] *hekdesh* funds for the poor would be more stringent than gleanings, forgotten sheaves and corners of the field which are the property of the poor that was given to them by

1. *"hekdesh" is like orphan money*: First, "*hekdesh*" (*tsedakah* funds) are deemed to have the same legal status as funds for orphans, a category of property that (like *tsedakah* in medieval times) was explicitly called *hekdesh* in the Talmud.[70]
2. *"hekdesh" is not like animal sacrifice*: It is clear, however, that "*hekdesh*" funds are not like the most sacred of property called *hekdesh* – sacrificial portions eaten by the priest in the Temple. What they eat is something that is owned by the divine, in the full sense of the word. What transpires in sacrifice is that: "when [the priests] acquire [their portion], it is from the table of the Most High that they acquire [it]."[71] כי קא זכו משלחן גבוה קא זכו
3. *"hekdesh" is like gleanings, etc.*: In fact, in this regard (as to the question of whether what the recipient receives is his property, something that is his to do with as he likes, as opposed to property belonging to God that can only be used in the manner directed, as is true with sacrifice[72]), *hekdesh* is not unlike *leket, shikhechah*, and *peah*, (gleanings, forgotten

the Bible...[But] there is a basis for deeming *hekdesh* exempt for we find in the [medieval Talmudic commentary of] the Mordechai [Mordechai ben Hillel Ashkenazi. 13c Germany (1240–1298)], that he analogizes *hekdesh* funds to the poor tithe, and such an analogy is made in a number of places in the Gemara. And we find in the Tosefta to Tractate Peah 4:16 that, as regards [produce set aside as] the tithe for the poor, 'they may not use it to repay loans, and they may not use it to repay favors received and they may not use it to ransom prisoners and they may not give any part of it as *tsedakah* but they may send part of it [to another] as an act of loving kindness [*gemilut chassadim*] but he must inform [the other person of the produce's status, and they may give it to a citizen who is known as a *chaver*, as a favor, etc.' For the poor tithe, even though it is not sacred (*kodesh*) it is not like the ordinary (*chol*), and it [may not be] used like pure ordinary property (*kechol gamur ukedin hedyot gamur*). Such is also the case with *hekdesh* for the poor. *For it was not for naught that it was called hekdesh.* Because [the funds] were connected to a *mitzvah*, they were prohibited for other matters, and it is not appropriate to deem them eligible to be taxed." (emphasis added).

70 There are theoretical reasons to suggest that these two sets of funds essentially have the same legal status. And, in fact, there are many similarities in their treatment in the Talmud. (E.g., orphan funds are entrusted to the court, Bava Metzia 7a, and regarding *tsedakah* funds the Talmud says that the court is the hand of the poor.) Just as a point of information, orphans' funds were declared, in Rabbi Joseph Caro's authoritative legal code, the Shulchan Arukh, to be exempt from the bans against overreaching, *ona'ah* (Hoshen Mishpat ["H.M."] 109:4–5) and lending money at interest (Y.D. 160:18), two exemptions that also apply to Temple *hekdesh*. They were also deemed exempt from the seventh-year remission of debts (*prozbul*) (H.M. 67:28) and, with some exceptions, from communal taxation (Y.D. 248:3). As for their treatment in the Talmud, see, e.g., B.T. Bava Batra 8a.

71 B.T. Kiddushin 52b.

72 By contrast to his portion of the sacrifice, the priestly tithe, *terumah* once given to the priest, is regarded as property that belongs to the priest (called *nikhsei kohen*, the property of the priest).

sheaves, and corners of the field), which fully become the property of the recipient as ordinary property (*hedyot*).

4. *"hekdesh" is like the poor tithe*: The poor tithe is an intermediate category, between pure *hekdesh* and *hedyot* (ordinary property). As opposed to the items in point 3, which are more like *hefker*, ownerless property that only the poor can take, there are restrictions as to how one is permitted to use the poor tithe funds.[73]

The Ran Responsum concludes that "it was not for naught that [the medieval *tsedakah* fund] was called *hekdesh*" (לא לחנם קראו לזה הקדש). It decides that, like the poor tithe, *hekdesh* funds are neither purely sacred nor purely ordinary, but something in between (one might call them quasi-*hekdesh*); in terms of the practical question, it decides that they are to be treated like sacred property and deemed exempt from taxation. This reasoned decision retains the theoretical significance of *tsedakah* as a type of *hekdesh* and recognizes it as such, as analogous to the poor tithe.[74]

There is one other medieval text that is helpful to this analysis, in the Talmudic commentary of the Ritva (Yom Tov ben Avraham Asevilli (1250–1330)). As in the above-described Responsum, the Ritva implicitly describes *tsedakah* as something that passes to the recipient not from another human being, but from heaven or God (*mishel shamayim*).

In his gloss on B.T. Bava Metzia 92a, the passage concerning the laborer, the Ritva provides a very clear explanation regarding the meaning of the Talmudic view that the laborer "eats from that which belongs to heaven" (*mishel shamayim hu ochel*).[75]

[73] See Tosefta Peah 4:16, which lists a variety of permissible uses for poor tithe funds. It should be noted that while this section of the Tosefta is often said to describe *maser sheni*, the second tithe, rather than *maser ani*, the poor tithe, Saul Lieberman, in his *Tosefta Kifshutah*, points out that all manuscripts reflect the latter version. (Although it is beyond the scope of this book, it would be interesting to delve more deeply into the theoretical similarities and other connections between the second tithe, which is explicitly called *kadosh*, and the poor tithe.)

[74] As a follow-up to the previous note, it is worth mentioning that various analogies could be appropriately drawn, and the one performed in this Responsum may or may not be the most persuasive. The complicated rules involving the different kinds of gifts and offerings means that there are different ways in which things can be seen as alike or different. For purposes of this book, which seeks a general understanding of the nature of *tsedakah*, the analogy to the poor tithe is useful and appropriate.

[75] *Chidushei Ha'Ritva*, B.T. Bava Metzia 92a. As will be seen, the Ritva's commentary takes off from and elaborates upon the shorter commentary offered by Rashi. Rashi's commentary on this phrase in B.T. Bava Metzia 92a is as follows: "'One person reasons that he eats of his own property' – and, therefore, he may not eat more than his salary, for a supplement cannot be greater than the principle. 'And [the other] person reasons that he eats of [property belonging to] heaven' – and he acquires it from God."

מר סבר משלו הוא אוכל והלכך לא יאכל יותר על שכרו, דאין תוספת מרובה על העיקר.ומר סבר משל שמים הוא אוכל וזכי ליה רחמנא

> [In the Talmud it states, "the rabbis] inquired: does the worker eat of his own [food] or does he eat of heaven's [food]?" Rashi, may his memory be blessed, interpreted [the view] "he eats of his own [food]" to mean that what was given to him by the Torah was a supplement that was addded to his salary. The alternative view, that "he eats of heaven's [food]" [implies that the Torah's grant of permission to eat was a salary increase but was] in the manner of acts of loving-kindness *like all the other other gifts to the poor.* (emphasis added)
>
> איבעיא להו פועל משלו הוא אוכל או משל שמים. פירש רש"י, זכרונו לברכה, משלו הוא אוכל דתוספת שכרו הוא שהוסיפה לו תורה,או משל שמים הוא אוכל בתורת גמילות חסדים כשאר מתנות עניים

The Ritva thus equates (and reads Rashi to equate) the laborer's food with the category of gifts to the poor.[76] This equivalence implicitly reinforces, or even expresses, the corollary fact that gifts to the poor represent property received from heaven (*mishel shamayim*).

The Ritva continues to track the text of the Talmud, explaining the significance of this distinction. If that which is eaten by the laborer belongs to him (as a supplement to his salary that he has earned) he should be able to direct that it be given to his wife and his son, whereas

> if ones says that "he eats of heaven's [food]," [he could not direct that it be given to someone else], because it was an acquisition given to him [*zachei lei*][77] by God *as tsedakah*, and he did not acquire [*lo zachi bei*] anything that he did not eat (lit: that did not come into his hands). (emphasis added)
>
> אי אמרת משל שמים הוא אוכל דלדידיה זכי רחמנא בצדקה,
> כמה דלא מטא לידיה לא זכי ביה.

The Ritva regards the laborer's entitlement as one of *tsedakah*. He also equates both of these things (the laborer's fruit and *tsedakah*) with gifts to the poor, and implies that all of three of these entitlements pass (are "acquired") directly from heaven (*mishel shamayim*) – presumably explaining why they all have the same legal status.

76 It should be noted that here, and in the continuation of the Ritva quoted below, he draws the same distinction made in Chapter 3, Section 4, between two possible conceptions of the laborer's entitlement to eat. (1) It could be regarded as a property entitlement that is part of the worker's salary, meaning that it is owed by the field owner for labor performed and it belongs to the worker, as a matter of normal contract or property law (applied with the gloss of a biblically guaranteed minimum wage). (2) Conversely, it could be seen as a property entitlement "from heaven,"meaning that it is a divine gift passing from God to the worker, like the poor tithe, rather than something earned. The implications of the fact that what the worker eats is a "divine gift" are concretely fleshed out in the continuation of the Ritva's comments.

77 The Ritva uses the familiar word *zokhe* (which I translate as "acquire"), the same word that was used consistently in the Talmud to connote acquisition via a divine gift (such as the priests' entitlement to their portion). See Chapter 3, *supra*.

The categorical similarities and distinctions highlighted in some of the medieval rabbinic texts help to flesh out the concepts, rules, and phrases from rabbinic literature (e.g., "acquiring from the table of the most high"), suggesting that the theoretical scheme outlined in the previous chapter continued.[78] What can be traced through much of the medieval literature is the recognition, among many, that *tsedakah* funds are not simply ordinary property. Comparing them to Temple sacrifices and poor tithes communicates the deeper conception of the obligation of aid to the needy as something that is embodied in the very property that one thinks one owns, articulating the legal and philosophical grounding that makes it much more pressing than the popular understanding of charity. One implication corresponds to something noted by the Rashba and other medieval scholars – that the failure to give *tsedakah* on the part of the rich constitutes stealing from the poor. With the overtones supplied by the theory of the divine lien, it can also be characterized as stealing from God[79] (or, at the very least, undermining the theoretical caveat of the divine lien that qualifies and justifies the institution of private property).

4.2 THE SUSTAINING/SAVING OF HUMAN LIFE AS A GIFT TO AND FROM GOD

There is a reason it was important for the rabbis to establish parameters defining the ontological nature of a pledge to *tsedakah* (such as their finding that,

78 Much more can be said about this, and a chart can easily be drawn up demonstrating the ways in which the various gifts described throughout this book are similar and distinct, in such a way as to clarify which concerns (e.g., what rights does the recipient have in the property) are significant for what categorizing purpose.

79 It is curious that more has not been made of this legal notion of divine ownership that is especially as it is borne out by the institution of *hekdesh*, given its legal, moral, and philosophical implications. Perhaps the reason for this lies in something that comes across in contemporary scholarly discussions as to the status of medieval *hekdesh*. One of the few places this topic does arise is in discussions regarding when and how the notion of the artificial legal person developed. The original institution of Temple-owned *hekdesh* is consistently cited by Jewish-studies scholars and by legal historians to represent the first rumblings of a notion of corporate personality. See, e.g., Gulak (1922), and Fink (1984) (who seems to quote Gulak [in translation] at length without attribution). Scholars then focus on the medieval institution of *hekdesh* as yet another step in the direction of such a theory. See, e.g., S. Eisenstadt, "*Al Hitpatchut Musag ha-Ishiyut ha-Mishpatit ba-Mishpat Ha'ivri*" [Hebrew: On the Development of the Concept of Legal Personality in Hebrew Law], *ha-Mishpat* 1/10 (1926), pp. 10–15. There is disagreement as to whether medieval *hekdesh* was considered a legal person and as to what that concept means in this context. What these discussions overlook is something that is made explicit by the theory outlined here – the assumption embedded in late antique and medieval texts, that there is such a thing as legal personhood in the divine; that this entity – with its own domain, its own property, its own rights (and perhaps its own responsibilities), interacts with humans,

following the destruction of the Temple, any ordinary – i.e., unspecified – pledge goes to the poor or to the synagogue[80]). As was true with the ancient institution of *hekdesh*, the vow of *tsedakah*, by its nature, subjects the status quo to an almost dangerous open-endedness[81] – a verbal statement, by itself, can alter the status of property and render it quasi-sacred.

An understanding of the (substantive) purpose and (procedural) operation of the *tsedakah* vow makes it possible to identify where the divine lien operates via this mechanism, including cases in which the character of the transaction is defined not by a verbal pledge, but by the context and circumstances of a transfer – that is, where human life is at stake.

4.2.1 *The Obligation to Sustain Human Life*

The matters discussed in the previous section, regarding the conceptualization of *tsedakah* as a *neder* and as a kind of *hekdesh*, although somewhat technical in nature, provide a clear basis upon which to extrapolate what the rabbis (both early and medieval) viewed as the theoretical underpinnings of *tsedakah*. As communicated by the biblical text, the rabbis had a clear understanding of the structural components of the early social system that entailed transfers to other human beings (e.g., tithes, gleanings) as institutions that were put in place to guarantee sustenance for the needy (a category that, for these purposes, included the class of supposedly landless priests.)[82] This comes across in the rabbinic construction of the legal institutions no longer in effect during their time; and it is this conceptualization that imbues the ongoing

and humans interact with it, through property in a real legal sense. Ironically, what might preclude contemporary scholars from appreciating the full legal personality of Temple-owned *hekdesh* is precisely the concept of "legal person" and the antipathy toward anthropomorphism when it comes to God. And yet, when one contemplates the possibility of the divine as legal person – playing with different rules but on the same field – this religious legal tradition's understanding of basic institutions such as property ownership, obligation, distributive justice and self-ownership becomes more clear and more compelling.

80 As quoted above, the Ri Migash B.T. Bava Batra 102b, asserted, "since we no longer have the Temple, in this day and age the unspecified consecration of property (*stam hekdesh*) is for synagogues or for the poor."
כיון שאין לנו עכשיו בית המקדש סתם הקדש בזמן הזה לבתי הכנסיות הוא או לעניים.

81 There is much discussion of the fact that one ought not readily undertake a *neder*. The recognition of the hazards (potential for even inadvertant desecration) presented by the fact that it is easy to render property *kadosh*, in an era in which there is no Temple, appears in numerous texts, such as those dictating that *hekdesh* created inadvertently or unthinkingly must be thrown into the sea. See, e.g., Ri Migash, B.T. Bava Batra 102b.

82 They also functioned to create parameters for, and regular reminders, of divine ownership. Other rules (that might otherwise be taken mistakenly for interhuman property transfers), such as *shemitah* and the Jubilee, play that role explicitly.

legal institution of *tsedakah*.[83] The rather obvious proposition, that gifts to God that are redirected to humans are those that entail the sustenance (if not saving) of human life, is explicitly articulated in the Talmud in the context of (at least) one of the property transfers considered a deflected "gift" to/from God – that involving the laborer in the field, who eats from that which belongs to heaven (*mishel shamayim hu ochel*).

Part of the Talmudic argumentation concerning the right of the laborer rests on the analogy between the entitlement of the laborer and the biblical prohibition against muzzling an animal while it is working, Deut 25:4: "You shall not muzzle an ox in its threshing" (לא תחסם שור בדישו). The differences between what might look simply like two "labor laws" is significant, for "one is commanded to keep [a person/the laborer] alive" (אתה מצוה להחיותו), but one is *not* obligated to keep an animal (an ox) alive (אי אתה מצווה להחיותו).[84] The text goes on to link this obligation to sustain human life to the laborer's entitlement to eat (in a manner that seems somewhat tongue-in-cheek), as follows:

> The verse [Lev 25:36] states: "And *your brother* shall live with you," your brother but not an ox (emphasis added).
>
> אמר קרא :וחי אחיך עמך אחיך ולא שור.

Although the requirement that the laborer be permitted to eat while working is mandated by specific verses that are construed to apply to specifically to him, the obligation to feed him is construed by the rabbis as an act that falls under the broader rubric of Lev 25:36, which establishes a general obligation to sustain human life. As was shown in the previous chapter, the right involved here is regarded, in the view of the majority of the rabbis, as an entitlement, on the part of the laborer to eat of God's property (*mishel shamayim hu ochel*, "he eats of that which belongs to heaven"). Rather than a guaranteed "minimum wage" owed by the field owner, it is an obligation that is essentially latent in the fruit itself; it is seen by the rabbis as something implicitly built into (and

[83] This section will follow this analysis through to its logical conclusion. It will be shown that the saving of a human life (*pikuach nefesh*) represents the pinnacle of the structure for giving to the divine by giving to others, and vice versa. The urgency of *tsedakah*, and the attendant implication of the divine lien on property when someone's life is at stake, is in conformity with (if not a part of) the general rule that, for the sake of *pikuach nefesh*, saving a human life, almost all other commandments are automatically rendered null. See B.T. Yoma 85b, in which the Amora Samuel explains why it is justified to break the laws of the Sabbath in order to try to save a human life. In a statement recognized explicitly to be unrefuted, Samuel quotes and interprets Lev 18:5 ("You shall keep my laws and my rules; which if a man do, he shall live by them") to mean: "He shall live by [the commandments], but he shall not die because of them."

אמר שמואל....[ויקרא יח] וחי בהם ולא שימות בהם

See also Mechilta on Exod 31:13.

[84] B.T. Bava Metzia 88b.

limiting) the property rights of the field owner. This transfer of ownership of the fruit from the field owner/employer to the laborer (via an automatic retrocession of the field owner's property to the divine domain) is expressly seen by the rabbis as part of the biblical directive itself. The word *kenafshecha*, in Deut 23:25,[85] although normally translated to mean "as is your desire," is interpreted by the rabbis, in this context, as follows:

> The verse states: "Like what belongs to you [the employer]," so is what belongs to the worker.[86]
>
> אמר קרא כנפשך כנפשו של פועל.

The property obligation to sustain human life – reflected, generally, in the systematized gifts to the poor and (as described in B.T. Bava Metzia 88b with respect to the laborer) embodied in the phrase "and your brother shall live with you,"[87] – is the very thing that gives rise to the *tsedakah* requirement. For there is no explicit mention of the obligation of *tsedakah* in the Bible. The rabbis derive this obligation from the verse quoted above [Lev 25:36], a verse that appears in the context of the related mandate to offer interest-free loans to the poor. Chapter 25 of Leviticus thus states, in part:

> (35) If your bother, being impoverished, comes under your authority, you shall strengthen him, proselyte or resident, so that he can live with you.
>
> (36) Do not take from him interest and increase; and you shall fear your God, and *your brother shall live with you.*
>
> (37) Do not lend him your money or your food [with a charge of] interest. (emphasis added)
>
> (לה) וכי ימוך אחיך ומטה ידו עמך והחזקת בו גר ותושב וחי עמך
>
> (לו) אל תקח מאתו נשך ותרבית ויראת מאלהיך וחי אחיך עמך
>
> (לז) את כספך לא תתן לו בנשך ובמרבית לא תתן אכלך

The theme of Leviticus chapter 25 is a rendition of many of the central property requirements that stem from the principle of divine ownership (with verse 23 providing, for example, "The land shall not be sold in perpetuity, for the

85 This is verse, which is interpreted to apply only to a laborer, states, "When you come into the vineyard of your fellow, then you may eat grapes *as is your desire*, to you satiety, but you may not put [any] into your vessel." .כי תבא בכרם רעך ואכלת ענבים כנפשך שבעך ואל כליך לא תתן The focus on this word is particularly interesting when read in parallel with organ transfer. (More can be said on "*kenafshekha*" in the verse and in the Talmudic interpretation.)

86 B.T. Bava Metzia 88b. Here the rabbis do not provide an actual quote of the verse; they essentially paraphrase the beraita's exposition thereof. (In some manuscripts of the Talmud, the last two words – "what belongs to the worker" (כנפשו של פועל) – do not appear. Thus, all that appears is the word used in the verse – *kenafshekha*.

87 Lev 25:36.

land is Mine…" (והארץ לא תמכר לצמתת כי לי הארץ), such as those related to the Sabbatical year, Levite cities, and the Jubilee year. The above-quoted verses regarding the obligation of aiding the poor are similarly understood by the rabbis, in accordance with their plain meaning (given their context), to be rooted in the divine lien on property.[88]

Thus, according to the rabbis, the requirement of *tsedakah* is implicitly embodied in the words "and your brother shall live with you." Appearing in B.T. Bava Metzia chapter 5, the Talmudic chapter that deals primarily with the prohibition against usury, the interpretation of this phrase to impose an affirmative obligation to sustain the lives of the poor makes perfect sense given the obligation to extend interest-free loans to the poor, with which it is biblically juxtaposed. Both of these rules are ownership limiting (in nature and in effect) with respect to one's property; they are property restrictions rooted in the divine lien. Together they make clear that, at the very least, one may not use one's property to profit from the desperation of those in need.

The ban against usury insists that the rich make resources available to the poor, and that they do so in a manner that, at most, requires only that the poor return that which they received and not one iota extra. As explained in the fifth chapter of B.T. Bava Metzia, in what amounts to a classic prohibition against commodification, the creditor is precluded from gaining anything from the debtor simply for having to wait for the return of his goods or money (which the creditor obviously did not need for himself during that time).[89] While the creditor retains ownership of the goods loaned (or the value of the money lent), he is directed to permit those in need to make use of them at no cost.

Out of a rule (banning interest) that is rather simple in principle the rabbis wove an intricate scheme of prohibitions affecting innumerable transactions. The complicated analysis set in motion by the rabbis to ensure the avoidance of even "the dust" of interest (*avak ribit*)[90] is strikingly similar to rules regarding

[88] The prohibition against usury is also anchored in the principle of divine ownership. There is no room to explore this particular prohibition here, but it is readily recognized as a prohibition against making a profit (getting benefit or *hana'ah*) from the neediness of the poor. See generally chapter 5 of Tractate Bava Metzia. When read in conjunction with the rabbis' enactment of the *prozbul*, which enabled the collection of loans past the seventh year for the express purpose of facilitating and encouraging loans to the poor, it offers a clue to the fact that, when it comes to enforcing or effectuating the justice-related purposes of the divine lien (see Chapter 3, Section 3.4, *supra*) the court and the community stand "in the shoes of" the divine. This conception of the role of the court can explain problems of *akirah*, "uprooting" of the Torah, that appear sporadically in connection with rabbinic nullification of ownership (e.g. *prozbul*), including categories that would appear to entail divine ownership (see, e.g., Mishnah Terumot 1:4).

[89] In its technical definition, interest is understood by the rabbis to be "money for waiting."

[90] This phrase refers to a large category of transactions that were rabbinically proscribed, in addition to those that, according to the rabbis, constitute biblically prohibited usury. In general, when the rabbis added a layer of prohibition, banning things more attenuated from that which is understood

the category of items, such as *hekdesh*, from which no human is permitted to benefit (*issurei hana'ah*). There is, in fact, no theoretical difference. In both cases, any benefit, no matter how slight, is prohibited,[91] and any infraction is extremely serious. More than simply an act of theft (a taking to which one is not entitled), benefiting from that which is explicitly set aside as something from which one is not permitted to profit is in the nature of a misuse of property; indeed, it is tantamount to an act of desacralization, a wrongdoing that is explicitly entailed when the property involved is inherently sacred in nature.

As explained above, the requirement of *tsedakah*, that is, of giving up one's property in order to sustain those in need, is also an ownership-limiting property rule rooted in the divine lien. It is this obligation that is (along with the divine lien) automatically triggered when a verbal pledge of *tsedakah* is made (even one that does not expressly mention the poor).

As witnessed with the case of the laborer and the obligation of *tsedakah* (a connection that will be made explicit by the Ritva), the phrase "and your brother shall live with you" appears in various contexts, to express a general obligation, upon the individual, to sustain and support human life – both one's own and that of the other.[92] The rabbinic conceptualization of this imperative as a property principle, one that is anchored in the idea of divine ownership, sheds light on the uses of this and other phrases that speak to the obligation to save and sustain human life.

4.2.2 Tsedakah *as a Transfer through the Divine Realm*

I have argued, based in the above-described textual derivations and linkages (e.g. between laborer, who eats from heaven's property, and the general sustaining of human life, particularly that of the poor), that a situation of (possibly or potentially) life-threatening human need triggers a property obligation in the

to be biblically proscribed, they did so in order to "make a fence" around the biblical prohibition, to ensure against even a near violation of its provisions. That purpose is made explicit with respect to the extensive range of transactions that were prohibited by the rabbis as "the dust of interest."

91 In the context of *hekdesh*, this can be seen, for example, in the following practice. When the Temple was in need of repair, the Temple treasurer would not actually purchase stones needed for the repair until after the stones were actually put in place and built into the wall, lest a tired worker improperly benefit by sitting on the stones for a brief respite while working. In the context of usury, a comparable ban on any benefit whatsoever can be seen, e.g., in the rule that precludes a debtor from even saying hello to the creditor when they pass on the street (in case the debtor, but for the loan, would not otherwise have acknowledged the creditor). *Id.*

92 Arising from the verse, "and your brother shall live with you," the property obligation of *tsedakah* reflects a broad claim on the individual; for example, as noted, this verse encompasses the requirement to feed the laborer. Given the correspondence between this verse and the general obligation of *tsedakah*, I will sometimes use the term *tsedakah* to refer to this broad obligation to sustain human life (which is the substantive content of the divine lien).

eyes of the rabbis. Yet, unlike the situation regarding the biblically derived mandatory givings (such as priestly gifts) discussed in the previous chapter, the idea that *tsedakah* passes through the divine realm might not necessarily seem conceptually intuitive to the contemporary reader. There is an intellectual tension here; probing it actually helps to reveal the deeper implications of this principle.

There are some things that might initially seem problematic but are readily resolved when comparisons are made to the other biblically mandated "divine" gifts. For example, the "ordinary" character of the recipient might seem to belie the fact that in the divine lien is in operation in the context of simple *tsedakah*, via the commandment to sustain life. And yet, it is not difficult to connect *tsedakah* to gifts to the poor (gleanings, etc.) and the fruit of the laborer in which property passes through the divine realm to people who have no special *kedushah* status.[93] Another, related, ostensible problem that is readily resolved is the failure to specify individual recipients in an open pledge of funds or goods to *tsedakah*. And yet, many institutions geared toward the satisfaction of the obligation to sustain human life, such as tithes, and corner of the field, do not identify a particular person to whom this entitlement is owed (although, some gifts to the poor are given by the donor to individuals of his choosing). Rather, they purport[94]

93 The comparison with other divine gifts is actually more complicated than this. For example, as discussed in the context of the Responsum of the Ran, another valence of analysis turns on the question of whether the property is going to "ordinary," *hedyot* ownership or not. In this regard, poor tithes are different from other gifts to the poor and bear a greater resemblance to the priestly tithe. Moreover, the priestly entitlements themselves fall into different categories for purposes of this type of analysis, as some items (e.g., portions of sacrifice) come to the priests directly from the table of the Most High (*mishulchan gavohah*) and do not become the property of the priests for all intents and purposes (i.e., other than eating), whereas *terumah*, the tithe going to the priest is called "*nikhsei kohen*" (נכסי כהן), or the property of the priest, as the priest is permitted to do more than eat it. As noted earlier, the spectrum of gifts that come under the rubric of what I refer to as the divine lien can be compared and contrasted in a number of ways, yielding a chart that would be quite interesting and informative for matters beyond those discussed in this book.

94 I say "purport" because these institutions under discussion during rabbinic and medieval times could not have been conceived the way one would today, using the legal institution of the trust, as such a legal entity did not exist. Hence the problem for medieval decisors in describing the status and ownership of the *hekdesh* funds before their distribution. Theoretically it is the legal personality of the divine realm that holds the funds until they are distributed – although, in reality, the community, court, or fund manager is the placeholder for the divine realm and, as such, is described as acting as "the hand of the poor." Related topics of the relationship (if any) between a divine legal personality and the development of a legal trust, a comparative examination of the "divine" (or something comparable) as a jural actor, and the relationship (if any) between the notion of the divine lien and political and legal theories regarding the commons suggest a fascinating area for future research in jurisprudence, political theory, and religion. See, e.g., Lynda Butler, "The Commons Concept: An Historical Concept with Modern Relevance," *William and Mary Law Review* 23 (1981), pp. 835ff; Joel Edan Friedlander, "Corporation and Kulturkampf: Time Culture as Illegal Fiction," *Connecticut Law Review*

to vest property rights in an entire class of people[95] – those who are needy.[96]

So, what is it that makes the idea of *tsedakah* as a "divine" gift less intuitive? I would suggest that the following facts are what make the operation of the divine lien in the case of *tsedakah* harder to conceptualize:

- unlike the poor tithe and the other aforementioned gifts to the poor, *tsedakah* is not necessarily given to a particular person, or group of people, as part of a regular ritual tied directly to permitting the use of the remainder of one's property (although it might function that way theoretically), and
- unlike gleanings, forgotten sheaves, and priestly tithes, an item given in satisfaction of the obligation of *tsedakah* is usually something that has no inherent sanctity to it (as does *terumah*, for example) and (like regular items dedicated to the Temple) is something that could just as well have been sold or loaned to the recipient.

The absence of a specific preexisting claim on particular property renders the operation of the divine lien less obvious in the usual case of *tsedakah*. Unlike the corner of the field waiting to be cordoned off, or the tithe (for the poor or otherwise) waiting to be designated by the erstwhile owner, a pledge of *tsedakah* can be made at any time, with respect to any property (that one owns).[97] Moreover, the fact that the item given as *tsedakah* (usually) has no inherent or implicit sacredness status[98] can make the divine lien difficult to

29 (1995), pp. 31ff; Assaf Likhovski, "The Invention of 'Hebrew Law' in Mandatory Palestine," *American Journal of Comparative Law* 46 (1997), pp. 339ff.

95 As for the non-*tsedakah* items in this category, they fall into two different groups, depending on whether the owner has the right to decide which individual, within that class, shall be entitled to receive the portion. In some cases the owner, who otherwise has no property rights in the item given, possesses this right of choice, called *tovat hana'ah*. (*Tovat hana'ah* is a matter as to which there is debate in the Talmud, particularly as to the question of whether or not it is worth money– טובת הנאה ממון או אינו ממון –with the majority opinion deciding that it is not.) By contrast, with respect to other gifts to the class of needy (e.g., the corner of the field, gleanings, and some poor tithes), the donor has no right to choose the recipient; the goods are left to be taken by any people who qualify.

96 Apart from the desire to explain priestly tithes by the presumption that, as a landless group, priests are categorically included in the group of those who are needy, for the purposes discussed here, "neediness" is explicitly *not* defined by a preexisting categorical status, but is purely circumstantial and pragmatic, based exclusively on actual and immediate need. Thus, for example, a wealthy traveler passing through town who, for some reason, has no money is entitled to take *tsedakah*. See Mishnah Peah 5:4, discussed *infra*. He incurs no property obligation to the *tsedakah* fund, or to the donors of the fund, that helped him in his hour of need. As will be seen below, rules such as these, making clear that there is no property obligation of repayment, are further evidence that the property is transferred in its entirety to the divine domain (and passes from one person to another through that domain).

97 This characteristic – the requirement that one must own that which one wants to give – is something that *tsedakah* shares with *hekdesh*.

98 Just as the recipient of a gift for the needy, unlike the priest, need have no special status.

imagine here. The item is almost always something that could have been loaned, rented, sold, or traded – something with respect to which one (otherwise) has full (human) ownership rights.[99]

By implication, there is a preexisting claim on the property that is given as *tsedakah* – that is, there is a preexisting claim (a divine lien for this purpose) on *all* property.[100] Conversely, under circumstances where the divine lien is automatically implicated by a transfer, that transfer must be characterized as an act of *tsedakah* even in the absence of declaration. Just as the mere pledge of a *sela* implicitly communicates that it is for the poor, so too a situation in which *tsedakah* is called for – most obviously, the most extreme situation, that of life endangerment – implicitly communicates (unless otherwise provided[101]) that a life-saving transfer is an act of *tsedakah*.

The category of *tsedakah*, in general, includes transfers that are gifts to sustain the needy, transfers that can be analogized to the poor tithe, corners of the field, and so on; they can be regarded as having passed through the divine domain on their way to the (as of yet) unidentified individual recipient(s). The usual case of *tsedakah* is where one who "has" gives to someone in the category of the "have-nots."[102]

The fact that a transfer is an act of *tsedakah* can also be identified by the given circumstances or situation at hand; in other words, someone who is in need in the moment is entitled to *tsedakah*, even if he otherwise has property. This is the view expressed by the majority of rabbis in Mishnah Peah 5:4:

> If a man of property[103] was traveling about from place to place and [due to his circumstances] needed to take gleanings, the forgotten sheaf, *peah* or the

99 Indeed, as noted, a person is not capable of sanctifying something he does not own and cannot give away entirely as a gift. See B.T. Nedarim 48a.

100 See Chapter 5 regarding the question of whether the human body, or a part thereof, can be given as *tsedakah*.

101 There is no room here to explore whether, when, and to what extent it is possible to successfully dictate otherwise.

102 Of course, the poor also have an obligation of *tsedakah*, so this is not entirely true. Yet, it is largely true, as is evidenced by the general rule that if one "has" property, one must give to those who do not. This becomes clear, for example, in the contrasting case of parental support by a child. While such support would also be characterized as *tsedakah* (as is child support, which lacks any other biblical basis, although the rabbis ordained that a person must support his children until they reach the age of six; B.T. Ketuvot 49b), it is also dictated (according to what appears to be the majority view) by the obligation to honor one's parents. See B.T. Kiddushin 31b–32a. Because of the involvement of the latter commandment, the situation that demands such support is understood to be different than the general obligation of *tsedakah*; whereas the general obligation of *tsedakah* applies when one has property, the parental support obligation applies whether the child has property or not.

103 This phrase, which literally means "a householder," refers to someone who would otherwise not be entitled to take things set aside for the poor. See Mishnah Peah 8:8: "If a man had two

poor man's tithe, he should take them; and on his return home, he must pay. So [says] Rabbi Eliezer. The Sages, however, say: *he was* [considered] *a poor man at that particular time* [and so he was entitled to take and need not make any restitution]. (emphasis added)

בעל הבית שהיה עובר ממקום למקום וצריך ליטול לקט שכחה ופאה ומעשר עני יטול וכשיחזור לביתו ישלם דברי ר' אליעזר וחכמים אומרים עני היה באותה שעה:

Whereas in the (minority) view of Rabbi Eliezer, a wealthy man who is temporarily needy owes a debt to the poor from that town,[104] the majority view treats the man as poor while he is in need. Accordingly, that which he takes is taken as *tsedakah*, something that gives rise to no property claim on the part of the donor (even if, as in this case, the recipient, under different circumstances, would not require help). Hence, there is no obligation of repayment whatsoever. Elsewhere it is suggested that, in the interest of fairness, he ought to donate the amount that he received to the poor of his own town – a payment that is clearly not the repayment of a debt (since they are not the ones from whom he took the property), but is more in the nature of an equitable concern of avoiding unjust enrichment[105] or, to be more exact, of returning the "gift" by giving the same type of gift to others in need – enacting precisely the type of cycle of giving (rather than debt repayment) that the obligatory gift (e.g., according to Mauss) can be said to engender.

Thus, aside from the case of categorical *tsedakah*, paralleling the case of the laborer, we see again that the law contemplates a purely circumstantial implication of the divine lien where there exists immediate need. A traveling "householder" is considered "poor," for purposes of the divine lien, even though, in other respects and under other circumstances, he is not a needy man. This category of what might be called situational *tsedakah* can be understood to include a case of life-threatening emergency – a case of *pikuach nefesh*. As in the case of the traveling householder, it is the set of circumstances that legally renders the person in need of life-sustaining (or life-saving) support as a *tsedakah*-recipient, and the transfer as an act of *tsedakah*, something that passes through the divine realm.[106]

hundred *zuzim* he may not take gleanings, the forgotten sheaf, corner of the field or the poor person's tithe…." ... מי שיש לו מאתים זוז לא יטול לקט שכחה ופאה ומעשר עני

104 The Jerusalem Talmud explicitly explains something that is described there as obvious – that in the view of Rabbi Eliezer, the repayment of the householder is owed to the poor of the town in which he had taken poor-support.

105 See, e.g., Yechezkel Rottenberg, "Unjust Enrichment," in Elon, Menachem (ed.), *Principles of Jewish Law*, Jerusalem: Keter Publishing House (1975), pp. 335–340; Nahum Rakover, "Unjust Enrichment," in Michael Chernick (ed.), *Essential Papers on the Talmud*, New York: New York University Press (1994), pp. 331–356.

106 This principle poses an interesting contrast to another context in which the law regulates the saving of human life – where it ranks the order in which people are to be saved. See Mishnah Horyot 3:7–8. While the triggering of the obligation of rescue and the divine lien is (obviously)

There is a clue to the temporal and situational sensitivity of the divine lien. It lies in the structural commonality between *tsedakah* and other *nedarim*: the biblical prohibition against delay.

Ironically, the very biblical mandate of "do not delay in fulfilling your vow" that the early rabbis use to link *tsedakah* to other categories of divinely related gifts is deemed, ultimately, to apply differently, and more stringently, to *tsedakah* than to any other item on the lists set forth in B.T. Rosh Hashanah 4a–b. Moreover, it is this take on the "do not delay" requirement that can be understood to reveal the purpose and application of the obligation to aid the needy.

At B.T. Rosh Hashanah 6a, the prohibition against delay in the fulfilling of one's vow of sacrifice is deemed violated with the passage of one year (three festivals.)[107] When it comes to *tsedakah*, however, the "period of delay" component to the "do not delay" requirement is essentially nullified; the Talmud determines that no time is allowed to lapse between pledging the funds and distributing them.

> Rava said, and in the case of *tsedakah* one is liable [not after three festivals have passed but] immediately. What is the reason? Because poor people [who need *tsedakah* without delay] are standing [before us].
>
> אמר רבא: וצדקה מיחייב עלה לאלתר. מאי טעמא דהא קיימי עניים

Following this statement, the anonymous voice of the Talmud asks why it is even necessary to teach this principle, as it is "obvious" (*peshita*, פשיטא)! The reply is as follows:

> You might have said that because [the prohibition against delaying *tsedakah*] is written in the context of sacrifices, [one is not liable for *tsedakah*] until three festivals have passed, as [is the case with] sacrifices. [Rava, therefore,] comes to teach us that it is only there [in the case of sacrifices] that God made [liability for delaying] contingent on the [passage of three] festivals; but here [with *tsedakah*, liability] is not [contingent on the passage of three festivals,] because poor people are plentiful.
>
> מהו דתימא כיון דבעניינא דקרבנות כתיבא עד דעברי עלה שלשה רגלים כקרבנות קא משמע לן התם הוא דתלינהו רחמנא ברגלים אבל הכא דהא שכיחי עניים.

situational, it is, nevertheless, apparently to be carried out in accordance with objective principles that rank the ordering of persons to be saved, without regard to the particular situation of any individual (a method that other ethical principles might dictate as more appropriate).

107 In fact, the reason the discussion concerning the "do not delay" requirement appears in B.T. Rosh Hashanah is that the point beyond which one has violated that requirement is deemed to be a year. This, and other year-long time limits, are discussed in this tractate with respect to the question of the date from which to count the year-long period. It should be noted that, whereas sacrifices have a one-year time limit, there is discussion as to whether some of the other vowed items carry a shorter period (e.g., the passage of one festival rather than three).

The unique urgency of the "do not delay" requirement as applied to *tsedakah* is further indication of the ideational significance of including *tsedakah* on the list of (otherwise biblically described) vowed items[108]; its inclusion in the "do not delay" category was more than a desire to simply include it under the umbrella of a legal technicality having to do with applicable temporal restrictions. As it turns out, *tsedakah* does not even share the same durational requirement. Rather, it is because *tsedakah* passes as a return gift to God on its way to the poor that it is on the list of items that are binding in the nature of a vow; inclusion in the "do not delay" prohibition is merely a surface indicator of that fact.[109]

Tsedakah is treated here more stringently than promises of gifts directly to the Temple and God, out of concern for the practical realities of the needs of the poor. Of course, there will always be poor people waiting, and the rabbis do not, in fact, insist that *tsedakah* always be disbursed the moment it is pledged or collected. As noted in texts described above, there are practical reasons related to the welfare of the poor that, depending on the circumstances, dictate a thoughtful, rather than a knee-jerk, structure to the operation of the institution of *tsedakah*.

This temporal directive reflects an important component in the larger theoretical framework of *tsedakah*. The practical considerations of circumstance – the presence of people in need who are waiting, and the urgency of their need, factor into the legal rules themselves. Indeed, when one traces the broader rabbinic conceptualization of *tsedakah* as a component of rules of property and distributive justice, it turns out that the rabbis are quite insistent: in a case of real and immediate need, "do not delay" means precisely what it says: let no time elapse between the designation (giving to the divine domain) and the receiving (from the divine domain).

In accordance with the reasoning suggested by the "do not delay prohibition," the very logic of *tsedakah* establishes that a circumstance in which a life is threatened is "the" ultimate case in which the divine lien kicks in. The prototypical case, in this context, is not necessarily gifts (e.g. corners of the field)

[108] It also helps provide an internal limiting principle to the obligation to feed others: one of geo-temporal proximity. See, e.g., Moshe Feinstein, *Iggerot Moshe, Hoshen Mishpat*, 1:103 (1968) (payment for donating blood to a blood bank – *choleh lefaneinu*); B.T. Bava Metzia 71a (prioritizing feeding those in your family before those in your town, those in your own town before those from other towns, etc.). Although it is fascinating (as well as potentially relevant to the question of distribution of human organs), there is no room, in this book, to explore this aspect of the *tsedakah* obligation.

[109] In calling it a "surface indicator," I do not mean to suggest that the temporal requirement is not intimately connected with the substantive meaning and operation of the requirement itself. For example, the immediacy of the "do not delay" rule as it is understood to apply to *tsedakah* dovetails with what the rabbis defined as the heart of the prohibition against usury (which derives from the same verse as the *tsedakah* requirement); that is, do not charge money for waiting (to get your money or property back from the debtor).

regularly left for the poor. Indeed, the quintessential case or ultimate expression of *tsedakah*, according to the Talmud, is the situation in which someone has been taken captive and his or her life is urgently at stake. In this context, money donated to redeem the captives, called *pidyon shevuyim* (redemption of captives), is deemed the most important case of *tsedakah*.[110] As recounted in B.T. Bava Batra 8a–b,

> Ifra Hormiz the mother of King Shapur sent a chest of *dinarim* (gold coins) to Rabbi Joseph. She said [to him] that they should be used for [carrying out] a duty of great importance (*mitzvah rabbah*). Rabbi Joseph was trying hard to think what [such a] duty of great importance would be. Abaye said to him: Since Rabbi Samuel bar Judah has taught that *tsedakah* is not to be collected from orphans even for the redemption of captives, we learn from this that *the redemption of captives is a duty of great importance*."[111] (emphasis added)
>
> איפרא הורמיז אימיה דשבור מלכא שדרה ארנקא דדינרי לקמיה דרב יוסף אמרה ליהוי למצוה רבה. יתיב רב יוסף וקא מעיין בה מאי מצוה רבה? אמר ליה אביי מדתני רב שמואל בר יהודה אין פוסקין צדקה על היתומים אפילו לפדיון שבוים שמע מינה פדיון שבוים מצוה רבה היא

As will be seen below, with respect to *pidyon shevuyim* in particular and *pikuach nefesh* in general, the act of giving to save a life – like money given to *tsedakah* to sustain life – is, by definition, a transfer of property implicating the divine lien. The two steps that silently comprise this type of interhuman giving-between-humans-via-God transaction are implicitly understood to occur simultaneously when a human life is at stake, something that is also true in the case of the laborer eating in the field and the (hopefully avoided) triggering of the dedication decreed in the so-called prohibitory vow. Giving to save a life cannot be considered a loan. By definition, it entails this type of property transfer. Indeed, these cases represent not only a subset but also perhaps the most important cases of *tsedakah* (which is also characterized, legally, as this type of transfer through the divine realm).

The fact that what is expended during the act of saving another's life is taken up by the divine lien, and thus does not give rise to a property claim on the part of the actor, is made clear in the Talmud, in Tractate Sanhedrin.

110 B.T. Bava Batra 8a–b. As will be seen in the general context of cases involving the saving of human life (*pikuach nefesh*), the financial obligation initially falls, theoretically, upon the captive; however, the community collects *tsedakah* in order to obtain their release. Theoretically, it is *tsedakah* because, if the captive does not have the funds, there will be no reimbursement. Thus, the donor's initial relinquishment of the money is final.

111 The text continues with a more theoretical and literary explanation for "the maxim of the rabbis that the redemption of captives is a religious duty of great importance…"
מאמור רבנן דפדיון שבוים מצוה רבה היא

4.2.3 *Fulfilling the Obligation to Save Human Life – The Divine as Primary Recipient*

The principles of *tsedakah* as divine gift lay the groundwork for a similar understanding of *pikuach nefesh*; concrete evidence to that effect is supplied by specific textual evidence and legal principles relating to the requirement, meaning, and significance of saving human life.

4.2.3.1 The Dualistic Obligation to Save Human Life

A lengthy section in the eighth chapter of B.T. Sanhedrin sets forth many of the broad parameters of the obligations and prohibitions that flow from the divine claim over human life, in rules ranging from the fact that a life may not be traded for another life (*ein dochin nefesh mipnei nefesh* אין דוחין נפש מפני נפש) to the rules that dictate when one is obligated to die for the sanctity of heaven (*al kiddush hashem* על קדוש ה').[112]

In this context, the Talmud sets forth the basic principles of the obligation of *pikuach nefesh*; specifically, the case involves a *rodef* – someone (or something) "pursuing" another person to kill him, and the question of what a bystander can, should, and must do to help. A beraita is brought, setting forth an affirmative obligation to rescue one whose life is in mortal danger and its derivation from Lev 19:16:

> From where [does one] know that one who sees another person drowning in a river, or being dragged by a beast, or being attacked by bandits, is obligated to save him? Scripture states [Lev 19:16]: "You shall not stand idly by the blood of your neighbor."[113]
>
> מניין לרואה את חברו שהוא טובע בנהר או חיה גוררתו או לסטין באין עליו שהוא חייב להצילו תלמוד לומר [ויקרא י"ט:טז] תלמוד לומר לא תעמד על דם רעך

As is common in the Talmudic text, this is succeeded by a discussion seeking a greater level of refinement. After quoting the above beraita, the Talmudic text proceeds as follows:

> [But] is this [law really] learned from [this verse? Is it not, rather,] learned from elsewhere? [As it was said,] "from where [do we know that one must save one's neighbor from] *the loss of his body*? Scripture states [Deut 22:2], "and you shall *restore it(him) to him(self)*." (emphasis added)
>
> והא מהכא נפקא? מהתם נפקא: אבדת גופו מניין תלמוד לומר והשבתו לו [דברים כב:ב]

[112] For this and other related rules and restrictions regarding the saving and forfeiting of human life, see B.T. Sanhedrin 73–75.

[113] B.T. Sanhedrin 73a.

The rabbis thus conclude that what gives rise to the obligation to rescue or save human life is not, as popularly assumed, the verse "do not stand idly by the blood of your neighbor." Rather, it is derived from the biblical obligation to restore lost property, which is found among the following verses at the beginning of in Deut 22:

1. You shall not watch your brother's ox or his sheep go astray and hide yourself from them; you must bring them back to your brother.
2. And if your brother [does] not [live] near you, or if you do not know him, then you shall bring it to your house, and it shall stay with you until your brother claims it and [then] *you shall restore it to him.*
3. You shall do the same with his ass; you shall do the same with his garment; and you shall do the same with everything that your brother has lost and you have found; you may not hide yourself [from them]. (emphasis added)

(א) לא תראה את שור אחיך או את שיו נדחים והתעלמת מהם השב תשיבם לאחיך
(ב) ואם לא קרוב אחיך אליך ולא ידעתו ואספתו אל תוך ביתך והיה עמך עד דרש אחיך
אתו והשבתו לו (ג) וכן תעשה לחמרו וכן תעשה לשמלתו וכן תעשה לכל אבדת אחיך
אשר תאבד ממנו ומצאתה לא תוכל להתעלם

Given its spelling, the phrase "and you shall restore it to him" can also be read as "and you shall restore him to him."[114] This is understood by the rabbis to impose an obligation to "return" to the other person his lost "body" (*gufo*), that is, to save his life.

Finally, the text at B.T. Sanhedrin 73a proceeds to explain why two biblical verses are necessary:

> From that [verse "and you shall restore it to him" at Deut 22:2,] I might think that it is [only an obligation] *on himself* [*benafshei*]. But I might have said [there is] no [obligation] to make an effort and hire workers [if he cannot save the person himself (e.g. if he cannot swim in order to save a person who is drowning)], [Therefore, this verse: "do not stand idly by", Lev 19:16] comes to teach that he must [hire someone else to perform the rescue under those circumstances]. (emphasis added)
>
> אי מהתם הוה אמינא הני מילי בנפשיה, אבל מיטרח ומיגר אגורי אימא לא קא משמע לן

The verse from Deuteronomy ("and you shall return it to him") establishes the basic obligation to act personally to rescue someone in need; one is obligated to do that which one is capable of doing with one's own body (*benafshei*).[115]

[114] The interpretation turns on the letter *vav* at the end of the word *vehashevoto*.

[115] As will be seen in Chapter 5, organ transfer would seem to represent perhaps the ultimate case of restoring someone else's life and body (*hashavat gufo*) by means of a "return" of the rescuer's

The additional directive from Leviticus, not to "stand idly by" makes it clear that, as part of the obligation, to save human life one is *also* required to spend money, to "make an effort to hire workers" – מיטרח ומיגר אגורי – to perform a rescue that one is not capable of accomplishing oneself.

What comes across most explicitly in the Hebrew text is the rabbis' vivid conceptualization of the basic obligation of *pikuach nefesh* (as distinct from the secondary property aspect of the obligation) as one that

1. *as regards the rescuer*, applies to his body or person. This is communicated by the use of the word *benafshei*. This word is used in this very Mishnah, and other parts of the accompanying Talmudic text, to refer specifically to the body/life of an individual (and not as a generic word to refer to "oneself")[116];
2. *as regards the person rescued*, is conceived as the physical "return" of himself to himself, in response to his loss of his own "body" (*gufo*).

The image depicted by the Talmudic language fully comports with the theory of the divine lien, whereby (from the perspective of the divine domain) the bodies of the two persons (or the ownership thereof) are somehow conceived as overlapping or somewhat interchangable for purposes of saving a life. This image, as well as the language used here, echoes another instance in which two bodies are theorized as interchangeable. At B.T. Bava Metzia 88b, the rabbis gleaned a critical aspect of the biblical mandate that the laborer eat while working (the question as to the amount or capacity in which he eats) from the word *kenafshecha* in the biblical verse. It is on the basis of this word that the rabbis essentially equate the laborer (his ownership status and even his body, in terms of its desire) with that of the field owner. See p. 149, *supra*.

The rabbinic conceptualization of *pikuach nefesh* as part of the obligation to return lost property has radical implications. It renders utterly transparent something that was implied by the rabbinic conceptualization of *tsedakah* described above: that in the face of the imminent loss of life, one's obligation to save the other is in the nature of a property obligation. When another life is at risk, a preexisting lien is triggered, such that to withhold life-saving support is the same as keeping property that belongs to someone else – it represents both an act of theft and a violation of the affirmative duty to return something lost.

person (*benafshei*). Indeed, regardless of the status of the secondary obligation of spending money (and of questions such as whether one is entitled to be reimbursed), the primary obligation of *vehashevoto lo* (you shall return him to himself) is in clear satisfaction of the divine lien.

116 The Mishnah here speaks of cases in which persons are to be saved "at the cost of their lives" – בנפשן and the phrase of saving a person "with his life" – *benafsho* בנפשו appears throughout the *sugyah*.

The "return" of the other person's life or health is, by definition (to a greater or lesser extent), a matter of ceding one's property (or body) to the other, who bears the legal entitlement thereto. The transaction is outside the ordinary flow of interhuman, commercial transfers. It is not contractual; it can be seen as neither a loan, nor a "pure gift", nor a sale. Given the circumstances, a shift occurs by operation of law, according to the rules of the economy of the sacred. Indeed, there is a ceding of one's property (or body) to another that takes place by means of a retroceding, or giving back, of one's property (or body) to God via the divine lien.

This is made clear on B.T. Sanhedrin 73a-74a. The first scenario listed in the *sugyah* for the obligation of rescue involves one who witnesses someone pursuing another person in order to kill him. The rescue obligation entails an obligation to run after the pursuer (known as a *rodef*). When discussing the question of who bears responsibility for damage caused to property during the course of the pursuit of the murderous *rodef* by the rescuer, the Talmud states unequivocally that there is no legal basis to exempt the rescuer from liability for property damage caused by him during the course of the rescue. If he breaks someone's dishes while chasing the *rodef* through the market, *min hadin*, as a matter of strict (property) law, he is responsible to pay for them. However, the rabbis consciously relieve him of this particular liability, for fear that the risk of open-ended financial exposure will be a disincentive to the act of rescue:

> If one pursuer [the rescuer] was pursuing another pursuer [a potential murderer] to save [someone's life] and broke some utensils, whether belonging to the [murderous] pursuer, the pursued [potential murder victim] or any other person, he is not liable [for damages]. *This is not the actual rule, but if you do not say [that] this [is the rule] no one will save his fellow from a [murderous] pursuer.* (emphasis added)
>
> ורודף שהיה רודף אחר רודף להצילו ושיבר את הכלים בין של רודף בין של נרדף בין של כל אדם פטור ולא מן הדין שאם אי אתה אומר כן נמצא אין לך כל אדם שמציל את חבירו מיד הרודף

Putting aside the rabbinic grant of immunity for damages to the rescuer, which is overtly done for purely pragmatic reasons, the genuine legal rule (*min hadin*) expects the person to perform the act of rescue even if it risks costing him money (whether in payment for broken utensils or for hiring a capable swimmer). This is in sharp contrast to the rules regarding the other type of obligatory "return" – that of returning lost property – where regular rules of property and contract law govern. The obligation to return lost property posits an affirmative obligation to pick up and return a lost item that one encounters (be it a stray ox or a wallet on the sidewalk). While this reflects respect for the property rights of others, in contrast to the obligation of rescue, it implicates no preexisting lien; it entails no shifts in the status of property and demands no ceding of property on the part of the one doing the returning. It is part of the ordinary, rather than the sacred, economy. The purely contractual nature of property obligations in the situation involving the "return of lost property" is in sharp contrast to the situation in which the act of saving, and the spending of money to save, human life is up to neither the person being rescued nor the person involved in the rescue.

A Mishnah in Tractate Bava Kamma illustrates this distinction quite vividly. It describes a situation in which the question of debt and liability is completely dependant on matters of consent and contract. This is in sharp contrast to the situation in which what is being "returned" is human life or health. Mishnah Bava Kamma 10:4 describes the following situation:

> If a person was coming along with a barrel of wine and another with a jug of honey, [and] the barrel of honey happened to crack, [if] the [wine-carrier] poured out his wine and rescued the honey into his [now empty barrel] he would be able to claim no more than the value of his services;[117] but if he said [at the outset], "I am going to rescue your [honey] and I [therefore] expect to be paid the value of my [wine]," the other has to pay him [for his wine].
>
> זה בא בחביתו של יין וזה בא בכדו של דבש נסדקה חבית של דבש ושפך זה את יינו והציל את הדבש לתוכו אין לו אלא שכרו ואם אמר אציל את שלך ואתה נותן לי דמי שלי חייב ליתן לו

In other words, the rescuer of property is under no obligation to go out of his way to expend his own money in the process, and if he chooses to do so, his entitlement to remuneration from the property owner is a contractual matter between them.[118]

By contrast, as noted above, the obligation of spending money to save another life is explicitly dictated by the biblical command not to "stand idly by." If the rescuer would succeed by pouring wine out of his barrel (something he would presumably be required to do), according to the ideal law (*min hadin*) it would

[117] How much money, if any, one might receive for the act of performing the *mitzvah* of returning lost property (or rescue) will be discussed below.

[118] Of course, there is something similarly noncontractual about the act of salvage and the act of saving another's life. In the words of Nahum Rakover, "[b]oth rest on a religious precept and accordingly involve a voluntary act without any legal obligation between the parties to do the act or any agreement as to indemnifying the salvor or rescuer." Rakover (1994), pp. 331–356, at 350. While I take issue with the first part of the sentence, which speaks of a pure "religious precept" and the lack of any "legal obligation", he correctly points out that the basic obligation itself is not a matter of contract between the parties.

be his loss, notwithstanding anything he might say to the person being rescued. While there might, in some cases, be a separate or special obligation on the person saved to reimburse the rescuer (to be discussed below), there is otherwise no basis for a debt of this sort.

4.2.3.2 Rendering Visible the Operation of the Divine Lien

Like the fruit eaten by the laborer that, according to the view that it belongs to heaven (*mishel shamayim hu ochel*), does not flow from the general rules regarding employment relations but passes as a divine gift, the property obligation entailed in the obligation to rescue is unlike an ordinary property obligation that arises out of the relations between the parties (contractual, tortious, etc.). As is true with respect to the broader category of *tsedakah*, the nature of, and basis for, the shift in property status in the context of *pikuach nefesh* – from the domain of the rescuer to that of the one who is saved – is anchored in the divine lien, in the very definitional or foundational structure of property law.

In this case, it is not a verbal pledge but the situation itself that automatically triggers the divine lien. The latent divine claim is triggered automatically by the circumstances in which the transfer takes place. As in the case of the laborer, the situation, as a matter of law, deems the property transferred something that has been reclaimed by the divine and given to the recipient in accordance with the principles of distributive justice outlined in the previous chapter.

In this regard, the case of *pikuach nefesh* helps clarify the operation of the divine lien in the broader context of *tsedakah*. In the absence of the immediacy and specificity provided in a situation involving *pikuach nefesh*, there is a general lack of temporal and spatial limitations circumscribing or identifying transfers that constitute vows of *tsedakah* (as there are with respect to corners of the field etc.). This lack of predetermined objective specificity as to what constitutes *tsedakah* (resulting in the fact that something given as *tsedakah* could, in the absence of exigent circumstances, simply pass as a sale or a loan) might be what allows for its mischaracterization as altruism/philanthropy – that is, as a "free gift," given from property one owns absolutely, in the absence of any obligation. For under normal circumstances, one has the choice as to whether a transfer constitutes *tsedakah*, and there is often a delay between the pledge or giving of *tsedakah* and its receipt by the (divinely vested) recipient.

Crucial to an understanding of the difference between *tsedakah* (an obligatory gift) and altruism (a free gift) is an appreciation of the way in which a transfer that might appear to be wholly voluntary is actually something else, due to its implication of a latent, preexisting property claim. In this regard, the case of *pikuach nefesh* is helpful, since it represents a *tsedakah* transfer that takes place instantaneously. Like the apple eaten by the laborer, the property ceded by the rescuer to the recipient passes simultaneously to and from God during the interhuman transfer. By analyzing the legal theory behind the mechanics of this transfer, the otherwise invisible operation of the divine lien is exposed.

A case recounted in B.T. Ketuvot 91b provides an analogy that illustrates how the attachment of a preexisting property claim like that entailed in *tsedakah* operates. The latent property obligation at play in that case is unrelated to the divine lien on property for the benefit of the poor and the needy (it has to do with the *mitzvah* of honoring one's parents). Nevertheless, it provides a very clear illustration of the way in which an apparently amorphous claim on property reveals itself in the way it operates invisibly – as a matter of law – to define and effectuate a shift in property.

In the tenth Chapter of B.T. Ketuvot (91b), the following case is recounted:

> [There was] a certain man who owed one hundred *zuzim* [coins]. [He] died, and left [his heirs] a small parcel of land that was worth fifty *zuzim*. The creditor came and seized [the parcel of land in partial satisfaction of the debt]. The orphans [who wanted to keep the parcel of land] went [and] gave him fifty *zuzim* [to purchase the parcel of land]. He [the creditor, came thereafter and] seized [the land] again. They came before Abaye, [who] said to them: It is a *mitzvah* for the orphans to repay their father's debt. [We,] *therefore, presume that* [*with that first payment of fifty zuzim*] *you performed the mitzvah* [of repaying your father's debt]. Therefore, [since your father still owes the creditor fifty *zuzim* after that payment, when [he] seizes [the land worth fifty *zuzim*] he seizes by right. And we only said this when the orphans [at the time of paying the fifty *zuzim*] did not say [to the creditor] "these fifty *zuzim* are payment for the [purchase of] the small parcel of land." But if they had said to him, "these fifty *zuzim* are payment for the [purchase of] the small parcel of land," [the creditor is] removed [from the land]. (emphasis added)
>
> ההוא גברא דהו מסקי ביה מאה זוזי שכיב שבק קטינא דארעא דהוה שויא חמשין זוזי אתא בעל חוב וקטריף ליה אזול יתמי יהבו ליה חמשין זוזי הדר קטריף לה אתו לקמיה דאביי אמר להן מצוה על היתומים לפרוע חוב אביהן הני קמאי מצוה עבדיתו השתא כי טריף בדין קטריף ולא אמרן דלא אמרו ליה הני חמשין זוזי דמי דארעא קטינא אבל אמרו ליה הני חמשין זוזי דמי ארעא קטינא סלוקי סלקוה

In this case, the orphans were not legally required to pay their deceased father's debt, although the obligation of honoring one's parents would have been satisfied had they done so. Because of this outstanding, preexisting legal/moral obligation, the law assigned a status to their unspecified payment to the creditor as payment made in satisfaction of this "voluntary obligation." When they paid fifty *zuzim* without specifying that it was for a purpose other than repaying their father's debt, the money was automatically deemed a payment in satisfaction of that *mitzvah*; as such, it was not a payment that the orphans could thereafter retract.

The divine lien inuring to the benefit of the poor operates in a similar fashion. It is obligatory and yet, under most *tsedakah*-related circumstances, voluntary. [119] However, because it exists, one need only say "this *sela* is for *tsedakah*," and the status or ownership of that *sela* is changed; it no longer belongs to the donor, and the transfer cannot be retracted.

The disposition of property given, damaged, or spent in a situation involving *pikuach nefesh* is also governed by the divine lien. The preexisting obligation to save the other attaches once property moves, ascribing it automatically to the divine lien in the way the *mitzvah* of honoring one's parents captured the fifty *zuzim* as soon as they were paid. When the lives of particular persons are immediately at stake, the situation identifies that which is given as a fulfillment of the obligation of *pikuach nefesh*, a form of *tsedakah*. A useful analogy for analyzing the life-saving transfer is another case in which the obligation to sustain human life (based on the phrase "and your brother shall live with you"[120]) is fulfilled – that is, the property transfer that takes place when the laborer eats while working; this is another case in which the circumstances are what define the property transfer as a gift passing instantaneously to and from God. Just as the food the laborer eats implicates the divine lien and is considered heaven's property (*mishel shamayim*), so too might one say that, by definition, that which is received by the recipient in a case of *pikuach nefesh* passes through the divine realm to sustain human life.

[119] The two cases are not exactly the same. For example, the obligations involved in *pikuach nefesh* in general (and organ transfer in particular) – the obligation to save human life and the prohibition against maiming the human body – cannot be waived by the individual. These obligations are unquestionably "embodied" in the human body as they are beyond the choice and consent of the person involved. By contrast, the *mitzvah* that creates a kind of preexisting lien in this case, that of honoring one's parents (which is what makes it a *mitzvah* for the orphans to repay their father's debt), is something that the parent is allowed to waive. See B.T. Kiddushin 32b. The use of this example to demonstrate the operation of the divine lien does not mean to imply that all *mitzvot* automatically create property liens to the extent applicable. (The question of whether that broader statement is true is something to be explored elsewhere; it is not necessarily implied by the argument in this book.)

[120] The general obligation to sustain human life generated in the phrase "and your brother shall live with you," (which lays the groundwork for the obligation of *tsedakah*), is also at play in other contexts invovling *mitzvot* of feeding people. This is made explicit in the case of the laborer and is implicit in the case of *pikuach nefesh*, notwithstanding the fact that separate verses are understood to specifically require these particular acts of giving (*ki tavo bekerem re'echa*, Deut 23:25, and *vehashevoto lo/lo ta'amod*, Deut 22:2/Lev 19:16, respectively).

The mechanics of this automatic status change in property is also what takes place when the laborer of the field eats the apple. As seen in Chapter 3, according to the majority rabbinic view, the two steps in interhuman giving and receipt of a divine gift occur simultaneously; this is like what takes place in the context of *pikuach nefesh* – what goes to (or, even more vividly, what might be ingested by) the recipient, in order to meet the (in this case immediate) need for sustenance or preservation, passes to him automatically and completely, as a matter of property law, via the divine domain.

As with the laborer reaching for an apple, when a person whose life is at risk is given sustenance, the preexisting obligation (the divine lien) is automatically implicated; as in the case in B.T. Ketuvot involving the payment of fifty *zuzim*, a transfer in this context (unless specified to the contrary, circumstances permitting[121]) is characterized, by operation of law, as the giving (and simultaneous receipt) of a "return" gift to God. This understanding not only is borne out in early rabbinic literature but, as will be discussed below, is also drawn out even more clearly by rabbis of the medieval period.

4.2.4 *Saving Human Life – The Question of Payment*

There is one final perspective from which the nature of the *pikuach nefesh* transfer ought to be explored – the question of subsequent (re)payment. We have seen that, in a life-threatening situation in which people are in the urgent position of having to act quickly and without calculation, the rescuer is obligated to expend funds if necessary to save the victim. Can the rescuer expect reimbursement for the costs of the rescue? Can the rescuer expect any other type of payment?

4.2.4.1 Who Bears the Costs of the Rescue?

Despite all that has been said regarding the nature of the life-saving expenditure as a divine gift, in which the divine lien is implicated such that no property claim arises on the part of the rescuer, there is one clear reason to suggest that the rescued, nevertheless, ought to repay the rescuer – the fact that the person rescued also has a legal obligation to save himself. For the divine lien applies not only to the saving of the other; it also – and, in fact, initially – applies to oneself. Parallel to one's obligation to sustain the lives of others is another obligation that comes first – to save and sustain one's own life. In the case of the person drowning described in the beraita in B.T. Sanhedrin 74a

[121] It is not necessary at this point, nor is there space, to delve into the details of the question of when one is permitted to withhold or is obligated to give up property that will save the life of a person in their presence.

and the erstwhile rescuer who cannot swim, even though the rabbis expressly described this obligation of *pikuach nefesh* to include the expenditure of funds to hire others, if the pants and wallet of the drowning man were on the side of the lake, the rescuer would be acting appropriately were he to first use the money in that wallet to hire someone who can swim.

The caveat to the rule that one must bear the expense of saving the life of another in need is the fact that primary responsibility for the act and expense of saving falls on the person in jeopardy. In fact, in the context of *pikuach nefesh*, this comes into play to preclude the saving of another life when doing so would mean (or might mean) the loss of the rescuer's life.

The parallel property (sovereignty-limiting) rule (here applicable to one's life/body and property) is derived from the same verse discussed above: "and your brother shall live with you." In a famous decision attributed to Rabbi Akiva, at B.T. Bava Metzia 62a, the limiting principle to the general requirement that one save the other is derived from the very verse in Leviticus (25:36) that gives rise to the general obligation to sustain human life: "and your brother shall live with you." Asked what a person must do if he finds himself in the desert with another, and with a flask containing only enough water to save the life of one of them, Rabbi Akiva learns from this verse that the flask owner *must* drink all the water himself. Not only does this verse require the sustaining of human life, but it also dictates that such an obligation applies to oneself as well and, moreover, that one's life must take priority. The requirement to preserve one's life precedes that of saving the life of the other (you must be alive in order for the other to be able to live *with you*[122]).

This can then be understood as yet another property principle, anchored in the divine lien, that circumscribes one's freedom of decision-making regarding one's life and one's property where the preservation of human life is concerned. The same obligation that requires one to preserve the life of others also requires one to save oneself – and, to save oneself first. These obligations could be seen as signifiers of the objectification of people (like all things) as the property of the divine. And yet, there is an (at least partial) offsetting of the potentially invidious implications that flow from this proposition. For the principle of divine ownership that gives rise to a lack of, or limits to, ownership (including self-ownership) on the part of the individual itself dictates the absolute prioritization of the life of the self over the life of the other. When combined, proscriptions regarding self-injury,[123] suicide, and so on suggest limits to

[122] This is the same logic used when a parent on an airplane is told that, in the event of an emergency, she must don her own oxygen mask before putting one on her child.

[123] The prohibition against injuring oneself is a separate prohibition, known as *issur chavalah*, which will be discussed in Chapter 5. Characterization of this prohibition as one anchored in

self-ownership attributable to the overarching ownership of the divine and the prioritization of the sustenance of human life.

The interplay of the obligations of both parties to a rescue (rescuer and rescuee) vis-à-vis payment is reflected in B.T. Sanhedrin 74a,[124] which explores the larger question of monetary liability when property is damaged in the course of the chase. A portion of this text was quoted above. The complete text provides as follows:

> If a [*rodef*, murderous] pursuer was chasing his fellow [to kill him] and he [accidentally] broke some utensils – [regardless of] whether they belonged to the person he was chasing or to a third part, he is free from monetary liability. Why? Because he is liable to be put to death.[125] If the utensils were broken by a [potential victim who was] being chased – if [the utensils] belonged to the [murderous] pursuer, [the pursued person] is exempt [from monetary liability, but] if they belonged to a third party he is liable [for monetary damages.] [The reason] he is exempt [from paying damages] if [the utensils] belonged to the [murderous pursuer] is that his property should not be more precious [to him] than his own body. However, if [the utensils] belonged to a third party, he is liable [for damages,] because, he *has [improperly] saved himself with the money of his fellow*. If one pursuer [the rescuer] was pursuing another pursuer [a potential murderer] to save [someone's life] and broke some utensils, whether belonging to the [murderous] pursuer ...or to any other person, he is not liable [for damages]. *This is not the actual rule, but if you do not say [that] this [is the rule] no one will save his fellow from a [murderous] pursuer.* (emphasis added)
>
> רודף שהיה רודף אחר חבירו ושיבר את הכלים בין של נרדף ובין של כל אדם פטור מאי טעמא מתחייב בנפשו הוא ונרדף ששיבר את הכלים של רודף פטור של כל אדם חייב של רודף פטור שלא יהא ממונו חביב עליו מגופו של כל אדם חייב שמציל עצמו בממון חבירו ורודף שהיה רודף אחר רודף להצילו ושיבר את הכלים בין של רודף בין שלנרדף בין של כל אדם פטור ולא מן הדין שאם אי אתה אומר כן נמצא אין לך כל אדם שמציל את חבירו מיד הרודף

In this discussion, there are two separate parties to whom one might think money might be owed by the rescued party after the rescue: (1) the person whose dishes are broken as the victim flees from the pursuer (perhaps a storekeeper

the idea of divine ownership of the human body, while logical and popularly assumed, is not easily demonstrated in the texts. Nevertheless, for purposes of this section, it suffices to say that the prohibition against maiming oneself does represent a limit to self-ownership *per se* since, as will be seen, it is not something to which one is legally capable of agreeing.

124 There is a parallel to this text in B.T. Bava Kamma 117b. Although there it is said in the name of Rabbah, and in Sanhedrin it is said in the name of Raba.

125 According to the principle *kam lei b'drabah minei*, קם ליה בדרבה מיניה, a person who is liable for the death penalty is exempt from the lesser penalty such as a fine or monetary damages. For another example see B.T. Ketuvot 29a.

with dishes on display in an outdoor market), and (2) the rescuer. With respect to the former, the obligation of the rescued party is asserted quite simply. He is obligated for the cost of the dishes, for he is saving himself with someone else's property. With respect to the rescuer, however, there is no explicit repayment obligation. We had been told earlier that the rescuer is obligated to expend funds for the rescue; no mention of repayment was made there. Here, what the rescuer is entitled to is relief from being obligated, himself, for dishes that he breaks while performing the rescue. Perhaps the debt will be paid by the rescued party, although this is not made explicit. Nevertheless, as noted earlier, the relief afforded the rescuer by the rabbis for this cost is explicitly given to avoid a disincentive to performing the rescue. According to the ideal law, we are told, the rescuer is responsible, financially, for the dishes.

It is possible, therefore, that there are different levels and types of repayment obligations for the absent third party and the rescuer. Before examining the obligation relating to the absent third party it is worth considering how the repayment to the rescuer, if any, might be different, legally, from that owed the absent third party.[126]

One might argue that the third party utensil-owner should be entitled to no reimbursement because the divine lien justifies the use of the other person's property. What differentiates the utensil owner from the rescuer, however, is the fact that he is not present, and his property is taken without his knowledge or permission, making the conduct more in the nature of theft; by contrast, the rescuer is present and exercising agency when he incurs property liability during the course of the (voluntary and obligatory) act of rescue. He is fulfilling the core "bodily" requirement of *pikuach nefesh* (Deut 22:2, *vehashevoto lo*), to which the monetary payment aspect (Lev 19:16, *lo ta'amod*) is appended. The costs incurred by the rescuer create no property debt on the part of the person rescued. It is possible (although this is not mentioned) that the rabbis might deem him entitled to reimbursement for expenditures if the rescued party has funds, in the interest of equity, on a theory of unjust enrichment. Nevertheless, according to the law, the rescuer (unlike the third-party utensil-owner who is not present) cedes property to save another, giving it up entirely to the divine lien; therefore, technically, the rescued party incurs no debt.

[126] As will be shown, the later medieval rabbis, based on a statement by the medieval Talmudist known as the Rosh, will treat both parties alike and assume that the rescuer is owed the same type of repayment as the absent third party. Nevertheless, there is not much discussion in the sources about this question to begin with, about the degree, type, and amount of repayment owed by one whose life has been saved, so there is clearly room for speculation, even within the tradition. This is in sharp contrast to the rules regarding repayment owed one who has saved someone's property, about which a good deal is written.

It is also possible (and perhaps more likely) that, as outlined earlier, the person saved has an obligation to expend his own funds to save himself; thus, the principle that it is wrong for someone to "save himself with the property of his fellow" applies to anyone who causes someone to incur costs in connection with the rescue, including the rescuer and the absent third party whose dishes are broken. This idea can be said to correspond to a principle known to other legal systems, including the common law in the United States. As phrased by a court in 1910:

> Theologians hold that a starving man may, without moral guilt, take what is necessary to sustain life; but it could hardly be said that the obligation would not be upon such person to pay the value of the property so taken when he became able to do so.[127]

While the Talmudic rule echoes this principle, it differs in one significant respect. Whereas in the above-quoted text the person rescued has a legal (and moral) obligation to pay for property used to save his life, under Jewish law this is only true *if he can afford it*. If he is poor, he has no obligation to pay – and the obligation of his fellow, to spend money in order to save his life, defines who bears the cost. In other words, if at the time of the rescue the rescued party has the funds, the lien attaches to it; however, if he is poor, the lien attaches to the property of the rescuer, and the rescued party owes nothing. There is no debt to be paid, and nothing is owed if, for example, he comes into money the next day.

The divine lien operates here as it did in the case we saw earlier, from Mishnah Peah 5:4, involving the traveling householder who runs out of money and must take from the *tsedakah* fund of the town he is visiting. When he returns home, he has no repayment obligation because, according to the sages, he was a poor person at the time he received assistance.[128] The *tsedakah* received was in the nature of a divine gift. Such is the case, as well, with funds expended for purposes of *pikuach nefesh*. It is true that the victim's obligation to pay comes first; however, the divine lien attaches to the funds of the rescuer if he has no funds.

The fact that this payment obligation on the part of the rescuer (where the rescued party is not obligated to pay) is in the nature of a lien, or encumbrance on his property, is reflected in the language of the medieval Talmudist Rabenu Asher ben Yechi'el (Germany/Spain, 1250–1327), also known as "the Rosh." The question of payment in the context of *pikuach nefesh* was debated among the medieval rabbis. Most of them interpreted the principle in B.T. Sanhedrin 74a, that one ought not save oneself with someone else's money, the way it has been described thus far – not as a prohibition against saving oneself with

[127] *Vincent v. Lake Erie Transportation Company*, 109 Minn. 456, 460 (Sup. Ct. Minn, 1910).

[128] See also Tur Y.D. 253, which analogizes the traveling householder to a poor person who, upon becoming rich, bears no obligation to repay the *tsedakah* fund.

another's property when necessary,[129] but as the basis for a claim for subsequent reimbursement against the rescued party.

The Rosh addressed the question of whether the rescued party is required to reimburse the rescuer for what he expended while discussing the command posited on B.T. Sanhedrin 73a, that the rescuer spend money to hire others. The Rosh states,

> the party rescued is required to repay [the rescuer] the amount that he spent, [on the rescue] because one is not obligated to save the life of his fellow with his own money *if the person saved has money*[130] (emphasis added)
>
> הניצול חייב לפרוע למציל מה שהוציא דאין אדם מחויב להציל נפש חבירו בממונו היכא דאית ליה ממונא לניצול

His support for the claim that the rescuer is entitled to reimbursement for what he spent is the statement (quoted earlier in this section (4.2.4.1)) at B.T. Sanhedrin 74a, "If the person being pursued [accidentally] broke some utensils ... if they belonged to a third party he is liable." This statement of the Rosh, that there exists an obligation of repayment *only* in the case where the rescued party has money, was codified in the Tur[131] and also recorded by Joseph Caro in his commentary to the Tur, the Beit Yosef.[132]

[129] On its face, the principle of "*assur lehatzil atzmo bemamon chavero*" (one is prohibited from saving oneself with the property of another) (אסור להציל עצמו בממון חברו) contravenes the general rule providing that none of the commandments save three (theft not being among them) can impede one from doing that which is necessary to save human life. And, indeed, there is a dispute about this among the medieval Talmudic commentators. Rashi reads this principle literally, finding that a person is actually prohibited from saving oneself with another's property. In a decision rendered in 1811 in Altuna, a modern decisor, Jacob Ettlinger (1798–1871), follows Rashi's interpretation (*She'elot u-Teshuvot Binyan Tziyon* number 167). However, most medieval (e.g., Tosafot, the Rosh) and modern decisors disagree with the view expressed by Rashi. See Israel Meir Lau, "*Sikun Iver Kedei Lehatzil*" [Hebrew: Endangering a Limb to Save [a Life]"], *She'elot U'Teshuvot Yachel Yisrael* 1:68, Jerusalem: Machon Masoret (1992), pp. 408–420. Like the Tosafot at B.T. Bava Kamma 60b (*s.v.*"*mahu lehatzil atzmo*"), they do not read this principle as a prohibition, but as the basis of a claim for subsequent reimbursement.

[130] *Piskei Ha-Rosh* Sanhedrin 8:2. A similar ruling was made by the Maharam of Rothenberg with respect to the funds used for *pidyon shevuyim*, ransom of captives (Responsa Number 32). If the person rescued has the money, he must refund the rescuer.

[131] Tur H.M. 426:1: "One who sees his fellow drowning in a river or being pursued by thieves is obligated to save him, both with his body and with his property; *however, if [the person rescued] has money to save himself, he is required to (re)pay [the rescuer]*" (emphasis added).

הרואה את חבירו טובע בנהר או שלסטין באין עליו חייב להצילו בין בגופו בין בממונו ומיהו אם יש לו ממון להציל עצמו חייב לשלם לזה

Note the mention, in the Tur, of the dual obligations of *pikuach nefesh* – the requirement to use one's body (*gufo*) and one's property (*mamono*).

[132] כתב הרא"ש (סי' ב) והניצול חייב לפרוע למציל מה שהוציא דאין אדם מחוייב להציל נפש חבירו בממונו היכא דאית ליה ממונא לניצולו הביא ראיה לדבר

The caveat that reimbursement is required only in the case of one who can afford it is decisive as to the legal status of the payment.[133] The person rescued does not owe an outstanding property debt to the rescuer; otherwise, the question of reimbursement would not turn on the wealth of the rescued party. Reimbursement is required by the wealthy because he has a primary obligation to save himself, and it would be unfair for him to benefit at the expense of an another other if he has the means to pay for it himself.[134]

Returning to Piskei Ha-Rosh Sanhedrin 8:2, the Rosh provides a particularly vivid description of the operation of precisely the type of lien described in this book (echoing the work of Marcel Mauss) as it relates to the property used by the rescuer to effectuate the rescue (where the rescued party has no duty of repayment):

> For the property of his fellow is obligated to [be applied] to the rescue; *[the property] is in the domain [reshut] of [the rescued party] in order to save him.* (emphasis added)
>
> שהרי ממון חברו מחויב להציל וברשות שברם כדי להנצל

Thus, anything used or spent by the rescuer with respect to which there is no entitlement to reimbursement (e.g., in the case of a poor victim) is understood to be legally encumbered by the obligation of rescue. Indeed, any utensils

"The Rosh wrote ([Piskei Ha-Rosh Sanhedrin 8] section 2), 'and the one saved is obligated to repay to the rescuer whatever he spent, for one is not obligated to save the life of his fellow with his money *where the one saved has money*,' and [the Rosh] brings proof for this" (emphasis added). For some reason, Caro did not repeat this statement in the Shulchan Arukh, but its commentators made note of his endorsement of the Rosh's statement in the Beit Yosef. Shulchan Arukh H.M. 426:1; Sma and Siftei Kohen ad loc. See also Rabbi Eliezer Waldenberg, Responsa Ziz Eliezer 19:2, who deduces from the statement of the Rosh that "when the person requiring rescue has no money the rescuer is, indeed, obligated to save the life of his fellow with his own money.

הכא דלית ליה ממונא לניצול כן מחויב המציל להציל נפש חברו בממונו

[133] Ernest Weinrib, a law professor at the University of Toronto, regards the possibility of restitution for the rescuer as significant, stating that "[I]f the rescuer can recover his disbursements from the person he has saved, the duty to rescue is less striking." Weinrib, Ernest, "Rescue and Restitution," *S'vara: A Journal of Philosophy and Judaism*, volume 1 (1989), pp. 59–65 at 65. On this basis he regards the decision of the Rosh as an example of the fact that "the idea of rights exercises a gravitational pull on legal reasoning even within this jurisprudence [of obligations]." In regarding this as a "right," Weinrib fails to take into account the conditional nature of the rescuer's so-called right to collect. This significant caveat makes clear that the obligation is not watered down but something quite serious. The rescuer must act without knowing the financial status of the victim and with the very real possibility that the divine lien will attach to his property and he will have no "right" of reimbursement.

[134] The fact that wealth disparity is decisive here comports with the broader theory of distributive justice driving the divine lien discussed in Chapter 3, and reconciles the (wealth-based) reimbursement requirement with the obligations imposed by the divine lien in the context of *pikuach nefesh*.

owned by an anonymous third party that happen to be broken by the victim are (after the fact) understood to have been similarly encumbered. Although somewhat randomly identified and possibly even sacrificed unknowingly, they are, as it turns out, bound by the divine lien such that they essentially belong to the rescued party for use in the rescue.

4.2.4.2 Other "Costs" to the Rescuer

As noted earlier, the obligation to rescue a life is twofold: one is obligated to use one's body (*benafshei* or *begufo*) and one's property (*bemamono*, e.g., to hire workers). As shown, it might turn out that property losses will be reimbursed, *if* the saved party can afford to pay. What is the rule regarding the possibility of reimbursement with respect to the expenditures one makes with one's body? As to this question the answer is quite simple – there is no basis for monetary payment, as reimbursement or otherwise. The sparse mention of reimbursement in connection with *pikuah nefesh* relates exclusively to property losses. The obligation to apply one's body anticipates an act that is done *gratis*.

That one cannot charge for one's "services" of performing the act of saving can, if nothing else, be gleaned from the rules with respect to returning lost property. As mentioned, that *mitzvah* is related to the obligation of *pikuach nefesh* (both are rooted in the idea of returning that which is lost, *vehashevoto lo*, Deut 22:2), but it is much weaker (given that no life is being saved). Thus, for example, whereas one is obligated to spend money to save a life, such is not the case with respect to saving or returning another person's property; nor can one obtain reimbursement in the absence of prior consent (as noted above in connection with Mishnah Bava Kamma 10:4).[135]

The medieval rabbis make clear that one is expected to return lost property without remuneration (although one can collect for legitimate expenditures). Thus, for example, the Shulchan Arukh (H.M. 265) states, "One who sees a lost article is obligated to return it for free."[136]

The only way one might receive money for one's (bodily) actions is if one had to abandon one's work in order to perform the *mitzvah*. This represents

[135] One can, however, recover reasonable out-of-pocket expenses.

[136] See also Tosafot to B.T. Bava Metzia 31b (s.v. "*im*"). The Shulchan Arukh (H.M. 265) provides in full: "One who sees a lost article is obligated to return it for free if he is not busy [working]. However, if he is involved in his work, and [to fulfill the commandment is forced to] desist from his work ... [the owner of the returned property] shall give him his wages as an out-of-work worker (*kefoel batel*) who has desisted from the particular work in which he was involved."
הרואה אבידה חייב להחזיר בחנם אם הוא בטל אבל אם היה עוסק במלאכה ובטל ממלאכתו ...נותן לו שכרו כפועל בטל שיבטל מאותה מלאכה שהיה עוסק בה

the recoupment of a monetary loss; it is not a fee for the performance of the *mitzvah*. Even here, the level of compensation is not open to negotiation between the parties; indeed, it is not even tied to the actual cost incurred. Jewish law provides a fixed, minimal wage that is less than the full salary lost by taking time off of work. (Mishnah Bava Metzia 2:9 provides the following: "[i]f his loss [of time] is worth a *sela*, he cannot say to [the person whose lost property he returned], 'give me a *sela*;' rather, he is to be paid as an unemployed laborer "*kefoel batel*."[137] (היה בטל מסלע לא יאמר תן לי סלע אלא נותן לו שכרו כפועל בטל)

To summarize, in the context of *pikuach nefesh*, one is expected to perform the *mitzvah* without negotiating the terms of payment or reimbursement. To the contrary, one is expected to dive right in (sometimes literally) and perform the act of rescue. Derived from two separate verses, the obligation of rescue demands the (free) application of one's body and one's property. While one *might* receive some payment for the latter, there will be no payment for the former. Not only do one's bodily and monetary expenditures satisfy the obligation of *pikuach nefesh*, but they are also gifts to God, in satisfaction of the divine lien. It also represents giving to someone something to which that person is entitled (as a gift from God). Asking for payment in that context is tantamount to theft.

The clearest expression of this idea that healing, in particular, is a form of *hekdesh* (a gift to and from God) is reflected in a Mishnah that parallels Mishnah Nedarim 11:3, quoted earlier. That text provided that a person who has forsworn benefit (*hana'ah*) from another human being is permitted to take from that person's gleanings, forgotten sheaves and corners of the field. As noted earlier, this expresses the fact that these benefits do not come from the property of the field owner, but they come from the realm of the divine (having been "placed" there by the field owner). Mishnah Nedarim 4:4 states,

> [regarding] one who is prohibited by vow (*neder*) from enjoying any benefit from his fellow, ... [if he is sick his fellow] can afford him a cure of *life* (*nefesh*), but [he can] not [afford him] a cure of *money (mamon)*. (emphasis added)
>
> המודר הנאה מחבירו....מרפאו רפואת נפש אבל לא רפואת ממון.

[137] What this means, according to the Talmudic exposition of the Mishnah (B.T. Bava Metzia 31b), is that he is to be paid as an "unemployed laborer" (*kefoel batel*) in his field. This term is understood differently by different medieval commentators, to call for either (1) the amount a person in his field would want to be paid in order to remain idle, or (2) the amount that is less than full pay that a person in his field would want to be paid in order to be able to return lost objects rather than work.

On its face, this Mishnah articulates the same principle laid down earlier regarding gifts to the poor – that in curing (saving) another human being one is not (personally or directly) giving that person a benefit. The Talmud proceeds to make clear that this is not a matter of providing a service for free; it is the cure itself that, legally, does not constitute the giving of benefit from one person to the other:

> [The Mishnah: states] "The latter may afford him a cure of life but not a cure of money, etc.." What does this mean? Shall we say that "a cure of life" means without payment, and "a cure of money" is for a fee? Then let [the Mishnah instead] state: He may heal him without payment, but not for a fee! Rather, [the phrase] *"a cure of life" [refers] to his body (gufo)*, [while] "a cure of money" refers to his cattle ... (emphasis added)
>
> מרפאהו רפואת הנפש כו'. היכי קתני? אילימא דרפואת נפש בחנם, רפואת ממון בשכר ליתני הכי מרפאהו בחנם אבל לא בשכר! אלא רפואת נפש גופו רפואת ממון בהמתו

Utilizing the now familiar binary of body (*gufo*) and property (*mamon*), the Mishnah makes clear that when providing a cure of "life," the healer does not impart to the recipient anything of value that would count as a "benefit" (*hana'ah*). This is not to say that a life cure has no value; indeed, as other areas of rabbinic literature suggest, its value is likely so high that it is incommensurable.[138] Rather, as was true in the case of gleanings and so on, that which is conferred upon the recipient does not come as a benefit from the human donor/actor. It implicitly passes through the divine realm and is received from the domain of the divine. This is in contrast with "a cure of money," such as curing one's cow (one's property). This is an ordinary (*hedyot*) commercial transaction that passes directly from one person to the other and is prohibited by the *neder*. Indeed, this Mishnah makes clear that a person does not have the legal capacity to forswear a cure via the mechanism of the *neder*, that one's life/health is not something that one has the power to give up (not even in the context of *hekdesh*, sacrificing for God).

This lien-like understanding in the context of *pikuach nefesh*[139] dovetails with the rabbinic interpretation of *vehashevoto lo* (Deut 22:2), "and you shall

[138] See generally Bava Kamma chapter 8 regarding the rabbis' attempts to assign value, for purposes of the calculation of monetary damages, to human body parts.

[139] The notion that, in the context of *pikuach nefesh*, a "cure of life" does not pass, as a benefit, from the person who performed the *mitzvah* of *pikuach nefesh* is bolstered by a more general Talmudic principle: "*mitzvot lav lehanot nitnu*," "commandments were not given to impart benefit (*hana'ah*)." According to this principle, whatever pleasure one receives from someone else's performance of a *mitzvah* (e.g., enjoyment of the sound of the *shofar*, ram's horn) does not, as a matter of law, entail the receipt of benefit (*hana'ah*) from the person who performed the *mitzvah*. See B.T. Rosh Hashanah 28a.

return [his body] to him." The situation depicted by all of these texts combined is that, in the context of *pikuach nefesh*,

1. the healer has no property interest in the life-saving aid provided,[140]
2. the recipient theoretically receives nothing (no benefit or *hana'ah*) directly from the healer, and
3. the healer is "returning" to the recipient something that already belongs to him; this situation is explained by the involvement of the divine as an intermediary in the transaction.

The conceptualization of healing as the return to someone of what is already his conveys the deep conceptual link between life-sustaining gifts to others and the original or predicate institution of Temple sacrifice – "return" gifts given to God, to whom (given his ownership of everything) these items *already* belong. *Pikuach nefesh* exposes the philosophical implications of the link between what were characterized as two types of gifts to God: those going to God, and those given to God and deflected to humans. Particularly in the absence of the Temple, the way to make "return" gifts to God is to save and sustain the lives of people; conversely, because it represents a gift to and from God, the life-saving assistance that one receives from another is a "return" gift to the recipient.

When the case of organ transplantation is considered, this analysis of *pikuach nefesh* is pushed to its limits. It is one thing to align the preservation of human life with the notion of sanctity and the teleology of the divine lien; the possibility of organ transfer presses the intersection of divine ownership, human life, and the human body (of both parties) to its ultimate limit.

[140] Mishnah Nedarim 4:4 makes clear that the healing, itself, is not something of value that passes between the healer and the recipient. The Talmudic discussion of the rescuer indicates that, by law, the healer is also not entitled to the reimbursement of expenses and costs. The obvious implication of these rules is that there is no basis upon which to pay a doctor, other than to incentivize him (as in the case of the broken utensils). As will be discussed below, the medieval debate over payment of doctors (like the debate over the payment of rabbis and other members of the community who spend all their time performing *mitzvot*) includes the view herein described. See Avraham Sofer Abraham, *Nishmat Avraham: Hilkhot Holim Rofim U-Refuah* [Hebrew: The Laws of Sick People, Doctors, and Medicine], Hoshen Mishpat, Hilkhot Chovel B'Chavero, Jerusalem: Erez (1982), section 326 (pp. 239–241). The question of payment to physicians, like that of paying rabbis, is resolved by the institution of *s'char batalah* (forgone salary), whereby the person is paid for the time spent performing the *mitzvah* that could have otherwise have been spent earning a salary. Of course, this mechanism was a legal evolutionary step that was necessary to allow for the professionalization of these functions within the community.

5

Returning a "Lost Body" with One's Own Body: Organ Transplantation as Retrocession and (Re)consecration of the Body

As it does for United States law, the possibility of organ transplantation poses unprecedented questions for Jewish law. Over the past three decades, legal scholars and religious authorities have, by analogy or otherwise, used Jewish legal principles derived from ancient, medieval, and modern texts to analyze this novel phenomenon. It is necessary to briefly summarize their findings before turning to a more in-depth analysis of organ transplantation, the divine lien and the question of the permissibility of payment for organs.

As noted earlier, the obligation to save human life takes precedence over almost all other obligations and prohibitions.[1] And yet, there is no general perception that organ transfer is obligatory. Why is that? What are the countervailing concerns that militate against articulating a straightforward obligation to give an organ to someone in need, whether *inter vivos* or postmortem? Contemporary writers and legal decisors point to two legal principles, both of which relate to the fact that one's primary obligation is to one's own life and body: the prohibition against self-mutilation (*issur chavalah*), and the prohibition against putting oneself in a life-threatening situation.[2] And yet, the question persists for, as noted, it would seem that the obligation to save life would operate to offset the effect of these prohibitions in a situation in which another person's life will be saved.[3]

Contemporary legal decisors balance these competing interests (*pikuach nefesh*, and the prohibitions against self-mutilation and life endangerment) and arrive at the following conclusions. Organ transfer is prohibited whenever

[1] Those not included are murder, idolatry, and certain sexual offenses such as incest and adultery. B.T. Sanhedrin 74a.

[2] See Mishnah Baba Kamma 7:6; Maimonides, *Mishneh Torah, Hilchot Chovel Umazik* [Hebrew: Laws of Injury and Damages] 5:1. See also David Daube, "Limitations on Self-sacrifice in Jewish Law and Tradition," in Calum M. Carmichael (ed.), *Collected Works of David Daube*, volume 1: *Talmudic Law*, Berkeley: University of California (1992), pp. 45–62.

[3] This book does not examine the complicating issues raised by the longstanding debate over the nature of this obligation when the person whose life is at stake is not Jewish.

there is a life-threatening risk to the donor;[4] some say that there is a small category of cases in which organ transfer is mandatory to save someone's life, if the procedure poses little risk and a slight burden for the donor (e.g., where the substances removed are replenishable, as are blood and bone marrow);[5] in the largest category of situations, organ transfer (being neither prohibited nor specifically mandated) is permissible (not mandatory).[6]

There is something missing in this analysis of organ transfer. Absent from the weighing of the competing interests (of protecting oneself and one's body and helping others) to ascertain permissibility of the practice is any information regarding regarding the meaning of the act itself.[7] The fact that something is missing in the above legal analysis becomes clear when one poses the question of question of whether organs can legally be bought and sold. The

[4] See, e.g., David J. Bleich, *Contemporary Halakhic Problems*, volume 4, chapter 12, "May Tissue Donations Be Compelled?" (1995), pp. 273–287; Mordechai Halperin, "Organ Transplants from Living Donors," *Israel Law Review* 27 (1993), pp. 566ff; Fred Rosner, *Modern Medicine and Jewish Law*, chapter 10 (1972); Nahum Rabinovitch, "What Is the Halacha For Organ Transplants?" in Fred Rosner and David Bleich (eds.), *Jewish Bioethics*, New York: Sanhedrin Press (1979), pp. 351–357; David Frenkel, "Transplants," in Nahum Rakover (ed.), *Jewish Law and Current Legal Problems*, Jerusalem: The Library Of Jewish Law (1984), pp. 195–201 at 195; Avraham Steinberg, *Encyclopedia Hilchatit Refuit* [Hebrew: The Halachic-Medical Encyclopedia], volume 2, Jerusalem: Schlesinger Institute (1991), pp. 191–244; Menachem Elon, Bernard Auerbach, Daniel Chazin, and Melvin Sykes, *Jewish Law (Mishpat Ivri): Cases and Materials*, New York: Matthew Bender and Co., Inc. (1999) (see Israeli Supreme Court decision on organ transplantation). There is one basic and significant disagreement that divides religious decisors over the legality of postmortem organ transfer. It relates to the legal definition of death. For heart transplantation, organ transfer is only a possibility for those who accept brain death. For those who insist on the traditional definition of cardiac death, based on a passage in B.T. Yoma 85a, in many cases organ transfer would be considered an act of murder.

[5] This obligation would likely not be considered mandatory unless the person in need is in physical proximity with the person capable of saving their life. This principle is known as "*choleh lefaneinu*" (an ill person in front of us). Cf. Moshe Feinstein, *Iggerot Moshe, Hoshen Mishpat* 1:103 (1968) (regarding donations to a blood bank, *pikuach nefesh* is found to be somewhat attenuated). Given the long list of people waiting to receive organs, this requirement is certainly met for kidneys, etc. This is not unlike the situation with respect to *tsedakah*, where the rabbis, in B.T. Rosh Hashanah 4b shortened the duration of the "do not delay" requirement because of the plentitude of poor people (see p. 156, *supra*). Cf. David J. Bleich, *Contemporary Halakhic Problems*, volume 4, chapter 12, "May Tissue Donations Be Compelled?" (1995), pp. 273–287, and Joel Roth, "Organ Donation" (YD 336, 1999), in Kassel Abelson and David J. Fine (eds.), *Responsa 1991–2000, the Committee on Jewish Law and Standards of the Conservative Movement*, New York: Rabbinical Assembly (2002), pp. 208–316.

[6] While all decisors agree that *pikuach nefesh* justifies what would otherwise constitute the illegal maiming of the human body, there are differences of opinion as to precisely how the exception is justified: e.g., does the saving of life override the prohibition or, because a human life is involved, does the prohibition of injury to the body not apply at all. See Michael WyGoda, "*M'chirat Eyvarim*" [Hebrew: The Sale of Organs], in *Shanah Beshanah*, volume 42 (5762) (2002), pp. 119–127.

[7] This might account, at least in part, for the low numbers of organ transfers by Jews.

few contemporary decisors who have confronted the question of sales treat it as nothing more than a gloss on the above analysis – are those findings (as to permissibility of the act of organ transfer itself), altered by the fact that money is changing hands? The presence of money in a transaction generally has no legal effect in Jewish law,[8] so the answer is found, quite simply, to be no.[9] Hence the conclusion by most who have written on the subject that the "sale" of human organs is permitted under Jewish law.

To demonstrate this phenomenon, whereby the introduction of money is often barely (if at all) relevant to questions regarding the legality of a transaction we turn to a contemporary Responsum that would sound like it ought to be on point. Rabbi Moshe Feinstein, one of the most renowned Orthodox rabbis of the twentieth century, was asked whether it is permissible, under Jewish law, to donate blood in order to receive payment.[10] For reasons that will become clear, the answer he gives is not particularly helpful in thinking about the sale of organs for transplant. Nevertheless, the Responsum is interesting in what it reveals about the role money does (and does not) play in Jewish law.

The question posed is: "whether it is permissible to allow doctors to draw blood [from a person] to enable [that person] to earn money."

אם מותר להניח לרופאים להוציא ממנו דם להרוחת ממון

The Responsum first presumes that the act of donating blood constitutes *chavalah* (injury), which is prohibited. He rules that giving blood is not an act of *pikuach nefesh* – which, if it applied, would render the act permissible – because there is no, proximate sick person capable of making immediate therapeutic use of the blood.[11]

[8] In other words, if an act is permitted, it will not become illegal because money is changing hands.

[9] The consensus is no, with very few exceptions. For an exception see Shabtai A. Rappaport, "Sale of Organs from a Living Donor for Transplant: Motivation and Decision-Making," in Alfred Mordechai Rabello (ed.), *An Equitable Distribution of Human Organs for Transplantation*, Jerusalem: Hebrew University Press (2003), pp. 97–108. For an overview of the writing of contemporary Orthodox decisors reflecting a consensus that there is essentially nothing seriously wrong with getting paid to supply an organ for transplant, see Daniel B. Sinclair, *Jewish Biomedical Law: Legal and Extra-legal Dimensions*, New York: Oxford University Press (2003), pp. 243–244; Fred Rosner, *Contemporary Biomedical Ethical Issues and Jewish Law* New Jersey: Ktav Publishing (2006), pp. 145–149; Mordechai Halperin, "Organ Transplants From Living Donors - Halachic Apsects," *Rambam Maimonides Medical Journal* 2(2):e0042 (April 2011), PMC3678940.

[10] Feinstein, Moshe, *Iggerot Moshe, Hoshen Mishpat* 1:103 (1968).

[11] The Responsum states, "who knows whether this blood ... will even reach a sick person for whom we would suspend prohibitions."

מי יודע אם יבא הדם הזה שיוציאו ממנו לחולה שדוחים איסורים בשבילו

This aspect of the decision raises other issues and will not be examined here. However, this section of the Responsum does implicitly recognize that had the requirements of *pikuach*

The Responsum then asks whether this otherwise illegal (non-life saving) act of bodily injury should be deemed permissible *because* of the money, that is: is it justified by the fact that the donor "needs" the money.[12] The answer is no – Jewish law prohibits any act of self-injury (*chavalah be'atzmo*), even when it is done to meet a "need" (*le'tzorech*).[13]

The Responsum then addresses (and rejects) an interesting argument as to why the payment ought to render the act of self-injury permissible. The view that it is illegal to injure oneself is traced to Rabbi Elazar HaKappar, who gleaned this from the fact that the Nazirite is biblically required to bring a sin offering at the end of his Nazirite period. According to Rabbi HaKappar, this is because the Nazirite improperly caused himself to suffer, or injured himself, when he forswore the drinking of wine. One might, therefore, argue that the receipt of money actually renders the (otherwise illegal self-injuring) act of giving blood legal; the money provides pleasure that more than offsets the pain to the individual! The Responsum rejects this argument, pointing out that, unlike the Nazirite, whose suffering inheres merely in depriving himself of the pleasure of wine (something that could theoretically be offset by substituting another pleasure), the blood donor suffers an actual physical injury, something that no amount of pleasure (or satisfaction of "need") will permit.

nefesh been met the donation would be permissible (if not obligatory?) as a *mitzvah*. In any event, because of this finding the Responsum never reaches the question of the propriety of receiving money for performing the *mitzvah* of *pikuach nefesh*.

12 The Responsum thus does not discuss the case where a person wants, but does not need the money (assuming that such a category of persons exists). The person's financial need seems to be presumed, as his "neediness" does not seem to be included in the question posed. It is also not clear how Feinstein defines "need" (given the fact that the amount paid for the blood was likely *de minimis*).

13 This rule is supported by Rabbi Akiva in Mishnah Bava Kamma 8:6, as well as Tosafot to B.T. Bava Kamma 91b (s.v. "*elu hai tanna*"), Maimonides, *Mishneh Torah*, *Hilchot Chovel Umazik* [Hebrew: Laws of Injury and Damages] 5:1, and Shulchan Arukh H.M. 420:31. This principle is established in the following story recounted in Mishnah Bava Kamma 8:6, which lists as an illegal act of injuring others the act of uncovering the head of a woman in the marketplace: "There was an incident in which someone bared the head of a woman in the marketplace. She came before Rabbi Akiva and he obligated [the perpetrator] to give her four hundred *zuz*. [The perpetrator] said to [Rabbi Akiva], "my teacher, give me time [to pay]!" So [Rabbi Akiva] gave him time. [The perpetrator] lay in wait for [the woman until he saw her] standing [outside,] at the entrance of her courtyard, at which point he broke a jug containing an *issar* [worth of] oil right in front of her. She uncovered her head and began sopping up [the oil with her head covering] and placed her hand on her head. [The perpetrator] set up witnesses against her and came before Rabbi Akiva and said to him, "To this one I must give four hundred *zuzim* [for damaging her by baring her head]?!" [Rabbi Akiva dismissed the man's arguments and] said to him, "You have said nothing. *One who wounds himself*, even though he *is not permitted to do so*, he is exempt [from paying damages] yet others who wound him are liable." (emphasis added).

In the end, the Responsum rules that giving blood is permissible because it does not entail any injury. This is because, (1) bloodletting was historically not only permitted but prevalent, as it was understood to improve health; therefore, rather than an act of *chavalah* (injury), it is in the nature of a therapeutic act (like undergoing surgery), which is always permissible, and (2) because donating blood is so simple and pain free today, it might not constitute injury for this reason as well. The Responsum ends with the decision that the act of donation, since it is not *chavalah*, is permissible – the question of the permissibility of payment is never even addressed. Thus, the decision about payment for blood donations turns completely on the permissibility of the act itself; the presence (or absence) of money is ultimately irrelevant to the legal analysis. No concern is demonstrated about matters of "commodification" of blood, the body or otherwise.[14]

This general approach to the question of commodification of the body (asking firstly whether the act itself is permitted and, if it is, taking it for granted that payment is permissible) does not yield anything insightful. Indeed, the fact that it provides no basis or resources for resolving the question (even if it is only secondary) of the legality of organ sales hints at thefact that there is more going on;[15] it reveals the need for a deeper analysis of what exactly takes place when an organ is given to save the life of another. It raises issues that go to the heart of the meaning of ownership itself (e.g., divine v. human), self-ownership, and health and welfare obligations owed to one another. The question of organ sales demands the fleshing out of the operation of the divine lien and its implications for organ transfer. If the sick

מעשה באחד שפרע ראש האשה בשוק באת לפני רבי עקיבא וחייבו ליתן לה ארבע מאות זוז אמר לו רבי תן לי זמן ונתן לו זמן שמרה עומדת על פתח חצרה ושבר את הכד בפניה ובו כאיסר שמן גילתה את ראשה והיתה מטפחת ומנחת ידה על ראשה העמיד עליה עדים ובא לפני רבי עקיבא אמר ליה לזו אני נותן ד' מאות זוז אמר ליה לא אמרת כלום החובל בעצמו אף על פי שאינו רשאי פטור אחרים שחבלו בו חייבים

[14] To the extent that money is shown to *potentially* register on the legal radar screen, a number of interesting insights into this ancient tradition's perspective on money are revealed in this Responsum. First, the payment is implicitly understood as something positive. Rather than being seen as something abhorrent, the payment for blood is presumptively regarded as something positive, that meets a "need" – the need to earn a living and to sustain oneself. As such, the payment supplies a possible (but rejected) justification for an impermissible act of self-injury. Secondly, the ban on self-injury reveals that the tradition has a legal problem with an individual who denies himself pleasure and, in this context, the offsetting benefit of receiving money could theoretically be a plus.

[15] See also the 2001 article by former Israeli chief rabbi Shlomo Goren, "*Mechirat Kelayot Lehashtalah al pi Hahalacha*"(Hebrew: The Sale of Organs for Transplant According to Jewish Law), in *Torat Harefuah: Mechkarim Hilchatiim Benosei Refuah* Jerusalem: Ha-idra Rabah (5761/ 2001), pp. 127–148. After a lengthy analysis regarding the legal permissibility of organ transfer leading up to the question of organ sales, the piece ends abruptly with a sentence or two on the actual question of sales.

person is actually entitled to a part of my body, by what right am I purporting to sell it to him?

The possibility of selling organs for transplant requires a deeper probing of the meaning of the act of organ transfer and its significance in Jewish law. It forces one to think about what had been the *assumed* parts of the analysis – the questions of ownership and obligation. These matters are precisely what are called into question by the prospect of organ sales.

The concerns of self-mutilation and self-endangerment might negate the existence of a technical legal mandate to give, but they neither imply absolute self-ownership nor do they vitiate the existence of an obligation. The fixation upon, and overprivileging of these two concerns give short shrift to the question of the obligation to donate and may reflect a contemporary distaste or repulsion for the idea that one might be expected to give of one's body to help another.

In fact, the two prohibitions themselves help to underscore the fact that there is an obligation. The act of organ transfer should be prohibited; it is permissible *only* because it fulfills the obligation of *pikuach nefesh*. There *is* an obligation, and it is doing significant work in the legal calculation. This is what gets lost in the typical analysis. Appreciation of the existence of this obligation and its meaning alters our understanding of the act of transfer itself. This altered understanding becomes apparent when the question of organ sales is posed.

This chapter will trace the significance of the act of organ transfer and the nature of the *mitzvah* or obligation to give a part of one's body to another. What becomes clear is that it is legally impossible to "sell" one's organ to another person according to the rabbis because the organ already belongs to them. Thereafter, in light of this analysis the question of what payment, if any, might be permitted will be considered.

5.1 ORGAN TRANSFER AND THE FULFILLMENT OF THE DIVINE LIEN

As noted in Chapter 4, the legal obligation to save human life comprises two elements, each of which is derived from a separate verse. (1) There is an obligation to personally undertake the life-saving act (בנפשיה), such as jumping into the water to save a person who is drowning. This is derived from Deut 22:2, "and you shall return it to him." (2) There is an obligation to spend one's own money, if necessary, to accomplish the saving (מיטרח ומיגר אגורי) ("make an effort to hire workers"). This is derived from Lev 19:16, "do not stand by the blood of your neighbor." In Talmudic law these two elements are regarded as distinct and are treated entirely differently. In perhaps the most salient distinction for our purposes, one might be compensated for one's monetary outlay (albeit only if the victim can afford it), whereas one is *not* compensated for the former – the use of one's body. (Note that such compensation is only a possiblity after-the-fact. Initially, the rescuer's property [just like his body] is captured by the divine lien via the obligation of *pikuach nefesh*.)

The dichotomy is preserved in the medieval sources, which all speak of a double-barreled requirement to save life "with one's body" (בגופו) (*begufo*) and "with one's property" (בממונו) (*bemamono*).[16] The category *begufo* (with one's body) captures precisely the donation of one's organ to save the life of another.[17] Tracking the language of Maimonides, that which actually makes one "able" to save the other person's life, that which actually accomplishes the saving,[18] is a part of one's body.[19]

There is an interesting symmetry established, in the framework set up by the Talmud in Sanhedrin 73, within the obligation of "returning." There are

[16] See, e.g., Tur H.M. 426; Shulchan Arukh H.M. 426; Maimonides' commentary to Mishnah Nedarim 4:4. The term used by all, בגופו, with one's body, corresponds to the Talmud's term בנפשיה, with one's person. In place of the phrase "make an effort to hire workers", (מיטרח ומיגר אגורי) the phrase *bemamono*, with his property, is used. Hereafter, the terms *begufo* and *bemamono* will be used to refer to these two principles.

[17] A body part could not, legally, be characterized as part of one's property for numerous reasons. No one, including those who claim that one "owns" one's body and, therefore, can sell it, characterizes the organ itself as a piece of property (ממון) in this manner. In any event, when given the choice of treating the organ as a person's body or his property, it is obvious that it falls in the former category.

[18] There is a way in which organ transfer differs from jumping in to save the drowning victim – one cannot single-handedly save the victim with one's organ; one needs the help of medical personnel. This makes no difference in terms of how to characterize the act. (The word *benafsho* in the Talmud, in reference to saving the drowning person personally, does not mean alone, but means "with one's body" or life, and thus is recorded by the medieval codes as *begufo*.)

[19] Maimonides' Commentary to Mishnah Nedarim 4:4 (which was analyzed in Chapter 4) states, in part, "And [healing] was not prohibited to the ill person himself [as opposed to the healing of his animal] because [the healing] is a *mitzvah*. In other words, the doctor is obligated by law to [heal] the sick of Israel. This is included by the interpretation of the verse [Deut 22:2], 'and you shall return it to him,' to include his body (*gufo*)…."

ולא נאסר זה לחולה עצמו מפני שהיא מצוה כלומר שחייב הרופא מן הדין לרפאות חולי ישראל והרי הוא בכלל אמרם בפירוש הכתוב והשבותו לו לרבות את גופו

(Note the reference in the Mishnah to the fact, discussed earlier, that there is a *mitzvah* to save and sustain human life but not animal life.) Parenthetically, were it not for the statements of the Radbaz (to be discussed, *infra*) in the context of the case of extortion, there would be no basis for denying the obvious applicability of the first prong of the *mitzvah* of "saving a life" (with one's body) to the act of organ transfer.

two types of returns required by law: returning (lost) property and returning someone's lost or endangered body/life/health (*avedat gufo*). With respect to the latter *mitzvah*, there are two paths to its fulfillment: with one's property (*bemamono*) and with one's body (*begufo*). On both dimensions of this conceptual matrix (what one saves: body or property; how one saves a life: with body or property), there is a subtle (or not so subtle) blurring of the presumed divide between persons and property. In a manner reminiscent of Mauss's speculation as to the ethos of various societies among whom this (and other related) binaries are not (so) fixed, both types of returns (lost property and life saving) are, by their nature, understood to be property returns, but of different types of property. When this matrix of legal principles is applied to the context of organ transfer, this blurring of the lines between people and things transmutes into a blurring of the lines between person and person (as one person's body, in an instant, is presumed to belong to another).

Intriguingly, when a person transfers an organ from her body to that of another, the two types of bodily returns (returning of the body of another, and using one's body to make a return) are accomplished simultaneously. A third type of "return" (albeit less visible) is also taking place. The transfer of the organ from one's body to another's, in fulfillment of the obligation to save a life, also fulfills one's obligation to make a return gift to God. It is this transfer to another to/for God, or to God to/for another, that defines the essence of the act; indeed, in this case the object of the transfer (on both the giving and the receiving end) is something that, as will be shown, intrinsically possesses a sacred quality. In this regard it can be regarded as nothing other than the ultimate *korban* or *hekdesh*. The fact that these dual legal obligations (of saving a life and giving a return gift to God) are automatically fulfilled thereby is what defines the character of the act.[20]

This chapter will explore this dual proposition, (1) that organ transfer is, perhaps, the classic case in which one is able, with one's body (*begufo*), to fulfill the obligation of saving (returning) the life (body, *guf*) of another, and (2) that it allows for the epitomy of return gifts to God, approximating human bodily sacrifice. The textual bases for recognizing an act of *pikuach nefesh* as an (ultimate) act of *tsedakah* and, as such, as a transfer implicating the divine lien, similar to the gifts to and from God were analyzed in Chapter 4. To gain further insight into the significance of the act of organ transfer, we pick up

[20] As with the giving of *tsedakah*, it is often up to the individual to decide to do so. That does not in any way detract from the nature of the act as fulfillment of an obligation. Indeed, it is an important part thereof.

where Chapter 4 left off to focus specifically on an act of *pikuach nefesh* that entails healing.[21]

As noted, the obligation to save human life is conceived in the Talmud as being twofold: *begufo* (with one's body), and *bemamono* (with one's property). Does *begufo* just means one's bodily actions, or, given the contemporary possibility of organ transfer, should it not be read to include the actual giving of one's body to accomplish the saving?

In illustrating what it means to use one's body to save the life of another, the Talmud in Sanhedrin describes someone who acts personally to save someone who is drowning or being mauled by animals. It seems implicit that the rescuer (or those hired by the rescuer) might (although will not necessarily) have to put his or her own body in harm's way in order to accomplish the rescue, and that this is what is contemplated by the word *begufo* (with his body). An even more vivid example of what is contemplated by *begufo* is reflected in the following incident that occurred in New York City in January, 2007:

> It was every subway rider's nightmare, times two. Who has ridden along New York's 656 miles of subway lines and not wondered: "What if I fell to the tracks as a train came in? What would I do?" And who has not thought: "What if someone else fell? Would I jump to the rescue?"
>
> Wesley Autrey, a 50-year-old construction worker and Navy veteran, faced both those questions in a flashing instant yesterday, and got his answers almost as quickly.
>
> Mr. Autrey was waiting for the downtown local at 137th Street and Broadway in Manhattan around 12:45 p.m. Nearby, a man collapsed, his body convulsing. Mr. Autrey and two women rushed to help, he said. The man, Cameron Hollopeter, 20, managed to get up, but then stumbled to the platform edge and fell to the tracks, between the two rails.
>
> The headlights of the No. 1 train appeared. "I had to make a split decision," Mr. Autrey said. So he made one, and leapt.

[21] Not surprisingly, the texts and debates relevant to this issue seem obviously to have implications for the question of payment for the services of a doctor. In the theoretical discussion of this issue, it is important to set aside the empirical fact that, in the present society, doctors are paid (indeed, they are well paid); focusing on that fact will make the following discussion difficult to comprehend. What comes across more clearly in the rabbinic texts soon to be discussed is that the Jewish tradition does, in fact, regard payment to physicians for treating, advising, and healing patients (depending how it is characterized) as something conceptually problematic. In fact, it turns out that exploring the relevant theoretical issues with the view to analyzing payment for organs yields insight into their implications with regard to payment for medical services, generally.

> Mr. Autrey lay on Mr. Hollopeter, his heart pounding, pressing him down in a space roughly a foot deep. The train's brakes screeched, but it could not stop in time.
>
> Five cars rolled overhead before the train stopped, the cars passing inches from his head, smudging his blue knit cap with grease. Mr. Autrey heard onlookers' screams. "We're O.K. down here," he yelled.... He heard cries of wonder, and applause.
>
> Power was cut, and workers got them out. Mr. Hollopeter, a student at the New York Film Academy, was taken to St. Luke's-Roosevelt Hospital Center... The police said it appeared that Mr. Hollopeter had suffered a seizure.
>
> Mr. Autrey refused medical help, because, he said, nothing was wrong .... "I don't feel like I did something spectacular; I just saw someone who needed help," Mr. Autrey said. "I did what I felt was right."[22]

In this scenario, Mr. Autry uses his body, in a very literal sense, to save the other person's body and life. He jumped down onto the tracks not to lift the victim up and off the tracks, but to use his own body to physically compress and shield that of Mr. Hollopeter from the oncoming train.

There is not much distance between this case and the case of organ transfer. In both situations, the rescuer is doing more than acting to save a life; the rescuer's body is, very literally saving (returning) the other person's body and life to him. Indeed, Mr. Autrey felt that what he did was not beyond the call of duty. It was not "something spectacular ... [he] did what [he] felt was right" – a perfect expression of the idea contemplated by the Talmud, that when one uses one's body to save another's life, one is simply returning to the other that which is his.

Of course, there is one significant difference between this case and that of organ transfer – there was no actual, physical transfer of a part of Mr. Autrey's body into that of Mr. Hollopeter. If Mr. Autrey's act is a dramatic illustration of *begufo* – using one's body to save another life, organ transfer is an even more explicit example of the same thing. Inasmuch as the act (of saving) and the property (the body or organ) are elided, there is no doubt that the giving of the organ constitutes giving *begufo*; indeed, it is clear that it does not fall in the only other possible category – that of giving *mamono*, one's property.[23] In this sense, a distinction between body and property – established explicitly by the

[22] Cara Buckley, "A Man Down, a Train Arriving, and a Stranger Makes a Choice," *New York Times* (Jan 3, 2007), p. 1.

[23] See *infra*, regarding the special status of the human body. One's body cannot be considered *mamon*.

Talmud itself – is preserved. In another sense, we see the distinction itself (or what we popularly understand as implications of it) fall away, as we read the Talmud to contemplate (when scientifically possible) not just an obligation to act, but an obligation to actually give of one's body (in a corporeal sense) – to feel the pull of the *in rem* duty of the divine lien on one's person – in order to save the life of another.

Conceiving of organ transfer as a return gift to God contemplates that the organ, in moving from person A to person B, is also moving into and out of the divine domain – as a return gift to God and, thereafter, as a gift from God to the recipient (much as the priest receives part of the sacrifice from the table of the Most High). Like the sacrifice eaten by the priest during the days of the Temple, it is imagined that the organ passes from one person to another via the "table [domain] of the Most High." Neither the donor nor the recipient can dispose of the organ as he sees fit; the recipient can no more sell (or do as he wishes with) the organ, once received, than the donor could. In a sense, the organ is and has always been in the divine realm; as it passes through the divine domain on the way to the recipient (the only way that it could legally be transferred to anyone[24]), its status remains the same. It is thus possible to understand organ transplantation as a phenomenon that was never previously conceivable, something that approximates Temple sacrifice and involves the direct transfer of (part of) the human body. Due to advances in science and medicine, one might suggest that something that in the rabbinic imagination was possible only symbolically during Temple (and biblical?) times[25] is now humanly possible: the returning or giving back to another person (and hence to the divine) of that which is the ultimate gift from the original donor – one's body and, hence, human life.

The donation of an organ cannot be understood as the expenditure of one's money or property because of the special status of the body. One's body is not something over which one otherwise has the power to transfer (for money or otherwise) except in the context of *pikuach nefesh*. This particular act of *pikuach nefesh* corresponds precisely to the lien on the body contemplated by the obligation of *vehashevoto lo*, and you shall return (his health or his body) to him with your body (*begufo*). With the divine lien, it is understood that one has not "lost" a body part, but ceded it or, more accurately, retroceded it to God. The lien, in this context, applies directly to the body of the donor, not

[24] Theoretically, this is what would take place if a person, in order to save his life, was forced to eat the body of a deceased human being.

[25] Temple sacrifice is a symbol of, or substitution for, giving a human back to God – something short of actual human sacrifice.

to his property. Of course this case was not in the minds of the authors of the Talmudic text; yet, this conceptualization of the act is almost demanded by the language used in the Talmud to describe what the act of healing represents for the recipient and for the rescuer.

The Talmudic language itself reinforces the conceptualization of organ transfer as a transfer that entails the attachment of the divine lien to the body of the donor, as his body part is then understood as returning, to the recipient, his own (health or) lost body part. While the Talmud did not intend this literal meaning, it does clearly communicate the rabbinic understanding of the "personal/bodily" (as opposed to the property) aspect of the rescue obligation (derived from the biblical text) as one that involves a lien on the rescuer's body in response to the other person's need to have his life saved, or his "body" returned.

In this sense, organ transfer operates, legally, in the same fashion as the Talmudic case of the laborer working in the field. Like the laborer who acquires something from God the moment he receives it, the situation is such that, whatever human domain of ownership the item might have originated in, when he receives it, he can be described as acquiring it "from heaven" (*mishel shamayim hu ochel*). Moreover, in connection with the laborer, the recipient "acquires" only that which actually passes to him to satisfy his entitlement;[26] he receives that which is entailed in the saving/sustaining of his life, nothing more and for no other purpose. Whatever property is given or used to save a life simultaneously leaves the ownership of the previous owner and becomes the property of the recipient. This automatic shift in status takes place, and the property is implicitly transformed, as it passes through the divine realm on the way to the recipient. This is a transfer that is outside the mundane human economy; it is part of the sacred economy of transfers that pass through the divine domain.

The case of organ transfer is, moreover, different from the usual case of saving a life, given the special nature of the property that is transferred. Something that is helpful here is the nuanced distinction suggested by the Ran (see Chapter 3, *supra*) between property acquired from heaven (*mishel shamayim*) and that acquired from the divine table (*mishulchan gavohah*) – the former being property that is not inherently sacred (e.g., an apple), but which passes through the divine domain and, as such, can be described as being eaten from heaven (*mishel shamayim*) as opposed to property, such as animal sacrifice, that possesses an inherent status of sacredness that is separate from the recipient's

[26] The Ritva makes this point regarding the laborer. See *Chidushei Ha-Ritva*, B.T. Bava Metzia 92a.

eating of it, and is thus described as being eaten (perhaps more directly) from the table of the Most High (*mishulchan gavohah*).

We turn now to a more detailed exploration of each step of the transaction in the case of organ transfer and its significance, from the perspective of the Talmudic texts.

5.2 WHAT IS GIVEN GOES (FIRST) TO GOD – THE HUMAN BODY AS *HEKDESH*

Does the divine lien (as an encumbrance on property gifted by God) apply to the human body? This deceptively simple question – implicating ideas such as human freedom and individual autonomy and the existence, extent, and meaning of a distinction between people and property – is the question ultimately raised by the issue of organ transfer and goes to the heart of the philosophical and normative framework of the Jewish legal tradition. The scenario of organ transfer and the issue of "sale" directly prompt this question and provide a conceptually useful and coherent mechanism for an analysis that provides concrete parameters and lays a foundation for further analysis. What follows is a brief outline of the place or meaning of the human body in the rabbinic legal system, followed by a specific examination of the question of how to characterize what it is that is being given in the context of organ transfer.

5.2.1 *The Body as an Object of Dedication and Retrocession*

The limits to the possibility of gifting oneself to God demonstrate that one's ownership of oneself is, in a sense, less absolute than one's ownership of ordinary property. Conversely, it is because the human person (more than other things) is owned by the divine[27] that one cannot give up one's life, one's freedom, or one's body parts (except as permitted by God).[28]

27 Or is a slave to God. See B.T. Bava Metzia 52a (according to God, humans "are my slaves, not the slaves of slaves") (*avadai hem velo avadim le'avadim*).

28 As will be seen, these limits to self-ownership often entail corresponding limits to the ownership of others. For example, with the institution of Arakhin, although one cannot consecrate oneself to the Temple one can consecrate one's value. Similarly, one cannot consecrate another person to the Temple, but one can consecrate the value of another person to the Temple. The impossibility of actual consecration, and the possibility of symbolic consecration, applies to both oneself and others. Much like the interpretation of the biblical punishment of "an eye for an eye" to mean compensation, here the practice of giving money in place of a person (or part of a person) can be seen not as any sort of "commodification" of the person but, rather, as an attempt to sanctify the person (not to mention an advance from actual human sacrifice, or a literal interpretation of an "eye for an eye.")

The rabbis did not conceive of consecrating oneself/one's body directly to the Temple.[29] However, there were institutional substitutes that can be said to represent a set of exceptions that prove the rule. For there were certain ways in which one was capable of "consecrating" oneself:

(i) *B.T. Arakhin* – As described in Tractate Arakhin, one of the formalized mechanisms for donating funds to the Temple in Jerusalem entailed pledging the "value" of a person – either oneself or someone else; either an entire body or a body part. In an interesting twist to the concern over commodification, in this context it was possible to symbolically sanctify a person by literally sanctifying the money donated to the Temple as a representation of the person.[30]

(ii) The Nazirite – This institution outlined in detail in Leviticus, and expanded upon by the rabbis, contemplated a possibility whereby a person could temporarily sanctify himself, to a limited extent, to God.[31] In short, the Nazirite vow and consecration (which could last for no more than thirty days) entailed refraining from drinking wine and from cutting one's hair. The termination of the thirty-day term involved rituals such as sacrifice (interestingly, a sin offering) and ritual cutting of the hair.

(iii) The so-called prohibitory vow. As described above (p. 123), it is possible to dedicate oneself to God in the sense of forswearing benefit from certain things (just as a Nazirite is precluded from drinking wine). While

29 (Apparent exceptional cases, including biblical narratives in which parents purport to consecrate their children to the Temple, raise separate issues that cannot be discussed here due to a lack of space.) There is debate about whether doing so, to the limited extent one is able (e.g., via the Nazirite vow), is something that is frowned upon. This view is expressed, for example, by those who find it significant that at the end of one's term as a Nazir, the type of sacrifice one is required to bring is a sin offering.

30 This is not to say that there are not aspects to this process that are problematic from the perspective of contemporary concerns like commodification and equality. For one thing, people were bought and sold as slaves, and the "market value" of a person as a slave was one way of appraising a person's worth. Furthermore, the more absolute valuation of people (derived from a list set forth in the Bible, Lev 27:1-8) was explicitly calculated on the basis of gender and age (in conformity with other texts that prioritize people according to (what seems like) their importance or value to the community. See Mishnah Horyot 3:7–8 and the Gemara there.

31 Notice that one of the main prohibitions attendant to Nazirite status is the prohibition against cutting one's hair. This is reminiscent of the rule against cutting the corners of one's beard. Indeed, as will be seen shortly, it seems that the hair is the one part of one's body that one owns fully, in the sense that one is permitted to cut it, sell it, and give it away. Hence the symbolism of not cutting one's beard or, in the case of the Nazirite, one's hair – selectively ceding to the divine (either a portion, or for a temporary period) this one part of one's body over which one has complete dominion. (Note also the significance of the requirement that a married woman cover her hair as the outward symbol of her marital status. As mentioned below, theoretically [and problematically] the status of being a wife entails a ceding of self-ownership to one's husband, in a manner analogous to the Hebrew slave.)

this type of vow presumes that no actual consecration will ever take place, the practical result of a prohibitory vow is to cede to God the right to benefit from certain things or people. By this means, a person effectively consecrates what amounts to the essence of "ownership" of one's body:[32] the use thereof to receive benefit or pleasure (*hana'ah*).[33]

(iv) Hair is a part of one's body that is the exception that proves the rule. It stands out in various contexts in rabbinic literature as the one part of the body that one may cut, sell,[34] and even "dedicate" to God, in a sense, via the Nazirite vow.

5.2.2 *Tithing the Body: Biblical Antecedents as Conceptual Analogues*

There are a number of biblical rules regarding the human body that are strikingly similar to the rules limiting and conditioning ownership of other property that were described in Chapter 2.[35] For example,

↔ Redemption of the firstborn son. Like firstborn animals, firstborn males are deemed to belong to God from birth. The animals are given to the priests, and it is necessary to redeem the firstborn males by paying money to the priests.

↔ The class of priests. The members of this group are explicitly described in the Bible as being *kadosh*, or sacred. With the numerous obligations, entitlements, and restrictions attendant to this status, the priests can be seen, in a sense, as the "firstborn" of Israel, as a corporate entity – in this case, a firstborn that is not redeemed, hence their special holiness status (*kedushah*).

↔ Circumcision. In apparent violation of what would otherwise apply as a prohibition against bodily mutilation (*chavalah*), circumcision literally entails separating a portion of the body. Indeed, the foreskin is called *orlah*, the same word used to describe the firstfruits that are, in a sense, set aside for God as a means of freeing up future fruit for human ownership (after year four).

↔ The corners of the beard. The restriction against shaving the corners of one's face (*peyot*) corresponds directly to the rule against harvesting the corners of one's field (*peyot*), with the latter being a gift to the poor, as

[32] As with many of the ideas mentioned in this chapter, the use-related focus of self-ownership, and the general relationships between use and ownership, and between *hana'ah* and ownership, represent rich areas for future research.

[33] "Benefit," *hana'ah*, can be physical or financial.

[34] See B.T. Arakhin 7b.

[35] Further research into each of the following examples would reveal the depth (and, for some perhaps, the legitimacy) of these items as parallel.

a diverted gift to God, and the former being simply a gift to God (i.e., a symbol of divine ownership).[36]

A case might be able to be made[37] that the rabbis read these institutions within the context of the overarching scheme of property ownership outlined above, regarding them (to a greater or lesser extent) as conceptual analogues to "returns" or gifts to God. For example, parallel to the tithing of one's produce, circumcision can also be understood as the ritual setting aside of a portion of the body as a type of prelude or precondition to self-ownership, with the circumcision itself understood as a marker of original, as well as lingering, divine ownership.[38]

5.2.3 *Limits to Bodily Destruction, Harm, and Sale*

There is a web of prohibitions and requirements that reflect limits to self-ownership, such as prohibitions against suicide and self-mutilation,[39] against giving one's life for another, and rules requiring the giving up of one's life under certain[40] circumstances.[41] Moreover, except when done in strict accordance with exceptional cases

[36] Refraining from cutting hair has a deeper meaning vis-à-vis the issue of self-ownership and divine ownership, as will be seen in the context of the Nazirite.

[37] There is no room in this book to examine these other legal institutions more closely, to see whether, or the extent to which, this understanding is suggested in rabbinic literature (although it would be useful to do so, in order to be able to flesh out more fully the rabbis' perception of the body's place within the larger scheme as described by the theory set forth here.)

[38] Similar, in this respect, to the rabbinic understanding of the ritual (described in Exod 21:6 and Deut 15:17) of making a hole in the ear of a slave who chooses to stay with his owner past the sabbatical year.

[39] The prohibition against self-injury is not as explicitly traceable to the limitation of divine ownership. There is no room, here, to expand upon this, but suffice it to say that there are indications from the rules of tort law laid out in the eighth chapter of Bava Kamma, and from elsewhere, that suggest that a person has some say over injuring his body, something that he does not have vis-à-vis his life. On the other hand, although this prohibition seems, in certain texts, to be linked to the general prohibition against waste, it is clear that there is more to the prohibition against self-injury than there is to the prohibition against cutting down one's plants wastefully. (This relates, as well, to the distinction between treatment, sustenance, and ownership of animals as opposed to people, something that was touched on in the context of muzzling one's cow, but that deserves greater explication elsewhere.)

[40] E.g., when necessary for God's sanctification (*al kiddush hashem*). Many of these related rules are recounted in B.T. Sanhedrin 74.

[41] The rabbis read the Bible to require that the human body, postmortem, be treated with respect. See Deut 21:23 and Josh 8:29. For example, the rabbis decree (based on Deut 21:23), that burial must take place as soon as possible after death. B.T. Sanhedrin 46b. There is also a prohibition against benefiting (receiving *hana'ah*) from a dead body. See B.T. Avodah Zarah 29b. For a review of these sources see the materials cited in J. David Bleich, "Fetal Tissue Research: Jewish Tradition and Public Policy," and "Utilization of Scientific Data Obtained Through Immoral Experimentation," *Contemporary Halakhic Problems*, volume 4, New York: Ktav Publishing House (1995), pp. 171–202, 218–236.

that are biblical in origin – such as slavery and marriage[42] – one is not permitted to sell oneself to, or to become the slave of, another human being. [43]

All of these rules relate to a person who is alive. The limit to human ownership of the body is unequivocal after death. For when a person dies, his body fits squarely within the category of things that (like *hekdesh*) are off limits to human benefit, and the prohibition against bodily mutilation is absolute. These rules apply equally to a limb or an organ that has been severed or removed. A body or body part must be buried and treated with respect and cannot be a source of human benefit (*hana'ah*).[44] Finally, rabbinic texts indicate that not only is the postmortem human body no longer in the realm of human ownership (in the senses described above), but to the extent that there was a degree of self-ownership (except, perhaps, for one's hair)[45] it seems that it does not extend beyond one's death. A person has no right to gift their body or body parts to another. This is asserted straightforwardly in B.T. Arakhin 7b:

> [The Mishnah states:] "[One may benefit from the hair of] a woman who has been put to death." [But why? There are prohibitions against benefitting from the dead.] Rav said: [this refers to the case] where [before being put to death] she said, "give my hair to my daughter." But if she said, "give my hand to my daughter," would we give it to her? [Of course not!][46]
>
> האשה שנהרגה [נהנין בשערה].אמר רב: באומרת תנו שערי לבתי. אילו אמרה תנו ידי לבתי מי יהבינן לה

As established in Chapter 4, "healing" does not entail the conferring of a benefit (*hana'ah*). To the contrary, the saving of human life is a *mitzvah* that is

[42] Marriage as *kinyan* (acquisition) is another example of the possibility, within prescribed limits, of purchasing a human being. The broader question of commodification of the human body or person would necessarily entail a much closer analysis of the institution of marriage (and of slavery –of both Jews and others).

[43] B.T. Bava Metzia 52a.

[44] As noted, this is a possible, but not necessary, indicator of divine ownership.

[45] The topic of human hair, by itself, presents a fascinating topic in connection with questions of ownership, self-ownership, and commodification of the body. There is contemporary relevance of the special status of human hair under Jewish law – of the need for married women to cover theirs, as something that can be "bought and sold" (unlike other body parts), and as something that would not carry an *issur hana'ah* (prohibition against deriving benefit). See, e.g., Daniel J. Wakin, "Rabbis' Rules and Indian Wigs Stir Crisis in Orthodox Brooklyn," *New York Times* (May 14, 2004), p. 1. In the case discussed in this article, another type of *issur hana'ah* is said to attach to the hair used to make wigs for married women – the prohibition against benefiting from items used in ritual of "idolatry."

[46] There ensues a debate between the rabbis as to whether the Mishnah is referring to the woman's hair or a wig. There are other Talmudic passages having to do with the requirement that the dead body, and severed limbs, be treated with respect. See, e.g., B.T. Sanhedrin 47a (commenting on Deut 21:22, "his body shall not remain all night upon the tree").

paramount. Hence, the above restrictions on the use or maiming of the body postmortem do not suggest that organ transfer (in the appropriate circumstances) would be problematic. To the contrary, it seems that organs ought to be used for that purpose.

In sum, there are numerous bases for limits to self-ownership, as well as conceptual analogues to consecration of the human body as a gift to God. Together these bolster the idea that the divine lien applies to the human body. And yet few, if any, contemporary legal decisors stress the way in which organ transfer fulfills this basic property obligation. In the section that follows, I examine and critique the theoretical framework commonly used to assess the meaning of organ transfer in Jewish law.

5.3 THE ERRONEOUS APPLICATION OF THE "PIOUS FOOL" IDIOM

While there is a considerable amount written on the issue of organ transfer under Jewish law,[47] there is little mention in the literature of the impact the introduction of money has on the legality of the transaction. That which has been written[48] either voices slight discomfort with the idea or, as in an article by Rabbi Israel Meir Lau, former chief rabbi of Israel, finds no legal

47 See, e.g., Joel Roth, "Organ Donation" (YD 336, 1999), in Kassel Abelson and David J. Fine (eds.), *Responsa 1991–2000, the Committee on Jewish Law and Standards of the Conservative Movement*, New York: Rabbinical Assembly (2002), pp. 208–316; Benjamin Freedman, *Duty and Healing: Foundations of a Jewish Bioethic*, New York: Routledge (1999); Elliott N. Dorff, "Jewish Law and Lore: The Case of Organ Transplantation," in *Jewish Law Annual* 12 (1997), pp. 65–114; J. David Bleich, *Contemporary Halakhic Problems*, volume 4, chapter 12, "May Tissue Donations Be Compelled?" (1995), pp. 273–287; Lau (1992); Mordechai Halperin, "Organ Transplants from Living Donors," *Israel Law Review* 27 (1993), pp. 566ff; Shaul Yisraeli, "*Terumot Evarim Min Hachai u'Min ha Met*" [Hebrew: Organ Donations from Live and Dead Donors], *First International Conference on the Law and Ethics of Medicine* (1993), p. 195 (also appearing in *Chavat Binyamin*, part 3, p. 1903); Noam Zohar, "Toward Justice in the Organ Trade," *Israel Law Review* 27 (1993), pp. 541ff; Avraham Steinberg, *Encyclopedia Hilchatit Refuit* [Hebrew: The Halachic-Medical Encyclopedia], volume 2, Jerusalem: Schlesinger Institute (1991), pp. 191–244; Frenkel (1984) at 195; Rabinovitch, (1979); Fred Rosner, "Heart and Other Organ Transplantation and Jewish Law," in *Studies in Torah Judaism: Modern Medicine and Jewish Law*, New York: Yeshiva University (1972), pp. 155–176.

48 Halperin (2011); Rosner (2006); Sinclair (2003); Zalman Nechemiah Goldberg, *Kinyanim Bemechirat Kelayot* [Hebrew: Acquisitions in the Sale of Organs], in *Ateret Shelomo* IV, Jerusalem: Machon Madaei Technologi Lehalacha (5757/1997), pp. 49–55; Goren (2001); Lau (2005); Rappaport (2003); Roth (2002), *supra.*; Michael WyGoda, "*Mechirat Eyvarim*" [Hebrew: The Sale of Organs], in *Shanah Beshanah* 42 (5762/2002), pp. 119–127; Yitzchak Zilberstein, "*Mechirat Kalya Lephar'on Chovot*" [Hebrew: Sale of Organs for the Payment of Debts], in *Yated Ne'eman, Musaf*, Israel: Bene Baraq (Dec 30, 1994/27 Tevet 5755), p. 7.

impediment under Jewish law to the "sale" of (or even the existence of a "market" in) human organs.[49]

The reason for the paucity of Jewish legal writing on the issue of organ sales is reflected in the decisions of Israeli chief rabbis Lau and Goren.[50] Generally, the question of whether financial payment renders the organ transfer impermissible is asked after the basic groundwork for organ transfer has been ascertained (the upshot of obligations to save life, not to harm oneself, etc.). This approach reveals something interesting, but not necessarily very illuminating for our purposes: that from a practical legal standpoint, the exchange of money is almost always beside the point in the determination of whether acts are permitted or prohibited under Jewish law. Something prohibited will still be prohibited; perhaps more importantly, unlike the many examples in contemporary Western law (e.g., prostitution), the exchange of money will not alter the inherent status of something otherwise permissible.[51]

While it might be true for United States law, it is not true that in Jewish law "no prior transactional idioms exist" for organ transfer.[52] I contend that the appropriate idiom is *hekdesh*, or the giving of a return gift to God; however, what contemporary Jewish decisors consistently invoke by way of analogy is not *hekdesh*, but a scenario depicted in the Responsum of a sixteenth-century rabbinic decisor, Rabbi David ben Zimra ("the Radbaz," 1479–1573).[53] The hypothetical situation described by the Radbaz is as follows:

> If a [tyranical] ruler says to a Jew, "Allow me to amputate one of your limbs (with an amputation that will not lead to your death), or else I will kill your fellow Jew," some [authorities] say that he is obligated to allow his limb to be amputated since he will not die.[54]

49 Lau (2005).

50 *Id.*; Goren (2001).

51 Laws against prostitution, for example, render the behavior illegal *because* money changes hands. By contrast, Jewish law would judge the conduct based on whether or not the sexual relations are themselves prohibited (e.g. as adultery, incest, etc.), according to the status of the individuals involved. It would not consider the payment of money a basis to outlaw an otherwise legal sexual encounter. It is in this sense that the involvement of money often will not even show up on the Jewish legal radar screen. Of course, there are outright prohibitions involving the exchange of money, such as the prohibitions against bribery and against usury.

52 Strathern (1998) at 216–217.

53 Everyone but Rabbi Shlomo Goren it seems. The Radbaz is taken as holding that one is not obligated to put one's life in danger in order to save the life of another. Rabbi Goren takes seriously a different view, articulated by Rabbi Joseph Caro (Beit Yosef to Tur H.M. 426 s.v. "*umah shekatav besheim harambam*") in the name of the *Hagahot Maimoniot* and based on the Jerusalem Talmud (Terumot 8:4) that one is obligated to risk one's life to save another, if only to reject the view that one who does so is a "pious fool." Interestingly, this alternate view, derived from the Jerusalem Talmud, finds support in a different Responsum of the Radbaz (5:18) that does not get much attention but will be discussed below.

54 Responsa Radbaz 3:627.

אם אמר השלטון לישראל הנה לי לקצץ אבר אחד שאינך מת ממנו או אמית ישראל חברך,
יש אומרים שחייב להניח לקצץ מאבר הואיל ואינו מת . . .

This presents something of a legal conundrum. Although the Talmud makes it clear that one need not and, indeed, is not legally permitted to give up one's own life to save the life of another (who is to say his blood is redder?[55]), perhaps one is nonetheless obligated to sacrifice a limb in order to fulfill the commandment to save the life of one's fellow. Two hundred and fifty years prior to the Radbaz, when asked about this scenario, Rabbi Menahem ben Benjamin Recanati (1250–1310) ruled that if the loss of the limb would not cause death, one would be obligated to give it up to save someone's life.[56] The Radbaz, however, disagreed with Recanati. His primary basis[57] was as follows:

> It is written, "And [the Torah's] ways are ways of pleasantness" (Proverbs 3:17); the laws of our Torah, therefore, must be in consonance with reason and intelligence. How can one imagine that a person would allow his eye to be blinded or his hand or foot to be cut off so that his fellow does not die?
>
> כתיב דרכיה דרכי נועם וצריך שמשפטי תורתינו יהיה מסכימים על השכל והסברא ואיך יעלה על דעתנו שיניח אדם לסמא את עינו או לחתוך את ידו או רגלו כדי שלא ימיתו את חברו?

He concluded that one who goes along with this threat, at a risk to his own life, is a "pious fool" (*chasid shoteh*). He also found that in a situation in which there is no significant risk to life, giving up the limb is an act of piety (*midat chasidut*), although still not obligatory.

As mentioned, this Responsum is seen by almost every contemporary thinker and religious decisor as the appropriate precedent for and definitive statement on the problem of organ transplants. Most decisors rely on it to find that there is no obligation (on the part of a live person) to donate an organ. Some go so far as to extrapolate from it that the *mitzvah* of *pikuach nefesh* cannot claim the

[55] "And how do we know that [murder may not be committed to save one's life]? It is a matter of human reason. [It is] like one who came to Rava and said to him, 'The governor of my town has ordered me: 'Go and kill so-and-so; if not I will kill you.' Rava answered, 'Let him kill you rather than you committing murder. What makes you think that your blood is redder than his? Perhaps his blood is redder than yours.'" (B.T. Yoma 82b).

ורוצח גופיה מנלן? סברא היא דההוא דאתא לקמיה דרבא [דרבה] אמר ליה אמר לי מרי דוראי קטליה לפלגיא ואי לא קטלינא לך אמר ליה נקטלך ולא תקטול מאי חזית דדמא דידך סומק טפי דילמא דמא דההוא גברא סומק טפי

[56] *Sefer Recanati* 470. Recanati reasoned *a fortiori*, as follows: saving a life comes before the Sabbath (one must violate the Sabbath to save a life), but the Sabbath comes before saving a limb (one is not permitted to violate the Sabbath to save a limb); therefore, saving a life comes before saving a limb.

[57] He actually listed six reasons. Many of his arguments were related to the fact that one could not be sure that one would not die from loss of the limb. For example, it could lead to a fatal loss of blood.

human body,[58] stating, in other words, that there is never an obligation to give anything of one's bodily substance to save the life of another.[59]

What stands out in this trend is the impoverished nature of the analogy for organ transfer supplied by the scenario of the despotic ruler. While both situations feature the surrendering of a body part with the goal of saving a human life, from the perspective of factors that are normatively and legally relevant, the situations could not be more different. In its fundamental conception, the tyrant scenario is almost an exact inversion or, more accurately, a perversion of what is entailed in the kind of gift transfer as described in Chapters 3 and 4. This model of the sacred economy in Talmudic law is a far more apt vehicle with which to analyze and analogize the contemporary situation of organ transfer. On that view, the transaction can be depicted as follows:

Divine
↗ ↘
(organ donor) Israelite ←··· ···→ Priest (organ recipient)

58 Not everyone does so. Numerous Orthodox rabbis have ruled that the donation of blood and bone marrow can, depending upon the circumstances, be mandatory. See Rabbi Samuel ha-Levi Woszner, *Teshuvot Shevut HaLevi*, part 5, Shulchan Aruch H.M. section 219, reprinted in *Halacha VeRefuah*, volume 4 (1985), pp. 139–142; Rabbi Moshe Se'ev Zorger, *Teshuvot Vayeshev Moshe* 1/84 (1989), p. 246; Rabbi Moshe Meiselman, *Halacha Verefuah*, volume 2, Jerusalem: Machon Regenshberg (1981), p. 118; Rabbi J. David Bleich, *Contemporary Halakhic Problems*, volume 4, New York: Ktav Publishing House, Inc. (1995), pp. 284ff.; see also Dr. Avraham Steinberg, *Encyclopedia Hichatit Refuit*, p. 218n62.

59 Based on the Radbaz, a number of rabbis have simply asserted something they seem to regard as self-evident, that the Talmudic requirement (echoed in the medieval sources) of saving another person with "one's body" (בגופו) means only bodily action, but not the body itself. In other words, they say that there is no obligation to make a live donation no matter what the circumstances. See, e.g., Lau (1992), "In a situation of possible danger there is no obligation to donate an organ to save one's fellow. And [even] if no danger is involved there still is no obligation, although it would be a pious act, as the Radbaz has decided."

במקום ספק סכנה אין חיוב לתרום איבר להציל חברו ואם אין בזה סכנה נמי חיוב ליכא אבל מדת חסידות איכא (וכפסק הרדב'ז)

Ziz Eliezer 13:101 (what is intended is some physical bodily action, "but not to giving him something of the very essence of his own body and the very structure of his own life"אבל לא לתת לשם כך ממח שבעצמיות גופו וממבנה חייו העצמיים); Rabbi Shaul Yisraeli, "Organ Donations From Living Donors: Danger to the Donor and Receipt of Payment," *Assia Journal of Medical Ethics and Halacha*, Questions and Answers, Volume 15, No. 57–58 (1997), p. 58. ("there is no obligation to donate from one's own body …even if the danger is not great [and even if it is something that will regenerate]…[however,] there is *midas chasidus* in such an act" אין חיוב לתרום מגופו הוא...אם כי "מדת חסידות" יש גם בזה. The article also appeared in English in M. Halperin and D. Fink (eds.), *The Proceedings of the First International Colloquium on Medicine, Ethics and Jewish Law*, Jerusalem: Schlesinger Institute for Medical-Halachik Research (1996), pp. 231–237; Joel Roth, "Organ Donation" (YD 336, 1999), in Kassel Abelson and David J. Fine (eds.), *Responsa 1991–2000, the Committee on Jewish Law and Standards of the Conservative Movement*, New York: Rabbinical Assembly (2002), pp. 208–316. For these decisors, one would not even be obligated to donate blood to a person standing in front of them who would die without it.

By contrast, in the scenario of the Radbaz, we have a cruel despot in place of God. In the place of the demand triggered by the divine lien, there is an irrational command and threat. In place of a curative transfer of the organ to another, there is the senseless destruction of a limb, with no certainty that the danger to the other is removed thereby.

To put it simply, there is something crucially significant about organ transfer that the Radbaz's scenario fails to capture, something that is precisely the focus of the story of the divine lien – that is, the transfer that takes place in the interest of saving a life between two human beings. The movement of the organ from one person's body (through the divine domain) into that of the other is what is most unprecedented and most amazing about organ transfer. This act, of giving a part of oneself to another in order to save her, is the heart of the matter here. It is this element that is highlighted when this action is analogized to the giving of a sacrifice to the Temple, or giving food to the priest and the poor, or the curative transfer of one's body, *begufo* in a double sense. It is, appropriately, this component that defines the action's legal and normative significance. And it is precisely this factor that is absent in the tyrant scenario depicted by the Radbaz (where there is no direct transfer between the person asked to give up the limb and the threatened victim; there is, in fact, a random and criminal intervening presence). It is also the absence of this element that explains this scenario's utter lack of legal and normative significance here. The relationship between the loss of the limb and the saving of the life is entirely random, uncertain, and even criminal; in the case of organ transfer, a part of one's body is literally taken into the body of the other and performs the act of healing.

The despotic ruler is precisely the inverse of the divine figure here: rather than mediating a preexisting obligation that arises out of his prior generosity (as does the figure of God in the case in which the divine lien comes into play in *hekdesh*-type scenarios), the ruler arbitrarily creates a link where there is and should be none (between A's limb and B's life), deploys coercion and brutality instead of obligation, and breaks down social relations rather than nurturing social bonding and an interpersonal sense of care. In this random economy of brutality, in what amounts to a parody of gift transfer and *pikuah nefesh*, the Radbaz's "pious fool" analysis makes sense; it does not make sense in the context of organ transfer.

The categorical difference between the two cases might actually be reflected in an additional, apparently contradictory, Responsum of the Radbaz.[60] There, the Radbaz asserts plainly that people *are* mandated to subject themselves

[60] Responsa Radbaz 5:218.

to physical risk to save the lives of others. What distinguishes this second Responsum from the first is that it deals with the typical act of life saving that the *mitzvah* contemplates – where one is able *directly* (e.g., through the direct use of one's body) to save someone's life, for example, by jumping into the river to save a drowning person. Unlike the problematic situation presented in the first Responsum, this situation (which he compares to and contrasts with the related requirement of saving of another's lost property) calls for one to risk one's life if necessary to fulfill the *mitzvah:*

> Within this prohibition [Lev 29:16, "do not stand idly by"] is [a prohibition against] refraining from saving the property of one's fellow, although one is not obligated to subject himself to possible danger for another's property. However, when it comes to saving the life of one's fellow, as it says in the Jerusalem Talmud [Terumot 8:4] *one is obligated to save the life of one's fellow even when it entails possible danger*.... (emphasis added)
>
> יש בכלל לאו זה שלא לעמוד על הפסד ממון חבירו אלא שאינו חייב להכנים עצמו לספק סכנה בשביל ממונו אבל להציל נפש חברו...אפילו במקום דאיכא ספק סכנה חייב להציל והכי איתא בירושלמי

Jewish religious decisors who would use the first Responsum as a basis upon which to generally exclude or limit organ transfer are confronted with the problem of having to reconcile these two Responsa.[61] And yet, if one reads the tyrant scenario as outlined above, it is not difficult to understand the complementary modes of reasoning behind both Responsa. In the case involving the tyrant, one is not actually saving someone's life; rather, one is succumbing to a capricious threat from a third party who is threatening harm. Giving in to the ultimatum is not the same as responding directly to, and removing the danger faced by, one's fellow who is drowning. The demand itself is irrational and the threat criminal, and no legal system (certainly not one whose ways are "ways of pleasantness") would demand such sacrifice in compliance with blatantly irrational cruelty.

Giving up one's limb under the circumstances of the tyrant is, therefore, rightly characterized by the Radbaz as (only) a pietous act (foolish or otherwise), rather than the fulfillment of an obligation. This is more like an act conceived as charity (or *caritas*, as opposed to *tsedakah*), an act of pure altruism, where one selflessly gives up something of one's own. Applying this assessment to the situation of organ transfer denies that the recipient (who, unlike the victim in the tyrant scenario, will directly receive and be saved by the organ itself) has some claim to the organ.

The inappropriateness of the application of the tyrant scenario (rather than the Talmudic sources on *hekdesh* etc.) to the case of organ transfer comes out

[61] They tend to subordinate this Responsum (5:218) to the other one about the pious fool (3:627).

most clearly when the question of "organ sales" is presented. Contemporary decisors mischaracterize the act of transfer as one of charity (rather than *tsedakah* as analyzed in Chapters 3 and 4). Like the theorists, in Chapter 1, debating the problem of commodification, these decisors approach the question of payment from the vantage point of the contrast between (pure) gift and sale (between charity and commerce). Absent the sense of lien or obligation, there is an implicit assumption that one can do as one wants with what is entirely one's own property – that is, they are stuck in the gift/commodity binary. Finding no clear basis upon which to outlaw the "sale" of an organ (in an otherwise permissible case of organ transfer), these writers conclude that the sale of organs for transplant is legally permissible. In other words, nothing special is presented by the question of sale. It gives us nothing new to think about. The analysis is the same as that used for the question of (pure) gift.

Following a misinterpretation of the Radbaz has led to a skewed perspective on not only the Talmudic principles and passages pertinent to the question of organ transfer, but also the Responsum's reasoning itself. Rather than taking the Radbaz to be stating unequivocally that Jewish law would not require an individual to succumb to a mad threat from a despot, these decisors interpret him to be declaring in no uncertain terms that Jewish law would not require an individual to give a body part (or even blood!) to save the life of another.[62] While this assertion of a near-visceral allegiance to individual corporeal integrity fits conveniently with modern ideas about the inviolability of a person's body (without consent) and individual autonomy, for the reasons described above, it does not necessarily comport with the ancient and medieval conceptions that are relevant here.

5.4 THE QUESTION OF PERMISSIBLE PAYMENT

Given the Talmudic understanding of organ transfer as an act of retrocession, or a return gift to God, how is one to think about money in this situation? What should be obvious by now is that asking whether one can "sell" one's organ is asking the wrong question.[63] It cannot be a sale for, as a matter of

62 This appears to be the position taken by the Conservative movement, according to a Responsum written by Rabbi Joel Roth, K. Abelson, and David J. Fine (eds.), *Responsa 1991–2000*, New York: Rabbinical Assembly (2002), pp. 208–316.

63 The possibility of providing some sort of minimal payment to the donor, albeit limited, does exist – e.g., as payment for lost time, suffering, or out-of-pocket expenses, either as a matter of incentivizing this behavior (as in the case of the broken utensils, see Chapter 4, Section 4.2.4.1) or avoiding a case of unjust enrichment (as with the travelling householder, see p. 154, *supra*). No payment, however, will change the status of the act of transfer into a sale. Moreover, given that, by definition, this is not a market transaction, there are strong, inherent constraints on the type and amount of compensation that can be provided.

law, it is a transfer of a different nature – a divine gift (that is, a gift or transfer to and then from God). Agreeing to give the organ (and actually giving it) is an act of *tsedakah*. By definition it calls for no remuneration, as it inherently represents the (retro) ceding of whatever ownership one had to God, the lien holder. Conversely, when the recipient receives the organ he (technically) gets nothing (no benefit) from the human donor; rather, what he receives from the divine domain is the minimum guarantee entailed in self-ownership: a basic entitlement of life.

The impossibility of sale in this context does not obviate the possibility that some form of payment might be permissible, or even appropriate. The principles concerning payment in the context of *pikuach nefesh* discussed in Chapter 4 have a particularly interesting application here, as do the more general concerns expressed in the texts regarding paying someone to perform a *mitzvah*. The fact that what is "given" here, to save a life, is a part of the human body renders the analysis particularly insightful, as to both obligation and the body, and the conceptualization of compensation.

There is no question about the characterization of organ (or even blood) transfer as an act of *pikuach nefesh*. That obligation, according to the text in B.T. Sanhedrin, is twofold: to act, personally, to save the life of another, and to spend money to try to bring about that result. There are two types of compensation contemplated in the relevant Talmudic passage – removing a disincentive and rectifying what would otherwise be unjust enrichment, each of which corresponds, respectively, to the two aspects of the obligation – to use one's body (literally, or just to take action), and to expend funds if necessary. The "unjust enrichment" payment (if any) relates directly to funds lost or expended in the process of rescue.[64] The "anti-disincentive" payment relates to the personal obligation to act in that it is intended, explicitly, to influence the individual's initial decision as to whether to act as a rescuer.[65] This latter payment,[66] which implicates a general concern in Jewish law that one ought not to get paid for performing a *mitzvah*, will be examined first.

[64] Note that, as described in Chapter 4, this is not a *property* obligation inasmuch as it is only required of some people after the fact (those who can afford to pay).

[65] Of course, the incentive payment entails repayment of the donor's financial loss, but this is done to remove the disincentive such a loss might otherwise represent, not because there is any legal (property) notion that the donor is entitled to have these costs reimbursed.

[66] The issue of payment to avoid a disincentive calls for clarification of an important side issue. As noted, the paradigmatic case under discussion is one in which the act of *pikuach nefesh* is not legally mandated, but is obligatory in the sense that it is a *mitzvah*; it is because this obligation can, in a sense, be seen as supererogatory that the matter of potential disincentive arises. There are extreme cases that define the spectrum within which our case falls. In one extreme case, the act itself would be prohibited (when the rescuer would be forfeiting his life to save the other),

5.4.1 *The Prohibition against Getting Paid to do a* Mitzvah

To what extent might the promise of payment (or, at least, of indemnification) be offered to remove a financial disincentive to the act of donation? The propriety of a payment of this sort is explicit in B.T. Sanhedrin 74a , a text that was examined above:

> If one pursuer [the rescuer] was pursuing another pursuer [a potential murderer] to save [someone's life] and he broke some utensils ... he is not liable [for damages]. This is not the actual rule, but if you do not say [that] this [is the rule] no one will save his fellow from a [murderous] pursuer.
>
> ורודף שהיה רודף אחר רודף להצילו, ושיבר את הכלים ...פטור. ולא מן הדין,
> שאם אי אתה אומר כן נמצא אין לך כל אדם שמציל את חבירו מיד הרודף

There are some important characteristics to this payment indicated by the language used here. As noted earlier, this is a payment (or, to be more exact, an exemption from a liability that would otherwise attach) that is explicitly intended to facilitate (or encourage) a person to assume the obligation of rescue. This is not an offer of a reward or financial incentive; the potential rescuer will not profit from his act. Nor is this a payment to which the rescuer is entitled as a matter of property law. This is simply an anti-disincentive measure; it ensures that a potential rescuer will not shy away from doing his duty for fear of exposure to potentially unlimited financial liability. In fact, to be more exact, the language that justifies this right of indemnification, "if you do not say [that] that this [is the rule] no one will save his fellow from a [murderous] pursuer," reveals that this is a purely pragmatic step, one that expressly takes into account the reality that, if this is not done, it is possible (if not likely) that no one will undertake a rescue and people might die as a result. (This reflects a cynical comment on human nature and/or a recognition that such behavior cannot realistically be expected of the average potential rescuer).

That the above is a correct description of the nature of this payment is made clear, also, by the fact that what is offered the rescuer is simply the promise of

and in the other, the act would be legally mandated (as when standing by a person drowning in the river). An incentive-oriented payment would be inappropriate in both of these cases, but would be appropriate in the broad range of cases that fall in between, in which someone could intervene to aid another but (due to proximity or other circumstances) would not be legally mandated to do so. In the context of organ transfer, the former "extreme" case (of prohibition) is obvious – e.g., heart transplant from a person who is not brain dead. The latter "extreme" case (of a mandate) could, arguably, involve a situation in which a person in front of the donor will die but for a blood donation from the donor (although the decisors discussed above, including the Conservative Movement [Roth (2002)], would not find an obligation even here). As with the rescuer, an incentive-oriented payment would be inappropriate in both of these cases (it would not render the act permissible in the former case, and it would be inappropriate – if not an act of extortion – in a case where there is a legal obligation.)

compensation for potential loss. What is not discussed is the degree to which it would be appropriate to relieve the potential rescuer of the possibility of financial loss, beyond this exact promise of exemption from liability for damage done to third parties. It is, nevertheless, clear that this sort of payment is necessarily in the nature of compensation for loss.

Militating against the propriety of profiting from the act of rescue is the special obligation to expend funds; doing so in the act of *pikuach nefesh* renders the expenditure, inherently, an act of *tsedakah*.[67] Even a policy that might provide for full compensation for any and all losses that the rescuer might suffer during the course of the rescue (including repayment of money expended) would not convert the nature of the expenditure itself – one of *tsedakah*, dictated explicitly by the commandment not to stand idly by (which, as noted above, is not simply a requirement to extend a loan to the person rescued) – into a payment giving rise to a property debt.

There is, moreover, another principle at play here besides the deep theoretical importance of recognizing the operation of the divine lien in the context of *pikuach nefesh*: what later became generally regarded as a principle precluding the payment of a salary (or profit) for performing a *mitzvah*. This is reflected in the fact, noted in Chapter 4, that although one is reimbursed for expenditures *bemamono* (of one's property) to save a life, one is not to be paid for what one does *begufo* (with one's body) to save a life.

The sources for the general prohibition against being paid to do a *mitzvah* in rabbinic literature are somewhat sparse. The doctrine developed much more fully during the medieval period in connection, for example, with the increased professionalization of the rabbinate and the question of whether a rabbi can get paid.[68] Interestingly, among the select practices that the medieval rabbis understood to fall under this prohibition was payment for a physician. The reason this is interesting is that, apart from the sources mentioned in Chapter 4 that discuss the reason *pikuach nefesh* does not generally warrant payment, the few Talmudic texts that speak to a prohibition against payment for a *mitzvah* do not mention doctors or healing in particular.[69] And yet, the medieval rabbis grouped doctors with rabbis, judges,

67 As noted in the previous chapter, *pikuach nefesh* is, inherently, a subcategory of *tsedakah*.

68 In his commentary to Mishnah Avot 4:7, Maimonides goes on at length about the question of whether rabbis ought to be paid.

69 This is one of the interesting questions with respect to the matter of payment for doctors. For there are, in fact, a number of Talmudic references that indicate that doctors could (or, at least were) paid. The discussion of payment for *pikuach nefesh* (and the operation of the divine lien in this context) described above, combined with the interpretation of relevant rabbinic texts below, provides a possible explanation for the inclusion of doctors within this category.

and witnesses – people who perform practices that the Talmud explicitly says do not warrant remuneration.[70]

While there is no room to fully enter into the topic of paying physicians here, it is useful to examine the rabbinic sources that speak to this overall problem. Before doing so, it is necessary to explain the notion of *schar batalah* (lost wages), the legal vehicle pursuant to which payment for professionals whose work involves the performance of a *mitzvah*, such as a rabbi, judge or doctor, was permitted. In accordance with the reasoning expressed in the Talmudic text quoted above (that without a promise of indemnity, no one will "save his fellow"), it is obvious that some provision for the sustenance of people in these categories must be provided, or else no one would (or would be able to) perform these functions. And yet, receipt of a salary (as such) was not permitted. Payments were permitted, as compensation for the time spent performing the *mitzvah* (*schar batalah*) – time one could otherwise have used earning a living. This notion appears in numerous places in the Talmud in connection with the performance of a *mitzvah*.[71]

The primary rabbinic text articulating a general prohibition against receiving payment for performing a *mitzvah* is in Mishnah Bechorot 4:6, which provides as follows:

> If one takes payment to act as a judge, his judgments are void; to give evidence, his evidence is void; to sprinkle or to sanctify [purification waters] the waters are considered [tantamount to] cave waters and the ashes are considered ashes of [ordinary] burnt [wood].
>
> הנוטל שכרו לדון דיניו בטילים להעיד עדותיו בטילין להזות ולקדש מימיו מי מערה אפרו אפר מקלה.

[70] See B.T. Bechorot 29a. Of course, this is a bit of an oversimplification, for there is a set of Talmudic texts on this question that are somewhat contradictory. For instance, regarding the first Mishnah in the thirteenth chapter of Ketuvot, there is a description of the fund from which civil judges were paid. A thorough study of these questions awaits additional research. On the question of paying physicians, see Fred Rosner and David Weinberger, "Jewish Concerns about Gifts to Physicians from Drug Companies," *Tradition* 32/3 (1998), pp. 19–30; Elliot N. Dorff, "Paying for Medical Care: A Jewish View," *Kennedy Institute of Ethics Journal* 7/1 (1997), pp. 15–30; Fred Rosner and Jacob Widroff, "Physician's Fees in Jewish Law," *Jewish Law Annual* 12 (1997), pp. 115–126.

[71] See, e.g., B.T. Bava Metzia 30b (this type of payment is permitted for the time taken to fulfill the obligation to return lost property). This concept is developed and used throughout medieval rabbinic texts as a matter of course. For instance, the Shulchan Arukh (Even HáEzer 13:13) states that (where no other woman can be found) a divorced woman can be forced to breastfeed her child (an obligation that is owed to her husband – see B.T. Ketuvot 59b – and not to her), and that she is to be paid *schar batalah*. Although there is no place to explore this topic more fully here, wet nursing and the obligation and/or availability of payment for breast-feeding, is an interesting topic to explore with the question of organ transfer (and possible "commodification" of the body) in mind. See, e.g., Valerie Fildes, *Wet Nursing: A History From Antiquity to the Present*, Oxford: Basil Blackwell (1988); George D. Sussman, *Selling Mother's Milk: The Wet-Nursing Business in France 1715–1914*, Urbana: University of Illinois Press (1982).

The Talmud at B.T. Bechorot 29a inquires as to the (biblical) source of this prohibition against payment:

> Whence do we know this? Rav Yehudah reported in the name of Rav: The verse [Deut 4:5] states: "[Moses says] see, I have taught you, etc.," which means *"just as I teach for free, so [shall] you teach for free."* This has also been taught [in a beraita]: The verse [Deut 4:5] states, "as the Lord my God commanded me," [intimating], "just as I teach for free, so shall you teach for free." And whence do we derive that if he cannot find someone to teach him for free, he must pay for learning? The verse [Proverbs 23:23] states: "Purchase the truth." And whence do we infer that one should not say "as I learned the Torah by paying, so I shall teach it for payment"? The same verse states, "[purchase truth] and do not sell [it]."
>
> מנהני מילי? אמר רב יהודה אמר רב דאמר קרא [דברים ד:ה] ראה למדתי אתכם וגו' מה אני בחנם אף אתם בחנם. תניא נמי הכי כאשר צוני ה' אלהי מה אני בחנם, אף אתם בחנם ומנין שאם לא מצא בחנם שילמד בשכר תלמוד לומר [משלי כ"ג:כ"ג] אמת קנה, ומנין שלא יאמר כשם שלמדתיה בשכר כך אלמדנה בשכר תלמוד לומר אמת קנה ואל תמכור

The statements in Deuteronomy refer to the giving of the Torah, as Moses says, "just as I received it for free, so [shall you] receive it for free."[72] What this statement encapsulates is the quintessential theory behind a deflected return gift to God – the idea that, in return for having received a gift from God, one ought to gift the same thing to another.

[72] There is an aggadic passage in the Talmud that is explicit in demonstrating that Moses did not regard his receipt of the Torah as something that conferred a benefit upon him. An aggadic passage in B.T. Shabbat 89a recounts the following: "Rabbi Yehoshua ben Levi said: When Moses descended from being before God, Satan came and asked him, 'Sovereign of the Universe! Where is the Torah?' [He said,] 'I have given it to the earth.' [Satan] went to the earth and said, 'Where is the Torah?' [The earth replied,] 'God understands its way, etc. [Job 28:23].' [Satan] went to the sea and it told him, 'It is not with me.' He went to the deep and it said to him, 'It is not in me,' … He went back and declared before [God], 'Sovereign of the Universe! I have searched throughout all the earth but have not found it!' [God said,] 'Go to the son of Amram'. [So Satan] went to Moses and asked him, 'Where is the Torah which God gave you?' [Moses said,] 'Who am I that God should give me the Torah? ' God said to Moses, 'Moses, are you a liar?' 'Sovereign of the Universe!' he replied, 'You have a stored-up treasure in which You take delight every day: *shall I keep the benefit for myself*?' God said to Moses, 'Moses, since you have disparaged yourself, [the Torah] will be named afer you, as it is said [in Malachi 3:23], 'Remember the law of Moses my servant, etc...'" (emphasis added).

אמר רבי יהושע בן לוי בשעה שירד משה מלפני הקדוש ברוך הוא בא שטן ואמר לפניו רבונו של עולם תורה היכן היא אמר לו נתתיה לארץ הלך אצל ארץ אמר לה תורה היכן היא אמרה לו [איוב כח] אלהים הבין דרכה וגו' הלך אצל ים ואמר לו אין עמדי הלך אצל תהום אמר לו אין בי.... חזר ואמר לפני הקדוש ברוך הוא רבונו של עולם חיפשתי בכל הארץ ולא מצאתיה אמר לו לך אצל בן עמרם הלך אצל משה אמר לו תורה שנתן לך הקדוש ברוך הוא היכן היא? אמר לו וכי מה אני שנתן לי הקדוש ברוך הוא תורה אמר לו הקדוש ברוך הוא למשה משה בדאי אתה אמר לפניו רבונו של עולם חמודה גנוזה יש לך שאתה משתעשע בה בכל יום אני אחזיק טובה לעצמי? אמר לו הקדוש ברוך הוא למשה הואיל ומיעטת עצמך תקרא על שמך שנאמר [מלאכי ג] זכרו תורת משה עבדי וגו'

We thus have clear textual support for the fact that certain roles – being a judge, a witness, a teacher of Torah, and performers of certain other practices – should not be paid a salary. As many medieval rabbis noted, if some mechanism for payment is not made, no one will perform these practices; since it is more important that they be done, the rabbis did something similar to that done in the context of the rescuer: to ensure that the overarching purpose be accomplished, they adopted what might, in some way, be considered a subterfuge – the notion of paying for lost time.

The appropriateness of extending to doctors the principle of *mah ani bechinam af atem bechinam* (just as I [received or gave it for free], so shall [I give it] to you for free) is illustrated, for example, in the work of the medieval rabbinic scholar Nachmanides.[73] He explained this extension by analogizing Torah knowledge (which was received freely and thus must be given freely) to knowledge about the human body and human health. This rationale is even more vivid when what is given (to heal) is not knowledge regarding the body, but a part of the body itself.[74] Indeed, imagining the case of organ transfer makes the comparison between Torah knowledge and body/health knowledge even more clear. For if there is anything that humans can be said to "receive for free" (apart from the Torah), it is their bodies and their lives.

As noted, Nachmanides makes this analogy between knowledge of Torah and knowledge of the body explicit, using reasoning that makes the application of this principle to organ transfer almost inescapable. He states,

> With respect to the matter of compensation for healing, it seems to me that [the physician] is permitted to collect from them compensation for lost time [*schar batalah*] and [compensation for] exertion. However, compensation for teaching [the patient what to do to be healed] is prohibited, as this represents the [return of] his lost body, and God said, "and you shall return it [him] to him [himself]."[75]
>
> ולענין שכר רפואה נראה לי דמותר ליטול מהן שכר בטלה וטרחה אבל שכר הלימוד אסור דאבדת גופו הוא ורחמנה אמר והשבותו לו

With respect to the Torah (or knowledge thereof), the Talmud offers the ultimate expression of the principle that one has a "return" obligation to God that can and should be satisfied by transferring (part of) what one received, as a gift

73 Moshe ben Nachman Girondi ("Ramban"). See C. D. Chavel, *Kitve Rabbenu Moshe ben Nahman*, Jerusalem: Mossad Harav Kook (1964) at 44–45.

74 There is a rich basis in the texts and in legal rules that suggests that a deep and meaningful analogy can be drawn between the Torah and the human body. For example, both must be buried.

75 *Id.* at 44.

from God, to another human being. Just as teaching Torah represents this type of divine gift (to and from God), so does organ transfer. The fact that this is an obligation that inheres in the property itself is made plain by the extension of this "return gift" principle to mere knowledge about the body. Like teaching about Torah, informing someone about how to be healthy (or, even more so, giving a body part to heal someone) is something that cannot, by definition, yield an income or, even worse, a profit.

There is another, particular reason to expect that acts of *pikuach nefesh*, and particularly the act of organ transfer, ought not to receive remuneration.[76] One of the specific rituals listed in Mishnah Bechorot 4:6 that must be performed at no charge is the act of sanctification (*lekadesh*). Indeed, the Talmud (B.T. Bechorot 29a) clarifies this in analyzing the Mishnah:

> [The Mishnah states: "if one takes a fee] to sprinkle or to sanctify [purification waters], the waters are considered [tantamount to] cave waters and the ashes are considered ashes of [ordinary] burnt [wood]." The following was cited in contradiction: If one betroths a woman with the waters of purification or with the ashes of purification, she is betrothed, although he is an Israelite? – Said Abaye: This offers no difficulty. Here, [in the case just mentioned,] it is payment for [simply] bringing the ashes [from Jerusalem] or drawing the waters, whereas there [in the case of the Mishnah], *it is payment for the act of sprinkling or sanctification*. (emphasis added)
>
> להזות ולקדש מימיו מי מערה אפרו אפר מקלה ורמינהו המקדש במי חטאת באפר
> חטאת הרי זו מקודשת אף על פי שהוא ישראל אמר אביי לא קשיא כאן בשכר הבאה
> ומלוי כאן בשכר הזאה וקידוש

As explained in Chapters 3 and 4, the act of organ transfer (like acts of *pikuach nefesh* in general) can, in a legal sense, be considered an act of consecration (making something *hekdesh*). In the context of *pikuach nefesh*, one is consecrating whatever property one gives, inasmuch as it is a gift to the divine domain, one that, like *tsedakah*, passes by means of a vow; it is then from the divine domain that it passes to the recipient. As explained above, the act of donating a part of the human body is unequivocally the closest one might get to sanctifying property to God – indeed, it is property that has a greater degree of sacredness (in the sense of a claim of divine ownership) to begin with.

Here, too, Nachmanides explicitly links the principle of "*mah ani b'chinam af atem b'chinam*" to the fee paid to a doctor, by citing this prohibition from

[76] There is no room here to address the larger question of when the principle of *mah ani b'chinam* (just as I received it for free so shall I give it for free) applies, with respect to *mitzvot* generally.

Mishnah Bechorot 4:6, and its interpretation. After quoting the aforementioned principle (*mah ani b'chinam*), Nachmanides deduces,

> therefore, compensation for [the physician's] knowledge and teaching is prohibited, as this would be [the same as] payment for sprinkling or sanctification. However, compensation for exertion is permissible, as this would be [the same as] payment for bringing the ashes or filling the waters, which is permissible.[77]
>
> הלכך שכר החכמה והלימוד אסור דהוה ליה כשכר הזאות וקידוש אבל שכר הטרחה מותר דהוה ליה כשכר הבאה ומילוי ומותר

Notwithstanding the contemporary reality regarding the amount doctors get paid, the notion of profiting from the act of giving one's body flies in the face of the basis for not paying someone to perform the particular *mitzvah* of healing. In fact, in the continuation of his discussion of payment for healing, Nachmanides relies on a fascinating discussion in B.T. Yevamot 106a[78] to explain not only that drugs must be charged at cost (and no more), but also that if it is necessary to promise to pay more to the doctor – for the drugs or, presumably, for the act of healing – the promise is null and void. The person who made the promise in a state of desperation is not held to it; for indeed, this is not a matter of contract. The law caps the amount that can be paid for the act of (or goods necessary for) life saving.[79] Profit is not permitted.[80]

5.4.2 *Concerns of Unjust Enrichment*

Finally, as described earlier, the question as to payment to avoid unjust enrichment might also apply. The following factors, specific to the context of organ transfer, are worth highlighting.

First, as demonstrated previously, the receipt of the organ, or the receipt of "healing," does not constitute "enrichment" derived from another human being; nor does providing the organ, or of healing *per se*, represent any actual

[77] *Id.*

[78] The context there involves a *yevamah* (woman whose husband has died while they are childless and is thus biblically married to her husband's brother) who is improperly compelled to promise to pay her brother-in-law to perform the ritual of *chalitzah* in order to free her of her *yibum* status. (This principle, which cannot be expanded upon here, has significant implications for the question as to whether a promise to pay is enforceable where initially asking for such a payment is improper.)

[79] For reasons explained throughout this chapter, it is not possible to argue that the "cost" to the organ recipient is the market value of the lost organ.

[80] Of course, as discussed elsewhere, there is a specific prohibition against having benefit (financial or otherwise) from a dead body or human organ.

loss when calculating loss and benefit between the two persons.[81] To the contrary, the above analysis suggests that the possession of, versus the need for, a (healthy) organ provides an independent measure of "wealth" and "poverty" for purposes of unjust enrichment. Just as the travelling householder is, due to his situation, temporarily (situationally) "poor" while he finds himself without funds for food (see p. 154, *supra*), so too the person who will die due to the absence of a healthy kidney is in the same category of need when it comes to divine gifts and divinely owned property. There is no need for some rectifying payment; the calculation in the context of organ transfer looks to the particular "goods" needed for sustenance.

Of course, once the issue of "payment" for the giving of the organ and restoration of the other person's body is dismissed, other costs can and should be analyzed in accordance with the equitable principles described earlier. Thus, if the organ recipient is wealthy, there is no question that he ought to cover the out-of-pocket expenses of the organ donor (separate and apart from any public-policy consideration that might also dictate that these costs be covered by someone). Other types of justice-oriented compensation might also be appropriate, depending on the circumstances. The important principle articulated by the Rosh[82] and other medieval rabbis pertains here: that fairness dictates that the rescuer be compensated for expenditures (and losses?) only so long as the recipient can afford it. In other words, the principle of wealth disparity as a relevant factor in the allocation of entitlements in the realm of divine gifts is decisive. Not only is there an absence of an outright property debt owed by the recipient to the donor, but a requirement of repayment is only triggered if the person can afford it.

One final observation regarding the question of payment in the context of organ transfer is that it is crucial to keep separate what amount to theoretically distinct categories of payment. There is the obvious concern that permissible payments ought not to be permitted to become subterfuges for what would, in fact, amount to impermissible payments of extortion and profiteering.

It is also important to retain the conceptual distinction between payments that ought to be made by the receiving party (e.g. on the grounds of unjust

[81] This is true notwithstanding texts in B.T. Bava Kamma chapter 8 (regarding compensation for injury). Not only is this obvious from the above analysis of what is entailed in the actual transfer of the organ, but there are texts from B.T. Bava Kamma that support the idea that, while it is necessary to calculate a value to compensate for injury, those provisions are not meant to be read as putting a "price tag" on body parts, or as suggesting that in a context like this the "loss" of the organ is something that ought to be compensated.

[82] See *Piskei Ha-Rosh* Sanhedrin 8:2.

enrichment), and payments motivated by public-policy concerns (e.g., to encourage people to act as rescuers), which ought (to some extent and when necessary) to be borne by the community at large. Certain costs could, and perhaps should, be borne by the community (paid, perhaps, out of a communal *tsedakah* fund). For while the obligation to sustain the lives of others is an individual one, owed by each individual to all others, as was true with the broader category of *tsedakah*, the logistics required for the effective management of a system that enables and ensures that individual obligations and entitlements are met, and met in a fair way, might require some centralized organization.

In this light, it becomes clear that it was no coincidence that, in the late middle ages, the word *hekdesh* took on the specific meaning of hospital for the poor. For in essence, the ultimate and, perhaps, most critical aspect of ensuring the mutual sustenance and preservation of human life lies in the guarantee of healthcare by the community.

5.5 THE FREE AND OBLIGATORY GIFT, AND THE QUESTION OF HUMAN OWNERSHIP

Chapter 3 started with a simple question: how is it possible to reconcile a blanket conception of divine ownership with a legal structure that, nonetheless, accommodates human property ownership, such that two separate institutions – *hedyot*, human owned property ownership, and *hekdesh*, divinely owned property ownership – can coexist?

Paradoxically, the answer lies in the question itself and provides the key to deeper conceptions of sanctity and implicit limits to human property ownership implied therein. For the fundamental notion that everything "belongs" to God – that everything is, ultimately, within God's domain – is subtly incorporated into the very conceptualization of these two realms of *hekdesh* and *hedyot*. The marker for the divide between these two realms is not spatial or material; rather, it is the goal of sustaining human life that provides the defining distinction. As a counterweight to the institution of property ownership, an important element within the Jewish legal tradition is a framework for (combined voluntary and obligatory) giving to nurture human life; this, in turn, represents a placeholder for the property realm of the divine. It is in this sense that one might say that the human body (along with human life) is "owned" by (owed to) God (to a greater extent than everything else in the world). This connection implies what amounts to both obligations and rights.

In terms of obligations, the relationship between the limitations of divine ownership and the human body is set forth in Tosefta Peah 4:1, a parallel to the passage in B.T. Berakhot 35a, with which our analysis of two overlapping realms of ownership began in Chapter 4, Section 4.2.4.1. The version in Tosefta Berakhot 4:1 provides as follows:

> A *person may not taste anything until* [*he recites*] *a blessing*, as it is written, [Psa 24:1]: *"The earth and all that is in it belongs to God."* A person who derives [any] benefit from this world without [first reciting a] blessing has committed *me'ilah* (sacrilegious theft from God)... Until all of the commandments (*mitzvot*) have [been satisfied, and have thus] rendered it permissible [for him to do so,] a person may not use his face, or his hands or his legs, except in honor of God (*konehu*), as it is written [in Prov 16:4:] "everything that God has made [is] for his/its purpose."[83] (emphasis added)
>
> לא יטעום אדם כלום עד שיברך שנאמר [תהילים כד:א] לה' הארץ ומלואה הנהנה מן העולם הזה בלא ברכה מעל עד שיתירו לו כל המצות לא ישתמש אדם בפניו בידיו וברגליו אלא לכבוד קונהו שנאמר [משלי ט"ז:ד] כל פעל ה' למענהו

The juxtaposition of the categorical restriction, based in the principle of divine ownership, on the use and/or ownership of anything (as set forth in Chapter 2, limitations calling for a return gift) – with an express limitation on the way one may use (own?) one's bodily limbs – is fascinating. The latter part of the passage can be read to bring the body within the ambit of the first, broad statement of divine ownership of everything. Indeed, the Hebrew word for God used here, *konehu* (related to the word *kinyan*, acquisition), is often translated as "his creator" but is more accurately translated as "his owner." Conversely, by singling out the human body for special mention, the passage can be read as an indication that, while the same (or a similar) principle might apply generally, there is, nevertheless, something categorically different about the human body.

There is no room, here, to explore the various possible readings and implications of this passage.[84] For these purposes, it is sufficient to take this statement for what it is: an unequivocal affirmative answer to the question posed above, a simple declaration that the limitations inherent in the overarching principle of divine ownership extend to the human body as well. Indeed, in reading this passage with the question of life-saving organ transplantation in mind, it would seem that such use of the body (certainly postmortem) is precisely what would be dictated by the principles

[83] This last quote refers to Prov 16:4, which reads, "everything that God has made [is] for his/its purpose" כל פעל ה' למענהו

[84] On matters such as the use of *konehu* for God vis-à-vis the body; restrictions on the "use" of one's body, and how that relates to limits on ownership (or hints at the limited degree to which one owns one's body – to use it, but not to consume, destroy, maim, sell it, etc.).

of ownership and appropriate use. Tracking the language of Tosefta Peah 4:1: to the extent that it is possible "to make use of" one's body parts for the purpose deemed paramount by God, its ultimate owner (sustaining and saving human life), it would seem that the dictates of divine ownership would *require* transplantation.

As promised, we return to complete the analysis of B.T. Berakhot 35a–b. As a larger literary entity, it provides a rich source for reviewing the thesis of divine ownership set forth in this book. The path taken by the discussion in this *sugyah* provides an excellent vehicle for recapping the theoretical perspective that the divine lien contributes to the analysis of the problem of commodification and the shortage of organs for transplant.

As noted in Chapter 3, the discussion in B.T. Berakhot 35a began with an attempt to ascertain the derivation of the principle that one may not receive pleasure (*hana'ah*) from eating without first reciting a benediction. The first part of the text, discussed above, found this to be a blanket expression of the deeper requirement that, for humans to enjoy things of this earth, they must be redeemed from God with an act of retrocession (or a symbol thereof, such as a blessing). The act of retrocession often takes the form of refraining from eating a portion of it and/or ceremonializing the eating of a portion of it as a kind of sacrifice. As noted earlier, it was concluded that no textual support is needed to teach this principle; it is something that is obvious and that can be derived from human reason (*sevarah*) alone.

Thereafter, the text proceeded to raise the question, also dealt with above, as to how it is possible for property to be owned both by humans and by God. Entailed in that question was a quotation from Deut 11:14 – "And you shall gather in your corn" (ואספת דגנך) – as representative of the domain of human ownership.[85] The Talmud proceeds to explore the implications of that verse, which they view as a signifier for human commercial enterprise.

A beraita is brought at B.T. Berachot 35b questioning the meaning of the above-quoted verse, in light of Josh 1:8, which seems to imply that one should spend all of one's time studying/teaching Torah: "This book of the law shall not depart from your mouth" (לא ימוש ספר תורה הזה מפיך). The juxtaposition of these verses poses the existential problem of how one ought to spend one's time – devoted to mundane commercial activity or to studying and teaching Torah.[86] The beraita recites the views of two rabbis, who have opposite

[85] This was contrasted with the verse making reference to divine ownership: "Therefore, I will take back my corn in its time, etc." (ולקחתי דגני בעתו וגו') (Hos 2:11).

[86] This is an activity that, as described above, entails a divine gift and ought not yield any income.

perspectives on this question. First, Rabbi Ishmael voices the more realistic or practical perspective:

> Our Rabbis taught: [Hos 2:11 states,] "And you shall gather in your corn." What is the verse coming to teach? Since it says, "This book of the law shall not depart from your mouth" [Josh 8:1], it would be possible to think that these words are to be taken literally. [Therefore] the verse [Deut 11:14] says, "And you shall gather in your corn," which [says that you are to live a life that has both Torah study] and a worldly occupation (lit: is conducted in the way of the world). This is the view of Rabbi Ishmael. (emphasis added)
>
> תנו רבנן ואספת דגנך מה תלמוד לומר לפי שנאמר [יהושע ח:א]
> לא ימוש ספר התורה הזה מפיך יכול דברים ככתבן תלמוד לומר
> ואספת דגנך הנהג בהן מנהג דרך ארץ דברי רבי ישמעאל

Recognizing that a person must earn a living, Rabbi Ishmael reads the two verses together and says that a person should undertake both to work (to earn a living), and to study Torah – an activity that (should, by right) yield no remuneration.

Thereafter, the *sugyah* recounts the idealistic view of Rabbi Shimon ben Yokhai:

> Rabbi Shimon ben Yokhai says: Is that possible? If a person ploughs in the ploughing season, and sows in the sowing season, and reaps in the reaping season, and threshes in the threshing season, and winnows in the season of wind, *what will become of [the study of] the Torah*? Rather, [the two verses can be reconciled as follows:] at a time when [the people of] Israel do the will of the God, their work is performed [for them] by others, as it says (Isa 61:5), "And strangers will arise and feed your flocks, etc.," [and the people of Israel will be able to devote all their time to studying the Torah.] But at a time when [the people of] Israel do not do the will of God their work is done by them, personally, as it says, (Deut 11:14) "And you shall gather in your corn." [87] Nor is this all, but [under those circumstances] the work of others also is done by them, as it says, (Deut 28:48), "And you shall serve your enemy, etc."
>
> רבי שמעון בן יוחי אומר אפשר אדם חורש בשעת חרישה וזורע בשעת זריעה
> וקוצר בשעת קצירה ודש בשעת דישה וזורה בשעת הרוח תורה מה תהא עליה
> אלא בזמן שישראל עושין רצונו של מקום מלאכתן נעשית על ידי אחרים
> שנאמר [ישעיהו ס"א] ועמדו זרים ורעו צאנכם וגו' ובזמן שאין ישראל עושין
> רצונו של מקום מלאכתן נעשית על ידי עצמן שנאמר [דברים י"א] ואספת דגנך
> ולא עוד אלא שמלאכת אחרים נעשית על ידן שנאמר[דברים כ"ח] ועבדת את אויבך וגו'

87 Interestingly, this view reverses the interpretation of Rabbi Hanina ben Papa that had been recited immediately preceding this discussion, who read the verse "And you shall gather in your corn" as referring to circumstances in which Israel does the will of God (whereas the phrase referring to God taking back the corn refers to the situation in which Israel does not perform God's will).

The notion that one's work will "get done," and that one will have the funds to sustain oneself if one spends all of one's time studying Torah, apparently proved to be as unrealistic as it sounds.[88] For the Talmud proceeds to recount the following in the name of Abaye:

> Said Abaye: Many have done as Rabbi Ishmael suggests [by combining the study of Torah with an occupation] and were successful; [others have] followed [the advice of] Rabbi Shimon ben Yokhai [devoting themselves to Torah study alone] and were not successful.
>
> אמר אביי הרבה עשו כרבי ישמעאל ועלתה בידן כרבי שמעון בן יוחי ולא עלתה בידן

The discussion of this debate ends with a recitation of the following statement of Rava (another indication that the view of Rabbi Ishmael prevailed):

> Rava said to the rabbis [his disciples]: I beg you, [do your work and] do not come before me [to study Torah] during [the months of] Nissan and Tishrei so that you will not be anxious about your food supply all year long.
>
> אמר להו רבא לרבנן במטותא מינייכו ביומי ניסן וביומי תשרי לא תתחזו קמאי כי היכי דלא תטרדו במזונייכו כולא שתא

The (perhaps obvious) fact that it was understood that one was supposed to spend time both studying Torah and earning a living is confirmed in this final statement. What is interesting about this portion is the recognition of the tension posed by the expectation that people will devote part of their time to an activity that is very much not like a "worldly occupation". The *sugyah* continues:

> Rabbah bar bar Hanah said in the name of Rabbi Yohanan, reporting Rabbi Yehudah bar Ila'i: Come and see how the later generations are unlike the earlier generations. The earlier generations made the study of the Torah [their] main [occucpation] and made their work incidental, and both [their Torah knowledge and their financial situation] remained with them. The later generations made their work [their] main [occupation] and their study of the Torah incidental, and neither remained with them.
>
> רבה בר בר חנה אמר רבי יוחנן משום רבי יהודה ברבי אלעאי בא וראה שלא כדורות הראשונים דורות האחרונים דורות הראשונים עשו תורתן קבע ומלאכתן עראי זו וזו נתקיימה בידן דורות האחרונים שעשו מלאכתן קבע ותורתן עראי זו וזו לא נתקיימה בידן

This statement, made in the name of Rabbi Yohanan further highlights the concern regarding the effect that the strong and, perhaps, growing pull of the commercial world was to have on the enterprise of Torah study.

88 I do not mean to attribute any historicity to Abaye's statement.

Ironically, the reasoning of Rabbi Shimon ben Yokhai – so idealistic when originally articulated – provided the practical rationale for the rulings of those who officially made it possible to earn a living while studying and teaching Torah, a compromise that did not entail profiting off of Torah knowledge, but that enabled people to earn a living while studying. In what ultimately became the way this tension was resolved, the institutionalization of Torah study and the professionalization of the rabbinate, the medieval rabbis (e.g., Nachmanides) argued that it is necessary to permit people to receive some type of funds while/for studying Torah (*schar batalah*), because otherwise "what will become of the Torah" as no one will (be able to) spend time in its study.

This reasoning mirrors that used to justify the indemnification of the rescuer in B.T. Sanhedrin 74a. The payments permitted in that context, and in the context of Torah study, were explicitly geared to the real-life actualization of the ultimate goal at hand – the saving of human life, or the continued study and teaching of Torah. At the same time, by openly creating the fictions that conceptualize payments as lost "wages" or indemnification for damages (and, presumably, by capping the amounts that could be paid as such), there was a consistent theoretical effort to maintain the underlying structure whereby the activity itself is seen as something altogether separate from the commerce-related activities – as something that represents the fulfillment of an obligation to give, something that does not yield a reward.

In the final relevant portion of B.T. Berakhot 35b, another statement, brought by the same rabbis in the name of Rabbi Yohanan, laments the dissolution of values that has transpired over the generations. Paralleling peoples' reduced commitment to Torah study over time was an attempt to wiggle out of the tithing obligation:

> Rabbah bar bar Hanah further said in the name of Rabbi Yohanan reporting Rabbi Yehudah bar Ila'i: Come and see how the later generations are unlike the earlier generations. The earlier generations used to bring their produce in[to their houses] by way of the kitchen garden purposely in order to make them liable to the obligation to [tithe], whereas the later generations bring their produce by way of roofs or courtyards or storage yards in order to make them exempt from [the obligation to] tithe. For Rabbi Yannai has said: Untithed produce is not subject to tithing until it has come within sight of the house [and has been brought into the house through a normal entrance.]
>
> ואמר רבה בר בר חנה אמר רבי יוחנן משום רבי יהודה ברבי אלעאי בא וראה שלא כדורות הראשונים דורות האחרונים דורות הראשונים היו מכניסין פירותיהן דרך טרקסמון כדי לחייבן במעשר דורות האחרונים מכניסין פירותיהן דרך גגות דרך חצרות דרך קרפיפות כדי לפטרן מן המעשר דאמר רבי ינאי אין הטבל מתחייב במעשר עד שיראה פני הבית

Whereas earlier generations behaved appropriately – by fully, generously, and whole-heartedly fulfilling their tithing obligation, later generations took advantage of what might be labeled a loophole in the law. By bringing their produce into the house through unusual entrances (via the back door, so to speak), they succeeded in avoiding the tithing obligation. This perfectly legal maneuver is a classic example of an act of evasion that contravenes the spirit of the law. In this case (unlike the case of reduced commitment to Torah study), there was no inherent penalty for such conduct.

Acknowledged, here, is the fact that it is possible to "cut corners" when an implicit property obligation is free and obligatory (as tithing – or perhaps any obligation – is, to the extent that loopholes always exist). The theoretical framework presumes, or proposes, that the force of the obligation be such as to impel one to fulfill the obligation fully, even if there is a cost (just as one ought to spend a good part of one's time studying Torah, even though it reduces one's overall income.)

This understanding of tithing – recognizing it, ultimately, as a kind of voluntary obligation, given the acknowledged degree to which an individual can evade it, or fulfill it in a less than whole-hearted manner – provides an even better parallel to the institution of *tsedakah*.[89] In the context of lamenting the absence of a sense that obligation inheres in the very property of which ownership is being taken, the Talmud here renders the tithing requirement a perfect stand-in for *tsedakah* and, indeed, for organ transfer. Ultimately, the nature of the act of tithing, studying Torah, or performing an act of *pikuach nefesh* remains the same: it fulfills the obligation, implicit in human property ownership generally, of making a return to God and to others. They inherently and ultimately rest on an individual sense of obligation (despite the possible availability of certain funds), and it is from that essence that they derive their meaning.

89 This point is emphasized further by the fact that no *schar batalah* (compensation for lost time or for effort) is provided for the time spent bringing the tithes to Jerusalem.

Conclusion and Public Policy Implications

There is a paradox at the heart of the Marcel Mauss's insight regarding exchange: if an item given continues in some sense to belong to the donor (or if the donor continues to reside as a presence within the item given), how is it possible to say that anyone ever owns anything received from another? This problem highlights the further Maussian insight that, in the end, what matters most is not ownership but the cycle of giving and continuing obligation to others. Starting with the premise that God is the original owner/donor of everything, one can recognize this same paradox in the complicated rabbinic understanding of ownership. The rabbis' intricate development of a biblical plan of giving reads as an effort on their part to work through this paradox. The biblical scheme they imagined ideally entailed the existence of the Temple in Jerusalem and an agricultural society. The legal vehicles they constructed to ensure the continuation of that model of social bonding and interdependence did not.

The complex scheme of property obligations to God is the theoretical cornerstone of the rabbinic property system. Retrocessionary obligations, or "return" gifts to God, are required for more than reasons of gratitude or atonement; many operate explicitly as legal preconditions to taking ownership or as continuing obligations of ownership. The imaginary domain of divine ownership is the central locus for an array of gifts to God and, more frequently (if not exclusively) later, to others. *Tesdakah* and certain other donations fall within this scheme. Thus, an analysis that assumes that *tsedakah* given from one person to another represents a gift of the human donor's property, a gift to the other person (rather than to God), or a gift from the human donor (rather than a gift from God) is incompatible with the Talmudic scheme.

The Talmudic texts presume that there is an alternative to the realms of commerce and (pure, altruistic) charity or *caritas*. In the subset of transactions that comprise the economy of the sacred, an act of giving has a different cultural meaning; it is understood not as an act of pure gift or sale, but as the fulfillment of an obligation, as the giving of something to which the other person has a claim. Contemporary Jewish legal decisors have largely overlooked and misread Talmudic law relevant to the question of organ transfer. The theory of property and obligation in Talmudic law offered here provides an alternative Talmudic rendering of the modern-day phenomenon of organ transfer.

Talmudic law is not being applied to the contemporary problem of organ transfer in a teleological sense, but as an intellectual experiment. It is in the tradition of the comparative enterprise described by Marilyn Strathern, whereby examinations of other cultures "[o]pen up a range of conceptual resources from which we [in Western society] might draw our models" in response to "the pressure of contemporary social change."[1] As she points out, "new resources are coming into being all the time," entities "for which no prior transactional idioms exist."[2] Such might readily be said with respect to the transfer of human organs from one person to another. However, Talmudic law does contain a prior transactional idiom – the phenomena of sacrifice, donations to the Temple, and so on. Making this cultural comparison, and applying an analysis of Talmudic law to the question of organ sales, illustrates what can be gained by approaching the moral complexities of the question not from the formal perspective of the presence of money, and the tension between gift and commodity, but from the perspective of property and obligation.

As this analysis of the problem of commodification of the sacred illustrates, it is particularly at the moment of encounter between novel possibilities realizable in the contemporary world and long-held conceptions and categories that the mutually revelatory potential of the project of comparison is at its greatest. It is this unexpected comparative challenge to central presumptions, such as the opposition between gift and commodity, which productively offers a new approach to the problem of commodification. The theory of the economy of the sacred in Talmudic law offered here contributes to the ongoing debate about limits to markets in a way that has ramifications beyond the question of "organ sales." This model stresses the unique nature of obligation as part of a larger theory of the limited nature of ownership.[3] Another innovation of Talmudic law is its conception of the natures of the person, which is seen as more porous, and of property, which is understood as more relational or inclusive.

1 Strathern (1998) at 231.

2 *Id.* 216–217.

3 Some would likely disagree with my qualified reading of the institution of private property under Jewish law. See, e.g., David Novak, "Economics and Justice: A Jewish Example," in *Jewish Social Ethics*, New York: Oxford University Press (1992), pp. 206–224; Menachem Lorberbaum, *Politics and the Limits of Law: Secularizing the Political in Medieval Jewish Thought*, Stanford: Stanford University Press (2001).

Echoing the idea that the donor remains in the property as the "spirit of the gift" to produce a feeling of debt in the recipient, the sense that one's blood, one's organs – the things that keep a person alive and sustained – were received as gifts signifies a lien in favor of those in need (starting with the self). In this sense, the removal of organ transfer from the "market" realm is not conceptualized as a "blocked exchange"; for indeed, it is not an "exchange" at all. It is a different type of transfer altogether, one that is both free, in that the undertaking is discretionary, and obligatory, in that it implicitly satisfies a preexisting lien in favor of the lives of others.

The category of ongoing gifts to God is nicely described by Mauss's notion that the original donor continues to animate the item given. It is understood, in Talmudic law, to create something that might be called an "embodied obligation" – that is, an obligation (to make a return gift to God/ to give to the needy) that is built into all property.[4] It is this prior obligation that comes with all property[5] and that generates a cycle of giving that continues indefinitely.

As opposed to the idea of pure gift, this theory contemplates a sacred economy that reflects the pervasive, embodied obligation to cede to the needy that to which they are entitled. Rather than giving from one's own in order to accrue ethereal credit, the (voluntary) decision to give a life-saving organ, like the decision to give *tsedakah*, is conceived as a relinquishment to God of what is due. Mauss correctly points out that *tsedakah* means justice; however, this idea of relinquishment reflects something quite different from what he describes.[6] It is an idea of distributive justice whereby divine ownership limits human sovereignty over property, where an obligation to others in need is built into "all property" or "all things."

This idea, of the lingering claim or (partial) ownership of the donor as something that is almost physical, helps explain the continuing obligation to God in Talmudic law embodied in all property, as well as why it is directed to

4 When giving to fulfill an embodied obligation, one gives something that one does not own. This conception is what can concretely instantiate the paradoxical mixture of the free and the obligatory. It is a confusing concept that is capable of being described by the legal fiction of the lien. At one point in his essay, Mauss alludes to the "fiction" of "the legal 'lien' [that] springs from things," but does not make much of it. Mauss (1990) at 48.

5 This is not to say that the desire to get "credit" in heaven is not contemplated as part of the motivation for giving *tsedakah* and doing other *mitzvot* within the Jewish tradition, for that would certainly be incorrect. However, what is explained here is the overriding conceptualization of what is taking place when one does such acts, mixed motives notwithstanding.

6 For example, Mauss's (unreciprocated) gift (of alms) makes the recipient inferior. Mauss (1990) at 65. By contrast, *tsedakah* does not represent an initiating gift (calling for reciprocation); rather, it is already a return gift to God given in fulfillment of an obligation. The recipient receives what, ultimately, belongs to her; there is no inferiority in this.

the poor. God – or the sacred – is resident in all property, including all people. This commonality bridges the gap between people and things, and between the individual and other persons. The notion of the porosity of the self, and of the inclusivity of property, is exemplified in the case of organ transfer. The ultimate giving back to God is the giving back of life.[7]

It is in this vein that Jewish law promotes (and in some life-saving circumstances might mandate) organ transfer as a *mitzvah*, while permitting (and, in some contexts, possibly encouraging) a certain kind of payment, when dictated by justice. This perspective could be seen to represent the kind of hybrid morality described by Mauss, one consisting of "a good but moderate blend of reality and the ideal," in which the "life of the monk, and the life of a Shylock are both equally to be shunned."[8]

According to this analysis, the transfer of an organ might be called a relinquishment of property or more accurately, an act of retrocession (of returning property to its original or rightful owner). It is not a (pure) gift or sale. Nor is it an "exchange" in the temporally and subjectively immediate sense that these categories connote. To the extent that the term "exchange" might be applicable to this transfer (as what Mauss calls a "gift exchange"), it refers to its status as a "return gift," as a transfer that completes (or continues) a larger debt cycle (one that incorporates more than two individuals.) Thus, one is not rendering it a "blocked exchange," as described by Walzer, when one states that it is a transaction that cannot be regarded as a sale. Indeed, the "blocked exchange" idea undermines the conceptualization of the transfer as one that transcends the gift/sale dichotomy. For whether or not money changes hands, the property transfer is an act of retrocession in the context of a lien that is triggered by the dictates of justice.

Nor is the transfer in the nature of what is contemplated by Titmuss. The element of altruism or "pure" gift is not what is critical; to the contrary, the polarities of pure self-interest and complete disinterest are both misplaced in this context. Rather than an anonymous act (selfless or otherwise), ideal transfer in this context is one that reflects and reinforces human interrelationality; rather than ensuring a pure, nonmonetary incentive, the public-policy perspective would be concerned with supporting and, indeed, cultivating a sense of (mutual) obligation when the well-being of others is at stake.

The obligatory gift instantiates an attitude that mixes concern for self with the concern for the other. Conceptual lessons can be drawn from the texts

7 Cf. Derrida's discussion of Kierkegaard's analysis of the sacrifice of Isaac in *The Gift of Death*.

8 Mauss (1990) at 69.

highlighted here, where even the principle dictating precedence of the self over the other is interrelational rather than atomistic. In the context in which it is cited by Rabbi Akiva, the phrase in Lev 25:36 that puts the self first – "and your brother shall live with you" (especially given the way it is interpreted elsewhere in rabbinic literature) reflects the notion of a "self" that is both built on a firm grounding of internal integrity and is also somewhat porous; that is, it is susceptible to the obligation to keep both the self and the sibling alive.

This approach is connected to some broader lessons derived from the first part of this book. Much of the current debate about commodification rests on assumptions associated with the meaning of money and the autonomy of the market. They make it somewhat difficult to perceive and to take into account the complexities of social exchange in our society, as well as the continuities between various forms of exchange (such as gift exchange and monetary exchange), and between our society and more "traditional" ones, past and present. Not only do these assumptions have the effect of circumscribing the perceived range of possible solutions to problems related to the pervasiveness of the market, but in the case of blocked exchanges, they actually serve to lock us into the very grid that gives rise to invidious effects of commodification.

The contrast case of Talmudic law provides an entirely different perspective, where money, by itself, is not ascribed a stigmatizing effect.[9] Indeed, with certain biblically prescribed roles (e.g., its use in the redemption of holy property[10]), it often plays a direct role in the realm of the sacred, having the capacity to become "sacred" itself (when "owned" by God/the Temple). In any event, according to the scheme of rabbinic law, the actual exchange of money is almost always beside the point in determining legality.

Arguably any attempt to fashion public-policy solutions to this problems posed by the pervasiveness of the market can benefit from analyses that strive for a more realistic appraisal of the social role of different modes of exchange, one that takes into account and seeks to foster the interrelationality of property. This is preferable to one that starts with a mythical atomistic individual who operates from an illusory position of absolute freedom, and invokes a set of mythical perceptions – such as pure contract, pure gift, and exclusive private property – that successfully conceal hierarchies and power relations that need to be addressed.

A number of concrete public-policy implications flow from this analysis of organ transfer (and sale) under Talmudic law, the first of which offers a model that would implement the theory proffered in this book: veteran-style health care benefits for organ donors.:

9 There are, possibly, some exceptions to this blanket statement, such as the ban from bringing money from a prostitute into the Temple. See Deut 23:18.

10 See Deut 14:24–26.

1. The obligation to save a life via organ transfer, even if not compulsory, can, nevertheless, be conceived of as a "real" obligation – indeed, as one that is essentially built into the property (the body) itself. Unlike the liberal perspective that conceptualizes organ transfer as a prerogative of the donor, the perspective that emerges from classical Jewish law would regard it as a transfer that entails a mixture of liberty and obligation; it is a right and an obligation in the sense that, as an imperative to be recognized in all human bodies, it impels one to give to others and enables one to expect that others will do the same. It is, perhaps, the most vivid example of the porosity of the human object, and of the interrelationality of property – including, if not especially, when it comes to the human body. On its face, this understanding might suggest that what is transpiring is the objectification of the human body. However, it accomplishes the support of human life and human interrelationships in a way that undercuts one of the main concerns of commodification. This analysis permits one to take into account the reality that human beings in need of organs are dying every day, and that this, in and of itself, might be sufficient to create a sense of obligation on the part of individuals and communities.

   As a matter of public policy, a perceived obligation to provide a life-saving organ can be analogized to the oft-felt moral obligation of (voluntary) military service. In both cases an actor chooses to put his life, health, and bodily integrity at risk in order to protect the health and well-being of others. Similar societal responses to this conduct would be appropriate. For example, as is commonly done in the case of military veterans, special mention or pictoral notation could be included as a matter of course in the obituaries of those who have donated.[11]

   Even more fitting given the analysis set forth in this book is the idea of extending lifelong healthcare benefits to organ donors (and possibly family members). Veterans' healthcare benefits have been in place since the late eighteenth century. While obviously serving an incentivizing purpose, these benefits are primarily justified as being morally compelled. Organ donors, like veterans, have jeopardized and/or sacrificed their own bodies, lives, and health to save other people's lives. Arguably, they, too, deserve to have their lives and health (or that of their families) looked after by society at large – the provision of healthcare is also not seen as "payback," but as an appropriate and symmetrical return gift.[12] As in the case of veterans, the community arguably ought to respond reciprocally (by protecting life and health) to those who sacrifice their

[11] See Madeline Kochen, "Mother's Final Gift," *Washington Post* (Sep 16, 2000), p. A19.

[12] The parallel is eerily complete as it has been established, relatively recently, that veterans' lifelong healthcare benefits are not a legal entitlement, even when promised during recruitment.

physical security to advance or protect the lives and health of others. And nothing could be more fitting than to have society recognize one who "returns" a "lost" body (life or health) than by offering to return to them (or to a family member, in the case of a postmortem donation) their body (life or health) with the offer of free healthcare.

2. Postmortem donations ought to be obligatory. To the extent that one does have "ownership" over one's body, this property interest does not extend beyond death. The movement of the organ from the divine realm to the recipient is most transparent in this case, such that withholding it can be considered tantamount to stealing from God.
3. While some nominal payment might be permitted (e.g., to avoid unjust enrichment or the disincentive of cost), this makes neither the transaction a sale nor the organ a commodity. Once it is understood as obligatory giving, as the performance of a *mitzvah*, the question of compensation can be dealt with utilizing the same principles developed to allow for the payment of doctors[13] and clergy or that accommodate the need to incentivize the giving of *tsedakah* (e.g., honor). However, special care needs to be applied to avoid the invocation of market-type incentives for donation.
4. The obligation entailed here is not simply an individual one; indeed, illness (especially when it is life threatening) is not a private problem. Like welfare (or *tsedakah*) and healthcare generally, the effective implementation of a guarantee that one's body will be "returned" in the form of an organ transplant if necessary requires the effective involvement of the community.[14] Moreover, beyond pragmatic considerations, the obligation in this context does not only reside in the body of the donor. In accordance with the theory of distributive justice described here, the community (even if regarded merely as a collective of individuals) is implicated. In the perspective outlined here, it is unjust to relegate to the market, to exchanges between individuals, a matter as important as the need to save lives that are imminently in danger.[15] A sense of

The provision of medical care to former veterans and their families really does come down to a "mere" moral obligation that society chooses to recognize and to fulfill.

[13] I do not mean to suggest that the way doctors are paid currently in the United States would comport with these rabbinic principles.

[14] See, e.g., Reed Abelson, "Blood Treatment's Promise Mired in Bureaucracy," *New York Times* (May 29, 2004), p. A1.

[15] This theory does, of course, support an argument for the free availability of healthcare. The moral imperative of providing for the poor, specifically for the health of those who are needy and whose needs can be met, ought to be felt by the community in the manner of the collection for the *hekdesh*, for the synagogue, and for the education of the young.

obligation is absent – one that would propel an individual and a community to act. As in the case of the general obligations of *tsedakah* and *pikuach nefesh*, it is necessary for the community to act – to regulate, to pay, and to organize, to ensure the availability (to the extent reasonably possible) of organs for the sick regardless of their wealth. The community has a responsibility to fill the gap between individuals – to organize a mechanism whereby postmortem donations are, for example, presumed and effectuated as a matter of course (albeit with the possibility of permitting an individual to opt out)[16] – to organize the fair distribution of organs, based on need and not on finances. As part of its power and responsibility in this area (and given the proposition that the human body, postmortem, is not "property" belonging to any individual), the community can be said to have a (refutable) presumptive claim on persons' bodies, postmortem, in favor of those who are ill.

5. Those in positions of leadership ought to promote the donation of organs. They should be active in rendering this a more pressing policy debate and should more clearly articulate the moral obligation at play here, given the fact that thousands of people are dying daily for lack of needed organs. Arguably clergy have a specific obligation to come forward and educate people as to the moral imperative involved here, especially given what appears to be a tremendous misunderstanding, among many Jews, as to the very permissibility of organ transfer. There tends to be a relatively low donation rate among Jews and Israelis; many attribute this to popular misconception that (like autopsy) organ transfer is illegal because it entails maiming the body. Indeed, the need to correct this misimpression is rendered even more important, given the central role played by Israel and Israelis in the international market in human organs – something that is both illegal and transgressive of classical Jewish legal principles outlined here.
6. In the theoretical and policy debate over problems of "commodification," consideration ought to be paid to unspoken assumptions, given the structure of our market-oriented society, that implicitly narrow the range of available options to solve problems that, like the organ-sales question, are matters of life and death. In this context, what obfuscates discussion is the reification of money, the fear of mixing the categories of "persons" and "things," and the presumptively all-encompassing nature of the liberal framework of contract and property.

16 Given the absence of a property right (but the desire to accommodate people's sensitivities), at the very least the law ought to presume (rebuttable) consent.

7. The obvious interrelationality entailed in the phenomenon of organ transfer ought to be recognized and built upon by policy makers. As mentioned in the Preface, when navigating the organ network apparatus myself, I was shocked at the degree to which the currently existing framework for organ transfer fails to contemplate, much less facilitate or encourage, people involved on the "giving" and "receiving" ends of the process to encounter one another. The manner in which social bonding is suppressed serves to reinforce a kind of market sensibility in the context of this most personal of transfers. With the caveat that the wishes of people who prefer not to be known ought to be honored, there are obvious pragmatic (incentive related and otherwise[17]) and ethical reasons for people to be able – or, indeed, encouraged – to meet if they so desire.

Titmuss expresses his intellectual debt to Mauss in *The Gift Relationship*, and yet (in Mary Douglas's words), Mauss "would have said 'Nonsense!' … to Titmuss's idea that the archetypal gift relationship is the anonymous, pure gift of blood."[18] Mauss would probably agree with Titmuss's desires to "see reciprocal or gift exchange have an enlarged scope in the modern world," and to see the world "bound together more by a community solidarity and a community feeling within which reciprocal exchange is more appropriate than market exchange";[19] yet, he would likely take issue with the idea that the archetypal gift is the anonymous gift of the stranger. One might say, paraphrasing Benjamin Nelson,[20] that Titmuss wants all strangers to be brothers. However, a faceless fraternity would not be the way to further the development of so-called gift relationships. Indeed, it is the notion of the gift as a debt of personal intimacy that leads to the relationality of property and the perpetuation of interpersonal implication.

This book offers what might be seen as an expansion of the notion of divine ownership at the heart of Locke's justification for limits to self-ownership, limits that, for Locke, seem to relate primarily to individual self-preservation. The Lockian theory of self-ownership (including its limits) is shown, in the context of organ transplantation, to be rather sterile. It fails to give rise to much, if any, sense of obligation; it might undergird the banning of organ "sales" while retaining only a "right" of altruistic alienation. By contrast, the alternative

[17] See Kochen (2000), p. A19.

[18] Douglas (1990) at viii. But see, e.g., Zelizer (1997) at 240n12: "Richard M. Titmuss' *The Gift Relationship* (New York: Vintage, 1971) provides a powerful update of Mauss with his comparison of paid versus voluntary blood transfusion services."

[19] Barber (1997) at 24.

[20] Benjamin Nelson, *The Idea of Usury*, Chicago: University of Chicago Press (1969) ("in modern capitalism, all are 'brothers' in being equally 'others,'" p. xxv.)

basis for limits to self-ownership suggested here, because of its origin in a theory of divine ownership understood in light of a neo-Maussian analysis, gives rise to a sense of obligation to others. Paradoxically, it would allow what might appear to be the "sale" of an organ for transplant, but what is actually an obligation-based act of donation, coupled with possible compensatory payment when appropriate to meet the demands of justice. The theory of divine ownership proposed here can provide a theoretical basis for a different understanding of how property might, even in a nondeistic context, be understood to be "sacred" in the sense that individual sovereignty thereover is internally limited by an inherent lien that inures to the benefit of others.

Apart from whatever its author may have intended, a statement in the Communist Manifesto could be seen as an emblematic epigram that encapsulates the theory of "the economy of the sacred" outlined here: that is, the observation that when the market (and an exclusivist conception of private property) is presumed to be all encompassing, "all that is solid melts into air, all that is holy is profaned."[21] The normative implications of the theory offered here recognizes a dimension in which obligation (the sacred) is something almost tangible, residing in all property – including the human body, something that is destroyed with an absolutist conception of private property and a pure market mentality.

The nearly invisible conceptual key described in these chapters – something that is hidden in plain view throughout rabbinic literature – is the role of the divine as intermediary in certain human transactions. This imaginary middle step provides the basis for a comprehensive theory of distributive justice – one that, indeed, need not require a divine personality.[22] In this analysis, God (or God's domain) simply represents the abstract legal or philosophical realm that is the source of property and property rights. The role of "the divine" in the justice scheme outlined here is filled by the (secular) sovereign; the idea of retrocession parallels familiar phenomena such as eminent domain. The legal/cultural phenomenon of a latent, voluntary property obligation inuring to the benefit of the needy (here called the divine lien) could theoretically exist in any property scheme that has an interest in nurturing a sense of mutual responsibility between individuals.

[21] D. Ryazanoff (ed.), *The Communist Manifesto of Karl Marx and Friedrich Engels*, New York: Russell and Russell (1930) at 28: "all that has been regarded as solid, crumbles into fragments; all that was looked upon as holy, is profaned."

[22] The divine property realm, which plays a critical role in the theory outlined in this book, is nothing more than the imaginary original domain from which all property rights devolve. The "meanings" engendered by the theory outlined here have "no need of *the event of a revelation*." Derrida, *The Gift of Death* at 49. What is proposed here, in the words of Derrida, is "a geneology of thinking concerning the possibility and essence of the religious that doesn't amount to an article of faith." *Id.*

Glossary

achilat ara'i: snacking
al kiddush hashem: [die] for the sanctity of God
am ha'aretz: uneducated person, lit: nation/people of the land
amirah: oral statement
amirah legavohah kemesirah lehedyot: an oral statement [giving property] to God is the functional equivalent of a [physical act of] transfer to a human being
aniyim: the poor
apotika/hiptik: treasury
arakhin: values [of persons pledged to the Temple]
assur lehatzil atzmo bemamon chavero: one is prohibited from saving oneself with the property of another
avadai hem velo avadim le'avadim: [God states: humans are] my slaves and not the slaves to slaves
azivah: leaving
bal te'acher : do not delay [in fulfilling a vow]
bal yichal : do not desecrate [your words]
bechor (s.), *bechorot* (pl.): firstborn animal(s)
bedek habayit: [fund for] Temple maintenance
bedisho: in his threshing
begufo: with one's body
bei gaza derakhmanah: God's property domain (lit. the Lord's treasury)
bemamono: with his property
berakha (s.), *berakhot* (pl.): blessing(s) or benediction(s)
beraita: Tannaitic text that does not appear in the Mishnah
beriyot: [God's] creations; humans
bikurim: first fruits

boreh: God (lit. creator)
brit melach: salt covenant
brit milah: circumcision
chalitzah. The ceremony by which a *yevamah* can avoid marrying her husband's brother
challah: dough offering (a portion of dough that must be given to the priest)
chasid/chasidut: pious person/piety
chavalah: bodily mutalation
cherem (s.), *charamim* (pl.): devoted property, for the Temple or for the priests
choleh lefaneinu: an ill person is in front of us
damim: values [of persons pledged to the Temple]
devarim haniknim be'amirah: items acquired with an oral statement [alone]
dinar: a coin used by the rabbis
ein dochin nefesh mipnei nefesh: one may not trade one life for another
gavohah: God (lit. high)
halakha/halakhic: Jewish law/Jewish legal
hana'ah: benefit
hatra'ah: warning (as in the obligation to warn a person about to commit capital crime that they will be subject to the death penalty)
hau: spirit
hedyot: ordinary (non-sacred)
hefker (*hevker*): ownerless property
hefker beit din hefker: property declared ownerless by the court is ownerless
hekdesh (s.), *hekdeshot* (pl.): sacred property; property owned by God and the Temple
issur chavalah: the prohibition against (self-)mutilation
issurei hana'ah: prohibitions against deriving benefit
ka zakhu/zokhe: merit; acquire
kadosh/kedushah: sacred/sanctity
kam lei b'drabah minei: a person liable for a greater punishment (e.g. the dealth penalty) is exempt from a lesser penalty (e.g. a fine)
kefoel batel: like an unemployed worker
kenafshecha: as is your desire
kerem revai: fourth year grapes
kiddushin: marriage
kinyan: acquisition
kodashim: holy things; donations to the poor or to a synogogue
kodashim kalim: less holy things
kodshei kodashim: most holy things

kohen: priest
konam: idiom meaning prohibited
koneh: acquire
korban: animal sacrifice
koreh shem: designation or specification that separates tithes (lit. calling a name)
kula: spirit of the gift
kupah: Temple fund for the poor, from which distributions were made every Friday
leket: gleanings, which must be left for the poor
lo ta'amod: don't stand [idly by the blood of your neighbor]
ma'aser (s.), *ma'aserot* (pl.): tithe(s)
ma'aser ani: poor tithe
ma'aser rishon: tithe for the Levite
ma'aser sheni: second tithe
mamon gavohah: property belonging to God (lit. property of the Most High)
mamzer: child born of certain prohibited sexual relations such as adultery and incest
matir: act required in order to render permissible something that is
me'ilah: sacrilege; stealing from God by illegally deriving benefit from *hekdesh*
mekablei matanot: gift recipients
mishel shamayim hu ochel: he eats from God's property
mishmar (s.), *mishmarot* (pl.): watch(es); block(s) of time used for rotational scheduling of priests performing services in the Temple
mitah beyedei shamayim: death at the hands of heaven
mitzvot lav lehanot nitnu: *mitzvot* were not given to impart benefit
nazir: Nazirite
nazirut: status of being a Nazirite
nedavah (s.), *nedavot* (pl.): voluntary offering(s) to God
neder (s.), *nedarim* (pl.): vow(s)
nikhsei cohen: property of the priest
ochel mishulchan gavohah: eating from God's food (lit. eating from table of the Most High
olelot: incompletely formed grape clusters that must be left in the vineyard for the poor
ona'ah: just price [requirement]; [prohibition against] fraud
orlah: prohibition against eating fruit from a free during the first three years after planting

peah (s.), *peyot* (pl.): corner(s) of the beard or reference to rule that produce growing on the corners of one's field must be left for the poor (lit. corner(s))
perutah: small coin used by the rabbis
pidyon: redemption
pidyon haben: redemption of the first-born son
pidyon shevuyim: redemption of captives
piggul: a sacrifice rendered invalid by improper intent at time of offering, such as intent to eat it outside its proper time frame
pikuach nefesh: saving a life
prozbul: rabbinic enactment that had the effect of permitting collection of debts past the seventh year
rasha (s.), *reshai'm* (pl.): evil person(s)
reshut: legal domain
ribit: usury
rodef: pursuer
schar batalah: lost wages; concept used to pay for performance of a *mitvah*
sela: coin used by the rabbis
sevarah: human reason
shamayim: heaven
shel gavohah: belonging to God or the Temple (lit. of the Most High)
shel hedyot: belonging to human beings (lit. of the ordinary)
shel shamayim: belonging to God or the Temple (lit. of heaven)
shelamim: peace offerings
shemitah: Sabbatical
shevuah (s.), *shevuot* (pl.): oath(es)
shikhechah: forgotten sheaves, which must be left for the poor
shulchan gavohah: God's property domain (lit. table of the Most High)
sugyah: pericope
tachat yado: in his possession (lit. under his hand)
tamchui: Temple food bank, from which distributions were made to people without food every day
terumah: priestly tithe
terumat ma'aser: tithe removed from the Levite's portion (*ma'aser rishon*)
tikun olam: repair the world
tovat hana'ah: right to choose recipients, e.g. of *terumah* (lit. benefit of gratitude)
tsedakah (s.), *tsedakot* (pl.): money or property for the poor
tsedek: justice

vehashevoto lo: you shall return it [or his body] to him
yehei shelo: it shall be his
yevamah: widow whose husband died while childless and must marry her brother-in-law or perform *chalitzah*
yibum: biblical system of levirate marriage
yovel: Jubilee; 50th year
zokhe: merit; acquire
zuz (s.), *zuzim* (pl.): coin used by the rabbis

Bibliography

Abelson, Reed, "Blood Treatment's Promise Mired in Bureaucracy," *New York Times*, May 29, 2004, p. A1.

Abraham, Avraham Sofer, *Nishmat Avraham: Hilkhot Holim Rofim U-Refuah* (Hebrew: The Laws of Sick People, Doctors, and Medicine) Jerusalem: Erez (1983).

Albeck, Chanoch, *Mechkarim B'vraita V'tosefta*, Jerusalem: Mosad Harav Kook (1913).

Albeck, Shalom, "*Yesodot Mishtar Ha'kehilot b'Sefard ad Ha-RaMah* (1180–1244)" (Hebrew), *Zion* 25/2 (1960), pp. 85–121.

Dinei Ha-Mamonot Ba'Talmud (Hebrew: The Law of Property and Contract in the Talmud), Tel Aviv: Dvir (1973).

Alexander, Gregory S., *Commodity and Propriety*, Chicago: University of Chicago Press (1997).

Anderson, Elizabeth, *Value in Ethics and Economics*, Cambridge: Harvard University Press (1993).

Andre, Judith, "Blocked Exchanges: A Taxonomy," *Ethics* 103/1 (Oct 1992), pp. 29–47.

Andrew, Edward, *Shylock's Rights: A Grammar of Lockian Claims*, Toronto: University of Toronto Press (1988).

Appadurai, Arjun (ed.), *The Social Life of Things: Commodities in Cultural Perspective*, Cambridge: Cambridge University Press (1986).

Arrow, Kenneth J., "Gifts and Exchanges," *Philosophy and Public Affairs* 1/4 (summer 1972), pp. 343–362.

Assaf, Likhovski, "The Invention of 'Hebrew Law' in Mandatory Palestine," *American Journal of Comparative Law* 46 (1998), pp. 339ff.

Assis, Yom Tov, "Welfare and Mutual Aid in the Spanish Jewish Communities," *Moreshet Sepharad* 1 (1992), pp. 318–345.

Baer, Yitzhak F., "*Hayesodot v'Hahitchalot Shel Irgun ha'Kehila haYehudit b'Ymei haBeynaim*" (Hebrew: The Foundations and Origins of the Jewish Community in the Middle Ages), *Zion* 15 (1950), pp. 1–41.

A History of the Jews in Christian Spain, Philadelphia: The Jewish Publication Society of America (1978).

Barber, Bernard, "Function, Variability, and Change in Ideological Systems," in Bernard Barber and Alex Inkeles (eds.), *Stability and Social Change*, Boston: Little, Brown (1971), pp. 244–262.

"Absolutization of the Market: Some Notes on How We Got from There to Here," in Gerald Dworkin, Gordon Bermant, and Peter Brown (eds.), *Markets and Morals*, Washington, D.C.: Hemisphere Publishing Corp. (1977), pp. 15–31.

Barclay, John M.G., *Flavius Josephus: Translation and Commentary*, Vol. 10: Against Apion, Leiden: Brill (2007).

Barfield, Thomas (ed.), *The Dictionary of Anthropology*, Oxford: Blackwell Publishers Ltd. (1977).

Baron, Salo, *The Jewish Community*, volume 2, Philadelphia: Jewish Publication Society of America (1942).

Baumgarten, Joseph M., "Qumran and the Halakha in the Aramaic Targumim," in *Proceedings of the Ninth World Congress of Jewish Studies: Panel Sessions, Bible Studies and Ancient Near East*, Jerusalem: Magnes Press (1985), pp. 45–60.

"The Laws of 'Orlah and First Fruits in the Light of Jubilees, the Qumran Writings and Targum Ps. Jonathan," *Journal of Jewish Studies* 38/2 (1987), pp. 195–202.

Becker, Gary, *The Economic Approach to Human Behavior*, Chicago: University of Chicago Press (1976).

Befu, Harumi, "Social Exchange," *Annual Review of Anthropology* 6 (1977), pp. 255–281.

Ben-Menahem, Hanina, "On the Talmudic Prohibition against Giving Gifts to Gentiles," *Israel Law Review* 29 (1995), pp. 95ff.

Benovitz, Moshe, "The Prohibitive Vow in the Second Temple Period and in the Literature of the Tannaim" (Hebrew), *Tarbiz* 64 (1995), pp. 203–208.

"*Kol Kinuyey Nedarim*" (Hebrew: Substitute Vow Formulas), *Sidra* 12 (1996), p. 5.

Kol Nidre: Studies in the Development of Rabbinic Votive Institutions, Brown Judaic Series 315, Atlanta: Scholars Press (1998).

Ben-Sasson, Menahem (ed.), *Dat V'Kalkala* (Hebrew: Religion and Economy: Connections and Interactions) Jerusalem: Zalman Shazar Center for Jewish History (1995).

Bernstein, Moshe J., "The Aramaic Targumim: The Many Faces of the Jewish Biblical Experience," in *Jewish Ways of Reading the Bible*, Oxford: Oxford University Press (1994), pp. 133–165.

"The Halakhah in the Marginalia of Targum Neofiti," in *Proceedings of the Eleventh World Congress of Jewish Studies (Jerusalem, June 22–29, 1993): Division A: The Bible and Its World*, World Union of Jewish Studies (1994), pp. 223–230.

Black, Henry Campbell, *Black's Law Dictionary*, 5th ed., St Paul: West Publishing Company (1979).

Bleich, J. David, *Contemporary Halachik Problems*, volume 4, New York: Ktav Publishing House (1995).

Blidstein, Gerald J., "Notes on Hefker Bet-Din in Talmudic and Medieval Law," in Zeev Falk (ed.), *Dine Israel*, volume 4 (1973), pp. 35–49.

Bloch, Maurice, "The Symbolism of Money in Imerina," in Jonathan Parry and Maurice Bloch (eds.), *Money and the Morality of Exchange*, Cambridge: Cambridge University Press (1989), pp. 165–190.

Bohannan, Paul, "Some Principles of Exchange and Investment Among the Tiv," *American Anthropologist* 57/1 (1955) , pp. 60–70.

Booth, William James, "A Note on the Idea of the Moral Economy," *American Political Science Review* 87/4 (Dec 1993), pp. 949–954.

Households: On the Moral Architecture of the Economy, Ithaca: Cornell University Press (1993).

"On the Idea of the Moral Economy," *American Political Science Review* 88/3 (Sep 1994), pp. 653–667.

Bourdieu, Pierre, *Outline of a Theory of Practice*, Cambridge: Cambridge University Press (1997).

Boyle, Nicholas, *Who Are We Now? Christian Humanism and the Global Market From Hegel to Heaney*, Notre Dame: University of Notre Dame Press (1998).

Bravmann, M. M., "Semitic Instances of 'Linguistic Taboo'," in G.F. Pijper (ed.), *Studies in Semitic Philology*, volume 6: *Studies in Semitic Languages and Linguistics*, Leiden: Brill (1977), pp. 465ff.

Brooks, Roger, *Support for the Poor in the Mishnaic Law of Agriculture: Tractate Peah*, Chico: Scholar's Press (1983).

Brown, Peter, *Poverty and Leadership in the Later Roman Empire*, Hanover: University Press of New England (2001).

Butler, Lynda, "The Commons Concept: An Historical Concept with Modern Relevance," *William and Mary Law Review* 23 (1982), pp. 835ff.

Caputo, John D., and Michael J. Scanlon (eds.), *God, the Gift, and Postmodernism*, Bloomington: Indiana University Press (1999).

Carrier, James G., "Property and Social Relations in Melanesian Anthropology," in C. M. Hann (ed.), *Property Relations*, Cambridge: Cambridge University Press (1998), pp. 85–103.

Clark, Ernest G. (translator), *Targum Pseudo-Jonathan: Deuteronomy (Aramaic Bible Vo. 5B)*, Collegeville, MN: The Liturgical Press (1998).

Cohen, Boaz, "*Hefker v'Yeush B'mishpat Ha'ivri v'Haromai*" (Hebrew: On Dereliction in Jewish and Roman Law), in *Jewish and Roman Law*, New York: Jewish Theological Seminary (1966), Vol. II, pp. 10–22.

Cohen, Felix S., "Dialogue on Private Property," *Rutgers Law Review* 9 (1954), pp. 357–387.

Cohen, G. A., "Capitalism, Freedom and the Proletariat," in Alan Ryan (ed.), *The Idea of Freedom*, Oxford: Oxford University Press (1979), pp. 9–25.

Self-ownership, Freedom, and Equality, Cambridge: Cambridge University Press (1995).

Cohen, Jonathan, "Charitable Contributions, Communal Welfare Organizations and Allegiance to the Community According to the Rashba," in *Hebrew Union College Annual*, volume 72, Cincinnati: HUC (2001), pp. 85–100.

Cohen, Lawrence, "Where It Hurts: Indian Material for an Ethics of Organ Transplantation," *Daedalus* (fall 1999), pp. 135–165.

Cohen, Mark, "*Halacha U'm'tsiut B'inyaney Tsedakah B'tedufat Hagenizah*" (Hebrew), in *Ha'Islam V'olamot Hashezurim Bo*, Jerusalem: Hebrew University (2002), pp. 315–323.

Poverty and Charity in the Jewish Community of Medieval Egypt (Jews, Christians, and Muslims from the Ancient to the Modern World), Princeton: Princeton University Press (2005).

The Voice of the Poor in the Middle Ages: An Anthology of Documents from the Cairo Geniza, Princeton: Princeton University Press (2005).

Cohen, Shaye, "The Place of the Rabbi in Jewish Society of the Second Century," in Lee Levine (ed.), *The Galilee in Late Antiquity*, New York: Jewish Theological Seminary of America (1992), pp. 157–173.

Cooley, Charles H., "The Institutional Character of Pecuniary Valuation," *American Journal Of Sociology* 18/4 (Jan 1913), pp. 543–555.
"The Sphere of Pecuniary Valuation," *American Journal of Sociology* 19/2 (Sep 1913), pp. 188–203.
Corinaldi, M., "The Legal Status of a Child Born from Artificial Insemination from an Alien Donor or a Donated Ovule" (Hebrew), *Shenaton Ha-Mishpat Ha-Ivri* 18–19 (1992–1994), pp. 295–328.
Cronbach, Abraham, "What Makes Jewish Work 'Jewish'? Historical Aspects," in Robert Morris and Michael Freund (eds.), *Trends and Issues in Jewish Social Welfare in the United States, 1899–1952*, Philadelphia: Jewish Publication Society (1966), pp. 209–214.
Dagan, Hanoch, *Unjust Enrichment: A Study of Private Law and Public Values*, Cambridge: Cambridge University Press (1997).
Dalton, George, "Theoretical Issues in Economic Anthropology," *Current Anthropology* 10/1 (Feb 1969), pp. 63–102.
Daube, David, "Limitations on Self-sacrifice in Jewish Law and Tradition," in Calum M. Carmichael (ed.), *Collected Works of David Daube*, volume 1: *Talmudic Law*, Berkeley: University of California (1992), pp. 45–62.
Davis, John, *Exchange*, Buckingham: Open University Press (1992).
Derrida, Jacques, *The Gift of Death*, translated by David Wills, Chicago: University of Chicago Press (1992).
Given Time, volume 1: *Counterfeit Money*, translated by Peggy Kamuf, Chicago: University of Chicago Press (1992).
Dolgin, J., "The 'Intent' of Reproduction: Reproductive Technology and the Parent-Child Bond," *University of Connecticut Law Review* 26 (1994), pp. 1261ff.
Donahue, Charles Jr., "The Future of the Concept of Property Predicted from its Past," in J. Roland Pennock and John W. Chapman (eds.), *Property*, Nomos 22, New York: New York University Press (1980), pp. 28–68.
Dorff, Elliot N., "Jewish Law and Lore: The Case of Organ Transplantation," *Jewish Law Annual* 12 (1997), pp. 65–114.
"Paying for Medical Care: A Jewish View," *Kennedy Institute of Ethics Journal* 7/1 (1997), pp. 15–30.
Douglas, Mary, "Foreword," in Marcel Mauss, *The Gift: The Form and Reason for Exchange in Archaic Societies*, New York: W. W. Norton and Co. (1990), vii–xviii.
Douglas, Mary, and Baron Isherwood, *The World of Goods: Towards an Anthropology of Consumption*, New York: Basic Books (1979).
Dubner, Stephen J., "Flesh Trade: Why Not Let People Sell Their Organs," *New York Times Magazine* (Jul 9, 2006), pp. 20–21.
Dworkin, Gerald, Gordon Bermant, and Peter Brown (eds.), *Markets and Morals*, Washington, D.C.: Hemisphere Publishing Corp. (1977).
Edan Friedlander, Joe, "Corporation and Kulturkampf: Time Culture as Illegal Fiction," *Connecticut Law Review* 29 (1996), pp. 31ff.
Edrei, Arye, "*Mitzvah al Hayetomim Lifro'a Chov Avihem*" (Hebrew: An Orphan's Obligation to Pay His Father's Debts: A Legal or Moral Duty), in Arnold Enker and Sinai Deutch (eds.), *Iyyunim Bemishpat Ivri Uvehalachah* (Hebrew: Studies in Jewish Law), Ramat Gan: University of Bar Ilan Press (1998), pp. 19–51.

Eisenstadt, S. "*Al Hitpathut Musag ha-Ishiyut ha-Mishpatit ba-Mishpat Ha'ivri*" (Hebrew: On the Development of the Concept of Legal Personality in Hebrew Law), *ha-Mishpat* 1/10 (1927), pp. 10–15.

Ellerman, David P., *Property and Contract in Economics*, Cambridge: Blackwell Publishers (1992).

Elon, Menachem, *Cherut Ha'Prat* (Hebrew: Freedom of the Debtor's Person [in Jewish Law]), Jerusalem: Magnes Press (1964).

Elon, Menachem (ed.), *The Principles of Jewish Law*, Jerusalem: Keter Publishing House (1975).

Elon, Menachem, *Jewish Law: History, Sources, Principles*, Philadelphia: Jewish Publication Society (1994).

Elon, Menachem, Bernard Auerbach, Daniel Chazin, and Melvin Sykes, *Jewish Law (Mishpat Ivri): Cases and Materials*, New York: Matthew Bender and Co., Inc. (1999).

Epstein, Richard A., "Organ Transplants: Is Relying on Altruism Costing Lives?" *The American Enterprise* 4 (Nov/Dec 1993), pp. 51–57.

"Are Values Incommensurable, or Is Utility the Ruler of the World," *Utah Law Review* (1995), pp.683–715.

Evans-Pritchard, E. E., "Introduction," in Marcel Mauss, *The Gift: Forms and Functions of Exchange in Archaic Societies*, London: Routledge (1974), pp. v–x.

Falk, Z. W., "On Talmudic Vows," *Harvard Theological Review* 59 (1966), pp. 309–312.

Faur, Jose, "The Targumim and Halkha," *Jewish Quarterly Review* 66 (1975–1976), pp. 19–25.

Fildes, Valerie, *Wet Nursing: A History From Antiquity to the Present*, Oxford: Basil Blackwell (1988).

Fink, David, "The Corporate Status of *Hekdesh* in Early Sephardic Responsa," *Jewish Law Association Studies*, volume 1, ed. B. S. Jackson, Atlanta: Scholars Press (1985), pp. 17–24.

Finkel, Michael, "This Little Kidney Went to Market," *New York Magazine* (May 27, 2001), p. 26.

Finley, M. I., *The Ancient Economy*, London: Penguin Books (1985).

Firth, Richard, *Primitive Polynesian Economy*, Hamden: Routledge and Kegan Paul, Ltd. (1965).

Fishbane, Michael, "Substitutes for Sacrifice in Judaism," in *The Exegetical Imagination*, Cambridge: Harvard University Press (1998), pp. 123–135.

Flesher, Paul, and Virgil McCracken, *Oxen, Women or Citizens? Slaves in the System of the Mishnah*, Atlanta: Scholars Press (1988).

Fraade, Steven, "Rabbinic Views on the Practice of the Targum, and Multiligualism in the Jewish Galilee of the Third–Sixth Centuries," in Lee Levine (ed.), *The Galilee in Late Antiquity*, Cambridge: Harvard University Press (1992), pp. 253–286.

Freedman, Benjamin, *Duty and Healing: Foundations of a Jewish Bioethic*, New York: Routledge (1999).

Frenkel, David, "Transplants," in Nahum Rakover (ed.), *Jewish Law and Current Legal Problems*, Jerusalem: The Library of Jewish Law (1984), pp. 195–201.

Friedman, Shamma Yehuda, "*Ha-Milon Ha-Mechkari L'lashon Ha'ivrit Shel Hatanaaim: Erech Hevker/Hefker; Bikoret*" (Hebrew: The Scholars' Dictionary of

Tannaitic Hebrew, a Critique of the Entry: *Hefqer/Hevker*), *Sidra: A Journal for the Study of Rabbinic Literature* 12 (1996), p. 113.

Frisch, Ephraim, *An Historical Survey of Jewish Philanthropy: From the Earliest Times to the Nineteenth Century*, New York: Cooper Square Publishers, Inc. (1969).

Galinsky, Yehuda, "Jewish Charitable Bequests and the Hekdesh Trust in Thirteenth-Century Spain," *Journal of Interdisciplinary History* 35/3 (winter 2005), pp. 423–440.

Gil, Moshe, *Documents of the Jewish Pious Foundations from the Cairo Geniza*, Leiden: Brill (1976).

Girard, Rene, *Violence and the Sacred*, Baltimore: Johns Hopkins University Press (1979).

Godbout, Jacques T., and Alain Caille, *The World of the Gift*, Montreal: McGill-Queens University Press (1998).

Godelier, Maurice, *The Enigma of the Gift*, Chicago: University of Chicago Press (1999).

Goitein, S. D., "Jewish Community Organization in the Light of the Cairo Geniza Documents" (Hebrew), *Zion* 26/2 (1961), pp. 170–179.

"The Local Jewish Community in the Light of the Cairo Geniza Records," *Journal of Jewish Studies* 12/3–4 (1961), pp. 133–158.

Goldberg, Zalman Nechemiah, "*Kinyanim Bemechirat Kelayot*" (Hebrew: Acquisitions in the Sale of Organs), in *Ateret Shelomo*, Jerusalem: Machon Madaei Technologi Lehalacha (5757/1997), pp. 49–55.

Goren, Shlomo, "*Mechirat Kelayot Lehashtalah al pi Hahalacha*" (Hebrew: The Sale of Organs for Transplant according to Jewish Law), in *Torat Harefuah: Mechkarim Hilchatiim Benosei Refuah* Jerusalem: Ha-idra Rabah (5761/2001), pp. 127–148.

Graeber, David, *Toward an Anthropological Theory of Value: The False Coin of Our Dreams*, New York: Palgrave (2001).

Gregory, C. A., "Gifts to Men and Gifts to God: Gift Exchange and Capital Accumulation in Contemporary Papua," *Man* n.s. 15/4 (Dec 1980), pp. 626–652.

Gifts and Commodities, London: Academic Press (1982).

"Exchange and Reciprocity," in Tim Ingold (ed.), *Companion Encyclopedia of Anthropology*, Oxford: Routledge (2000), pp. 911–939.

Grey, Thomas C., "The Disintegration of Property," in J. Roland Pennock and John W. Chapman (eds.), *Property*, Nomos 22, New York: New York University Press (1980), pp. 69–85.

Grossfeld, Bernard, "Targum Onqelos, Halakha and the Halakhic Midrashim," in Beattie and McNamara (eds.), *The Aramaic Bible: Targums and Their Historical Context*, Journal for the Study of the Old Testament, supplement series 166, Sheffield, U.K: JSOT Press (1994), pp. 228–246.

Gulack, Asher, *Yesodei Hamishpat Ha'ivri* (Hebrew: The Foundations of Hebrew Law), vol. 1, Berlin: Devir (1922).

Haas, Peter J., *A History of the Mishnaic Law of Agriculture: Tractate Maaser Sheni*, Chico: Scholars Press (1980).

Halperin, Mordechai, "Organ Transplants from Living Donors," *Israel Law Review* 27 (1993), pp. 566ff.

"Organ Transplants From Living Donors – Halachic Apsects," Rambam Maimonides Medical Journal 2(2): e0042 (April 2011), PMC3678940.
Halperin, Mordechai and D. Fink (eds.), The Proceedings of the First International Colloquium on Medicine, Ethics and Jewish Law, Jerusalem: Schlesinger Institute for Medical-Halachik Research, (1996).
Hamel, Gildas, *Poverty and Charity in Roman Palestine, First Three Centuries C.E.*, Berkeley: University of California Press (1990).
Hands, A. R., *Charities and Social Aid in Greece and Rome*, Ithaca: Cornell University Press (1968).
Hann, C. M. (ed.), *Property Relations: Renewing the Anthropological Tradition*, Cambridge: Cambridge University Press (1998).
Harrington, Hannah K., *Holiness: Rabbinic Judaism and the Graeco-Roman World*, London: Routledge (2001).
Hart, J. H. A., "Corban," *Jewish Quarterly Review* (old series) 19 (1907), pp. 615–650.
Heineman, Joseph, "Early Halakhah in the Palestinian Targumim," *Journal of Jewish Studies* 25/1 (1974), pp. 114–122.
Hengel, Martin, *Property and Riches in the Early Church*, Philadelphia: Fortress Press (1974).
Henry Maine, *Ancient Law*, London : Everyman's Library (1972).
Herzog, Isaac, *The Main Institutions of Jewish Law*, London: Soncino Press (1980).
Henschke, David, "*L'tiv Zikato shel HaTargum HaMeyukhas L'Yonatan Lemidrashe Ha-halakha: L'parshayot Ama Ivriyah*" (Hebrew), *Tarbiz* 68 (1998–1999), pp. 187–210.
Heydebrand, Wolf (ed.), *Sociological Writings of Max Weber*, New York: Continuum (1994).
Hirschman, Albert O., *The Passions and the Interests*, Princeton: Princeton University Press (1977).
Hohfeld, Wesley Newcomb, "Some Fundamental Legal Conceptions as Applied in Judicial Reasoning," *Yale Law Review* 23 (1913), pp. 16ff.
Horner, Robyn, *Rethinking God as Gift: Marion, Derrida, and the Limits of Phenomenology*, New York: Fordham University Press (2001).
Horowitz, Elimelech, "*V'yhi Ani'yim Hagunim Bney Beitecha*," in Menahem Ben-Sasson (ed.), *Dat V'kalkala Yachasey Gomlim* (Hebrew: Religion and Economy, Connections and Interactions), Jerusalem: Salman Shazar Center for Jewish History (1995), pp. 209–232.
Hubert, Henri, and Marcel Mauss, *Sacrifice: Its Nature and Functions*, Chicago: University of Chicago Press (1964).
Hunwick, J. O., "Wakf," in Bearman, Bianquis, Bosworth, van Donzel, and Heinrichs (eds.), *The Encyclopeaedia of Islam*, volume 11, Leiden: Brill (2000), p. 60.
Hyde, Lewis, *The Gift: Imagination and the Erotic Life of Property*, New York: Vintage Books (1983).
Hyde, Alan, *Bodies of Law*, Princeton: Princeton University Press (1997).
Jackson, Bernard S., *Theft in Early Jewish Law*, Oxford: Clarendon Press (1972).
Jaffee, Martin S., *Mishnah's Theology of Tithing: A Study of Tractate Maaserot*, Chico: Scholar's Press (1981).
Jenson, Philip Peter, *Graded Holiness*, Sheffield: Journal for the Study of the Old Testament Press (1992).

Joel Edan Friedlander, "Corporation and Kulturkampf: Time Culture as Illegal Fiction," *Connecticut Law Review* 29 (1996), pp. 31ff.

Katz, Jacob, *Divine Law in Human Hands: Case Studies in Halakhic Flexibility*, Jerusalem: Magnes Press (1998).

Tradition and Crisis, Syracuse: Syracuse University Press (2000).

Katzoff, Ranon, "Oral Establishment of Dowry in Jewish and Roman Law: *D'varim Haniknim Ba'amira* and *Dotis Dictio*," in John Cairns and Olivia Robinson (eds.), *Critical Studies in Ancient Law, Comparative and Legal History*, Oxford: Hart Publishing (2001), pp. 157–171.

Kindler, Arie, "Donations and Taxes in the Society of the Jewish Villages in Eretz Israel During the 3rd to 6th Centuries CE," in Rachel Hachlili (ed.), *Ancient Synagogues in Israel: Third–Seventh Century C.E.*, BAR International Series 499, Haifa: University of Haifa (1989), pp. 55–59.

Kochen, Madeline, "Mother's Final Gift," *Washington Post* (Sep 16, 2000), p. A19.

"It Was Not for Naught that They Called it Hekdesh: Divine Ownership and the Medieval Charitable Foundation," *Jewish Law Association Studies*, volume 17, Binghamton: Global Academic Publishing (2008), pp. 131–143.

"Tracing the History of a Legal Term of Art: The Word *Azarah* in Biblical, Tannaitic and Targumic Literature," in Eric Meyers and Paul Flescher (eds.), *Aramaic in Postbiblical Judaism and Early Christianity*, Winona Lake, Indiana: Eisenbrauns (2010), pp. 105–126.

"Debt, Debts (Judaism)", in D. Allison Jr. (ed.), *Encyclopedia of the Bible and Its Reception, Vol. VI: Dabbesheth – Dreams and Dream Interpretation* Berlin: de Gruyter (2012), pp. 424–426.

Komter, Aafke E. (ed.), *The Gift: An Interdisciplinary Perspective*, Amsterdam: Amsterdam University Press (1996).

Lau, Israel Meir, "*Sikun Iver Kedei L'ehatzil*" (Hebrew: Endangering a Limb to Save [a Life]), *She'elot U'Teshuvot Yachel Yisrael* 1:68, Jerusalem: Machon Masoret (1992), pp. 408–420.

"The Sale of Organs for Transplantation," in Daniel B. Sinclair (ed.), *Jewish Law Association Studies*, volume 15, Binghamton: Global Academic Publishing (2005), pp. 285–305; translated from the Hebrew in *Tehumin* 18 (5758/1998), pp. 125–136.

Lea, David, *Melanesian Land Tenure in a Contemporary and Philosophical Context*, Lanham: University Press of America, Inc. (1997).

LeClair, Edward E., and Harold K Schneider (eds.), *Economic Anthropology*, New York: Holt, Rinehart, and Winston, Inc. 1968.

Levenson, Jon, *Death and Resurrection of the Beloved Son*, New Haven: Yale University Press (1993).

Levine, Hillel, *Economic Origins of Antisemitism*, New Haven: Yale University Press (1991).

Levine, Lee, *The Ancient Synagogue: The First Thousand Years*, New Haven : Yale University Press (2000).

Lewin, B. M., *Otzar Hageonim* [Hebrew: Thesaurus of the Geonic Responsa and Commentaries Following the Order of the Talmudic Tractates], Haifa & Jerusalem: Hebrew University Press (1931).

Lie, John, "The Concept of the Mode of Exchange," *American Sociological Review* 57/4 (Aug 1992), pp. 508–523.

Lieberman, Saul, *Greek in Jewish Palestine*, New York: Jewish Theological Seminary (1942).
"How Much Greek in Jewish Palestine?" in Henry A. Fischel (ed.), *Essays in Greco-Roman and Related Talmudic Literature*, New York: Ktav Publishing House (1977), pp. 325–343; reprinted from Alexander Altmann (ed.), *Biblical and Other Studies*, Cambridge: Harvard University Press (1963), pp. 123–141.
Tosefta Kifshuta, Jerusalem: Jewish Theological Seminary (1992).
Lightstone, Jack N., *The Commerce of the Sacred: Mediation of the Divine among Jews in the Graeco-Roman Diaspora*, Chico: Scholar's Press (1984).
Likhovski, Assaf, "The Invention of 'Hebrew Law' in Mandatory Palestine," *American Journal of Comparative Law* 46 (1998), pp. 339ff.
Little, Lester K., *Religious Poverty and the Profit Economy in Medieval Europe*, Ithaca: Cornell University Press (1983).
Lock, Margaret, *Twice Dead: Organ Transplants and the Reinvention of Death*, Berkeley: University of California Press (2002).
Loewenberg, Frank M., *From Charity to Social Justice*, New Brunswick: Transaction Publishers (2001).
Long, N., "Commoditization: Thesis and Antithesis," in N. Long et al. (eds.), *The Commoditization Debate: Labour Process, Strategy and Social Network*, Pub. Dept. Sociol. 17, Wageningen: Agricultural University (1986), pp. 8–23.
Lorberbaum, Menachem, *Politics and the Limits of Law: Secularizing the Political in Medieval Jewish Thought*, Stanford: Stanford University Press (2001).
Lynda Butler, "The Commons Concept: An Historical Concept with Modern Relevance," *William and Mary Law Review* 23 (1982), pp. 835ff.
Macpherson, C. B., *Political Theory of Possessive Individualism*, Oxford: Oxford University Press (1962).
Malinowski, Branislaw, *Argonauts of the Western Pacific*, London: Routledge and Kegan Paul (1922).
Maloney, Robert P., "Usury in Greek, Roman and Rabbinic Thought," *Traditio* 27 (1971) pp. 78ff.
Malowicki, Sinai, *An Illustrated Guide to Korbonos and Menachos*, Brooklyn: Torah Umesorah Publications (1991).
Mandelbaum, Irving, *A History of the Mishnaic Law of Agriculture: Kilayim*, Chico: Scholars Press (1982).
Maori, Yishayahu, "*Al Yachaso Shel Targum HaTorah HaMeyukhas L'Yonatan ben Uziel L'mekorot HaHalakhah*" (Hebrew), in M. Friedman, A. Tal, and G. Brin (eds.), *Te'uda*, volume 3: *Studies in Talmudic Literature in Post-biblical Hebrew and in Biblical Exegesis*, Tel Aviv: Tel Aviv University (1983), pp. 235–250.
"The Aramaic Targum and Rabbinic Exegesis" (Hebrew: *HaTargumim Ha-Arami'im LeTorah U'midrash Hazal*), in *Proceedings of the Ninth World Congress of Jewish Studies: Panel Sessions, Bible Studies and Ancient Near East*, Jerusalem: Magnes Press (1985), pp. 1–12.
The Peshitta Version of the Pentateuch and Early Jewish Exegesis (Hebrew), Jerusalem: Magnes Press (1995).
Marcus, Jacob R., *Communal Sick-Care in the German Ghetto*, Cincinnati: Hebrew Union College Press (1947).

Mauss, Marcel, *The Gift: The Form and Reason for Exchange in Archaic Societies*, New York: W. W. Norton and Co. (1990).
McFall v. Shimp, 10 Pa. D. & C.3d 90 (1978).
Milgrom, Jacob, *Cult and Conscience*, Leiden: Brill (1976).
Studies in Cultic Theology and Terminology, Leiden: Brill (1983).
Leviticus 23–27, New York: Anchor Bible (2001).
Miller, Daniel, "Consumption and Commodities," *The Annual Review of Anthropology* 24 (1995), pp. 141–161.
Nelson, Benjamin, *The Idea of Usury*, Chicago: University of Chicago Press (1969).
Neusner, Jacob, *A History of the Mishnaic Law of Holy Things*, Leiden: Brill (1978).
The Economics of the Mishnah, Chicago: University of Chicago Press (1990).
Newman, Lewis E., *The Sanctity of the Seventh Year: A Study of Mishnah Tractate Shebiit*, Chico: Scholars Press (1983).
Novak, David, "Economics and Justice: A Jewish Example," in *Jewish Social Ethics*, New York: Oxford University Press (1992), pp. 206–224.
Jewish Social Ethics, New York: Oxford University Press (1992).
Ohrenstein, Roman A., and Barry Gordon, *Economic Analysis in Jewish Law: Rabbinic Thought in the Light of Modern Economics*, Leiden: Brill (1992).
Ouroussoff, Alexandra, "Illusions of Rationality: False Premises of the Liberal Tradition," *Man* 28/2 (Jun 1993), pp. 281–298.
Pahlitzsch, Johannes, "The Concern for Spiritual Salvation and *Memoria* in Islamic Public Endowments in Jerusalem (XII–XIV C.) as Compared to the Concepts of Christendom," in U. Vermeulen and J. Van Steenbergen (eds.), *Egypt and Syria in the Fatimid, Ayyubid and Mamluk Eras*, Leuven: Uitgeverij Peeters (2001), pp. 320–344.
Parry, Jonathan, "The Gift, the Indian Gift and the 'Indian Gift,'" *Man* 21/3 (Sep 1986), pp. 453–473.
"On the Moral Perils of Exchange," in Jonathan Parry and Maurice Bloch (eds.), *Money and the Morality of Exchange*, Cambridge: Cambridge University Press (1989), pp. 64–93.
Parry, Jonathan, and Maurice Bloch (eds.), *Money and the Morality of Exchange*, Cambridge: Cambridge University Press (1989).
Peck, Avery, *The Priestly Gift in the Mishnah: A Study of Tractate Terumot*, Chico: Scholars Press (1981).
Penner, J. E., *The Idea of Property in Law*, Oxford: Oxford University Press (2000).
Penslar, Derek J., *Shylock's Children: Economics and Jewish Identity in Modern Europe*, Berkeley: University of California Press (2001).
Polanyi, Karl, "Aristotle Discovers the Economy," in Karl Polanyi, Conrad M. Arensberg, and Harry. W. Pearson (eds.), *Trade and Market in the Early Empires: Economics in History and Theory*, Glencoe: Free Press (1957), pp. 64–97.
"The Economy as Instituted Process," in Karl Polanyi, Conrad M. Arensberg, and Harry. W. Pearson (eds.), *Trade and Market in the Early Empires: Economics in History and Theory*, Glencoe: Free Press (1957), pp. 243–270.
The Great Transformation, Boston: Beacon (1957).
Posner, Richard A., and William A. Landes, "The Economics of the Baby Shortage," *Journal of Legal Studies* 7 (1978), pp. 323–348.

Posner, Richard A., "The Regulation of the Market in Adoptions," *Boston University Law Review* 67 (1987), pp. 59ff.
Rabello, A. M. (ed.), *An Equitable Distribution of Human Organs for Transplantation*, Jerusalem: Hebrew University (2003).
Rabinovitch, Nahum, "What is the Halacha For Organ Transplants?" in Fred Rosner and David Bleich (eds.), *Jewish Bioethics*, New York: Sanhedrin Press (1979), pp. 351–357.
Rader, Michael, "The 'Good Samaritan' in Jewish Law," *Journal of Legal Medicine* 22 (2001), pp. 375–399.
Radin, Margaret Jane, *Reinterpreting Property*, Chicago: University of Chicago Press (1993).
Contested Commodities, Cambridge: Harvard University Press (1996).
Rajak, Tessa, "The Gifts of God at Sardis," in Martin Goodman (ed.), *Jews in a Graeco-Roman World*, Oxford: Clarendon Press (1998), pp. 229ff.
Rappaport, Shabtai A., " Sale of Organs from a Living Donor for Transplant: Motivation and Decision-Making," in Alfred Mordechai Rabello (ed.), *An Equitable Distribution of Human Organs for Transplantation*, Jerusalem: Hebrew University (2003), pp. 97–108.
Rakover, Nahum, "Unjust Enrichment," in Michael Chernick (ed.), *Essential Papers on the Talmud*, New York: New York University Press (1994), pp. 331–356.
Rivlin, Joseph, *Inheritance and Wills in Jewish Law* (Hebrew), Ramat Gan: Bar Ilan University Press (1999).
Robison, Jeffrey K. "Note: The Debtor's Right to Restrict Lienholder Recovery to the Value of the Encumbered Property under Section 506 of the Bankruptcy Code," *Journal of Corporations Law* 11 (spring 1986), pp. 433–455.
Rohter, Larry, "Tracking the Sale of a Kidney on a Path of Poverty and Hope," *New York Times* (May 23, 2004), pp. 1, 8.
Rosenthal, Franz, "*Sedaka*, Charity," *Hebrew Union College Annual* 23/1 (1950–1951), pp. 411–430.
Rosner, Fred, "Heart and Other Organ Transplantation and Jewish Law," in *Studies in Torah Judaism: Modern Medicine and Jewish Law*, New York: Yeshiva University (1972), pp. 155–176.
"Payment for Healing on the Sabbath," *Journal of Halacha and Contemporary Society* 40 (fall 2000), pp. 59–67.
Contemporary Biomedical Ethical Issues and Jewish Law, New Jersey: Ktav Publishing (2006), pp. 145–149.
Rosner, Fred, and David Weinberger, "Jewish Concerns about Gifts to Physicians from Drug Companies," *Tradition* 32/3 (1998), pp. 19–30.
Rosner, Fred, and Jacob Widroff, "Physician's Fees in Jewish Law," *Jewish Law Annual* 12 (1997), pp. 115–126.
Roth, Joel, "Organ Donation" (YD 336, 1999), in Kassel Abelson and David J. Fine (eds.), *Responsa 1991–2000, The Committee on Jewish Law and Standards of the Conservative Movement*, New York: Rabbinical Assembly (2002), pp. 208–316.
Rottenberg, Yechezkel, "Unjust Enrichment," in Menachem Elon (ed.), *Principles of Jewish Law*, Jerusalem: Keter Publishing House (1975), pp. 335–340.
Ryan, Alan, *Property and Political Theory*, New York: Basil Blackwell Inc. (1986).

Ryazanoff, D. (ed.), *The Communist Manifesto of Karl Marx and Friedrich Engels*, New York: Russesl and Russell (1930).
Rzepka, Charles J., *Sacramental Commodities*, Amherst: University of Amherst Press (1995).
Sahlins, Marshall, *Stone Age Economics*, Chicago: Aldine Publishing Company (1972).
Sandel, Michael J., "You Bet Your Life," *The New Republic* (Sep 7, 1998), p. 11.
"What Money Can't Buy: The Moral Limits of Markets," in Grethe B. Peterson (ed.), *The Tanner Lectures on Human Values*, volume 21, Salt Lake City: University of Utah Press (2000), pp. 87–122.
Sarason, Richard, *Mishnaic Law of Agriculture: A Study of Tractate Demai*, Leiden: Brill (1979).
Schlatter, Richard, *Private Property: The History of an Idea*, London: George Allen and Unwin, Ltd. (1951).
Schrift, Alan D., *The Logic of the Gift: Toward an Ethic of Generosity*, New York: Routledge (1997).
Schwartz, Earl, "Lands, Liens and Ts'daqah," *Journal of Law and Religion* 14/2 (1999–2000), pp. 391–404.
Shapiro, James, *Shakespeare and the Jews*, New York: Columbia University Press (1996).
Sherman, A., "Donation of Organs for the Purpose of Financial Profit" (Hebrew), *T'Chumin* 20 (2000), pp. 353ff.
Simmel, G., *The Philosophy of Money*, London: Routledge and Keegan (1978).
Shinan, Avigdor, *Targum V'aggadah Bo – Ha'agadah B'targum HaTorah Ha'arami Ha-Meyukhas L'yonatan ben Uziel*, (Hebrew: The Embroidered Targum: The Aggadah in Targum Pseudo-Jonathan of the Pentateuch), Jerusalem: Magnes Press 1992.
Sinclair, Daniel B., *Jewish Biomedical Law: Legal and Extra-legal Dimensions*, New York: Oxford University Press (2003), pp. 243–244.
Singer, Isidore (ed.), "Tombstones", *The Jewish Encyclopedia*, New York: Funk and Wagnalls Co. (1916), pp. 190–195.
Singer, Joseph William, *The Edges of the Field*, Boston: Beacon Press (2000).
Smelik, Willem F., "The Rabbinic Reception of Early Bible Translations as Holy Writings and Oral Torah," *Journal for the Aramaic Bible* 1 (1999), pp. 249–272.
Sokefeld, Martin, "Debating Self, Identity, and Culture in Anthropology," *Current Anthropology* 40/4 (Aug–Oct 1999), pp. 417–447.
Soloveitchik, Haym, "Can Halakhic Texts Talk History?" *AJS Review*, volume 3, Cambridge: Association for Jewish Studies (1978), pp. 153–196.
Sombart, Werner, *The Jews and Modern Capitalism*, New York: Collier Books (1951).
Steinberg, Avraham, *Encyclopedia Hilchatit Refuit* (Hebrew: The Halachic-Medical Encyclopedia), Jerusalem: Schlesinger Institute (1991).
Strathern, Marilyn, "Subject or Object? Women and the Circulation of Valuables in Highlands New Guinea," in Renee Hirshchon (ed.), *Women and Property – Women as Property*, New York: St. Martin's Press (1984), pp. 158–175.
The Gender of the Gift: Problems with Women and Problems with Society in Melanesia, Berkeley: University of California Press (1988).

"Divisions of Interest and the Languages of Ownership," in C. M. Hann, (ed.), *Property Relations*, Cambridge: Cambridge University Press (1998), pp. 214–232.
Sussman, George D., *Selling Mother's Milk: The Wet-Nursing Business in France 1715–1914*, Urbana: University of Illinois Press (1982).
Tao, Dominick, "Worldwide Market Fuels Illegal Traffic in Organs," New York Times (July 29, 2009), p. A26.
Tawney, R. H., *Religion and the Rise of Capitalism*, Harmondsworth: Penguin Books (1972).
Titmuss, Richard M., *The Gift Relationship: From Human Blood to Social Policy*, New York: New Press (1997).
Twersky, Isadore, "Some Aspects of the Jewish Attitude Toward the Welfare State," in *Studies in Jewish Law and Philosophy*, New York: Ktav Publishing (1982), pp. 108–129.
Urbach, Ephraim E., "*Magamot Datiyot V'chevaratiyot B'torat Ha'tsedakah shel Chazal*" (Hebrew: Political and Social Tendencies in Talmudic Concepts of Charity), *Zion* 16 (1951); also appearing in Ephraim E. Urbach, *Me'Olamam Shel Chachamim* (Hebrew: The World of the Sages: Collected Studies), Jerusalem: Magnes Press (1988), pp. 97–124.
"*'Hefker' – Mashehu al Hamosad U'm'komo Hahistorit*" (Hebrew: On the Place of *Derelictio* in Historical Reality), *Shenaton Ha-Mishpat Ha-Ivri* 6–7 (1979–1980), pp. 17–28; also appearing in Ephraim E. Urbach, *Me'Olamam Shel Chachamim* (Hebrew: The World of the Sages: Collected Studies), Jerusalem: Magnes Press (1988), pp. 257–268.
Collected Writings in Jewish Studies, Jerusalem: Magnes Press (1999).
Wakin, Daniel J., "Rabbis' Rules and Indian Wigs Stir Crisis in Orthodox Brooklyn," *New York Times* (May 14, 2004), p. 1.
Walzer, Michael, "Socialism and the Gift Relationship," *Dissent* (fall 1982), pp. 431–441.
Spheres of Justice, New York: Basic Books (1983).
"A Note on Positive Freedom in Jewish Thought," *S'vara* 1/1 (winter 1990), pp. 7–11.
Wegner, Judith Romney, *Chattel or Person? The Status of Women in the Mishnah*, New York: Oxford University Press (1988).
Weiner, Annette B., *Inalienable Possessions*, Berkeley: University of California Press (1992).
Weinman, Zvi, "*Hekdesh Mishpachti Eyno Hekdesh*" (Hebrew), *Tehumin* 21 (2001), pp. 237–247.
Weinrib, Ernest, "Rescue and Restitution," *S'vara: A Journal of Philosophy and Judaism* 1 (1990), pp. 59–65.
Werbner, Pnina, "Economic Rationality and Hierarchical Gift Economies: Value and Ranking Among British Pakistanis," *Man* n.s. 25/2 (Jun 1990), pp. 266–285.
Wilk, Richard R., *Economies and Cultures*, Boulder: Westview Press (1996).
Wilson, Rodney, *Economics, Ethics and Religion: Jewish, Christian and Muslim Economic Thought*, London: Macmillan Press, Ltd. (1997).
Woodburn, James, "Sharing Is Not a Form of Exchange: An Analysis of Property-Sharing in Immediate-Return Hunter-Gatherer Societies," in C. M. Hann (ed.), *Property Relations*, Cambridge: Cambridge University Press (1998), pp. 48–63.

Wygoda, Michael, "*Mechirat Eyvarim*," (Hebrew: The Sale of Organs) *Shanah Beshanah* 42 (5762/2002), pp. 119–127.

Yaron, Reuven, *Gifts in Contemplation of Death in Jewish and Roman Law*, Oxford: Clarendon Press (1960).

Yavrov, Tzvi, "*Ba'alut Ha'adam al Gufo Venafsho: Haneshama lach Vehaguf Shelach*"(Hebrew: Self-ownership of One's Body and Soul), *Yated Neman, Musaf* (Dec 30, 1994/27 Tevet 5755), pp. 6–7.

Yerkes, Royden Keith, *Sacrifice in Greek and Roman Religions and Early Judaism*, New York: Charles Scribner's Sons (1952).

Yisraeli, Shaul, "*Tikrit Kivyeh L'or Ha-halacha*," *Ha-Torah ve-ha-Medina* 5 (1953–1954), pp. 71–113.

"*Terumot Evarim Min Hachai u'Min ha Met*" (Hebrew: Organ Donations from Live and Dead Donors), in *First International Conference on the Law and Ethics of Medicine* (1993), pp. 195; also appearing in *Chavat Binyamin* part 3, p. 1903.

"Organ Donations From Living Donors: Danger to the Donor and Receipt of Payment," *Assia Journal of Medical Ethics and Halacha*, Questions and Answers, Volume 15, No. 57–58 (1997), p. 58; also appearing in English in M. Halperin and D. Fink (eds.), *The Proceedings of the First International Colloquium on Medicine, Ethics and Jewish Law*, Jerusalem: Schlesinger Institute for Medical-Halachik Research (1996), pp. 231–237.

Yuval, Israel Jacob, *Chachamim B'Doram* (Hebrew: Scholars in Their Time), Jerusalem: Magnes Press (1988).

Zeitlin, Solomon, "Korban: A Gift," in *Studies in the Early History of Judaism: History of Early Talmudic Law*, volume 4, New York: Ktav Publishing House, Inc. (1978), pp. 348ff.

"*Hefker V'Yeush*" (Hebrew), in *Studies in the Early History of Judaism: History of Early Talmudic Law*, volume 4, New York: Ktav Publishing (1978), pp. 438ff.

Zelizer, Viviana A., *Markets and Morals: The Development of Life Insurance in the United States*, New Brunswick: Transaction Books (1983).

Pricing the Priceless Child, Princeton: Princeton University Press (1994).

The Social Meaning of Money, Princeton: Princeton University Press (1997).

Zevin, Shlomo, "*Mishpat Shylock*" (Hebrew: The Case of Shylock), in *L'or Ha'halacha*, Jerusalem: Beyt Hillel (1946), pp. 311–335.

Zilberstein, Yitzchak, "*Mechirat Kalya Lephar'on Chovot*" (Hebrew: Sale of Organs for the Payment of Debts), *Yated Ne'eman, Musaf* (Dec 30, 1994/27 Tevet 5755), p. 7.

Zohar, Noam, "Toward Justice in the Organ Trade," *Israel Law Review* 27 (1993), pp. 541ff.

Alternatives in Jewish Bioethics, Albany: State University of New York Press (1997).

General Index

Abaye, 158, 165, 208, 215
akhilat ara'i, 119n122
acquisition. *See kinyan*
Akiva, Rabbi, 63n2, 168, 181n13, 222
al kiddush hashem, 159, 193n40
Alfasi (the "Rif", Rabbi Isaac Alfasi (1013–1103)), 140
alms, Mauss' theory of, 13
am ha'aretz, 62n1
amirah, acquisition with, 72
amirah legavohah kemesirah lehedyot, 72n23
amoraim, defined, 62
ancestral fields, priestly redemption of, 88n58, 94
Andaman Islanders, 54
Anderson, Elizabeth, 23
anthropomorphism, 71n19, 147n79
apotika, 74n28. *See hiptik*
Appadurai, Arjun, 24–25n12, 36
Aquinas, Thomas, 30
arakhin, 14n41. *See damim*
Aristotle, 30, 31
Assis, Yom Tov, 137n49, 138
assur lehatzil atzmo bemamon chavero, 172n129
Autrey, Wesley, 186–87
azivah,105n92

Babylonian Talmud, defined, 62
bal te'akher, 125
bal yichal, 103n89, 125
Barber, Bernard, 27n22, 29, 30, 35n51, 226n19
Barfield, Thomas, 32n37
Baumgarten, Joseph, 74n28
beards, rules about, 10n28, 191n31, 192
bechor (s.), *bechorot* (pl.), 13n34, 65
Becker, Gary, 22n3, 42
bedek habayit, 79
bedisho, 87n55
begufo, 174, 184–88, 194, 204
bei gaza derakhmanah, 74
Beit Hillel, 110
Beit Shammai, 105n92, 110
Beit Yosef, 172, 173n132, 196n53
bemamono, 174, 184–86, 204
Ben Patura, 63n2
benediction before eating, 13n34, 67–69, 213
benefit. *See hana'ah*
Benovitz, Moshe, 14n40–41, 72n20, 73n25, 124, 125n12, 130–31
berakha (s.), *berakhot* (pl.). *See* benediction before eating
Berger, Samuel, xiii, xiv
beriyot, 103, 105
Bernstein, Moshe, 74n28
bikurim, 95–97
Binyan Tziyon (Rabbi Jacob Ettlinger, 1798–1871), 167n127
Binyan Tziyon (Rabbi Jacob Ettlinger, 1798–1871), 172n129
black market organ sales, xiii, 20
Bleich, Rabbi J. David, 179n4, 193n41, 195n47, 198n58
Bloch, Maurice, 29, 30n29, 32n37, 33n43–44, 34n46, 35n52, 39, 40–50
blocked exchanges, 1n2, 22–24, 26–27, 220–22
blood donations, 23, 182, 203n66
bloodletting, 182
bodily mutilation, 15n43, 192, 194
Bohannon, Paul, 32n37, 34
bone marrow transplants, 2n4, 179, 198n58
boreh, 103
Bourdieu, Pierre, 45n12, 47
breastfeeding, payment for, 205n71
brit melach, 119
brit milah, 13n34
burial, laws of, 10n28, 193n41
burnt offering, 126n19, 127

captives, redemption of, 158, 172n130
Caro, Rabbi Joseph, 143n70, 172, 173n132, 196n53
Carrier, James, 44n3, 48, 56
chalitzah. *See yevamah*
challah, 86–87n53, 95, 107
charity. *See* the poor; *tsedakah*
caritas; as inaccurate definition of *tsedakah*, 13, 17, 126n21, 200, 218
chasid/chasidut, 197, 198n59
chasid shoteh, 197
chavalah, 10n28, 168n123, 178, 180–82, 192
cherem (s.), *charamim* (pl.), 14n41, 72n21, 88, 95, 127, 135n43
Chisda, Rav, 127n24
Chiya, Rabbi, 117
choleh lefaneinu, 157n108, 179n4
circumcision, 10n28, 192
Cohen, Felix S., 44–45
Cohen, G. A., 46
coins mentioned in rabbinic literature
- *dinar* (s.), *dinarim* (pl.), 158
- *perutah*, 89
- *sela*, 135, 140, 154, 166, 175
- *zuz* (s.), *zuzim* (pl.), 155n104, 165–67, 181n13

Communist Manifesto, 227
Conservative Movement, 179n5, 195n47, 198n59, 201n62, 203n66
Cooley, Charles, 25, 42n83
corners of the field, 13n36, 79, 100n84, 101, 103–5, 107, 110, 143, 153n95, 154, 155n103

Dalton, George, 34
damim, 127n23. *See arakhin*
de Modena, Leon (Judah Aryeh, 1571–1648), 11n31
dead body
- requirement of respectful treatment of, 193n41, 194n46, 209n80

death
- legal definition of, 174n4
- obligatory postmortem organ donation, 224

Derrida, Jacques, 7, 51–54, 221n7
devarim haniknim be'amirah, 72n23
dinar (s.), *dinarim* (pl.), 158
"do not delay" prohibition, 74, 125–29, 132, 156–57, 179n5
doctors, payment of. *See* physicians, payment of
domain, legal (*reshut*), 87, 91n66, 94–95, 173
dough offering, 86–87n53, 95, 107
Douglas, Mary, 14, 29, 32n37, 47n25, 50n37, 226
Durkheim, Emile, 58

ein dochin nefesh mipnei nefesh, 159
eye for an eye, 190n28

Eliezer, Rabbi, 155, 173n132
embodied obligation, 7, 19, 57, 220
Ettlinger, Jacob, 172n129
Evans-Pritchard, E. E., 18n53, 47n22

Feinstein, Rabbi Moshe (*Iggerot Moshe*), 157n208, 179n5, 180–82
festivals, 127, 156
first fruits, 12n33, 74n28, 95–97
firstborn
- animal, 82, 84n45, 85n51, 95, 96n73, 118, 126–28, 192
- son, 10n28, 12, 13n34, 95, 192

forgotten sheaves, 97, 100n84, 101, 126–28, 142n69, 153, 175
Formalist paradigm of exchange, 31, 33
Foucault, Michel, 56n62
fourth year grapes, 68
Fraade, Steven, 75n28
Friedman, Shamma, 109

gavoha. *See shel gavoha, mamon gavoha*
Gemara, defined, 62
The Gender of the Gift (Strathern), 25n13, 37
Gersonides, 2, 85–86n5
The Gift (Mauss). *see* Mauss, Marcel
gift economy, concept of, 34n46, 38, 47n25
Gil, Moshe, 135n44, 137n49, 138
gleanings, 79, 100n84, 101, 103–5, 107, 126–28, 132–33, 142n69, 143, 147, 152–55, 175–76
Goren, Rabbi Shlomo, xxi*n*5, 182n15, 195n48, 196
Gregory, C. A., 32n38, 34n46, 34n49
Grey, Thomas C., 45n12
Grossfeld, Bernard, 75n28

Hadza people of Tanzania, 49
hamakom, 103
hair, rules about, 191–94
Hakappar, Rabbi Elazar, 181
hana'ah, 175–77, 192–94, 213. *See issurei hana'ah*; *tovat hana'ah*.
Hanina ben Papa, Rabbi, 66n12, 214n87
Hann, Chris, 3n7, 6n16, 29n28, 34n47–48, 35n50, 36n54, 42n83, 44n3–4, 46n16–18, 49n30–32
hatra'ah, 10n28
healthcare benefits for organ donors, 223–24
hedyot. *See shel hedyot*
hefker, 14, 72n21, 79, 101, 102n87, 105n92, 107–10, 115n116–17, 117n120, 135n43, 144
hefker beit din hefker, 14, 115n116, 117n120, 135n43
hevker. *See hefker*.
Heineman, Joseph, 75n28
hekdesh (s.), *hekdeshot* (pl.), 11, 12n32, 14, 18n52, 64–67, 69–71, 73, 77, 78n34, 79,

80n36, 86, 103, 122–25, 127, 129, 147, 151, 152n94, 153n97, 175–76, 185, 190, 194, 196, 199–200, 208, 211, 224n15. *See also mamon gavoha*; shel gavoha; *shel shamayim*
hiptik, 74. *See apotika*
Hobbes, Thomas, 45
honoring one's parents, the *mitzvah* of, 154n102, 165–66
Hollopeter, Cameron, 186–87
Hubert, Henri, 14n42
human donor, defined, 84n44
human life, obligation to save. *See pikuach nefesh*
human reason, 68, 197n55, 213
human sacrifice, 127n23, 188n25, 190n28

The Idea of Usury (Nelson), 1, 226n20
Ifra Hormiz, 158
Iggerot Moshe (Rabbi Moshe Feinstein, 1895–1986), 157n108, 179n5, 180–82
inheritance, 63n4, 91n65, 102, 114, 118
interest-bearing loan, ban on, 21, 52, 77, 136, 139, 142, 150, 151n91, 157n109, 196n51
Isaac Alfasi, Rabbi ("Alfasi" or the Rif, 1013–1103), 140
Isaac ben Moses of Vienna, Rabbi (*Or Zarua*,1200–1279), 141
Isaac, sacrifice of, 221n7
Ishmael, Rabbi, 214–15
Israel, organ donation and black market organ sales in, xii–xiii, 225
Issi ben Yehudah, 117
issur chavalah, 10n28, 168n123, 178, 180–82, 192. *See* self-mutilation
issurei hana'ah, 1, 70, 76–77n3, 87, 134n39, 150n88, 151

Jackson, Bernard, xv, 65, 72, 137
Jerusalem Talmud, defined, 61
Jewish law, defintion, xii*n*4
Jews and money, stereotype about, xi, 60
Jose the Galilean, Rabbi, 83n43
Joseph, Rabbi, 158
Josephus, 80n39, 123
Jubilee year, 13n34, 64, 71, 88, 89n58, 91–92, 94, 107–9, 113, 118, 147n82, 150. *See yovel*

ka zakhu. *See zokhe*
kadosh/kedushah, 66, 70–71, 72n23, 76, 79n36, 82, 84n46, 86, 88, 100, 126, 135–36, 144, 147n81, 152, 192
  hierarchy of, 79n36
kam lei b'drabah minei, 164n124
Katz, Jacob, 5n13
Katzoff, Ranon, 72n23
kefoel batel, 174n136
kenafshecha, 149, 161
kerem revai, 68
Kibbutz movement, 60
kiddushin, 14n41, 32n37, 61, 72n23, 76, 194
Kierkegaard, Søren, 221n7
King Shapur, 158
kinyan/koneh, 11n31, 72, 77n33, 85n49, 90, 108, 194n42, 212
  amirah, acquisition with, 72
  amirah legavohah kemesirah lehedyot, 72n23
  devarim haniknim be'amirah, 72n23
kinyan sudar, 11n31
Kochen, Madeline
  "Property and Its Limits: Jesus, the Pharisees, the Rabbis and the Targumists," 75n28
  "Mother's Final Gift," 223n11
kodashim, 61, 77, 84, 95, 130, 136
koinos, 131
konam, 103–5, 123, 131. *See* prohibitory vow
koneh. *See kinyan*
konehu, 212
korban, 103n89, 123–24, 131, 185
koreh shem, 73n25
kula, 56n63
kupah, 132, 134n37

Lacan, Jacques, 56n62
Lau, Rabbi Israel Meir, xxi*n*5, 4, 172n129, 195–96, 198n59
Leon (Judah Aryeh) de Modena (1571–1648), 11n31
leket, 79, 100n84, 101, 103–5, 107, 126–28, 132–33, 142n69, 143, 147, 152–55, 175–76
Levi, Rabbi, 66–67
Levi ben Gershon ("Ralbag," or "Gersonides", 1288–1344), 2, 85–86n5
Levinas, Emmanuel, 56n62
Levite (s.), Leviyim (pl.), 102, 104, 114, 118
Levite cities, 150
Lie, Jon, 41n78
Lieberman, Saul, 123, 144n73
limb given up to save life of another, 16–17, 196–201
lo ta'amod, 166n120
loan, ban on interest-bearing, , 21, 52, 77, 136, 139, 142, 150, 151n91, 157n109, 196n51
Locke, John, 45, 226
lost property, obligation to restore, 62, 160–63, 174–75, 185, 200, 205n71
Luke 6:1, 117

ma'aser ani, 13n35, 79, 86, 100–6
ma'aser rishon, 101, 103
ma'aser sheni, 13n35, 86–87, 97, 100–1, 103, 113
Maharam (Meir of Rothenburg, c.1215–1293), 141–42, 172n130

Maimonides (Rabbi Moses ben Maimon, "Rambam," 1135–1204), 81n40, 113n110, 140, 178n2, 181n13, 184, 204n68
Maine, Henry, 50n36
Malinowski, Branislaw, 26n16, 28n24, 33
mamon gavohah (property belonging to God; lit. property of the Most High), 70n18, 76–86. *See also shel gavohah*; shel shamayim; *hekdesh*
mamon hedyot (ordinary property), 86–87
mamzer, 76n29
Maori, Yishayahu, 75n28
Maori gift exchange, 12, 53–55
Mark 2:23, 117
Mark 7:1–3, 131n32
marriage, 14n41, 32n37, 61, 72n23, 76, 194
Marx, Karl, 30–31, 33, 227n21
matir, 118–19
Matthew, 12:1, 117
Matthew, 15:1–9, 131n32
Mauss, Marcel, 3n8, 6–10, 13–14, 18n53, 23, 26, 27n23, 28n24, 29, 33–34, 44n3, 47n22, 48n27, 49–59, 68–69, 113, 155, 173, 185, 218, 220–21, 226
McFall v. Shimp, 1c Pa.D.&C. 3d 90 (1978), 2n4
Mechilta, 111n116, 112, 144n83
me'ilah, 67, 76, 124, 212
Meir, Rabbi, 86–87, 124
Meiselman, Rabbi Moshe, 198n58
mekablei matanot, 95, 111
Melanesia, exchange practices in, 14, 38, 48, 53n47, 55n56, 56n63
menorah, 134n37
The Merchant of Venice (Shakespeare), xi, 16n46, 17
Merleau-Ponty, Maurice, 56n62
midat chasidut, 197
mitah beyedei shamayim, 71n19
Miller, Daniel, 36n56, 42n79
Mishnah, defined, 61
mishmar/mishmarot defined, 90n63
mitzvah,defined, xxin9, 15n44
Money and the Morality of Exchange (ed. Parry and Bloch), 30n29, 35n52, 39
Mordechai ben Hillel Ashkenazi (1240–1298), 143n69
murderer, no monetary redemption for, 10n28
muzzingling an ox, biblical prohibition against, 87n55, 120, 148

Nachmanides (Moshe ben Nachman Girondi or "Ramban", 1194–1270), 113n110, 207–9, 216
Native Americans, 55
nazir/Nazirite/*nazirut*, 61, 73n25, 95, 181, 191–92, 193n36
nedavah (s.), *nedavot* (pl.), 125, 134n38, 136
neder (s.), *nedarim* (pl.), 72n21, 73, 74n27, 103n89, 109, 122–27, 129–36, 140, 147, 175–76
Nelson, Benjamin, 1, 226
New York Organ Donor Network, xiii
New York subway system rescue (2007), 186–87
nikhsei cohen, 96–97, 143n72
Non-Jews, 70n16

olelot, 68, 100n84, 107
Or Zarua (Rabbi Isaac ben Moses of Vienna, 1200–1279), 141n64
ona'ah, 77, 143n70
Orders of the Mishnah, 61
Origen, 131
orlah, 13n34, 74n28, 192
Otzar Hageonim, 135, 136n45
Ouroussoff, Alexandra, 3n6, 33n40, 40n73, 47n25, 49n29, 56n62
ox, biblical prohibition against muzzling, 87n55, 120, 148

Palestinian Talmud, defined, 62
Papa, Rav, 102
paschal lamb, 127
Parry, Jonathan, 4n12, 9n24, 29, 30n29, 32n37, 33n43, 35n52, 39, 40n71–72, 42n80, 46n16, 50n35, 50n37
peah (s.), *peyot* (pl.), 13n36, 79, 100n84, 101, 103–5, 107, 110, 143, 153n95, 154, 155n103
peace offerings, 83n43, 102, 126n19, 127
pericope, defined, 66
perutah, 89
Philo, 80n39
physicians, payment of, 2n3, 15n45, 177n140, 186n21, 204–9, 224
pidyon, 14n41, 86, 158, 172n130
piggul, 81n40
pikuach nefesh, 10n28, 122, 148, 155, 158–59, 161, 164–88, 197, 202, 204, 208, 217, 225
pious act, 198n59
pious person, 62n1
Polanyi, Karl, 31–35, 40n73, 42, 50
potlach, 55
priestly gifts, list of 24, 95
private property, general discussion of, 44–46
prohibitory vows, 123–24, 129n27, 130n30, 131, 158, 191–92
prozbul, 115n116, 143n70, 150n88
Pseudo-Jonathan, Targum of 74

Quasi-*hekdesh*,131, 144

Raba, 169n124
Rabban Gamiliel, 120

Rabi, 120
Rabbah, 169n124
Rabbah bar bar Hanah, 215–16
Radbaz (Rabbi David ben Zimra, 1479–1573), 16–17, 140n60, 184n19, 196–201
Radin, Jane, 1n2, 22–23
Rajak, Tessa, 122–23
Rakover, Nahum, 155n105, 163n118, 179n4
Ralbag (Levi ben Gershon, "Gersonides", 1288–1344), 2, 85–86n5
Rambam. *See* Maimonides
Ramban (Rabbi Moshe ben Nahman Girondi or "Nachmanides," 1194-c1270), 113n110, 207–9, 216
Rami bar Chana, 94
Ran (Rabbi Nissim ben Reuven, 1320–1376), 142–44, 152n93, 189
rasha (s.), *reshai'm* (pl.), 61n2, 86n52
Rashba (Rabbi Shlomo ben Aderet), 137n49, 138n53, 139n58, 141, 146
Rashbash (Rabbi Solomon ben Simon Duran, c.1400–1467), 140
Rashi (Rabbi Shlomo Yitzchaki, 1040–1105), 101, 144n175, 145, 172n129
Rav, 73n26, 117, 194, 206
Rav Chisda, 127n124
Rava, 88, 95, 111, 129, 156, 197n55, 215
Recanati, Rabbi Menahem ben Benjamin (*Sefer Recanati*, 1250–1310), 197
reshut, 87, 91n66, 94–95, 173
Ri Migash (Rabbi Joseph ibn Migash, 1077–1141), 139–40, 147n80–81
ribit, 21, 52, 77, 136, 139, 142, 150, 151n91, 157n109, 196n51
Rif (Isaac ben Jacob Alfasi ha-Cohen or "Alfasi,"1013–1103), 140
Ritva (Yom Tov ben Avraham Asevilli, 1250–1330), 144–45, 151, 189n26
rodef , 159, 162, 169, 203
Rosenthal, Franz, 128
Rosh (Rabbi Asher ben Yechi'el, 1250–1327), 170n126, 171–73, 210
Roth, Rabbi Joel, 16n47, 179n5, 195n47, 198n59, 201n62

Sabbatical year, 13n34, 18n52, 64, 79, 86, 107–10, 116–18, 147n82, 150
sacred property. *See hekdesh*
Sahlins, Marshall, 9n23, 34, 49
salt covenant, 119
Samuel, 66n12, 73, 74n26, 148n83, 158
Samuel bar Judah, Rabbi, 158
Sandel, Michael, xv
Sardis Synagogue, 122–23
schar batalah, 205, 207, 216, 217n89
Sefer ha-Terumot (Samuel ben Isaac ha-Sardi, written in 1225), 139n58
Seidman, Naomi, xv, 11n31
sela, 135, 140, 154, 166, 175
self-endangerment, prohibition against, 18, 183
self-interest. *See* altruism/self-interest
self-mutilation, prohibition against, 178, 183, 193. *See chavalah*
self-ownership, xiv, 10, 16n47, 17, 121, 147n79, 168–69, 182–83, 190n28, 191n31, 192n32, 193–95, 202, 226
sevarah, 68, 197n55, 213
Shakespeare, William, xi, 5n12, 16–17, 60
She'elot u-Teshuvot Binyan Tziyon (Rabbi Jacob Ettlinger, 1798–1871), 172n129
shel gavohah, 65, 71, 77, 83, 97
shel hedyot, 71, 83
shel shamayim, 70n18, 87, 97, 107, 128n25, 144–45, 148, 164, 166, 189
shelamim, 95, 102
shemitah, 13n34, 18n52, 64, 79, 86, 107–10, 116–18, 147n82, 150
shevuah, 73n25, 123
shikhechah, 79, 100n84, 101, 103–7, 143
Shimon, Rabbi, 124
Shimon ben Lakish, Rabbi, 74n26
Shimon ben Yokhai, Rabbi, 214–16
Shinan, Avigdor, 75n28
Shulchan Aruch, 139n58, 140n60, 143n70, 173n132, 174, 181n13, 184n16, 205n71
Simmel, George, 30
sin offering, 126–27, 181, 191
Singer, Joseph William, xv, 45n12
slaves and slavery, 14n41, 27, 64, 108, 127n23, 190n27, 191n30–31, 193n38, 194
Smelik, William, 75n28
Smith, Adam, 30
social contract theory, 3n5, 9n23
Sodom, 62n1
Sombart, Werner, 4n12, 60
"spirit of the gift," 8–9, 12, 36, 55–58, 220
Strabo, 80n39
Steinberg, Dr. Avraham, 179n4, 195n47, 198n58
Strathern, Marilyn, 3, 6n16, 25n13, 37, 43–44n2, 48n28, 196n52, 219
Substantivist paradigm of exchange, 31, 32n37, 33n44
sugyah, defined, 66
synagogue, 122n5, 134n37

tachat yado, 91–92, 95
Tacitus, 80n39
Talmud, definition of, 62
Talmudic law, definition, xii*n4*
tamchui, 132, 134n37
Tannaim, definition of, 61
Tarfon, Rabbi, 120

Targum, 8, 74, 74–75n2
terumah, 70, 79, 86, 95–97, 101, 103, 105, 119, 143n72, 152n93, 153
terumat ma'aser, 86, 95
Teshuvot Shevut HaLevi, 198n58
Teshuvot Vayeshev Moshe, 198n58
tevel, 82, 119n122
theft from God, some Talmudic sources, 65n12
tikun olam, 116
tithes. *See ma'aser*; *terumah*
Titmuss, Richard, 23–24, 26, 29–30, 50, 221, 226
tombstone epitaph, 11n31
Tosafot, 68n13, 84n47, 172n129, 174n136, 181n13
Tosefta, defined, 61–62
tovat hana'ah, 79, 83, 100, 103–6, 153
Trobriand Islanders, 56n63
tsedek, 13, 15, 113, 115, 128
Tur, 171n128, 172, 184n16, 196n53

Urbach, E. E., 14n41, 109, 137n49
usury, prohibition against, 21, 52, 77, 136, 139, 142, 150, 151n91, 157n109, 196n51

Value in Ethics and Economics (Anderson), 23n6
value pluralism, 23
values of persons, pledged to the Temple. *See arakhin*; *damim*
vehashevoto lo, 161n115, 166n120, 170, 174, 176, 188
veterans, healthcare benefits for, 222–24
Vincent v. Lake Erie Transportation Company, 171n127

Waldenberg, Rabbi Eliezer (*Ziz Eliezer*, 1915–2006), 173n132, 198n59
Walzer, Michael, 1n2, 22, 25–29, 50, 221
watches (in the Temple), defined, 90n63
waqf, 138, 139n56
Weber, Max, 4n12, 60
Weinrib, Ernest, 173n133
Werbner, Pnina, 34n49
wet nursing, payment for, 27, 205n71
Woodburn, James, 49, 56–57
Woszner, Rabbi Samuel ha-Levi (*Teshuvot Shevut HaLevi*), 198n58

Yachel Yisrael (Rabbi Israel Meir Lau), 172n129
Yannai, Rabbi, 135n42, 216
Yehoshua ben Levi, Rabbi, 206n72
Yehudah, Rabbi, 86
Yehudah, Rav, 66n12, 67, 206
Yehudah bar Ila'i, Rabbi, 215–16
Yehudah ha-Nasi, Rabbi, 61
yibum/yevamah, 209n78
Yisraeli, Rabbi Shaul, 17n50, 195n47, 198n59
Yohanan, Rabbi, 74n26, 215–16
Yosef, Rav, 102
"you shall return his body to him", 161n115, 166n120, 170, 174, 176, 188
yovel, 13n34, 64, 71, 88, 89n58, 91–92, 94, 107–9, 113, 118, 147n82, 150. *See* Jubilee

Zeira, Rav, 91n64
Zelizer, Viviana, 29, 29n68, 40–42, 47n25, 49n29, 226n18
Zevin, Rabbi Shlomo, xin2, 17–18
Ziz Eliezer. *See* Waldenberg
zokhe/ka zakhu, 85, 87–88, 91–97, 101, 145n77
Zorger, Rabbi Moshe Se'ev (*Teshuvot Vayeshev Moshe*), 198n58
zuz (s.), *zuzim* (pl.), 155n104, 165–67, 181n13

Index of Bibical and Talmudic References

Bible
Exodus
13:7 77
21:6 193n38
23:11 110n104, 115
30:14–15 115n115
31:13 148n83
Leviticus
2:13 119
5:21–26 89n60
7:18 81n40
7:35 114n112
18:5 148n83
19:10 107n96
19:15 114n114
19:16 159–160, 166n120, 170, 183
23:30, 32, 96n72, 101
25:1–7 64
25:8–13 64
25:13–16 88n57
25:23 64n5
25:35 120
25:36 63n2, 148–149, 168, 222
25:42 64
25:55 64n6
27:1–8 127n23, 191
27:14, 16, 64n8
27:16, 20–21, 88
27:21 88n58, 90, 92
27:26 65, 85n51
27:29 82n42
27:30, 32, 65n9
27:32–33 84n48
Numbers
5:6–8 89n60
5:8 89–90, 111n105
5:10 93–95
15:20 86n53, 107n97
18:7 119
18:8–19 119
18:8–29 114n112
30:3 123n7, 125
35:1–2 114
35:8 114
Deuteronomy
4:5 206
11:14 213–214
12:17 87n56
14:24–26 222n10
14:27 100n83, 102, 114n113
15:17 193n38
18:6–7 93n70
21:22 194n46
21:23 193n41
22:2 159–160, 166, 170, 174, 176, 183–184
23:18 222n9
23:22 74
23:22, 24, 126n20
23:22–24 125
23:25 74n27, 117, 149, 166n120
23:25–26 97n94, 106, 116
25:4 87n55, 148
28:48 214
Joshua
1:8 213

8:29 193n41
19:51 135n43
1 Samuel
2:12 85n52
1 Chronicles
29:14, 16, 122n3
Ezra
10:8 135n43
Job
28:23 206n72
Psalms
24:1 66, 74, 212
40:7–8 80n40
50:8–15 80n40
115:16 66
Proverbs
16:4 212
23:23 206
Hosea
2:11 213n85, 214
6:6 80–81n40
Amos
5:21–27 80n40
Micah
6:6–8 80n40
Isaiah
1:11–17 80n40
Jeremiah
6:20 80n40
7:21–22 80n40

Mishnah
Arakhin
7:3 88, 91
Avot
3:10 103
4:7 204n68
5:13 62n1
6:1 103
Bava Kamma
7:6 178n2
8:6 181n13
9:5 89
10:4 163, 174
Bava Metzia
2:9 175
7:4–5 98n78
Bechorot
4:6 205, 208–209
Berakhot
3:3 103
6:1 68
Bikurim
2:1 96
3:12 96
Eduyot
5:1 116n119
Hagigah
2:5 120
Horyot
3:7–8 155n106, 191n30
Kiddushin
1:6 11n30, 72n24, 73, 77n33
2:8 76n30, 87n54
Kinim
1:1 125n13
Nedarim
4:4 175, 177n140, 184n16, 184n19
11:3 103–105, 175
Peah
5:4 153n96, 154, 171
6:1 110
8:7 132n34
8:8 154n103
Sanhedrin
4:5 103
8:2 172n130, 173, 210n82
Shekalim
2:5 100n82
3:2 103
Sheviit
4:2 116n119
Terumot
1:4 150n88
1:5 101n86
8:4 196n53, 200

Tosefta
Bava Batra
5 103
Bava Kamma
7:1 103
Berakhot
4:1 212

Kiddushin
1:9 73–74
Nedarim
2:9 124n10
7:4 105
Peah
4:1 211, 213
4:16 143n69, 144n73

Babylonian Talmud (B.T.)
Arakhin
6a 129, 133, 135n41
6a-b 133–134
6b 135n42
7b 192n34, 194
24b 88
29a 82n42, 85n51
34a 92, 94
Avodah Zarah
29b 193n41
Bava Batra
8–10 132–135
8a 134n39, 143n70
8a–b 158
8b 132n34
102b 139n58, 147n80–81
Bava Kamma
chapter 8, 176n138, 210n81
12b 83n43, 84n47, 99n81
13a 85n50
36b 140n60
60b 172n129
109 83n43
109a 102n87
109b 89, 90n62, 92–93
110 111
110b 91, 95, 119
117b 169n124
Bava Metzia
chapter 5, 150
7a 143n70
30b 205n71
31b 174n136, 175n137
52a 190n27, 194n43
57b 141
62a 63n2, 168
70 134n39
70a 136n47
71a 157n108
87a 106n94
87b 106
88b 120, 148n84, 149, 161
89b 101
90a 86, 86n53
92a 97, 98n79, 111n107, 117, 144, 189n26
Bechorot
29a 15n45, 205n70, 206, 208
Berakhot
35a 68n13, 212–213
35a–b 66–67, 213
35b 213, 216
Bezah
21a 85n50
Chullin
12a 85n50
Gittin
36b 135n43
Ketuvot
29a 169n125
49b 154n102
59b 205n71
91b 165, 181n13
Kiddushin
22b 64n6
31b–32a 154n102
32b 166n119
52a 87n55
52b 83n43, 85, 143n71
Megilah
Chapter 4, 129n28
Meilah
13a 87n55
Menachot
6a 85n50
Nedarim
7a 129n27
29b 140n60
48a 154n99
84b 100n84
84b-85a 104n91
85a 104n90

Pesachim
23a 77n32
Rosh Hashanah
4a–b 126n16, 127, 131–133, 156
5a 127n24
5b 126n18
6a 156
6b 134n37
28a 176n139
Sanhedrin
37a *xxin7*
46b 193n41
47a 194n46
73 184
73–75 159n112
73a 159n113, 160, 172
74 193n40
74a *xxin6*, 167, 169, 171–172, 178n1, 203, 216
112a 97n74
112b 86n53, 99n81
Shabbat
89a 206n72
Yevamot
73a 97n74
106a 209
Yoma
82b 197n55
85a 179n4
85b 148n83

Jerusalem Talmud (J.T.)
Kiddushin
1:6 73
Nedarim
11:3 (42c) 105
Peah
5:4 155n104
Rosh Hashanah
56a-c 126n17
Terumot
8:4 196n53, 200

Lightning Source UK Ltd.
Milton Keynes UK
UKOW07n1302250115

245063UK00003B/13/P

9 780521 493383